History and Structure of Languages

JAPANESE AND THE OTHER
ALTAIC LANGUAGES

Mutsuko Endo Hudson

History and Structure of Languages

Japanese and the Other Altaic Languages

ROY ANDREW MILLER

THE UNIVERSITY OF CHICAGO PRESS
Chicago and London

International Standard Book Number: 226-52719-0
Library of Congress Catalog Card Number: 79-151129

THE UNIVERSITY OF CHICAGO PRESS, CHICAGO 60637
The University of Chicago Press, Ltd., London

Contents

Illustrations

Foreword

The question about the relation of Japanese to the Altaic languages was for the first time treated in a manner satisfactory to linguists by the Austrian scholar Anton Boller, who in 1857 published a work aimed at proving that Japanese was a language related to the Ural-Altaic languages, i.e., Uralic, which comprises Samoyed and Finno-Ugric, and on the other hand Altaic, which comprises Turkic, Mongolian, and Manchu-Tungus, to which some linguists have also added Korean. In that stage of investigation, the affinity of Japanese and the Altaic languages could not be proved beyond doubt, although Boller advanced serious reasons for genetic affinity and illustrated his observations with convincing examples.

A considerable step forward was made by Ramstedt, who published a number of interesting comparisons of Japanese words with Mongolian and Turkic. A brilliant linguist and an expert in Mongolian and Turkic, Ramstedt was, however, too little acquainted with Japanese and lacked knowledge of Chinese, which is of paramount importance to anyone who is engaged in the study of the history of the Japanese language and the problems of its origin.

Roy Andrew Miller's work differs from those of his predecessors in that he, being a specialist in Japanese, approaches the problem of Japanese and Altaic affinity from the position of a historian of the Japanese language. His comparative method is that of the neogrammarians who insisted on the 'Ausnahmslosigkeit der Lautgesetze'. A number of etymologies offered by Miller are absolutely convincing, e.g., OJ *irö* < **yirö* < **yurö* 'color, facial appearance' = Mo. *düri* 'appearance, shape' = Tk. *yüz* 'face'; J *ir-e-* < **yir-* 'to insert' = Mo. *düre-* 'id.'; OJ *yö* 'four' = Mo. *dörben* 'id.', etc., which illustrate the rule that **d-* is J *y* (as in Turkic), and ∅ before *i*. Very interesting is J *s*, which goes back to Common Altaic **l_2* (which was probably **l'*) > Tk. *š*, Mo. and Manchu-Tungus *l*. Applying the comparative method, Miller has established a number of words common to Japanese and the Altaic languages. The correspondences discussed by him are hardly coincidental.

The fact that the common elements in the Japanese and Altaic vocabulary and morphology are not very numerous, so that in most cases only a few examples for a given sound correspondence or a suffix can be given, is of secondary importance. First of all, there is no rule concerning the obligatory minimum number of common stems that can be regarded as proof of linguistic affinity. Second, it is known that undoubtedly genetically related languages may have little in common. In this connection, Collinder's remark should be remembered, that the number of words common to modern Swedish and modern Greek is so small that, on their basis, it would be difficult to regard the two languages in question as related (*Acta Societatis Linguisticae Upsalensis*, NS 1:4, p. 117).

Acceptance of the theory about the Altaic origin of Japanese does not yet provide the means to assign Japanese a strictly defined place among the other Altaic languages. It is possible that Japanese, together with the other Altaic languages, has branched off from Proto-Altaic in the manner demonstrated in Miller's scheme (Fig. 1), but, on the other hand, it is also possible that Proto-Altaic and the oldest ancestor of Japanese go back to a common source considerably older than Proto-Altaic. I do not think, however, that this is an important problem at this time. What we need at this stage are a careful investigation of Japanese words and suffixes in comparison with Altaic words and suffixes respectively and a collection of acceptable etymologies. This task seems to me to have been achieved successfully by Miller, even if a good deal of his etymologies may be rejected at a later time.

Some scholars, like Polivanov, regard Japanese as a hybrid language consisting of Malayo-Polynesian, Altaic, and other, undetermined elements. The problem of hybrid languages cannot be discussed here, although it is quite possible that Japanese does have a Malayo-Polynesian stratum. In the event that several strata can be established in Japanese, Miller's work would be affected insignificantly and would retain its validity with regard to the Altaic stratum in Japanese. It would still be of great help in reconstructing that ancient Altaic language that continues to live as one of the strata in Japanese.

NICHOLAS POPPE

16 February 1971
Seattle, Washington

Acknowledgments

So much of this book has grown out of my almost daily discussions with my colleague at Yale, Samuel E. Martin, and I am so much in debt to him for specific suggestions and guidance, particularly with regard to Korean and Mongol, that it has not been possible to make individual acknowledgment of each item for which I am in his debt. Of course, this does not imply that Martin is in agreement with me on every idea or theory advanced here, or even that he supports my views on the precise nature of the relationship of Japanese to Altaic— much less that he is responsible for my errors of fact or opinion.

Earlier versions of portions of § 4.1 first appeared in *JAOS* 88.753–65 (1968, published 1969); of § 4.3 in *UAJr* 42.127–47 (1970); and of

§ 5.3 in *JNATJ* 6:2.14–29 (1969); but all these have been rewritten and revised for the present work. Preliminary drafts of other sections of this book were read at meetings at Columbia and Harvard universities, and also at a panel on 'The Periphery of the Japanese Language' held in Boston in March 1969. In preparing them for final publication here, I have had the benefit of the discussions on those occasions. In addition to Professor Martin, Eric Hamp (Chicago), John C. Street (Madison), and Nicholas N. Poppe (Seattle) have also been kind enough to read through my manuscript, and I have profited from their comments and suggestions. In particular, I am greatly in debt to Professor Poppe for a large number of detailed criticisms and corrections, and also very grateful to him for being kind enough to contribute a foreword to this volume.

But more than anything else, I must acknowledge my debt to Yale University, for the facilities and atmosphere that have made it possible for me to continue to work on a book with as little relevance to the times and conditions in which we live as this one will surely be held to have.

R.A.M.

5 February 1970
New Haven, Connecticut

Abbreviations and

Transcription Conventions

Reconstructions

pA	proto-Altaic (see Poppe 1960)
pKJ	proto-Korean-Japanese (see Martin 1966)
pT	proto-Tungus (see Benzing 1955)
pTk	proto-Turkish
pM	proto-Mongol (see Poppe 1955)

Languages

Bur.	Buriat
Chag.	Chaghatai

Chu.	Chuvash
Ev.	Evenki
Go.	Goldi
J	(new, modern, standard Tokyo) Japanese
MJ	Middle Japanese
OJ	Old Japanese
Jak.	Jakut
K	(new, modern) Korean
MK	Middle Korean
Kaz.	Kazakh
Kirg.	Kirgiz
Lam.	Lamut (or, Even)
Leb.	Lebed
Ma.	Manchu
Mo.	(written) Mongol
MMo.	Middle Mongol
Mongr.	Monguor
Negd.	Negidal
Oi.	Oirot
Olc.	Olcha
Osm.	Osmanli
R	Ryūkyū
Skt.	Sanskrit
Sogd.	Sogdian
Sol.	Solon
Tat.	(Volga) Tatar
Tg.	Tungus (a few citations, not further identified as to individual language, from Ramstedt/Aalto 1952, 1957)
Tk.	Turkish
MTk.	Middle Turkish
OT	Old Turkish
Tkm.	Turkmen
Uig.	Uigur
Udh.	Udehe

Texts

NKBT	Nihon koten bungaku taikei. Tokyo: Iwanami.
M	glosses in the NKBT edition of the *Man'yōshū*, Ōno, Takai, and Gomi, 1957–62 (= NKBT vols. 4–7), cited by volume number and page.

M poems in the NKBT edition of the *Man'yōshū*, cited by the numbering in that edition.

Note also that *Kojiki* and *Nihon shoki* poems are cited in the numbering of Tsuchihashi and Konishi 1957 (= NKBT 3), whose numbers however do not always correspond to those of other texts, as for example those in Philippi 1968. For abbreviations of titles of journals, series, etc., see the Bibliography.

Transcription Conventions

Old Japanese is transcribed using *ë*, *ö* and *ï* for the *otsu*-vowels of the written records (Miller 1967: 177), and *F* for the labial phoneme that was probably a voiceless stop somewhat earlier than the bulk of the Old Japanese corpus, but a voiceless bilabial spirant for most of the Old Japanese period (see Miller 1967: 201). In modern Japanese citations the syllabic nasal is always written *n*, even in those cases where it assimilates to a following consonant to become [m] or [ŋ]. With this single modification the Hepburn romanization has generally been used for all modern Japanese forms, except in cases where it has been more relevant to the discussion to cite these forms in some other transcription; in these cases long vowels (*ō*, etc.) have sometimes been rewritten as phonemic clusters (*oo*, etc.), and the affricates and pre-palatal spirant rewritten morphophonemically (*tu* for *tsu*, *si* for *shi*, etc.).

Chinese is written in the Wade-Giles transcription, with the addition of the so-called Yale tone-marks; numbers in [ ] following Chinese forms indicate the numbers of the corresponding Chinese characters in Mathews 1956. One exception to this rule has been the citation of the Middle Chinese rhyme-finals (pp. 63 ff.) in the 'tonal spellings' of Stimson 1966, to facilitate easier correlation of the Old Japanese data within the framework of Chinese historical phonology as arranged by Stimson.

All other languages have been cited according to the transcription conventions most generally found in the literature; the aim has been to alter all cited forms as little as possible. The only important exceptions to this rule are the following: *ñ* has been used throughout for the palatal nasal, often written elsewhere as *ń;* *i̇* has been used for the symbol *ι* as sometimes used, for example, in writing Chuvash

(Krueger 1961), and in proto-Tungus (Benzing 1955); and *x* has been used for Chuvash χ (Krueger 1961), also written *h* (Benzing 1959). The symbol ': :' is to be read 'corresponds regularly to'. The symbols // enclose phonemic, and [ ] enclose phonetic, transcriptions, but both sets of.symbols have been used sparingly and only when the context makes it important to distinguish either variety of transcription.

Chapter 1

Introduction

Well over a century has now passed since the publication of Anton
Boller's *Nachweis, dass das Japanische zum ural-altaischen Stamme
gehört* (1857). The present study aims at a rather less ambitious goal,
contenting itself solely with the Altaic relationships of Japanese, but
apart from this limitation of scope, its aims and method are not very
much different from those of the pioneer Viennese linguist of the last
century.

Like Boller's study, this is an attempt to apply the methodological
findings of the neo-grammarians, particularly as developed in their
study of the relationships among the Indo-European languages, to the
problem of the relationship of Japanese to the Altaic languages. Also

like Boller, we will begin by determining, as far as possible at the present state of our knowledge, what the regular correspondences in phonology are that may be revealed by the comparison of lexical items similar or identical in both meaning and form in the various languages involved, and then on the basis of these phonological correspondences advance the technique of comparison into the areas of morphology and lexicon.

For its time, Boller's study was a monument to his impressive grasp of the essentials of the comparative method and to his rigorous methodological concern. If it did not indeed 'prove' the relation of Japanese to any of the many other languages that it dealt with, this was in part because it attempted rather too much in relating Japanese to Ural-Altaic rather than simply to Altaic; also it was in part because at the time Japanese linguistic materials were available to Boller only on the most primitive and haphazard basis. The wonder is not that he accomplished relatively little, but that he was able to accomplish anything at all, given his sources for Japanese; and we will note below (p. 258) that at least one of Boller's original etymologies relating Japanese to Altaic is still of considerable linguistic value.

In this and many other ways, Boller's *Nachweis* remains a landmark among such studies. It shows the incredible energy and industry of European orientalists in the mid-nineteenth century; it documents the strong impression that the findings of the Indo-European comparativists had already made throughout European linguistic scholarship, even a decade before the first edition of Brugmann's *Grundriss;* and at the very least, it provides a lasting monument to the all but incredible skill and patience of the European printer, reproducing as it does a great variety of 'native orthographies' from poorly designed but beautifully hand-cut types—including a memorable if almost unreadable nineteenth-century Viennese font of Japanese *katakana!*

If Japanese was indeed an 'Ural-Altaic' language, and hence a later changed form of the proto-'Ural-Altaic' linguistic unity, then it was immediately apparent to students of the problem that Japanese was distinguished among almost all the other languages that might be considered to belong to this family by reason of the antiquity of its written records—of no great age when compared with the written records of Indo-Iranian, or other Indo-European sources, to be sure, but of extremely impressive antiquity for the 'Ural-Altaic' area. For an age of scholarship that too easily and too often confused the use of written records with historical linguistics, and did not always understand the difference between the study of written records and the recovery of linguistic prehistory by means of the comparative method, this single fact seemed to give Japanese a particularly fascinating advantage.

Dickens, for example, wrote of the Old Japanese corpus in glowing terms as 'the primal extant deliverances of the whole Ural-Altaic stock' (1906: 2.xxv). This is much further than we would think it proper to go today, in content as well as in style. Our concern in the present study is with Japanese as an Altaic language. This, by and of itself, is an undertaking of major dimensions, and the Ural-Altaic hypothesis plays no part in our considerations. Our Old Japanese texts are in the main extremely sophisticated literary texts; they are neither 'primal' nor in any sense of the word 'primitive'. But they are, for the Altaic area at least, extremely old, and Dickens was not by any means completely misleading in his effusive expressions of enthusiasm.

Actually, it is an interesting, and a curious—and perhaps even a significant—fact that in the Altaic area, where in general we lack the advantage of very old written records for any of the languages concerned, it happens to be just these two languages found at the geographical extremes of the area—Old Turkish on the one hand and Old Japanese on the other—for which we have the oldest written records; and a further coincidence is involved when we note that these two important bodies of old written records happen to date from substantially the same period.

For Old Turkish, our oldest written records are those of the Orkhon dialect, the language of the second East Turkic empire of ca. A.D. 680–740. They consist of five monumental inscriptions on stone dating in the main from a period of fifteen years beginning about 720. The inscription of Kül tigin may be dated in correspondence with August 732; the inscription of Bilgä kagan is dated in correspondence with 735; the Tonyukuk inscription is to be dated ca. 720; the İšbara tarkan (or Ongin) inscription is to be dated in 732 or one or two years later; and the Kül čor inscription is to be dated sometime in the period between ca. 719 and 723 (details in Tekin 1968: 9 ff.).

Meanwhile, far across the vast Asian expanse, the year 720, that in the reaches of the Orkhon probably saw the composition and erection of the Tonyukuk inscription, saw in Japan the completion of the *Nihon shoki*, one of the most important literary remains of Old Japanese (the *Kojiki* had been completed in 712, shortly before the earlier possible date for the Küli čor inscription). But our chief textual resource for Old Japanese is, by all means, the some 4,500 poems of the *Man'yōshū* (to be precise, 4,516 as numbered in the NKBT edition, but systems for counting and numbering the corpus differ). It is precisely the peak of *Man'yōshū* poetic art, the period between 710 and 733, that corresponds most closely to the period of the Old Turkish inscriptions on the Orkhon.

The *Man'yōshū* is, in most general terms, a text from the last half of the eighth century. Internal evidence in Bk. 14 indicates that it was finally put into its present textual form sometime after 771, and it is not possible to think of the present text of the *Man'yōshū* apart from the editorial activities of the poet Ōtomo Yakamochi (718?–785). But the *Man'yōshū* contains a great many linguistic materials earlier than the date of this final textual redaction; it is, in effect, in fact as well as in form, an anthology of some four hundred years of Japanese poetic experience.

It is possible to distinguish elements within this anthology going back to the first of the four periods of time into which an analysis of the contents of the *Man'yōshū* usually divides itself, i.e., earlier than the year 672. These selections are of course of extreme interest as language, if not always of equal interest as poetry. The second period, between 672 and 710, is one in which the art of the Old Japanese poet reached accomplished maturity; we note that this immediately precedes, in time, the bulk of the Old Turkish corpus. The third of the *Man'yōshū* periods is that between 710 and 733, generally conceded by Japanese literary critics to be the period in which the art of Old Japanese poetry reached its ultimate fruition; and this is the period that coincided almost exactly, if fortuitously, with the Orkhon Old Turkish corpus.

This 'Hochblüte der *M[an'yōshū]*-Dichtung' (Lewin 1965: 42) was distinguished by the work of such poets as Yamabe Akahito (d. ? 736), who together with the great Hitomaro is revered as one of the two 'divine poets' of the Old Japanese period; Yamaoe Okura (? 660–? 733); Takahashi Mushimaro (fl. ca. 730), and finally, the celebrated and colorful Ōtomo Tabito (665–731). These men

were members of a group of civil servants of lesser rank. . . . their poetry reflects their varied interests in Chinese philosophy as well as a new sense of literary discrimination. Around Tabito, . . . a group of officials with Chinese tastes formed a kind of literary coterie whose elegant gatherings and poetic exchanges were the last word in fashionable behavior *à la chinoise*. Some of these poets played a major role in the compilation of the *Man'yōshū* from pre-existing anthologies and private collections of verse, exhibiting high liter-ary standards and an ability to distinguish clearly between the crude and the elegant, the old and the new in poetic composition. The height of fashion-able elegance was reached at the famous party held by Tabito at his Viceroy's mansion on the thirteenth day of the first month of 730. The season was early spring, the occasion the flowering of the plum trees, and officials under Tabito's command gathered from all over the island to feast and drink sake, hold literary converse, and compose graceful tanka in praise of the beauty of the blossoms and the generosity of the host. . . . The significance of poems written on such occasions lies in the evidence they provide of the degree of sophistication of the Nara poets, and the existence of what might be called a society of esthetically-minded poets with fashionable literary tastes (Brow-er/Miner 1961: 90).

From this celebrated meeting of this accomplished group, we have preserved in *Man'yōshū* Bk. 5 a group of thirty-two poems, *M* 815–46, recorded entirely in phonograms and following the generally archaic phonological characteristics that distinguish much of *Man'yōshū* Bk. 5.

For example, these poems maintain the distinction between OJ *o* and OJ *ö* following OJ *m-*, a feature of the early language that other-wise and generally is maintained only in the *Kojiki* of 712, and one that had disappeared from the texts by the time of the *Nihon shoki* of 720, as well as the bulk of the *Man'yōshū* (Ōno in M 2.423–24). It could not have been too many months following Tabito's celebrated and well-remembered poetic party that the Old Turkish scribes at the other end of Asia set themselves in earnest to the task of composing a text for the monumental inscription of Prince Kül.

We surely do not have, in our Old Japanese texts any more than in our Old Turkish texts, anything approaching 'the primal extant deliverances' of any 'stock', Altaic or otherwise; but we do have the fortunate preservation of a considerable body of early written records.

Of and by itself, this corpus alone would tell us little about the early history of Japanese, and still less about the relationship of Japanese to other languages. Linguistic history does not result from reading old texts. Written records, no matter how plentiful or ancient, do not really tell us anything about the 'history of language', at least in the technical sense of that expression. To write the actual history of any language, the comparative method and internal reconstruction are the necessary techniques; but the fortunate existence of these two major bodies of old written records will greatly facilitate both the application of these methods to our materials and our ultimate interpretation of the results. The written records of Old Turkish and Old Japanese by themselves tell us little, but when they are studied together with comparison and reconstruction, it becomes possible to recover much of the earlier common history of the languages concerned, sometimes in considerable and often surprisingly intricate detail.

The present work takes the successful reconstruction of the essential structural features (phonology, morphology, lexicon) of proto-Altaic as an accomplished fact. This reconstruction implies the earlier existence of an Altaic linguistic unity, in relation to which the attested languages (Turkish, Mongol, Tungus) are all simply later, changed forms. The existence of this earlier linguistic unity is of course also taken both as accomplished and as the point of departure of the present work. But it would not do to overlook the unfortunate fact that it is still somewhat in vogue, in certain quarters, to continue to speak of the Altaic language family as if its inner relationships had not been demonstrated, and indeed as if the historical relationship of the attested languages to an original, and now lost, though partially recoverable, linguistic unity, were for some mysterious reason not even susceptible of scientific demonstration.

The present work limits itself to this already successfully demonstrated Altaic, and does not become involved in 'Finno-Ugric' or 'Ural-Altaic'. The former is a fairly well-established linguistic unity, but the reconstruction of the latter (which would, if recovered, be a gigantic 'super-stock' indeed), is not sufficiently advanced to encourage its utilization in our present study. And even in the case of the former, so much remains to be done with the reconstruction available that an attempt to involve Japanese at the present time would clearly be premature. In the meantime, there is no need for Japanese studies to become involved in these other and still fairly nebulous entities, particularly since so much can be done in relating it simply and directly to proto-Altaic.

For our immediate ends, as well as for more general purposes, proto-Altaic may now simply and accurately be defined as that original linguistic community or unity attested by the sound correspondences established in Nicholas Poppe's *Vergleichende Lautlehre*, Teil 1 of his *Vergleichende Grammatik der altaischen Sprachen* (1960). Many of the etymologies in this monumental work derive from earlier studies in the field; in particular the great pioneering contributions of G. J. Ramstedt (1873–1950) cannot be forgotten in this connection. But it remained for Poppe's *Vergleichende Lautlehre* to establish proto-Altaic as a historical fact; and with the publication of this volume, the original Altaic linguistic community became at least as well established as was the original Indo-European linguistic community by the time of the publication of the first edition of Karl Brugmann's *Grundriss der vergleichenden Grammatik der indogermanischen Sprachen* (1886–1900). Poppe's first successful reconstruction of proto-Altaic may actually be dated as early as his classic paper 'Altaisch und Urtürkisch' (Poppe 1926; see Pritsak 1957: 15), finally culminating after decades of careful refinement of detail in his 1960 *Lautlehre*. His accomplishment has been elegantly summed up in the following encomium, upon which it would be difficult to improve, either for style or for content: 'In exakter Arbeitsweise, auf der Basis des Prinzips der Ausnahmslosigkeit der Lautgesetze hat er [i.e., Poppe] der Urverwandtschaft des Türkischen mit dem Mongolischen und Tungusischen (sowie mit dem altaischen Substrat des Koreanischen) nachgewiesen' (Pritsak 1957: 15). With the publication of Poppe's *Lautlehre*, 'no one should remain unconvinced' (Krueger 1961: 71); the proto-Altaic linguistic unity 'is now in effect proven' (Street 1962: 92). (Perhaps the elaboration of the Japanese evidence for Altaic undertaken in the present work will make it unnecessary to retain, in future statements, even the cautious hedging represented by Street's 'in effect'.)

The parallel with the history of Indo-European studies suggested immediately above—Poppe, as against Brugmann—is of course not to be taken too literally. It could be argued, and with considerable point, that Brugmann's *Grundriss* rested on a much fuller accounting of the interrelationships among the sub-branches of Indo-European than we have in hand, even now, for Altaic, and that Poppe's work is more nearly comparable to that of Franz Bopp (1791–1867). But this comparison, too, would be somewhat misleading, since Poppe's greatest single contribution to the field has been his insistence upon the introduction of rigorous linguistic methodology at every step, and nothing could be farther from a description of Bopp's pioneering contributions to Indo-European studies. Perhaps Poppe's work is more closely analogous to that of August Schleicher (1821–1868). There are many significant points on which it is possible to compare the state of Indo-European studies by the time of the publication of Schleicher's *Compendium der vergleichenden Grammatik der indogermanischen Sprachen* (1861–62), and the state reached by proto-Altaic studies with the publication of Poppe's *Lautlehre*. But the question is essentially insoluble, since (in this particular field, at least) man has learned from the mistakes of his past, and Poppe has come to his lifework prepared with all the methodological equipment of the Indo-Europeanists; hence it has not been necessary for his work to retrace each of the early stages of Indo-European scholarship. Poppe is neither Bopp, nor Schleicher, nor Brugmann—he is, of course, Poppe; but in the sense of giving some concrete indication of the role of his *Lautlehre* in the history of proto-Altaic studies, probably the comparison with Brugmann's *Grundriss* remains the most informative.

But no matter how well-worked-out the scholarly solution for a longstanding scientific problem may be, apparently there are always certain elements (generally, to be sure, on the fringes of academic circles) for whom the very fact that a solution finally has been attained proves, in some peculiar psychological way, to be a deep disappointment. Their chagrin will be evidenced in their continued refusal to admit that a solution has been achieved, and in their protracted attempts to reintroduce as refutations older positions of argumentation and data that have, as a matter of fact, already been satisfactorily taken into account in the course of reaching the solution. This is what has happened in the history of Indo-European studies, and it is also what has happened in Altaic. The principal difference between the two areas has been that, in Indo-European studies, the fringe of pretenders who once attempted to refute the entire hypothesis and methodology of the comparative method has all but disappeared, while in Altaic studies it is still very much with us. But this disparity is due in large part simply to differences in the chronology of scholarship in the two fields. If the reconstruction of the proto-Altaic linguistic unity has lagged nearly a full century behind Indo-European studies, so have its critics, who still level against it the same charges that were once current in Indo-European circles, but which, mercifully, have all but ceased to be heard there.

But because of curious psychological factors, we still have our critics of proto-Altaic, even given the irrefutable evidence of Poppe's *Lautlehre*. They continue to argue, despite the detailed sets of regular sound correspondences that have been demonstrated among many different Turkish, Mongol, and Tungus languages, that these correlations in matters of precise detail are either the result of chance or borrowing, or of other circumstances not generally too well defined; above all, they maintain that these precise correlations do not result from the fact that all these languages are later, changed forms of a very much earlier language, one that we can recover only through the comparative method (i.e., 'reconstruct'), and also one that without the techniques of that method—in other words, without the assumption of regular sound change—would be totally beyond our knowledge as well as beyond our grasp.

To follow these critics of proto-Altaic is to abandon the findings and techniques of the comparative method. It is to hold that Indo-European too—as well as proto-Algonquian, and all the many other earlier linguistic unities that have been recovered through its assumptions—is a false and misleading figment of the scholarly imagination. It is to hold that since sound change is not regular, no historical statements of any kind can be made about language at all and that no earlier form of any variety can be recovered. It is, in total effect, not to criticize the assumptions and methodology of Altaic linguistic studies, but instead simply to abandon them.

The most serious charge that may be brought against the few that would still attempt to refute proto-Altaic and deny the existence of an original Altaic linguistic unity is that even though they deny the validity of the processes of linguistic comparison and reconstruction upon which the demonstration of this original linguistic unity is based, they themselves most inconsistently employ the identical techniques of comparison and reconstruction when these happen to suit their own purposes. Poppe himself (1965: 153) has given the most striking examples of this internal contradiction, showing how one such critic attempts to explain similarities in form and meaning between Mongol and Turkish solely in terms of borrowings of forms that are never attested in either language, or in other words, forms that we know only through the very assumption of genetic relationship and regular sound change that this particular critic is at one and the same time attempting to deny. Thus, essential to the argument of the critic of a proto-Altaic original linguistic unity is the very assumption that he is attempting to demonstrate as invalid.

In this particularly classic instance of internal inconsistency, a critic of the Altaic unity has attempted to explain the semantic and formal similarities between Mo. *dayir*, OT *yaɣïz* 'brown' as resulting from a borrowing of an earlier Turkish *daɣïz* into Mongol—quite conveniently forgetting that no such form as Turkish *daɣïz* is ever attested, and that this very form is known only to the extent that it has been recovered, or reconstructed, on the basis of the assumption of regular sound change as well as on the assumption of an earlier

Altaic linguistic unity—both of which assumptions he is attempting to overthrow.

It happens that among the forms often invoked in precisely this same variety of circular argument a few have particular relevance to Japanese. It will not take us too far afield to consider them briefly here, since they will immediately show how evidence from Japanese may on more than one occasion correlate with the other Altaic data, and incidentally in the process help to clarify details in the reconstruction of the proto-Altaic linguistic unity. Poppe points out that Mo. *yašil* 'purple; also name of a plant' and Tkm. *yāšil* 'green' are in a loanword relation to each other, the Mongol form having been borrowed from the Turkish (Poppe 1965: 153). But we also know, thanks to Poppe's reconstruction of proto-Altaic, that both these forms go back to pA *$\check{n}al_2$-, with various suffixal materials in the different languages (Poppe 1960: 39, 77, 97–98). The Japanese offers two striking reflexes for this same etymology; the first is OJ *nasi* 'pear', the second, J *nasubi* 'eggplant'. The first of these two forms is abundantly attested in the Old Japanese texts; the second does not appear in the earliest texts, but is recorded in lexical sources from ca. 940 on, and both have survived unchanged in meaning down to the present time.

OJ *nasi* goes directly with pA *$\check{n}al_2$-, with the most usual and best attested Japanese reflex for pA *l_2, i.e., J -*s*- followed by -*i*-, this vowel reflecting also the original palatal articulation of pA *l_2. Together with these forms goes K *nal* 'raw' (on which cf. Martin 1967: 232, #95, where, however, a different and less satisfactory Japanese etymology is suggested). The relationship of this particular Korean form within Korean to K *na-* 'become', going with both J *nar-* 'id.' and J *nas-* 'create' (Martin 1967: 225, #11), provides additional evidence for the original pA *l_2 that appeared in final position in this root in the original language (see pp. 37–38 below).

The important point to note here is that OJ *nasi* 'pear' cannot possibly have been a loanword into Japanese from any of the other attested forms, even if simply for the sake of argument we admit the possibility of early language contacts (not too difficult to imagine in the case of Korean perhaps, but extremely farfetched in the case of Turkish). Korean has *nal*, Turkmen has *yāšil*, Mongol has *yašil*. OJ *nasi* could not come directly from any one of these; only our reconstruction pA *$\check{n}al_2$- can bring all these forms into a meaningful historical relationship with each other; and of course no loan could ever have been made from this reconstructed form, since we have recovered it solely through our study of the regular correspondences in other cognate forms in the languages involved. The conclusion imposes itself: the attested forms are all later, changed versions of a now lost, but recoverable, original form. J *nasubi* 'eggplant' is also extremely valuable; its suffix *-bi* shows the Japanese reflex of the same velar suffixal element (pA *-w-*) that must be reconstructed to account for the -γ- of Mo. *nilaγun* 'roh, unangenehm nach rohem Fisch schmekkend, widerlich', and other related forms (Poppe 1960: 39). Before this labial element, the J *-i-* that we would normally expect with a reflex of pA *l_2 has most understandably been assimilated to become *-u-*. Again, a loanword cannot possibly account for all this, since the labial *-w-* of the original form is a reconstruction to account for a complex set of correspondences in the attested languages, and does not appear precisely as such in any of the attested Altaic forms— except, of course for the Japanese. The precise correlations in meanings as well as in phonology among these forms will also be noted. The correspondences in sounds could not possibly, in these cases, be the result of borrowing; the correspondences in meaning all but rule out coincidence, that other favorite argument of the amateur attempting to refute the comparative method. These two Japanese forms tell us a great deal about the Japanese relationship to Altaic; at the same time they play their own independent part in the establishment of an original Altaic linguistic unity. To refute them, it is necessary entirely to abandon the comparative method, together with the assumption of regular sound change.

The present work, needless to say, chooses not to abandon these major findings of linguistic science. It assumes, with the neo-grammarians, that sound change is regular (or, in Bloomfield's terms, that 'phonemes change'). On the basis of this assumption, earlier linguistic forms not known from written records may be recovered—or, in the usual terminology, 'reconstructed'. On the basis of these reconstructions, and working also with written records (when and if such are available), as well as through internal reconstruction (a technique for applying the same assumption of regular sound change to a single language, rather than to the comparison of several languages), we can recover linguistic facts that are also and at the same time historical events. We can, in a word, learn a great deal about the prehistory of the languages in which we are interested. This is what Poppe has done for proto-Altaic, in the course of summing up the work of others as well as in his own original contributions. He has recovered that lost original language of which the attested Turkish, Mongol, and Tungus languages are all much later, and greatly changed, forms. The present work attempts to present evidence showing that Japanese too is a later changed form of that same earlier, original language that we call proto-Altaic. Viewed from this perspective, it is hoped that the obvious echo in our title of Holger Pedersen's *Hittitisch und die anderen indoeuropäischen Sprachen* (1938) will be instructive rather than misleading or offensive, particularly to those with a special interest in the history of studies in the comparison of languages.

Previous attempts to relate Japanese to the Altaic languages have, of course, not been lacking. There have also been attempts to refute the relationship, clearly beside the point so long as none of the attempts to demonstrate the relationship was rigorous enough or extensive enough completely to demonstrate its thesis. Some of the attempts to relate Japanese to the Altaic languages have compared Japanese to a single Altaic language; others have compared it to more than one, but generally not to the original proto-Altaic linguistic unity (this was at any rate all but impossible before the appearance of Poppe's 1960 *Lautlehre*). Most of this earlier literature is essentially amateur work, unscientific in its data and approach alike, and nothing would be gained from a complete survey of it here. Instead, this summation will limit itself to a few particularly significant items within this body of the earlier literature, selecting for special comment works that because of their scientific orientation and approach (atypical for the field) merit particular consideration, or works that because of their sheer bulk or ambitious scale simply must be noted. In the first of these two categories, Boller (1857), Pröhle (1916/17), Ramstedt (1924, = Ramstedt 1951), Murayama (1950, 1957, 1962, 1963, 1966) and Martin (1967) are important; in the second, we have Haguenauer (1956), Kwon (1962), and Ozawa (1968).

Boller (1857) has already been noted above. That his study can still be read with profit by a student of the Japanese relationship to the other Altaic languages is the greatest possible compliment to the skill and perception of Anton Boller (1811–1869) as a comparativist, particularly in view of the primitive Japanese materials at his disposal. The organization and methodology of Boller's paper are excellent. He begins with comparative phonology (395 ff.), goes on to derivation (450 ff.), and concludes with morphology (471 ff.), under which he also includes a certain amount of comparative lexical material, in particular the numerals. Thus it can easily be seen that

Boller's approach is not unlike that of the present work; both attempt to proceed from the demonstration of phonological correspondences toward the identification and recovery of larger linguistic segments on the basis of those correspondences. Boller's weakness was not in his method but in his materials. The Indo-Europeanists were working with well-known and, in general, well-described languages. They were able to base almost all their comparisons on their exceptionally solid control of the major languages with which they worked. But with Japanese and the other Altaic languages Boller was working in virtual darkness on many important points. Even elementary lexical information was not easy to obtain for several of the languages vital to his comparisons, including Japanese, not to mention the total lack of reliable data about their structural essentials. Still, the wonder is not that he was often misled into comparisons that cannot be maintained today, but rather that he so often found himself led in the right direction. For example, his amazingly perceptive comparativist's intuition, working with a few Japanese verb forms along the lines of what today we should call internal reconstruction, led him to the correct historical explanation of Japanese *e* as resulting from internal changes within Japanese, notably from contractions of earlier combinations of *i* plus another vowel (Boller, 452, writes *ija*, neatly anticipating the modern formulation of OJ *e* < pre-OJ *i* + *a*).

Had descriptive and lexical data of the necessary degree of refinement been forthcoming, it would have been possible for Boller and others to have followed up his 1857 study with more and more precise treatments of the issues raised there, and it is entirely possible that Altaic and Japanese comparative studies would have progressed toward the same fruition and with the same rapidity as did Indo-European studies. Unfortunately, this was not the case. The data that would have been necessary were not soon forthcoming; some of them are still not yet available even today, more than a century later. Their delay has in the meantime strikingly inhibited the further development of the kind of study that Boller so promisingly began.

Even when Japanese materials of far greater accuracy and value were at hand, continuing interest in the 'Ural-Altaic' hypothesis and unwillingness to limit the investigation to Altaic materials alone continued to hamstring research. Pröhle (1916/17) is a good example; in its handling of Japanese materials it shows great advances over Boller (1857), but since it treats these materials against the overwhelmingly vast horizon of 'Ural-Altaic', few if any of its etymologies continue to be of interest today, except for their incidental role in the history of Japanese comparative studies.

A comparison of Boller⁻ (1857) and Pröhle (1916/17) with Ramstedt (1924, = Ramstedt 1951) at once shows the great ingenuity and perception of the Finnish linguist but at the same time demonstrates how little progress, in absolute terms, had been made in the half-century that by now had elapsed. The non-Japanese materials have somewhat improved, but not as much as might have been expected from the passage of so much time; and Ramstedt's methodology is hardly as impressive as Boller's. Still, Ramstedt (1924) remains a model study among others of the same period that might be cited; it is generally cautious; it makes a certain number of important suggestions; but it leaves one with the ultimate conclusion that the great promise of Boller's early studies was not lived up to, in any important respect, during the first three decades of this century.

It remained for the years following World War II to see the publication of the most massive attempt yet at studying the possible Altaic connections of Japanese. Haguenauer (1956), representing three decades of continuous and painstaking, if disorganized, scholarly labor, brings together almost everything that had been found out about Japanese as an Altaic language in the century separating Boller from the present; but this turns out to be disappointingly little. This massive volume of 640 pages is a veritable mountain in bulk as well as in the scope of the problems that it attacks (it does not limit itself to language, but ranges widely over comparative anthropology, archeology, and several other disciplines); but out of this mountain comes only a very tiny mouse. Worst of all, it has no index, no outline of contents, no bibliography, no apparent plan, and almost no internal organization. A second volume was promised for 1959; a decade later, it still has not appeared.

The only substantial attempt at an over-all evaluation of Haguenauer (1956) is from a political scientist (Reischauer 1956), who concluded that it is 'a major contribution to Japanese linguistic studies and one that will be long utilized and cited by other students of comparative linguistics' (207). Probably no linguist would say as much. Haguenauer's attempts at handling comparative materials are marked by his innocence of the techniques of the comparative method as well as by his almost total disregard of the basic methodology that alone makes such study possible.

Haguenauer speaks in the most vague terms of a *japonais commun*

(365 ff.), but it is never clear to the reader (or apparently to the author either) exactly what this means: is *japonais commun* a *koiné?* is it a reconstructed protolanguage? is it a kind of 'lowest common linguistic denominator' embracing elements of all possible varieties of Japanese from all possible times and places? For Haguenauer, *japonais commun* apparently is all these things, and moreover all of them at one and the same time; by that same token, it is of course absolutely without value for any serious linguistic purpose. His reviewer credits him with 'a careful and stimulating analysis of materials (particularly in the field of linguistics)' (Reischauer 1956:205); it would be good also to be told where to find the same in Haguenauer's massive tome, where the linguist will search for it in vain. We are also told that '[Haguenauer] attempts to identify on the basis of the phonetic laws he has built up [*sic*] the words that are common to these various languages' (Reischauer 1956: 206), an amazing statement that would be false even if it were true—which it is not!

Haguenauer fails to establish a single historical phonological correspondence between the Altaic languages and Japanese. He makes it clear he does not understand that the comparative method can operate quite satisfactorily in the absence of ancient written records (220; 365–66), and that, indeed, the comparative method is a technique that makes it possible for us to recover much of the prehistory of languages even in the total absence of such early documentation.

It is impossible even to guess according to what principles Haguenauer's 'comparative vocabularies' (380–442) are put together, so that when he finally approaches the necessity for drawing conclusions from these materials (451 ff.), nothing but the vaguest expressions can be employed—'un élément humain qui pouvait se rattacher à une ethnie 'altaïenne' par des ancestres déjà trés lointains' (638) is typical. For the political scientist, such conclusions 'may seem vague, [but] they are all the more convincing because of his caution' (Reischauer 1956: 207). This provides the outsider with a fascinating if unexpected insight into the methods and standards of political science (apparently, the more nebulous a statement is, the more convincing it becomes, is what Reischauer is trying to say); but the linguist whose interest has not completely expired by this time can only note in dismay that among the 1,310 'radicals and simple words' that Haguenauer assembles, he claims that only 349 are found in Altaic, after having excluded all terms likely to be loanwords. But what is very much wrong here is the fact that the principles according to which a word in

Altaic is 'identified' with a word in Japanese, as well as the principles according to which a word is 'excluded' as a loanword, are never stated, so that the apparent statistical dimension of Haguenauer's work becomes little more than a mirage; moreover, even his own attempts to provide statistical summaries of his findings (451–53) are misleading and often do not correlate with his own materials. Of the 23 Japanese words with initial *e-* that he treats in his 'comparative vocabularies', Haguenauer claims that 10 go with ('seraient rattachables à') Altaic (451). But this number seems curiously large, in view of the special historical nature of Japanese *e*, and, indeed, it is possible to locate only two actual examples among Haguenauer's materials, in the form of extremely unlikely comparisons for J *ebi* 'crustacean' (246) and MJ *esemono* 'fraud' (442). This last is compared with Ma. *ehe* 'bad, unlucky, inauspicious', but the Japanese form must go together with, as a doublet, J *nisemono* 'id.', and clearly involves different developments of an original nasal initial in different Japanese dialects, perhaps ultimately with significance for the problem of the Japanese reflexes of pA *$\tilde{n}$-. At any rate, it has nothing whatever in common with the Manchu form cited, to which it is similar neither in form nor in meaning. The others simply defy tracing.

In a word, Haguenauer's findings about the 'origines de la civilisation japonaise' may be of interest to and satisfy the academic standards of the political scientist, but the linguist will find in them virtually nothing of concern or value. He may even end up in agreement with the archeologist who, after looking through Haguenauer's book, concluded in despair, '[it] makes one feel that attempts at reconstructing the prehistoric features of the language are undoubtedly more difficult than reconstructing a prehistoric Ainu' (Kidder 1960: 216).

Kwon (1962) is a somewhat different kind of study, an attempt to deny rather than to prove linguistic relationship. He attempts to investigate the problem of the relationship, if any, between Korean, the (other?) Altaic languages, and Japanese by means of a scrutiny of the formation and 'conjugation' of the verbs in the various languages. He reaches an essentially negative conclusion:

Bei dieser Vergleichung der Verbalformen des Koreanischen mit denen der genannten Sprachen muss ich hinsichtlich der Verwandtschaftsverhältnisse zwischen dem Koreanischen und den genannten Sprachen eine negative Antwort geben (Kwon 1962: *Vorwort*, xi).

Since Kwon's dissertation is primarily interested in Korean and in the possible relation of Korean to the other languages with which he concerns himself, it is not actually very surprising that his investigation concluded in this completely negative and uninformative fashion. For reasons that in the main still escape us, Korean actually shares remarkably few grammatical elements with those other languages to which it must, however, in the final analysis almost surely be related. We can verify this situation, anomalous though it is, most conveniently and most confidently with respect to the Korean-Japanese relationship, where despite the large amount of lexical evidence available (Martin 1966), which cannot be dismissed, the grammatical evidence for the relationship remains remarkably, strikingly, and disappointingly sparse. This means that even if Kwon had gone about his investigation on the basis of a more satisfactory and more rigorous methodology than the one he employed, he might very well still have ended up with 'eine negative Antwort' to the problem he set for himself. But in that case his negative answer would have been a significant even though a negative conclusion, which unfortunately is not now the case. The difficulty is that Kwon's methodology is not sound, and this means in turn that to an already extremely vexatious area of study he has simply added new problems, rather than (as might have been hoped for in a serious work of the scope and scale of his Munich dissertation) clearing away at least some small part of the earlier accumulations of scholarly underbrush.

What Kwon has done is to rely almost exclusively upon grammar and dictionary glosses and definitions for the forms that he attempts to compare. At the same time his comparison is carried out on the basis of the false assumption that there is a normal expectation that forms from different languages glossed with identical terms in lexical and grammatical sources will, if they are historically related, always look alike in addition to meaning the same thing and being used in the same fashion. Of course, no such assumption may be seriously advanced. If all of these several variables on a number of different levels do not immediately fall into place, Kwon then holds that the possibility of historical relationship and diachronic inheritance of earlier common forms is at once and totally ruled out. (That the grammars and other sources Kwon has used for most of the languages studied, and particularly for Japanese, are generally unsatisfactory in their data and less than rigorous in their analysis and description adds another dimension of serious difficulty to his study, but one about which it is possible to be silent here, since his methodological problems already preclude success quite apart from the quality of his materials.)

Nothing of course could be further from the methodology and techniques of the comparative method than the above. As time passes and languages change, we are fortunate indeed if we can continue to locate and identify a relatively few surviving elements and forms, and the ones that we can trace become fewer and fewer as more and more time passes. Forms change, meanings change, grammatical uses and morphological categories change, everything changes; and the wonder is not that things end up looking very different, but rather that they sometimes still manage to look anything alike, after centuries and centuries of change and alteration. We will never know enough about all the changes that operate to affect the forms we study—particularly when we are working on the level of the great original linguistic unities such as Indo-European and Altaic, with their staggeringly remote time-depths—but we are only short-circuiting any genuine possibility of finding out the little that probably is to be learned if we go about our work in the fashion adopted by Kwon.

Suppose that we have three languages, A, B, and C. Suppose further that we would like to study whether a particular morphological indicator, for example, 'future', in the verbal formations of each of these languages is related to any of the others, i.e., whether or not it belongs to a set of later changed forms all of which go back to a common form in an original linguistic unity, proto-ABC. What will we find out if we: (a) check a grammar or dictionary of each of the three languages, (b) line up glosses from each language illustrating 'future' alongside each other, and (c) then try to see how much they do or do not look alike? Very little at best, and most likely nothing. By applying this method, which is Kwon's method, we could easily 'demonstrate' that English, French, and German are all unrelated to one another, or indeed virtually any other proposition that we might wish to 'demonstrate'. In effect, Kwon ends up saying, over and over again, 'you see, these forms are not related at all'; to which the answer is simply, but accurately, 'yes, but who ever said they were?'.

Furthermore, even when his method does, in spite of itself, turn up obvious cognates, forms that clearly are historical continuations of an earlier linguistic unity, Kwon simply dismisses their evidence without discussion. Thus, in his treatment of the imperatives (56–60), he cites Old Korean imperatives in -*ra*, which clearly go directly (through the *ö/a* ablaut relationship) with the Old Japanese imperatives in -*rö*, which in fact he also cites (though not in that particular form); but he then goes on to 'conclude' that the imperative formations provide no basis for relating Japanese to Korean (60). Grammatical, as distinct from lexical, correspondences between Korean and Japanese are far too few and far too valuable to be dismissed in this cavalier fashion.

An even more striking example of Kwon's methodological difficulties is to be found in his treatment of the future verbal structures in the various languages (73–77). For Tungus he cites what are historically totally irrelevant forms with a -*j(i)*- formative; and for Japanese he writes, most surprisingly of all:

Das Futurum wird mit den Suffixen -*mu* und -*muzu*(-*nzu*) und ferner [*sic*] in der Umgangssprache auf -*u* und -*yo* [*sic*] gebildet (76).

Apparently Kwon is not aware that the modern Japanese optative-dubitive forms in -(*y*)*ō* all go back directly and regularly to earlier forms in -*mu*, and that this is one of the portions of the Japanese verbal system preserving important traces of a direct cognate relationship with Tungus, in the form of the optative formations in proto-Tungus *-*ma*-, *-*mu*-, so that pT *ǯ*äb.mä*- 'essen wollen, Hunger haben', not only goes directly with Ev. ǯ*əmū*-, Lam. ǯ*əm*- 'id.,' and Go. ǯ*əmusi*-, Udh. ǯ*əmu.hi* 'er will essen' (Benzing 1955: 1069), but also directly with J *tabeyō* 'let's eat' < *tab-e-mu. Here historical correlations of the most important kind lurk beyond the grammar glosses and modern forms with which Kwon attempts to operate, and his conclusions are incorrect because his investigation does not extend beyond the superficial level of his method and materials. The same is true of his treatment of the negatives (95–99), where, as we shall see below, the related forms may be traced in considerable detail in Japanese as well as in the other Altaic languages, even though the changes here have helped conceal many of the traces of the earlier linguistic unity.

Since one of the continuing difficulties with all attempts at relating Japanese to Altaic has been the problem of handling the philological sources for Japanese linguistic data accurately and effectively, it is hardly surprising that it remained for Japanese scholars themselves to make the first really impressive contributions to the field. The techniques of the comparative method have not, in general, been well received or even completely understood by modern Japanese scholarship, and this has imposed a severe limiting condition on their work in this area; but there have been exceptions. Most deserving of mention in this connection is the work of Murayama Shichirō (1950, 1957, 1962, 1963, 1966, to cite only those papers of Murayama that have been of particular utility in preparing the present study). Murayama generally works in the best traditions both of traditional Japanese scholarship on Japanese, and of the western techniques of the neo-grammarians, while his familiarity with both camps (something that few of his Japanese colleagues can aspire to, much less emulate) has given his work on the Japanese relationship to Altaic remarkable value and scope. Since much of his technique is western, and partly also because his findings are of an order of complexity and importance that put most other contemporary Japanese linguistic scholarship in the shade, Murayama's *œuvre* is little known and less appreciated in Japan. It has received more realistic evaluation abroad, where he fully deserves his reputation as Japan's best-known and most active comparativist. The debt of the present work to Murayama will be obvious time and time again.

Another recent study to which the present work is greatly in debt is Martin (1966), the first comprehensive monograph irrefutably to demonstrate the relationship of Japanese to another language on the Asian mainland. Martin's reconstruction of proto-Korean-Japanese put the entire possibility of a scientific demonstration of the relation of Japanese to the other Altaic languages on a new and exciting footing, and one of the chief aims of the present work has been to attempt to follow up at least a few of the possibilities thus opened up by Martin. The debt of the present study to Martin (1966) will be obvious throughout; for an evaluation of his study and an estimate of its importance, see especially pp. 57–58 below. The precise relationship to the original Altaic linguistic unity of the proto-Korean-Japanese linguistic unity for which Martin makes such a convincing case remains a vexatious problem, with many unsolved conundrums awaiting comprehensive treatment by others in the future. We shall see shortly below some of the different possibilities that have been suggested for incorporating Korean into a reconstruction of Altaic; further refinement of the relationship demonstrated by the Korean data is certainly the most urgent single task now facing Altaic-Japanese comparative studies.

Finally, Ozawa (1968) must be noted, as an example of a massive work that deserves mention if only (and almost solely) for its bulk. Its problems and shortcomings are described below (pp. 66 ff.), and it has been held up to the clear light of rigorous method and scientific approach in a detailed review by Murayama (1969). It attempts to compare Japanese with Mongol, and in the process introduces other Altaic materials from time to time. One has only to compare Ozawa (1968) with Martin (1966) to see that, even in the year of its publication, the Japanese study was already a living fossil, carrying over into the last decades of this century a haphazard, unmethodological approach to linguistic comparison that would have appalled Boller a century earlier. The more things change, the more they are the same: this is never true of languages, but unfortunately, it often seems to be true of their study.

The present treatment stresses phonological, lexical, and to a certain extent morphological correspondences among the languages held to be cognate with Japanese, but it pays rather less attention to other features of these languages that might more generally be considered 'grammar', especially the grammatical and/or inflectional particles, and most notably syntax, which is all but ignored. This last omission will probably not strike any traditional comparativist as in the least strange, but it will surely appear to be a crippling omission to younger persons trained over the past decade to think of syntax as the only aspect of language worth serious study. The answer to the omission of syntax is of course extremely simple; we lack techniques for dealing with comparative syntax on any but the crudest level, and this level is still too crude to provide any useful findings. The comparative syntax of the Altaic languages including Japanese will one day probably become the subject of profitable investigation, but that day can come only after the phonological, lexical, and morphological correspondences are even better understood than they are at present.

But even apart from the orders and patterns of syntax, the present study pays relatively little attention to many elements that might be said to belong to the 'grammar' of the language pure and simple, and a word both of explanation and of extension on this point will not be out of place. First of all, it might be noted that in this selectivity we are in good company; Martin (1966) elects the same choice in his reconstruction of proto-Korean-Japanese, which is why, as his title indicates, his study is concerned almost entirely with 'lexical evidence'.

The major reason for this decision, and at the same time the major difficulty that the solely grammatical elements in the languages concerned introduce on the comparative level, is found in their forms as well as in their meanings. In contrast to the lexicon in general, these grammatical elements are always extremely short in phonetic shape and extremely difficult to pinpoint semantically. The longer the form, the longer the 'fit', i.e., the number of precise phonological correlations possible in diachronic comparison, and the more valuable a comparison involving such a form is as a result. At the same time, the more precisely we can define the meaning of a form, the more valuable is a comparison involving such a form. But grammatical elements are short, typically consisting of a single vowel or consonant, or at most one of each, and their meaning is generally difficult to state except in the most general terms. From this it follows that such elements are of relatively little utility for the study of the Altaic relationships of Japanese, at least in the present state of such studies.

The little that actually can be done in relating the essentially grammatical elements of Japanese to presumably cognate elements in the other Altaic languages has by and large been surveyed by Murayama (1957), a study that vividly demonstrates all the pitfalls of this area. At the same time, its materials and findings are comprehensive enough to inhibit a full-scale reconsideration of the problems here or elsewhere in the immediate future. Two of the grammatical elements treated by Murayama, however, are worth reinvestigation, if only briefly, both for the interest that naturally attaches to the forms themselves as well as in order to illustrate the problems of applying the comparative method to this particular area.

Murayama suggests that the Old Japanese attributive adjective inflection *-ki* may be identified with a proto-Altaic adjective suffix **-ki*, a form that can be traced in Turkish, Mongol, and Tungus, and therefore a form that must be reconstructed for the original linguistic unity (1957: 130). His argument is a persuasive one, though presented by him with extreme brevity, and it will therefore be to our advantage to investigate the relevant data with somewhat more care.

For Old Japanese, this attributive inflectional element is customarily described by grammars in the shape *-ki;* note that the vowel was *-i*, not *-ï* (Yamada 1954: 98–135, especially 111 ff.). The traditional Japanese grammarians have little or nothing to say on the origin of this element (Ōno 1955: 280–81). A purely descriptive approach to Old Japanese would make it necessary to treat this element not as a single morpheme but rather as two, with *-k-* the adjectival marking morpheme and *-i* a 'contingent mood morph' (Yokoyama 1950: passim and 35, n. 44). In such a case, then, the morphological elements bifurcate at the cost of halving their length, and the problem of historical identification becomes just that much more difficult. So much for the shape of the morpheme; its meaning is not difficult to state: it serves to mark attribution of a quality or characteristic to a following noun-head.

In Altaic, the original genitive marker is to be reconstructed as pA *-n*. This appears in Tungus as pT *-ŋī* (Benzing 1955: 1038), to be analyzed in turn as pA *-n* + *-ki*, but the *-ki* involved is not restricted to Tungus. It may be traced in Mongol, cf. Mo. *endeki* 'being here, belonging to this place' (Poppe 1955: 187), and is widely (and significantly) attested in Turkish. In Old Turkish, *-ki/-qï* is an important adjectival formant; examples include *ayqï* 'monatlich' (*ay* 'Mond, Monat'), *söki* 'einstig' (*sö* 'Zeit'), *tabγačγï* 'being or living in China' (von Gabain 1950: §§ 49, 74, 410; Tekin 1968: 104, 105). Various modern Turkish languages provide excellent evidence for the widespread employment of this same element in proto-Turkish, where it appears to have become specialized early in the history of this branch of Altaic as a formant for time- and place-related adjectivals, though still maintaining abundant traces of its original role as a general marker of attribution. Bashkir has *qïš-qï* 'winterlich' (*qïš* 'Winter') (Benzing 1959: 428). The same formant is well represented in Kazan Tatar (Thomsen 1959: 414). Uzbek is particularly rich in examples of the use of a cognate element in forming the 'Adjektive der Zugehörigkeit', thus *yaz* 'sommer', *yaz-gi* 'sommerlich', *aγïz* 'Mund', *aγïz-ki* 'Mund . . .' (Wurm 1959: 495, 498). Chuvash too inherited the same element, which appears there as Chu. *-hi* (Benzing 1959: 717). The shape and conditions of the Tungus reflex of this form have already been noted; here it is part and parcel of the 'genitive', and of pT *-ŋī* Benzing notes, 'Wir finden Wörter mit diesem Suffix überall als Eigenschaftswörter der Zugehörigkeit' (1955: 1038). His examples make this clear: Ev. *hawamnīŋī* 'zum Arbeiter gehörig, Arbeiter . . .', Lam. *am.ŋī* 'Vaters . . .', Ma. *ama.i boo* 'das Haus des Vaters' (loc. cit. 1039).

These correspondences in form and meaning are sufficiently precise to make it possible to reconstruct the following historical linguistic scenario for the development of adjectival morphemes with the attributive formant *-ki* in the original Altaic linguistic unity, and in Japanese as well. Originally, adjectives were not distinguished from other forms; they were identical with nouns, or at best, a minor subclass of nouns. The attributive formant *-ki* was essentially a genitive, or perhaps still better, a general referent marker. It became specialized in usages together with a certain group of nouns, in Turkish with place and time words, in Japanese with quality and characteristic terms. In Japanese these later developed other formations with still other formants, or with compound formants encapsulating this same *-ki*, and from this eventually attained morphological class identity as adjectives. In Tungus the process did not go that far, so that there the earlier general use of the attributive marker in its original genitive, or general referent role, remains clear.

The form is not impressively long, even when taken as the *-ki* of Japanese school grammar, much less as the smaller *-k-* and *-i* elements revealed by a purely synchronic analysis. Hence the 'fit' with the proposed cognates in other languages is, inevitably, less than striking. Its meaning is also difficult to categorize with the precision that would be necessary in order for the semantic correlations in the other languages to be very striking. Since there is so much evidence from other areas, and importantly from other phonological and lexical correspondences, showing that Old Japanese and Old Turkish are cognate, the evidence for OJ *-ki* and OT *-ki/-qï* going together becomes of value; but it would not be so if it were the only evidence of its kind, or if all other evidence available were of the same size, form, and type. But taken in the context of the rest of our knowledge of the relationship between these two languages, and of their common relation to proto-Altaic, it does make it possible to write the history of OJ *-ki* with considerable confidence: this form descends directly from an earlier Altaic form of similar shape, meaning, and function.

Incidentally, these data also make it possible to refute a historical account for the same Japanese form based solely upon internal reconstruction within Japanese itself, proposed by Martin (1967), by which OJ *-ki* would be interpreted as a contraction of the adverbial *-ki* + *ari* (1967: 260). This would be difficult to accept at best, but particularly in view of these data from the related languages, making it clear that Japanese inherited this *-ki* intact and in that very shape from the original Altaic linguistic unity, there is neither need nor justification to see in it a contraction of anything. Martin's formulation is justified in terms of internal reconstruction within Japanese, but it remains essentially a descriptive, not a historical statement, and it cannot be maintained against historic evidence from the comparative method when that evidence clearly contradicts it (see Hill 1950: 97, on the nonhistoricity of descriptive statements, even those couched in historic terms, as is Martin's formulation).

Another instructive example pointing up some of the difficulties generally encountered in treatments of purely grammatical elements on the comparative level is provided by the modern grammatical particle J *o*. Bloch's categorization of this particle as 'emphatic object referent particle' (Bloch 1970: 52, 57, 96) exactly sums up its role in the modern language; but what can we discover of its history? We assume that J *o* is the modern descendant of an older *wo*, and although this assumption is made largely on orthographic evidence, there are no reasonable grounds upon which to challenge it. But the difficulty then immediately becomes that Old Japanese appears to have not one but at least two, and possibly more, homonymous particles of the shape OJ *wo*. The broadest, most clear-cut differentiation between the two varieties of OJ *wo* is provided by syntactic evidence. One occurs in utterance-final position, where its sense is clearly exclamatory or ejaculatory, while the other is found internally in syntactic structures. If all the instances of this second variety of OJ *wo* are to be considered merely different employments of the same particle, then about the only statement concerning its meaning that can be made is the very general one that it 'indicates the referent (J *taishō*, not *mokuteki*, which would be 'object'!)' of a verb. If an attempt is to be made to subdivide the occurrences of this second variety of OJ *wo* somewhat more precisely, then a case can be made for an OJ *wo*₁ marking emphatic direct objects (thus, in *M* 10, 334, 843, 4219, 4348, etc.), to be distinguished from another OJ *wo*₂ marking the place or time at which or during which an action transpires (thus, in *M* 462, 769, 1881, 1934, etc.). The usual Japanese grammarians' classifications of OJ *wo* are based solely on semantic values and as a result switch back and forth across what are actually very different uses. For example, even though the classification of OJ *wo* in Sanseidō (1967: 829ᶜ–830ᶜ) represents a great advance over most of the presentations in the traditional grammars and suggests several useful innovations in the treatment of this form, it does not hesitate to include a case of the utterance-final exclamatory *wo*, *M* 1022, under the examples that we have categorized above as OJ *wo*₂, simply because a place is mentioned in that particular text passage. When, as in this fashion, all other possible criteria are made secondary to semantic considerations, the description naturally is all but useless for comparative purposes. The exclamatory, utterance-final *wo* of Old Japanese is clearly distinguished from all other instances of this form by the conditions of its syntactic occurrence, and while there are certain problems in the further subdivision of the other instances of this form, the least we can expect is that these clearly marked exclamatory occurrences will not be brought into the picture needlessly. Nor is other recent Japanese scholarship on the problems of this form of any great assistance. Oyama (1964) suggests that OJ *wo* in all its varieties was simply manufactured out of whole cloth by the speakers of Old Japanese in order to prevent possible misunderstanding of their own language and concludes that the form was 'developed in accordance with human mental development' (463). Since her methods and assumptions are roughly those of linguistic science a hundred and fifty years ago, her findings tell us nothing, except insofar as they remind us of the sorry state of most *kokugogaku* studies in modern Japan. Even if her method and assumptions were less antique, her study would still tell us nothing of the origin of this form, since she ignores the evidence of Old Japanese and does not investigate any texts earlier than the *Genji monogatari*. Hirohama (1967) is somewhat more useful. He includes interesting statistical data, but he does not depart from the usual school explanations for OJ *wo*, in which all its employments, including its use as emphatic direct object marker, are seen as later developments from the exclamatory usages. He does not attempt to explain just how one may have led to the other, and he ignores the syntactic dichotomy that separates the two usages.

Murayama (1957: 130) treats the Old Japanese form simply as an accusative marker, and compares it directly with Ma. *-be*, pT **-wa* ∼ *-*we;* but he does not go further into the semantics of the comparison. Because of this, he misses most of the important historical correlations of the materials, since it is clear from the evidence of the Old Japanese texts that OJ *wo*, no matter how many subdivisions we may choose to set up in order to describe it, is not simply an 'accusative particle'. Murayama's treatment is satisfactory as far as it goes, but it does not go far enough; it falls down on the score of treating only the phonology of the forms, while at the same time all but ignoring their meanings and functions.

A closer inspection of the Tungus materials will show that there are important correlations between the meanings and functions of the so-called accusative particle in these languages and those of OJ *wo*. Precisely like our OJ *wo*$_2$ above, the Tungus languages use their reflexes of an original accusative particle, pT **-ba* in Benzing's reconstruction, for indications of time and place, quite parallel with the time- and place-structures with OJ *wo*. The parallel of Go. *mi duəntəwə* *pulsihəmbi* 'ich ging durch den Wald' (Benzing 1955: 1028) with OJ *kasugano wo yuki* 'going through Kasugano . . .' (*M* 1881) is immediately apparent. Other striking parallels might be cited; they are available in Benzing (1955: 1028–29; 1047–48; 1096–97), and make clear the possibility of establishing precise correlations in sense and function between the Tungus 'accusatives' and OJ *wo*, quite apart from the problems of the phonological relationship of the forms. Along with these employments for place, Tungus also has characteristic examples of the accusative used for expressions of time (Benzing 1953: 113–14), where again the parallels with the Japanese materials in sense and function are striking. Even the 'emphatic object' employment of J *o* in the modern language has an impressive parallel in Manchu; with Ma. *bithe-be arambi* 'écrire un livre' beside Ma. *bithe arambi* 'écrire des livres' (Sinor 1968: 265), compare J *hon o kaku* 'write a book (emphatic object)' beside *hon kaku* 'write books'. Parallel to the Manchu use of its accusative particle to mark a subordinate clause, as in Ma. *hafan oǰoro-be buyembi* '(Il) désire être fonctionnaire' (Sinor, loc. cit.), we have the well-known Japanese construction *hito no kuru o matsu* 'to wait for someone to come' (Lewin 1959: 79).

All of this can only remind us of what Ramstedt said about the accusative particles in all the Altaic languages in general:

Der Akkusativ ist natürlich adverbal, d.h. er gehört direkt zum Verb. . . . Über den Gebrauch des Akkusativs in allen diesen Sprachen ist im allgemeinen noch zu bemerken, dass der Akkusativ nicht nur als Kasus für das Objekt des Verbs angewandt wird, sondern auch die Entfernung in Zeit oder Raum ausdrücken kann (Ramstedt/Aalto 1952:29, 31).

Ramstedt was not far from the mark here; and the Japanese evidence helps to show just how close he was to estimating the original Altaic situation. In the light of our other information on the relationship among these languages, the correlations in sense and function of OJ *wo* with the accusative particles in Tungus are striking and important; taken by themselves, of course, they would tell us nothing.

These two examples illustrate the problems of comparisons involving purely grammatical elements in these languages, and also some of the difficulties in Murayama's generally useful study of these features. A few other details may be mentioned in this same connection, before going on to other subjects. Murayama's treatment of J *ga* (1957: 129–30) is generally satisfactory, but like his treatment of J *o*, it requires considerable refinement in details of meaning and syntactic function. Murayama writes *ŋga*, but this form is never attested, and should therefore properly carry an asterisk. The problem of the connection between OJ *ga* and OJ *nö* is a very vexatious one, and far from solution; simply to make up a form, as Murayama has done, that puts both their initials together into a single unit carrying the vocalization of the first is a tempting but rather irresponsible solution. All that we can say for certain is that in some of the earliest portions of the Old Japanese corpus, OJ *ga* and OJ *nö* appear to be 'vowel harmony' alternants of each other; thus in the *Bussokuseki* inscription poem 1 we have *titiFaFa ga* 'of father and mother' beside *moröFitö nö* 'of all men'; and later in the same inscription, poem 14 has *waga yö* 'our world' beside *könö yö* 'this world', presaging the same pattern thanks to which the modern language has inherited such expressions as *waga kuni* 'our land', and similar clichés. These syntactic occurrences explain the alternation in vowels, but they do not explain the alternation in the consonants.

Tōgō (1968) has studied the Heian usage of *ga* and *no*, but his analysis is completely along semantic lines, and ignores even the possibility of an old phonological alternation ever having been involved. He concludes that the choice between *no* and *ga* was determined by the 'psychological distance between the writer and the person denoted by the noun taking the particle', and while his massive statistical evidence is impressive, his findings are unconvincing due to his failure to base his study on a more rigorous linguistic method. He does not consider the Old Japanese evidence, nor does he show any familiarity with the important early examples, such as the *Bussokuseki* evidence. As a result, his study is important chiefly for its statistical data and for its citation of the relevant earlier Japanese literature on the problem. A well-known tale in the *Uji shūi monogatari* (§ 93, ed. Watanabe Tsunaya and Nishio Kōichi, NKBT 27.221) documents a Middle Japanese semantic distinction between *no* and *ga*, but it is difficult to relate this to the Old Japanese materials, and to the earliest stages of the language.

Murayama's study by no means exhausts the possibilities for pointing out genetic relationships between Japanese grammatical elements and similar forms in related languages. For example, he does not touch upon the obvious relationship between the Old Japanese plural suffix *-ra* and the 'vocalized' reflexes of the Altaic collective suffix **-l* for which we have the magisterial demonstration of Pritsak (1957). This and many other similar Japanese grammatical elements await comprehensive treatment on the comparative level.

One further word should be added concerning a grammatical element whose absence from the present study may well be surprising to many, who will search in vain here for a comparison of OJ *i* as a nominative marker with K *i* of similar meaning. This is one of the most often suggested comparisons between Japanese and Korean (Ōno in M 1.258; Murayama 1950: 45 and n. 14), and involves a grammatical particle that appears a few times in the *Man'yōshū* (e.g., M 237, 545, 537) and other early texts, but then mysteriously all but disappears from the language.

Occurrences of this particle in the glosses to Nara Buddhist texts have been collected by Yamada (1954: 421–34). Its frequency in these early glossed scriptural texts and its subsequent rapid disappearance from the language make it extremely likely that what we have to deal with here is simply an early loan from Korean, used by the Buddhist scribes and clerics under the tutelage of their Korean masters to gloss their texts, and subsequently imitated in Japanese compositions for a short period, as a variety of literary elegancy, but never really adopted into the language proper, and hence disappearing completely and rapidly once the early period of Korean-dominated Nara Buddhism had drawn to a close. We have clear evidence of other Korean words being employed to gloss Japanese texts in a similar fashion (e.g., Miller 1967: 66), and this loanword explanation for the rare grammatical element OJ *i* fits in perfectly with that other evidence. Since this form was in all likelihood, and for these reasons, an early loan from Korean, it plays no part in the present study.

Something else conspicuous by its absence from these pages is glottochronology or, as it is sometimes called, 'lexicostatistics'. This is a pseudoscientific technique that has in recent years attempted to develop a means for estimating the amount of elapsed time that separates an earlier common language from its later, changed forms, somewhat along the lines by which carbon-14 dating now provides a technique for estimating the age of archeological specimens. Unfortunately, what is often lost sight of is the fact that glottochronology tells us nothing at all about whether or not the languages it studies ever were in fact actually related; it estimates the time elapsed since their separation under the assumption that they were once the same, but it provides no information of any kind on the critical question of whether or not this genetic assumption is correct. If the genetic assumption is false, then of course the time-lapse figures generated by glottochronology are not only completely meaningless but totally misleading, since in such a case there never was any earlier unity. Roughly speaking, glottochronology stands in the same relation to the comparative method and internal reconstruction, the techniques employed in this study, that phrenology does to brain surgery and psychoanalysis. The time-lapse figures that have been calculated for various assumed relationships involving Japanese are summarized in Miller (1967: 82–83); this provided the materials for Chew's perfectly justified burlesque of the technique and its pseudoscientific pretensions (Chew 1969: 204).

The logical point of departure for all comparisons involving Japanese with other languages is provided by the forms of Old Japanese, for which we have a corpus of written records of considerable size, dating in the main from the late seventh and early eighth centuries. Early written records are by no means essential to, nor are they even an integral part of, the comparative method, and there are more than a few cases where a modern Japanese linguistic form apparently unattested in the Old Japanese corpus can be shown to be a direct inheritance from the Altaic linguistic unity from which Japanese itself is descended. But while it would be folly to ignore the evidence of the modern language except when it is supported by citations from the older stages of the language, so also it would be perverse in the extreme to attempt comparative and historical work, in the case of a language as richly supplied with earlier written records as is Japanese, without a consideration of the forms preserved in those records.

Fortunately we are now well served for Old Japanese by the comprehensive, accurate, and extremely useful lexicon of the language recently compiled by a committee of twelve modern Japanese scholars under the chairmanship of Omodaka Hisataka. This work is cited throughout the present study simply as 'Sanseidō 1967'; for the names of the other eleven scholars concerned, see the Bibliography under the name of the chairman. The publication of this work has brought the written records of Old Japanese under convenient philological control for the first time and thus immeasurably facilitated their use in historical and comparative work. Until its appearance, Old Japanese forms could be cited only by a variety of haphazard half-measures, all of them more or less unsatisfactory; there was always the risk of overlooking important forms, or of misciting forms from carelessly edited secondary sources. This was still true as late as Miller (1967ᵇ), in which the Old Japanese forms cited were assembled by this hit-and-miss method. With Sanseidō (1967), everything has changed, and we can refer to the Old Japanese corpus with confidence both in the forms we are citing and in our comprehensive control of the corpus itself.

Probably the single most important innovation of Sanseidō (1967) is its listing of the Old Japanese *kō* and *otsu* vowel distinctions in the case of every form for which such distinctions can be documented from the texts. With this, we have for the first time a convenient and complete guide to the vocalization of Old Japanese forms, something of capital importance to all Japanese historical linguistic studies. For an interpretation of these vowel distinctions, and for other features of Old Japanese phonology, taken as already demonstrated for the purposes of the present study, see Miller (1967: 172–200 and passim).

Apart from the evidence for the Old Japanese corpus as presented in Sanseidō (1967), almost no attempt has been made here to consider other, still earlier Japanese forms, such as for example those preserved in the third-century Chinese history *Wei chih* (Miller 1967ᵇ: 278), because of the still unsolved philological difficulties that these written records generally present. Nevertheless, it has been possible from time to time in the body of this work to cite a few forms from the important early linguistic fragments that have been collected from Korean historical sources; the nestor of Japanese linguistics, Shinmura Izuru (1876–   ), was the first to call attention to the fact that these fragments obviously preserve a number of vocabulary items, including numerals, from an ancient language having a close genetic connection with Old Japanese. Unfortunately the full utilization of these fragments for linguistic study is still somewhat hampered by unsolved philological problems in their interpretation, but they may be cited in a few instances with profit (notably, below, under the numerals [§ 5.3], and in connection with the word for 'rabbit' [pp. 116 ff.]). They have been studied most recently in detail by Murayama (1962ᵇ), and somewhat less usefully by Lee (1963). Murayama does not commit himself on the precise relationship of the ancient language preserved in these fragments to Old Japanese; Lee considers them to be fragments of the Koguryŏ language, naming it after the Korean state that between 313 and 552 dominated the peninsula, and finds them 'most closely related with Japanese' (103). He also concludes that 'the language of those who brought the Yayoi culture to northern Kyūshū some 2,300 years ago was the Koguryŏ language, or one very close to it' (100).

It is probably safer, at least for the time being, simply to consider the language preserved in these fragments to be an early variety of pre-Japanese found on the Korean peninsula sometime around the fourth century of our era. (A personal communication from Bruno Lewin, dated 20 April 1970, promises a forthcoming full-scale study of these fragments, which should greatly enhance their value for the study of the genetic relationship of Japanese.)

For Korean, and above all for the reconstruction of proto-Korean-Japanese, the source has of course been Martin (1966). This reconstruction systematically treats all features of the languages being compared, reconstructing an earlier set of suprasegmental features along with the vowels and consonants of proto-Korean-Japanese. These suprasegmentals have not been considered in the present work, since we lack parallel data for almost all the other languages involved, and hence even if they had been taken into account in carrying over Martin's proto-Korean-Japanese forms, there would have been nothing in most of the other languages with which to compare them. But this omission of the proto-Korean-Japanese suprasegmentals should not be understood as in any way underestimating their importance. It should go without saying that the suprasegmentals are fully as important as any other feature of that linguistic unity, and they too must one day be accounted for on the Altaic comparative level, when our other materials are sufficiently detailed to permit such study. Unfortunately, that day does not appear to be close at hand. As in the case of Japanese, one of the major problems in introducing Korean materials into Altaic comparative studies has always been the initial difficulty of proper philological control of the sources. Martin's pioneering study has broken through this barrier and has at last placed Korean materials on a level of control sufficient for serious historical linguistic work.

For proto-Altaic, the data and reconstruction of Poppe (1960) have, in general, been taken as the point of departure for all further comparisons, and in particular for the attempt to demonstrate the genetic relationship of Japanese with proto-Altaic that is the principal aim of the present work. This makes it possible immediately to relate all new comparisons proposed herein to the totality of Poppe's painstaking reconstruction of the phonology of the proto-Altaic linguistic unity, with obvious gains in the significance as well as in the accuracy of our conclusions.

Almost nothing in the Japanese materials suggests the necessity for minor, much less for any major, revisions in Poppe's reconstruction of proto-Altaic phonology. This is a rather significant fact, since of course Poppe's reconstruction was performed without using Japanese materials (his use of Korean in the *Lautlehre* is so slight as not actually to affect his reconstructions in any substantial way). The possible exception to this general statement that is important enough to be noted here has to do with the vowels that Poppe reconstructs for his proto-Altaic. They comprise an unusually rich vocalism of nine different vowels, each appearing in both a short and a long variety, for the rather remarkable total of 18 different contrasting vowel phonemes in the original language. We shall have occasion elsewhere below (pp. 153, 185) to point out that comparison with Japanese appears to indicate that there is at least a good possibility that the original vocalism of the linguistic unity underlying all the Altaic languages, Japanese included, was rather less formidable than that reconstructed for proto-Altaic by Poppe (notably in his 1960 *Lautlehre*), and that it probably more closely resembled the vocalism reconstructed by Benzing for proto-Tungus, i.e., a total of eight different contrasting vowel phonemes, comprising a front and back variety for each of four different vowels; thus, it would be this rather simpler system from which Japanese originally inherited only four cardinal vowels without the front and back distinction, though that distinction was indeed a relevant one in the original linguistic unity from which Japanese is descended, with the result that traces of it may be found in the Japanese treatment of certain inherited consonants.

Comparison with Japanese indicates the strong probability that the long vowels presently reconstructed for the original Altaic linguistic unity are instead secondary developments in the individual languages, or in some later, secondary stage of proto-Altaic, and hence need not be reconstructed for the earliest stages of proto-Altaic; this would of course reduce the total number of vowel phonemes in Poppe's reconstruction by half.

These long vowels have not always been held to be original in proto-Altaic. Poppe himself long considered them secondary developments (Poppe 1965: 140–41), and only later came to his present position according to which they are part of the original language. There is a considerable literature on the problem (see, among other examples, Poppe 1962, Poppe 1967, and Murayama 1969ᵇ), and the issue is one that cannot be gone into here, except to note in briefest possible fashion how the Japanese evidence may in future perhaps cast new light on this involved question. Unfortunately the relevant Japanese evidence is still far too fragmentary to do more than provide suggestive indications, but it does appear to point out the way in which at least one of the so-called original Altaic long vowels may have developed from an earlier sequence of two vowels separated by a consonantal semivowel.

The vowel in question is pA *ŏ̄. In general terms, this is the reconstruction representing the correspondence of Mo. ö, Mongr. ō, Ma. *u*, Jak. *üö*, Tkm. ō̄, and Chu. -ăvă- or -ăva- (Poppe 1960: 107). These Chuvash reflexes are of great importance, both in themselves and because of a possible correlation with the Japanese materials. As is so often the case, here too a more careful inspection of the data at once shows that while the statement pA *ŏ̄ :: Chu. -ăvă-, -ăva- generally holds true, many unsolved problems remain that urgently require future study and more precise restatement. In briefest terms, when these sequences appear in Chuvash, it seems to be fairly safe to assume that they represent earlier *ŏ̄, but it is by no means equally safe to assume that an earlier *ŏ̄ is always going to appear in Chuvash as -ăvă- or -ăva-; instead, the correspondence represented by pA *ŏ̄ turns up often enough as Chu. *u* or *ü* (Benzing 1959: 704).

Two types of evidence relevant to this problem may be cited from Japanese. One appears to indicate that Japanese may have preserved a sequence of two vowels separated by a consonantal semivowel exactly parallel to the Chuvash sequences -ăvă-, -ăva-, leading to the tentative conclusion that in these words at least *ŏ̄ is not to be reconstructed for the original proto-Altaic linguistic unity, but rather that an original sequence of two vowels separated by a consonant is indicated, and that this sequence, with the loss of the intervocalic consonant, later assimilated, contracted and simplified into a long vowel (for that matter, in precisely the same way that later in the history of Japanese sequences of the type -aFu-, for example, shifted to -ō-, etc.).

The most striking lexical evidence for this involves OJ *kaFa* 'skin; leather', when compared with the following two Altaic etymologies, each of which involves the word 'skin; leather' and must, according to Poppe's reconstruction, go back to original pA *$\bar{\bar{o}}$:

1. pA *$k\bar{\bar{o}}$- in Mo. *küisün* < *$k\ddot{o}p\bar{\imath}sün$*, Chu. *kăvapa*, Tkm. *gŏbek*, all 'Nabel' (Poppe 1960: 109).

2. pA *$k\bar{\bar{o}}$- in Mo. *körge*, Ev. *kürge̯* (a loan from Mongol), Jak. *küört*, all 'Blasebalg' (Poppe 1960: 110).

Further lexical evidence of the same variety is provided by the following:

3. pA *$s\bar{\bar{o}}k$-, Mo. *söge-* 'schelten, schimpfen,' Bur. *hüge-* 'Unsinn sprechen', Tkm. *$s\bar{\bar{o}}k$-*, Jak. *üöχ-* 'tadeln, schelten' (Poppe 1960: 109), beside OJ *saFag-u* 'create a fuss, carry on, cause a disturbance'.

4. pA *$\bar{\bar{o}}č$-, Mo. *ös* 'Rache, Hass', *ösije* 'Hass', Tkm. *$\bar{\bar{o}}č$* 'Rache', OT *öč* 'id.' (Poppe 1960: 109), beside OJ *aFat-as-u* 'scorn, spurn'.

Certainly this lexical evidence opens up the possibility that Japanese and Chuvash have here preserved the original phonological structuring of the roots in question, and that the lingusitic community underlying all these languages had a sequence of vowel + labial semivowel + vowel instead of original long vowels in these roots. This problem is one that urgently requires further study, but one that also raises so many unsolved problems that it has not been possible to pursue it further in the present work.

The other variety of evidence is somewhat different, but probably of equal importance; moreover, it is surely interrelated with the first variety. We do not at present have any clue as to how the Old Japanese *ö* ~ *a* ablaut variation originated. But we must notice that in two of the best attested Altaic roots in Japanese, where our reconstructions and control of the forms are particularly secure, this ablaut variation is attested in roots that, in Poppe's terms, would be reconstructed with original long pA *$\bar{\bar{o}}$; these are '4', OJ *yö*, going with pA *$d\bar{\bar{o}}$-*, Chu. *tăvată* '4' (Poppe 1960: 110), and 'self', OJ *ore* (i.e., *$\ddot{o}re$*), going with pA *$\bar{\bar{o}}r$*, Chu. *var* 'Mitte, Bauch, das Innere' (Poppe 1960: 109). But OJ *yö* '4' has its ablaut partner in OJ *ya* '8', and OJ *ore* 'self' has its ablaut partner in OJ *are* 'that one over there'.

In other words, it is precisely in words that have, on independent grounds, already been suspected of originating not in *$\ddot{o}$ but rather in an earlier sequence of the order *-a-ṷ-a-, that the *ö* ~ *a* ablaut variation turns up in Japanese. Another case in point is that of the obvious Japanese reflex for pA *$\check{g}\bar{\bar{o}}l$-, represented in Mo. *ǧol* 'Glück, gutes Geschick', Mo., MMo. *ǧolgo-*, var. *ǧolga-* 'treffen, begegnen', Tkm.

jōl- 'Weg', Jak. *suol* 'id.', OT *jol* 'Weg, Schicksal', *joluq-* 'begegnen' (Poppe 1960: 99; cf. ibid. 75). It is difficult not to associate this root with OJ *yör-*, as in OJ *yör-u* 'approach, depend upon, encounter', and in OJ *yörös-i* 'auspicious, satisfactory, pleasing', cf. OJ *yörödu* 'myriad; an auspicious high number'. The semantic correlations are striking, but the phonological correspondence is unsatisfactory, since the bulk of the other evidence indicates that before original *-o-*, whether short or long, pA *ǯ́-* normally appears as J *t-* (see § 4.1 below). But before *-a-* followed by a continuant we would expect J *y-*, and one wonders whether it might not be justified to postulate an earlier stage of the Altaic linguistic unity in which, instead of an original long *-ō-*, the form in question had instead the vowel *-a-* followed by the same labial semivowel element postulated above for sequences of the order *-a-u̯-a-* > *-ȫ-*, with the difference that in this case a sequence *-a-u̯-* resulted instead in *-ō-*, so that *ǯ́au̯l-* relates directly to OJ *yör-*, according to the normal statements for the relevant phonological correspondences, and the *ǯ́ōl-* reconstructed by Poppe for his proto-Altaic system is in reality a somewhat later development by and large reflected in all the Altaic languages except Japanese. In this connection it is also probably important to note that Jakut has the vowel clusters *üö* for *-ȫ-* and *uo* for *-ō-*; these are customarily re-garded as later developments within Jakut (e.g., Poppe 1959: 674; Poppe 1963: 54), but in view of the Japanese evidence it is certainly worth reconsidering whether they might not instead preserve traces of a rather earlier stage in proto-Altaic phonology.

This would mean that something resembling the following scheme could be set up, clarifying many of these developments and incidental-ly suggesting for the first time a possible origin for the Old Japanese *ö* ~ *a* ablaut variation:

earliest pA	later pA	Attested forms in Turkish and Japanese
*däu̯-	*dȫ-	Chu. *tăvată* Jak. *tüört* OJ *yö-* '4'
[cf. *dä-		OJ *ya-* '8']
*ǯ́au̯l-	*ǯ́ōl-	Tkm. *jōl* Jak. *suol* OJ *yör-* 'luck; en-counter'

In still another case of pA *ō* (and also perhaps one of *ā*), there is further evidence pointing again in the direction of an early contrac-tion. It is tempting, at first glance, to follow Murayama (1950: 41) and connect OJ *wor-* 'to be, exist' with pA *bōl-*, Mo. *bol-*, OT *bol-*, Jak. *buol-* 'werden' (Poppe 1960: 99), but a more careful study of the data shows that this is an oversimplified and rather deceptive comparison. It is necessary instead to survey the entire range of words for 'to be; exist; become' in the Altaic languages, including Japanese and Korean; and when this has been done, it becomes clear that in many of these languages, and particularly in Turkish and Japanese, we must reckon with very old contractions of a prior element originally meaning 'to be; to exist (of animates)' with another element originally meaning 'to have; to exist (of inanimates)'. Poppe (1960: 112) reconstructs the equivalent of this first element as pA *bü-, but the vocalism of this reconstruction is entirely based on the written Mongol cognate, and it is more systematic to follow instead the -*i* vocalization more widely attested both in the Tungus cognates and elsewhere in Mongol as well, reconstructing pA *bi-* (cf. Benzing's reconstruction pT *bi-,* 1955: 1093). It is this original pA *bi-* that was sporadically altered to assume the shape attested in Mo. *bü-,* and it was also this pA *bi-* that entered into the contractions responsible for OT *bōl-* 'become', as well as OT *bar-* 'to be, exist'. It is also cognate with OJ *wi-ru* 'to be, exist', while in a completely parallel fashion OJ *wi-* also entered into quite similar contractions, as did another semantically parallel (but etymologically independent) form OJ *ni-*.

These complicated formations are best illustrated in tabular form, with the symbols '+ . . . >' to be read '. . . contracts with . . . to form . . .':

pA	OT	pKJ	OJ
bi-			*wi-ru* 'to be, exist'
är-	*är-* 'to be, exist' [cf. *ir-* once in Orkhon, Tekin 1968: 336]		*ar-u* 'have; exist'
	*bi+är- > *bär- > bar-* 'to be, exist' [on *-ā- in this form, Tekin 1968: 177]		*wi+ar-u > wor-u* 'to be'
äl- (*ol-?)	*bü+äl > bōl* 'become' or, *bi+ol > id.* [for *ol-,* cf. *ol-* 'take one's stand' (Nadelyayev et al. 1969: 366ª), and *olur-* 'sit, stay, dwell'. With *äl-,* cf. also perhaps *el* in *el bol-* 'reach agreement', ibid. 169ᵇ]		
äl₂-		*ni+äl₂ > *nar-/*nas-*	*nar-u, nas-u* 'become'

In connection with the proto-Korean-Japanese forms above, Martin has suggested that the abbreviation took place 'in the proto-language, with the unabbreviated forms continuing only in Japanese' (Martin 1966: 226). The Japanese 'pseudocopula infinitive' *ni-* must surely be of great importance for the history of this entire interconnected network of forms, particularly when we recall that original **ni-* would have given **i̯i-* in proto-Turkish; hence the form *ni-* may very well be concealed behind the militantly front vocalism that characterizes the Altaic 'be, exist' paradigm as a whole.

In other words, the same contraction that is represented in Japanese by *ni + ar-* > *nar-* might very well also have taken place in Turkish; but even if it had, its normal representation there would be **ni-* > **i̯i- + *är-* (or even, **i̯i- + ar-* > *är-!*), and hence it would be all but impossible to trace. At any rate, it is surely in the front-vocalism of pA **är-* that we find the ultimate historical explanation for the morphological anomaly exhibited by the two Old Japanese verbs *ari* and *nari*, when they elect to employ the 'conjunctional form' in *-i* in place of the otherwise general and distinctive 'final form' in *-u* (for an essentially nonhistorical statement of this anomaly in terms of the internal reconstruction of the Old Japanese verb, cf. Miller 1967: 323). OJ *ari* and *nari* appear as such (and not as **aru* and **naru*) because they go back to pA **är-* and **ni + är-*; the final *-i* of OJ *ari* and *nari* is a nonetymological paragogic vowel added in 'vowel harmony' with the original **-ä-* vocalization of the verb root, and hence it is exactly parallel to the final *-i* of OJ *nani* 'what?', also added because of the original **-ä-* of that interrogative (cf. OT *nä* 'id.', and § 5.2 below). In this same connection, we must note that the **l₂* indicated by the *-r-/-s-* alternation in the proto-Korean-Japanese forms, going with J *nar-u, nas-u*, cannot be reconciled with the Turkish evidence, which points in the direction of **l₁* (or in other forms, **r₁*), never **l₂* (or **r₂*). But we will realize that there is probably still more to all this than at present meets the eye when we recall that the evidence from the Turkish languages generally is that even in proto-Turkish the form underlying OT *bol-* was employed as a copula replacing forms missing for OT *är-*, and also that *ol-* and *bol-* apparently stood in much the same sort of relationship to each other early in the history of these languages (see the references collected s.v. *bōl-* in Deny et al. 1959: 791[a]; cf. also Poppe 1965: 34). Gō (1959) contains a certain amount of material on OT *bar-* and *är-*, and proposes a comparison with OJ *ar-*, but is able to reach no conclusive results.

One cannot escape the impression that in this portion of the common Altaic lexical inheritance there is much still to be learned, and that the Japanese segment of that inheritance will in time yield important evidence helping to clarify some of the basic problems encountered here. But at present it is difficult to go beyond these extremely tentative suggestions and, apart from this possibility for a simpler solution for Poppe's original Altaic long vowels, it is not necessary to depart from his reconstruction of proto-Altaic phonology in any significant respect in order to bring Japanese into its proper historical relationship with this language stock.

For proto-Mongol, the data and reconstruction of Poppe (1955) have been employed. In a perceptive review Street (1957) suggests several unsolved problems raised by Poppe's reconstruction of proto-Mongol; fortunately none of these is critical to the use made of Poppe's proto-Mongol in the present study.

It is interesting to note in passing, however, that the Japanese data may possibly shed some light on one of the problems Street discusses. Poppe's reconstruction of proto-Mongol implies a double development for pM *γ. In a large number of cases where this consonant phoneme was found between vowels in the original language it is observed to have dropped in this position by the time of Middle Mongol, and the vowels between which it was originally found are seen to have contracted to result in a long vowel in most of the attested languages; but in many other cases it appears to have remained as such. Street correctly points out that rather than allow this double development of pM *γ, it would be better to postulate two proto-Mongol (and by the same token, probably also two proto-Altaic) voiced back velars, *γ and *$\acute{g}$, the former dropping sometime before Middle Mongol, the latter being maintained in the descendant languages (Street 1957: 84–85). Later Poppe turned his own attention to this problem (Poppe 1960: 56–62), and in the course of working out its over-all solution on the proto-Altaic level was able to demonstrate the interrelationship of the voiced/voiceless (or *lenis/fortis*) contrast in certain proto-Altaic consonants to the development of the proto-Altaic long vowels and accent (Poppe 1960: 143–47; see also his subsequent treatments of these problems in Poppe 1962, 1967). Surely Street is correct in his evaluation of this set of findings as 'undoubtedly Poppe's greatest single contribution in [the *Lautlehre*]' (Street 1962: 97).

Fortunately, secure Japanese cognates are available for the two words that best illustrate this problem and the solution Street proposes, and while they do not completely solve the question, they do throw additional light on it.

Cognate with Street's pM *saɣa- 'milk a cow' is J *sag(e)- 'hang it down', *sagar- 'come down', cf. J. *saka* '(down) slope', all going with pKJ *swag(ʔa)-, K *suk- 'droop' (Martin 1966: 230, #69). Cognate with Street's pM *daġa- 'follow' is J *tagai (ni)* 'together' (see p. 85 below). For proto-Altaic Poppe would now reconstruct *sagā- for the first (1960: 59), and *daka- for the second (1960: 22, 120); and of the shift of original *-k- > *-g- in Mo. *daga-* 'folgen', he writes, 'Ausserdem findet sich diese Entwicklung in einigen unklaren Fällen im Inlaut des Stammes' (Poppe 1960: 56). It is clear at the outset that the Japanese reflexes preserve no overt, linear phonological features correlating with the original difference Street proposes to reconstruct with his *ɣ and *ġ; the linear features of the Japanese forms neither confirm nor deny his hypothesis. The light these Japanese reflexes do cast on this problem is involved rather with their suprasegmental features, another indication that, as pointed out above, to ignore such features at this stage of our comparative studies is nothing more than a convenient expedient that must not be taken to imply that such features did not play a part in the proto-Altaic phonology inherited by Japanese. The Japanese forms going with pA *sagā- are tonic (J *sagár-, J *saká*), while going with *daka- we have atonic J *tagai* (also atonic is the verb J *sitagaF-u*, from the infinitive of which it is a derived noun, minus the prefix *si-*). Other attempts have also been made to correlate the Japanese pitch accent system with the consonantism of earlier historical periods (Miller 1967[b]: 285-86, n. 14); but since we still lack a comprehensive reconstruction of the proto-Japanese pitch system, working as then (and as here) solely in terms of the modern Tokyo accentuation can hardly be expected to lead to comprehensive results.

In other words, from the point of view of the Japanese evidence, the original distinction that Street reconstructs as *saɣa- beside *daġa- was a contrast of *sagá- beside *daga-. When we are able to cite suprasegmental descriptive data of the requisite degree of accuracy for most of the other languages involved in the comparison of Altaic with Japanese, and when the proto-Japanese pitch system has been reconstructed in detail, it is almost certain that this and many other similar correlations of suprasegmentals with linear phonological features will prove to explain many other present difficulties in our systems of reconstruction.

For proto-Tungus, the data and reconstruction of Benzing (1955) have proven to be the most useful, and accordingly have been employed in the present study, despite criticisms that have been leveled against them (Poppe 1965: 142). Benzing's own views on the original proto-Altaic linguistic unity are not those underlying the present study (Benzing 1953; cf. Poppe 1965: 150–51), but this has in no way lessened the value of his proto-Tungus reconstruction for our present purposes.

No reconstruction of proto-Turkish is conveniently available. While this remains a major desideratum in the field of Altaic studies, the lack is to a large extent remedied by the fairly complete treatment of the Turkish languages in the literature and by the control of the earlier written records provided for by a variety of sources. For Old Turkish, the grammars of von Gabain (1950) and Tekin (1968) are invaluable, and for the lexicon we now have the sizable assistance of Nadelyayev et al. (1969). Poppe is, of course, the great pioneer in the reconstruction of the Turkish linguistic unity, a field in which he has distinguished himself since his early work with Chuvash (beginning with Poppe 1924/25). Much of the lacking integral reconstruction of proto-Turkish may be supplied from Poppe's 1960 *Lautlehre;* otherwise, for both the older written forms of Turkish and for the living languages, there are the generally informative and carefully written articles in the great *Philologiae turcicae fundamenta* ... of 1959, edited by Deny et al. Individual articles in this volume have been cited below by author, and appear also under author in the Bibliography, with references to their location in the *Philologiae turcicae fundamenta* . . . . The preparation of a handbook of equal detail and utility for each of the other branches of Altaic, including Japanese and Korean, would greatly accelerate progress in Altaic studies of every variety. Volumes dealing with Turkish, Mongol, and Tungus have recently appeared in the *Handbuch der Orientalistik,* under the general editorship of Spuler, but unfortunately they are not on the same level as the *Philologiae turcicae fundamenta* . . . , nor do they prove as useful to the comparativist. Articles from the *Handbuch der Orientalistik,* when employed in the present study, have also been cited by author, with cross references in the Bibliography.

Graphic representations of reconstructed language relationships are always of interest, partly because they provide a way of displaying a large body of evidence that otherwise is often difficult to summarize, and partly because the conspectus of findings that they provide is naturally more striking and attractive than a detailed recounting of that data itself would be. At the same time, of course, such schematic representations have a great built-in weakness, if not danger, since in the process of arranging all such diagrams, including 'trees' and similar graphic schemes, a certain degree of violence to the subtle niceties of the language relationships that can be recovered by the comparative method is inevitable. But so long as the end is not mistaken for the means—in other words, so long as we remember that the only purpose of such diagrams is simply to summarize other detailed data in broad outline, and also that they never replace, or serve as substitutes for, or (most importantly) in any way substantiate the findings they illustrate, they can do no real harm.

Poppe (1960: 8) presented a graphic representation illustrating the interlanguage relationships revealed by his reconstruction of proto-Altaic; this has been commented upon in useful detail and certain modifications have been suggested by Street (1965: 95); and Poppe again (1965: 138; 143–48) has reviewed these and other attempts at graphic representations. For the purposes of the present work, little or nothing need be altered in Poppe's basic scheme as evolved in his *Lautlehre* (1960: 8), apart from the position of Korean within the over-all system—and of course, that of Japanese. In the *Lautlehre* (1960: 8) Poppe depicts Korean as a later changed form of an earlier 'Urkoreanisch', and this 'Urkoreanisch' is then depicted in his diagram as descending directly from the 'Altaische Spracheinheit' that is Poppe's terminological equivalent for our 'proto-Altaic'. Street (1962: 95) suggested instead that it would be useful to reconstruct a 'proto-North-Asiatic' (this term is originally due to Samuel E. Martin) as a still-earlier antecedent to proto-Altaic, and that Korean, and probably also Japanese and Ainu, would be later changed forms of this 'proto-North-Asiatic' rather than relating directly to the proto-Altaic unity. Pritsak (1957: 15) has written of Poppe's work with Korean as dealing with the 'altaische Substrat' of Korean; but this term might very well be misleading, and should probably be abandoned. The inherited Altaic elements in Korean are no more 'substratum' than are the original, inherited elements in any other of the Altaic languages, nor do they differ in any significant respect from the inherited Altaic elements in Japanese. In the case of both Japanese and Korean, we have a great many innovations in and later accretions to this inherited portion, particularly in lexicon (mostly in the form of massive borrowings from Chinese of several different periods), but the discernible Altaic elements in both Korean and Japanese are no more 'substratum' than are, for example, the discernible Indo-European elements in English, French, or Hindi.

In the absence of a rigorous account of the Korean-Japanese relationship, and in the absence of a full-scale treatment of the Japanese relationship to all the other Altaic languages, it was of course impossible for Poppe and Street to do more than speculate on the proper locations for both these languages when drawing up their diagrams. Martin's account of the Korean-Japanese relationship has already solved one portion of this puzzle, and it is hoped that the present work will in large measure complete the picture.

Figure 1 is a graphic display of the historical relationship of Korean and Japanese to the other Altaic languages, as well as to each other, as recovered and reconstructed partly in Martin (1966) and partly in the present work. It now relates these two languages to the over-all horizon of proto-Altaic in a more precise fashion than has been possible to date. In particular, this figure is designed to direct special attention to the specific relationship, noted from time to time in the present work, that connects several of the inherited Altaic features in Japanese with the proto-Tungus linguistic unity in an especially direct fashion. Like all such graphic displays, this figure inevitably oversimplifies much important detail, but it should nevertheless be useful in indicating the main directions of historical development that now have been established.

The principal innovation introduced in Figure 1 is the postulation of an original proto-Peninsular and Pelagic unity to account for the common inheritance of Korean, Japanese, and Ryūkyū from proto-Northern and Peninsular Altaic. The term 'Peninsular and Pelagic' follows usual usage for reconstructed linguistic unities by incorporating the two geographical extremes that identify the area where the unity may be tentatively located, according to the evidence provided by the actual location of the later, attested languages (as for example in 'Indo-European'). 'Peninsular' of course stands for the Korean peninsula; 'Pelagic' (Grk. πέλαγος 'the sea') indicates the languages now attested from the seas extending beyond that peninsula.

FIGURE 1

Japanese and the Other Altaic Languages

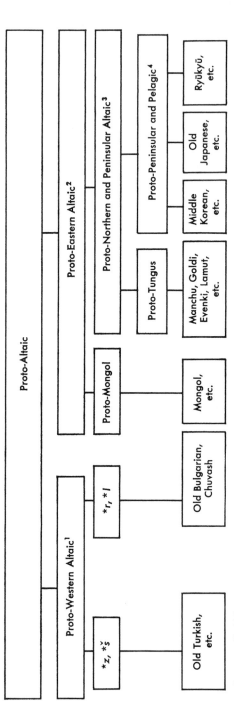

[1] i.e., proto-Turkish
[2] i.e., proto-Mongol-Tungus-Korean-Japanese
[2] i.e., proto-Tungus-Korean-Japanese
[4] i.e., proto-Korean-Japanese

Figure 1 hints at (but cannot show in the necessary graphic detail) the special set of relationships between Japanese on the one hand and a few of the Tungus languages, in particular Manchu, on the other. These special relationships can only be explained in terms of a close geographical association between the earlier forms of both, somewhere and sometime in the proto-Northern and Peninsular Altaic linguistic unity. This geographical association may best be thought of in terms of an area characterized by a great deal of common habitation by the different linguistic groups concerned—a kind of linguistic 'commons' that permitted large-scale symbiosis among the various groups over a long period of time—a symbiosis, moreover, in which the different groups preserved their individual linguistic and ethnic entities while still engaging in their daily activities in close proximity with each other. Since these are essentially areal relationships—or more exactly, perhaps, historical relationships that can best be explained in areal terms—it is difficult to summarize them in a simple linear diagram; but Figure 2 shows what can be done to give some graphic indication to the probable loci of earlier linguistic unities within the larger proto-Northern and Peninsular Altaic area.

The question of the ultimate geographical orientation of the scheme set forth in Figure 2—in other words, of precisely where in the world each of these linguistic areas was originally located—is a problem of vast proportions whose investigation cannot yet be undertaken in any significant detail, and which therefore will not further concern us here. Jettmar (1952, especially p. 498 and following) has broached the subject for the original homeland of the Tungus speakers, but a great amount of further study will be necessary before we will be able to begin establishing approximate geographical loci for each of the early linguistic unities that enter into the reconstruction of proto-Altaic. At the very least, the ultimate location of the proto-Altaic 'Urheimat' will, without any doubt, turn out to involve a complex of problems all quite as thorny, and all quite as difficult to fit out with convincing solutions, as has been the case with the proto-Indo-European home-land.

In Figure 2 we can more easily visualize the geographical area of linguistic symbiosis (crosshatched in the drawing) that must have been shared in common, during the proto-Northern and Peninsular Altaic period, by speakers of earlier forms of Tungus on the one hand and those of earlier forms of Korean-Japanese on the other. The existence of this old area of common, shared habitation best explains

the several important shared features between Japanese and the
Tungus languages, notably between Japanese and Manchu, that are
noted from time to time in the present work. The detail-projection of
proto-Peninsular and Pelagic in the lower-left of Figure 2 contains
several graphic oversimplifications; in particular, the close association, if not unity, of Japanese (J) and Ryūkyū (R) prior to their move
from the original continental homeland site to their eventual island
domiciles has not been indicated in the drawing.

A reviewer of Poppe's *Lautlehre* attempted to explain the neglect
of Japanese data in the studies of proto-Altaic reconstruction up to
that point as being due to the fact that, in Japanese-Altaic compari-

FIGURE 2
Proto-Northern and Peninsular Areal Relationships

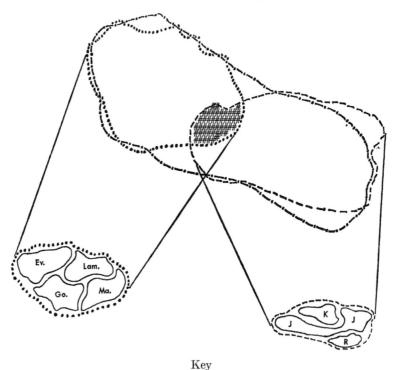

Key

·—·—·— limits of proto-Northern and Peninsular area

········ limits of proto-Tungus area

— — — — limits of proto-Peninsular and Pelagic area

————— original language areas

######## area of linguistic symbiosis

sons, 'phonological and morphological material is rather scanty, but . . . syntactic correspondence is very great' (Krueger 1961: 72). If the present work shows nothing else, it should demonstrate that the two terms in this statement must be exactly reversed. We are still not at the state in our comparative studies where the apparent syntactic correspondences between Japanese and the other Altaic languages (striking though they may be) can be manipulated to reveal anything significant about the history of these languages; but the phonological and morphological correspondences in matters of precise detail that can now be established between Japanese and Turkish, Mongol, and Tungus leave no reasonable doubt that Japanese is a later, changed form of the earlier linguistic unity to which Turkish, Mongol, and Tungus must also be referred; in other words, Japanese is another one of the Altaic languages

---

Chapter 2

Phonological Conspectus

The correspondences in phonology that can be established among the various Altaic languages may be accounted for by reconstructing a total of 18 different original consonants for the earlier linguistic unity (Poppe 1960: passim). Even though Japanese considerably simplified this rich Altaic consonantism, it is still possible to recover evidence for many segments of it from within the Japanese materials.

Most important of all the changes that transpired between the stage of proto-Altaic and the attested forms of Old Japanese was the uniform unvoicing of initial pA *b* and initial pA *g*, so that their reflexes in Japanese cognates fell together with the Japanese reflexes of original pA *p* and pA *k*, resp., giving OJ *F* for the two original labials (*p and *b), and so also OJ k for the two original velars (*k and *g). (This is to treat the original major contrast within the Altaic consonantism as if it were one of voice/voiceless, even though it was probably, in the earliest stages of the linguistic unity, actually a *fortes* [p, etc.]/*lenes* [b, etc.] contrast [Poppe 1960: 9]. But the exact nature of the phonetic qualities involved at any particular state in the history of Altaic does not alter the patterning of the Japanese developments being accounted for here.) The Japanese developments in certain cases of initial pA *b are unfortunately somewhat less than completely understood, and under circumstances that cannot yet be stated, *b sometimes did not unvoice but rather shifted from stop to continuant, to result in OJ w. The developments just described obtained only in those cases in which original *b or *g were found in word-initial; internally (in intervocalic position) original *b and *g sometimes appeared as OJ b and g, sometimes as OJ F and k, again under circumstances that require further refinement of formulation in the future. The Japanese reflexes in these internal cases are further complicated by a frequently observed phenomenon of secondary voicing in Japanese, in which intervocalic F and k often, but not regularly, became b and g; this secondary Japanese voicing was probably in some way associated with the original location of a pitch accent on the forms concerned, and genetically related to parallel developments that the proto-Altaic labials and velars underwent according to whether they were found before or after the accented vowel (Poppe 1960: 40–49, 57–60; Miller 1967[b]: 286, n. 14).

Proto-Altaic *s was regularly inherited, unchanged, as OJ s; original *j (i.e., -i̯-) appears normally as OJ y, though this phoneme was not frequent in the proto-Altaic lexicon, and in one of the few but important words in which it is well represented, the general Altaic interrogative morpheme, it can be traced only by allowing for a considerable amount of analogic change (see pp. 190–97 below). The original nasals *m and *n were also inherited unchanged in Japanese; original *ŋ, which occurred in proto-Altaic only in postvocalic position, never in word-initial (Poppe 1960: 71), is difficult to trace in Japanese. Etymologies illustrating the Japanese developments of the nine proto-Altaic consonants described in this paragraph (i.e., pA *p, *b, *k, *g, *s, *j, *m, *n, and *ŋ) will be found passim below and are also summarized in the Index of Correspondences.

The Japanese developments for the other nine proto-Altaic consonants (i.e., pA *t, *d, *č, *ǯ, *ñ, *l₁, *l₂, *r₁, and *r₂) are somewhat more involved, and therefore are treated in order and in somewhat greater detail below. In the case of $*t$, $*d$, $*č$, $*\overset{\vee}{\gamma}$, and $*ñ$, the Japanese developments may be understood only by reference to the original front- and back-vocalism contrasts of the Altaic linguistic unity, and it is in this sense that the original system of Altaic vocalism is reflected in the Japanese evidence. In the case of the two contrasting orders of liquids ($*l_1$, $*l_2$, $*r_1$, $*r_2$), the Japanese materials preserve clear traces of the original Altaic distinctions among these four original phonemes in a rather striking fashion; that Japanese should have inherited unmistakable relics of this unique quadruple contrast is one of the most significant indexes of its ultimate relationship to the other Altaic languages.

In the same way, it is necessary to reconstruct the surprisingly large total of 18 different and contrasting vowel phonemes for the original Altaic linguistic unity; there appear to have been both short and long varieties of each of the following nine vowels: $*i$, $*ï$, $*u$, $*ü$, $*e$ ($=ä$), $*ė$, $*o$, $*ö$, and $*a$ (Poppe 1960: 90–117). Speaking in the most general terms possible, we may summarize the Japanese inheritance of this rich original vocalism by pointing out that, by and large, Japanese simplified the Altaic vowel system by leveling out the differences between long and short vowels, and at the same time by maintaining the contrast between front- and back-vocalization (which it did, however, inherit) only in a relatively limited set of circumstances. But these general statements do not take cognizance of a large number of special correspondences in particular context. Even Old Japanese had what at least superficially appeared to be a relatively simple vowel system. Old Japanese, at its richest, knows only eight vowels (a, i, u, e, o, $ï$, $ë$, and $ö$), and even this modest repertoire is by the time of our written records severely limited in its distribution vis-à-vis the consonants (see Miller 1967: 180), as if to presage the wholesale destruction of this eight-vowel system and its replacement by a virtually modern five-vowel system that transpired early in the history of the language. But despite this superficial simplicity of vocalism, Japanese did actually inherit important traces of almost every segment of the original proto-Altaic 18-vowel system, with the possible exception only of the contrast between short and long vowels in the case of $*a$, $*ö$, $*i$, $*u$, and $*ü$. These considerations apart, the Japanese materials reflect the proto-Altaic vowel system quite closely, with OJ i corresponding to pA $ï$ and i both short and long, OJ u corresponding to pA $*ü$ and $*u$, both short and long, and OJ a corre-

sponding to short and long *a, *e, and *ė. Etymologies illustrating
these correspondences are found below passim; see also the Index of
Correspondences below. In the case of pA *ö and *o, short and
long, OJ corresponds with its own ö and o, but the Old Japanese ö/o
contrast was surely not inherited from the proto-Altaic *ö/*o contrast, nor does it correspond regularly to it. The evidence is not
abundant enough to make it possible to verify all the details, but
from what materials there are it appears that OJ ö is the normal correspondence for both pA *ö and pA *o, whether short or long in each
case, while OJ o is a secondary development within pre-Old Japanese,
whose appearance in certain inherited roots is to be explained by
developments within Japanese after the separation from the original
linguistic community. We have already noted (pp. 34 ff. above) the
possibilities presented by the Japanese evidence for recovering some
of the prehistory of the Altaic long vowels, particularly the vowel reconstructed as pA *ȫ; perhaps in the future this kind of historical
analysis will result in a far simpler view of the entire original Altaic
vocalism.

Given the structural imperatives for the prehistory of Old Japanese
(see § 3 below), we would expect and are not disappointed to find
that the Japanese correspondences for pA *ē and pA *e are all simply
a, in parallel with the Japanese correspondences for pA *ē and *ė;
because of their special importance for the history of Japanese as an
Altaic language, the Japanese reflexes for long and short pA *e and
*ė are discussed in detail (see § 4.5 below). All these statements are
for the developments of individual vowels, in first-syllable position,
and uncomplicated by the effects of certain consonants, notably labials, immediately following or preceding, which at times also determined the precise nature of the Japanese developments.

With this, we have accounted for the Altaic origins of the Old
Japanese vowels i, u, ö, o, and a, or in other words, for the Altaic
origins of those Old Japanese vowels that may be considered to have
been primary in terms of the internal history of Japanese, since the
remaining three vowels, OJ ï, e, and ë, result from secondary developments within Japanese, and hence these three vowels are without
direct significance for the history of the relationship of Japanese to
the other Altaic languages (pp. 55–81 below).

If we survey the Japanese treatment of the original Altaic phonology in terms of the similarities and differences shown thereby as
against the treatments that these same phonemes received in the

other branches of Altaic, many of the contrasts thus revealed are
extremely instructive. Japanese shares with Tungus an important
archaism in consonantism; both preserve unchanged the original
inheritance of the velars *k and *g, without splitting these up into two
series, to go with the front- and back-vocalism of the immediately
following vowels, as for example Mongol and Turkish did. Further,
in its treatment of the four contrastive *l and *r phonemes, Japanese is
even more conservative than in the case of the velars, since it preserves traces both of the *l_1/*l_2 contrast, and also traces of the
r_1/r_2 contrast; one must look to Turkish to find any other branch
of Altaic that preserves this unique Altaic characteristic to this extent,
since Mongol and Tungus both content themselves with the reduction
of these four original phonemes to a simple l/r contrast.

In its treatment of the original initial pA *p, Japanese goes along
in common with all the other Altaic languages that have in general
shifted this original stop initial to a spirant, so that OJ F and its later
developments in the course of the history of the language are completely in keeping with the drift of Altaic developments. Only Goldi,
Olcha, and Orok in Tungus, along with Korean, preserve this original
*p unshifted as p, while otherwise throughout the Altaic linguistic
community the spirant has generally prevailed. Thus, for pA *$pül$-
we have Mo. *ülije*- 'blasen', Ma. *fulgije*- 'id.' (Poppe 1960: 12) :: K
pul-, MK *pïl*- 'blow', going either with OJ *Fuk*- 'blow' (pKJ *$p_{\vartheta}l\hat{g}$-)
or with OJ *Fur*- '(rain, snow) fall, come blowing' (pKJ *$p_{\vartheta}r$-) (Martin
1966: 226, #16); or possibly even with OJ *Fir*- 'break wind' (Murayama 1962: 108). Japanese also shares with Turkish many charac-
teristics of its treatments of *d, *$\check{c}$, *$\check{\j}$, *$\tilde{n}$, and *j, while at the same
time these treatments provide a certain amount of evidence for the
relationship of the Japanese vowel system with the original contrasting back vs. front vocalism that it inherited from proto-Altaic. Finally,
Japanese, like all the other related languages, preserves original *s,
*m, and *n unchanged. It should also be noted that Japanese knows
absolutely nothing of such clearly secondary Tungus phenomena as
its characteristic development of initial *x- or *η- in certain roots, and
under certain phonetic conditions (see Poppe 1960: 31 on Tungus
*x-; ibid. 24, 71 on *η-). These Tungus innovations must therefore
be dated at a period sometime after the separation of proto-Tungus
from proto-Peninsular and Pelagic.

In the vowels, it is surely worth noting that the primary pre-Old
Japanese vowel system (i, u, $ö$, o, and a) closely parallels the proto-

Tungus vowel system (back *a, *ï, *o, *u, front *ä, *i, *ö, *ü; see Benzing 1955: 967–73), particularly when we recall that OJ *ö* and *o* do not (as noted above) reflect an original Altaic vowel contrast, but rather most likely resulted from developments within Japanese, so that we have, in effect, pre-Old Japanese *a, i, *o,* and *u* (where *o* is the original vowel later differentiated, solely within Japanese, into *ö* and *o*), parallel with the two series of proto-Tungus *a, *ï, *o,* and *u*. Japanese, as usual, has leveled out the original Altaic contrast between front and back vowels that survived in Tungus; but otherwise, in the essential patterning of its rearrangement of the larger Altaic vowel repertoire, it displays significant parallels with Tungus that are not without their historical implications for the prehistory of both language groups. Samuel E. Martin has suggested the useful term 'temporary hypertrophy' as a characterization of the rich 8-vowel Nara system, when viewed against the historical perspective afforded by the far simpler systems out of which it more or less suddenly grew, and to which it was eventually to revert (personal communication, 19 January 1971).

We have already noted several times in this chapter that the original Altaic contrast between front- and back-vocalism was in fact inherited by Japanese—not as such, to be sure, but in the form of distinctive reflexes for certain Altaic consonants when found occurring before front or back vowels (particularly pA *d, *ǯ, and *č). An earlier statement implying that this front- and back-contrast was probably not an original Altaic feature (Miller 1967: 69) is misleading and should be corrected; the distinction is at least as old as the ultimate Japanese relationship to the Altaic linguistic unity, and hence as old as anything in Altaic. This original front- and back-contrast is not to be confused with the limitations on occurrences of various Old Japanese vowels in successive syllables ('Arisaka's Law'), first formulated by Arisaka (1934), and summarized in Ōno (1955: 270–71) and Miller (1967: 197–98). This phenomenon of restricted occurrences of vowels in successive syllables is a Japanese innovation, and totally without relevance for the genetic relationship of Japanese to other languages (though it has often been mistaken for a continuation of the Altaic front- and back-vocalism distinction, as is implied for example in Tsukishima 1965: 133).

It is impossible, at the present state of our knowledge, to relate any of the proto-Altaic suprasegmentals reconstructed by Poppe (1960: 143–47) directly to the Japanese evidence, but many suggestive indications exist in this area, and there can be little doubt that future studies will clarify historical developments in the suprasegmentals also. For example, Poppe has demonstrated that the developments in vowel quantities in Altaic can only be accounted for by assuming that at various times in the history of different areas within proto-Altaic, original long vowels were shortened to fall together with the original short vowels, except when these original long vowels happened to occur in syllables with a phonemically distinctive high pitch; and in other changes, vowels in noninitial open syllables, whether originally long or short, dropped out entirely unless they too had the same high pitch (Poppe 1960: 118, 154, usefully summarized in Street 1962: 97–98). This situation in the broad sense must account for the characteristic nature of the Japanese inheritance from the Altaic vocalism, and in particular for the nonsurvival of the original (if indeed they are original) Altaic long vowels in Japanese; but its precise formulation in terms of the Japanese data awaits further study.

Finally, comparison of Japanese with the other Altaic languages provides evidence that makes possible the recovery of a process of assimilatory change that appears to have been widespread enough throughout all these languages for us to postulate its frequent operation within the proto-Altaic linguistic unity itself. In this assimilatory change, C_1 in the sequence $C_1 + V + C_2$ is assimilated to the manner of articulation of C_2, to result in secondary $C_2 + V + C_2$. Ramstedt long ago noted some of the problems that this assimilatory process causes (Ramstedt/Aalto 1957: 70–71). Other evidence for the operation of this type of assimilatory change in Altaic is not difficult to locate; for examples, all (perhaps significantly) from Tungus, see Poppe 1960: 24, on pT *g > *η; ibid. 27, on pT *$\check{\jmath}$ > Ma. n, and Benzing 1955: 984, 990, again on developments in Manchu. Comparisons with Japanese now show the importance of this same phenomenon in determining the reflexes of pA *d and pA *$\check{\jmath}$ before original -a-, -$ä$-, and -$ê$- (pp. 82 ff. below). In these cases the change was not a sporadic one but a regularly operating condition for the Japanese developments of the Altaic consonants in question; in certain other cases of pA *$t + V + r$, the change appears to have been sporadic. Standing in some type of ultimate relationship to this phenomenon, but clearly separate from it, are the characteristic Japanese reflexes of pA *r_2, which show a dissimilatory rather than an assimilatory pattern, with C_2 turning up as OJ -t- when C_1 was a continuant in pre-Old Japanese, but as OJ -r- when C_1 was a stop.

Chapter 3

Structural Imperatives

The morphology of Old Japanese provides internal evidence pointing in the direction of the following conclusion: the variety of Japanese known from our earliest written records (with eight vowels: *a, i, u, e, o, ï, ë, ö*) was itself immediately preceded in time by a still earlier stage whose vowels consisted of the following five: *i, u, ö, o,* and *a;* conversely, we may also conclude that it was out of this five-vowel variety of pre-Old Japanese that the language of our earliest texts developed, principally through the regular morphophonemic replacement of the earlier sequence *i + a* with later OJ *e;* the replacement of the sequence *a + i* with OJ *ë;* and the replacement of the sequences *ö + i* and *u + i* (among others, perhaps) with OJ *ï*. We have already noted above (p. 13) how Boller, as early as 1857, correctly identified some of the evidence pointing to this conclusion.

If this conclusion is correct, it should be possible to verify it with evidence from the comparative method. In other words, if the earlier stage of pre-Old Japanese that is postulated in this way, largely from the evidence preserved in the morphological structure of the language itself (internal reconstruction) and from the details of the orthography (inspection of written records), is historically accurate and valid, it should then be possible to verify this postulation by means of the comparison of the Japanese forms involved with cognate forms in related languages (the comparative method). If such utilization of the comparative method then substantiates these postulations earlier and independently arrived at from internal reconstruction and from the inspection of written records, it will provide a valuable vindication for the same postulations; at the same time, the coincidence of the findings of these three disparate methods will provide necessary substantiation for certain views on the ultimate genetic relationship of Japanese. If, on the other hand, the comparative method proves to be unable to provide any evidence that will undergird the findings of internal reconstruction and the inspection of written records with respect to the vowel system of this postulated earlier stage of pre-Old Japanese, this will be a serious objection to the postulations earlier advanced.

The phonological structure of a language does more than simply impose certain limits upon the forms of that language at any given time in its history. It also imposes restraints upon the occurrences of forms and sequences of items, restraints that will in turn to a greater or lesser degree be imposed upon and reflected through all the later, changed forms of that language—later, changed forms that will then be 'genetically related' to each other and at the same time 'descended from' the earlier common, undifferentiated form of that language, to indulge the biological figure of speech usually employed to describe these relationships. The comparative method will not only recover the forms and constituent elements (phonemes) of the original, earlier language that underlies these later changed forms (cognates), but in that process it will also recover the structural dimensions and limitations of that original. Its findings should be (and as it turns out below, actually are) particularly striking in this respect in the case of Old Japanese, because of the fairly unique skewing exhibited by the phonological structure of that language (cf. Miller 1967: 197–98). The phonological patterning of Old Japanese, as well as that of pre-Old Japanese, imposed a number of critical limiting conditions upon those languages, upon their structures, and upon their historical development. These limiting structural conditions must have come from somewhere; they must have been inherited by both Old Japanese and by pre-Old Japanese from the language or languages that are actually attested or that we can reconstruct as being the earlier forms out of which both Old Japanese and pre-Old Japanese have developed as later, changed varieties.

These inherited structural conditions were the phonological limiting factors within whose boundaries and under whose restraints the development of pre-Old Japanese into Old Japanese took place. Since they permit us to extend our knowledge of the history of Japanese back into that still earlier period for which written records are totally lacking, they are what may be termed the 'structural imperatives' for the prehistory of the language.

If OJ *e*, *ë*, and *ï* are indeed the result of secondary developments within late pre-Japanese, as suggested above, it is then clearly to these vowels that we must initially direct our attention. What do the available comparative materials tell us of the historical development and structural status of these vowels?

The only full-scale systematic consideration of Japanese on the comparative level to date is that of Martin (1966), in which for the first time a major corpus of Korean-Japanese lexical correspondences was analyzed and made the basis for a rigorous reconstruction of proto-Korean-Japanese. In this paper Martin worked almost entirely with modern Japanese forms, and all his Japanese forms are cited with the five-vowel system of modern Japanese, not with the eight-vowel system of Old Japanese. Miller (1967[b]) attempted to survey these same materials in terms of the Old Japanese eight-vowel system as preserved to some extent in the early written records and as revealed to a somewhat greater extent by internal reconstruction, making suggestions for changes in some of the details in Martin's proto-Korean-Japanese reconstructions. (The findings of this chapter will, as we shall see below, make it necessary again to revise the reconstructions, if not the essential conclusions, of both Martin [1966] and Miller [1967[b]] in a number of important details.) Among the many advances that Martin (1966) represented for the field, not the least was the fact that for the first time a large body of comparative material, from a language often held to be cognate with Japanese, had been subjected to a rigorous investigation, an investigation, more-over, that was presented in such a methodical fashion that both its materials and its findings may be used, even apart from Martin's conclusions themselves, for a variety of purposes. Our present study of the structural imperatives for the prehistory of Japanese consti-tutes, in part, one such independent employment of Martin's ma-terials.

Let us begin by making a simple count of the number of recon-structed proto-Korean-Japanese roots for which Martin offers lexical evidence, according to the modern Japanese vowel reflex that each such root exhibits (Table 1).

TABLE 1

Proto-Korean-Japanese Roots

Japanese vowel	Number of proto-KJ roots in Martin 1966
a	136
u	81
o	78
i	62
e	17

Here we are at once confronted by the most striking statistical skewing possible. It would in a sense be almost possible to write at least a portion of the prehistory of the Old Japanese vowel system from this numerical evidence alone, particularly when we recall that the Japanese *o*, *i*, and *e* of Martin's lexical comparisons are modern Japanese *o*, *i*, and *e*, and that therefore his *o* subsumes both OJ *o* and *ö*, his *i* both OJ *i* and *ï*, and his *e* both OJ *e* and *ë*. Thus, not only does Martin's *e* in the table above have to account historically for both OJ *e* and OJ *ë*, but we further notice that the total of 17 given above is an absolute and most generous maximum figure, since actually two lexical items from his correspondences involving J *e* are repeated under his correspondences involving J . . . *e*, and that furthermore both these are queried with '?', so that it would be possible (and probably would actually be well advised) to reduce the total for J *e* to 4 and that for J . . . *e* to 9, for an even smaller total of only 13 roots for this entire category. Clearly, the lexical evidence for J *e*, whatever its source, that is to be elicited from a comparison of Japanese and Korean is only a fraction of the evidence that may be elicited for J *a*, *u*, and *o*; it is also significantly less than the evidence on the same comparative level for J *i*, particularly when we recall that Martin's J *i* must account for both OJ *i* and OJ *ï*, just as his *e* must account for both OJ *e* and *ë*, and so in effect further halving the statistical weight of his evidence for *i*.

It is at once apparent from the above that J *e* (i.e., OJ *e* and *ë*, which fell together as J *e*) is significantly different, in terms of its role relative to the over-all, diachronic phonological structuring of the language, from all the other Japanese vowels; and it would also seem a reasonable hypothesis to postulate that at least a portion of the historical constituency of J *i* (i.e., either OJ *i* or OJ *ï*) also represents a segment of the language that developed under circumstances of special, if not unique, structural limitation. No other hypothesis can satisfactorily account for the heavy statistical weight of the evidence in Martin's proto-Korean-Japanese corpus for J *a*, *u*, and *o*, first of all as against *i*, but most particularly as against *e*.

Having said this, we find that we have arrived, in all but the most precise details, exactly at the same point in linguistic history as that which internal reconstruction and the written records reveal for pre-Old Japanese: *e*, the result of a coming together and subsequent replacement of *i* + *a*; *ë*, the result of *a* + *i*; and *ï*, the result of *ö* + *i* or *u* + *i* (and hence turning up somewhat more often in Martin's materials because of its greater number of possible prior sources— at least two, *ö* and *u*, as against only one each, *i* for *e*, and *a* for *ë*).

It is important to note at this point that the numerical data for Martin's proto-Korean-Japanese reconstructed roots presented above has significance over and above the statistical occurrences of the vowel phonemes in Japanese itself; in other words, we are not here simply picking up a reflection of the frequency of occurrence of *a*, *i*, *u*, *e*, and *o* in modern Japanese. This may be verified by a comparison of our count of Martin's reconstructions with three sets of data on the occurrence of the vowel phonemes in modern Japanese, from Bloch (1970). In Table 2, (a) gives the vowels in descending order according to their freedom of distribution in the language, with (in order for each phoneme) the number of phonemes that precede it, the number of those that follow it, and the total number of combinations in which it appears (Bloch 1970: 151–52); (b) gives phoneme frequencies in a sample text analyzed by Bloch, where the range was from 296 for /a/ to 2 for /x/, and two phonemes, /p ž/, did not occur at all; the numbers given are relative frequencies expressed in terms of occurrences per 19,000 phonemes (i.e., the actual percentage multiplied by 100)

(Bloch 1970: 154); finally, as a rough indication throwing some light on relative initial list frequency (in contrast to text frequency) of the vowel phonemes, (c) gives figures for the number of pages occupied by words with the vowels as initial phonemes in Kenkyusha's *New Japanese-English Dictionary* (Bloch 1970: 153, n. 37) and (d) repeats the data from Martin (1966), as above.

In Table 2, (c) is of relatively little importance, but the evidence of (a) and (c) taken together with (d) is highly significant. Clearly it is only to be expected that the vowel *a* should have turned up most often in Martin's reconstructed roots; but for the other vowels, it is difficult to see how their simple frequency of occurrence alone in the language could have been ultimately responsible for the distribution of the data in (d). Thus, (a) appears to group *o* and *u* together on the

TABLE 2

The Modern Japanese Vowels

(a)		(b)		(c)		(d)	
a	27/29/56	a	1333	i	102	a	136
o	26/29/55	o	1081	o	76	u	81
u	25/29/54	i	734	a	72	o	78
e	22/29/51	e	464	u	39	i	62
i	21/29/50	u	297	e	24	e	17

one hand, and *e* and *i* on the other; but in this (a) is totally unlike (d), where *u, o,* and *i* go together in a group and as a group contrast together with *e;* so also for (b), where *o* and *i* this time group together against *e* and *u,* in a system quite unlike anything in (a) or (d). We must conclude that the striking statistical imbalance of *e* against *u, o,* and *i* in Martin's reconstruction corpus (d) is of genuine significance for the history of the language.

Working in this same direction, two other related sets of statistical evidence may also be introduced into the discussion at this point. Table 3 gives the gross numbers of pages in the Old Japanese corpus as it appears in Sanseidō (1967); it thus provides a survey of the approximate segment of the Old Japanese corpus occupied by forms with each vowel as initial and by forms with each of the consonant + vowel combinations as initials. The vowels in Table 3 are simply those of modern Japanese, and it does not distinguish the eight vowels of the Old Japanese written records, since the purpose of this table is only to survey the approximate portions of the Old Japanese corpus, and for this purpose the modern vowels serve satisfactorily. Table 4 again presents data from Sanseidō (1967), but in a somewhat more refined fashion. This table lists the number of different lexical items (both free and bound) appearing in this source with OJ *e* and OJ *ë*, both as zero-initial and also in the case of those Old Japanese consonants following that the *e/ë* contrast was still maintained in the written records. Note that Sanseidō (1967) departs slightly from general Japanese scholarly practice in its treatment of Old Japanese *e* with zero-initial. Most Japanese reference sources treat zero-initial

TABLE 3

The Old Japanese Vowels

	zero-initial	*k-, g-*	*s-, z-*	*t-, d-*	*n-*	*F-, b-*	*m-*	*y-*	*r-*	*w-*
a	64	65	29	44	29	32	32	23	3[1]	12
i	44	15	33	5	11	26	25	-	1[2]	3
u	31	28	17	24	6	18	12	34	0[3]	-
e	3	5	3	4	5	4	5	-	0[3]	3
o	28	33	10	26	8	11	17	18	1[4]	14

[1] all bound-morphemes; no free forms in *ra-*
[2] less than one page; one bound-morpheme, one Chinese loanword
[3] less than one-quarter of a page, one bound-morpheme
[4] less than one page; bound-morphemes and two Chinese loanwords

TABLE 4

Old Japanese *e* and *ë*

	zero-initial	*k-, g-*	*F-, b-*	*m-*
e	12	9	19	15
ë	10 (= *ye*)	31	11	27
E	6	7	6	2

OJ *e* as always OJ *ë* (i.e., an *otsu*-vowel), and parallel this with *y*-initial OJ *e* that for them is always OJ *e* (i.e., a *kō*-vowel). Sanseidō (1967) puts both these together under zero-initial, and as a result has no entries under OJ *ye-*. In Table 4 the third row, *E*, represents those cases in which the written records do not preserve any unambiguous writing indicating, in the case of a particular lexical item, whether the vowel was *kō* or *otsu*, i.e., OJ *e* or *ë*. Sanseidō (1967) is particularly meticulous about distinguishing this important third category of lexical entries, a concern that makes it all but unique among similar lexical sources. Tables 3 and 4 should be considered together, since

Table 4 provides the necessary breakdown, in terms of Old Japanese phonology, of the undifferentiated J *e* entry in Table 3.

If we accept the pre-Old Japanese origins of OJ *e*, *ë*, and *ï* as set forth earlier in this chapter, largely on the basis of internal reconstruction and the written records, we might then also go a step further and postulate the following approximations of phonetic shapes for the same OJ *e*, *ë*, and *ï:*

(a) if OJ *e* derives from the earlier combination *i* + *a*, then we might expect that it was pronounced something like *[ᶦä] or *[ᶦɛ], with a mid-high vowel and an initial *i̯*-glide; by the same token,

(b) if OJ *ë* derives from the earlier combination *a* + *i*, then we might expect that it was pronounced something like *[äⁱ] or *[ɛⁱ], with the same mid-high vowel as in (a) but with a final *i̯*-glide; finally,

(c) if OJ *ï* derives from the earlier combinations *ö* + *i* and *u* + *i*, then we might expect that it was pronounced something like *[əⁱ], with a central vowel and a final *i̯*-glide.

The next question that logically arises following this speculative formulation is, of course, whether or not the early written records of Old Japanese can be made to provide any evidence to affirm or deny this hypothesis. As it turns out, the *man'yōgana* phonograms of the Old Japanese texts substantiate this working hypothesis on the pronunciation of OJ *e*, and *ë*, and *ï* in a most striking fashion.

Wenck (1954: II) makes it possible to survey the *man'yōgana* phonograms as employed in the different historical levels of the Old Japanese texts with considerable convenience. One does not, of course, find a perfectly neat one-to-one compartmentation of the phonograms with respect to the *kō* and *otsu* distinctions of the Old Japanese vowel system. There is a considerable amount of shifting back and forth between the two categories, a situation rendered even more complex by the fact that the Old Japanese orthography was diachronically accumulative, so that once a writing was used it was more often than not quickly canonized by usage and subsequently employed with little or no consideration of its original phonological rationale. Still, and despite all these obvious historical and philological problems, it is nevertheless possible to sort out major groups of the *man'yōgana* phonograms in terms of their Middle Chinese rhyme-finals, and to draw certain over-all conclusions about the pronunciation distinctions that went to make up the *kō* and *otsu* vowel oppositions in Old Japanese. Simply to verify the Middle Chinese pronunciations of all the *man'yōgana* phonograms in terms of Karlgren's or some other

reconstruction of Middle Chinese, and then to attempt to reach conclusions about the pronunciation of Old Japanese on that basis, is a
circular and almost completely pointless exercise, though one often
attempted. Summaries of several such attempts are arranged in convenient tabular forms in Wenck (1959: IV.15). But by working with
the over-all patterns of occurrence of the phonograms as presented in
Wenck's meticulous survey of the materials one may nevertheless
arrive at worthwhile findings, findings that moreover substantiate to
a considerable extent the above speculative formulations about the
probable pronunciation of OJ *e*, *ë*, and *i*.

We begin with OJ *ë*, which in the written records is found only
following OJ *k-*, *g-*, *F-*, *b-*, and *m-*. The relevant *man'yōgana* phonograms are arranged and discussed in Wenck (1954: II.84) for the velars, (II.259) for *F* and *b*, and (II.280) for *m*. If we cull from Wenck's
materials and discard as irrelevant those examples in which the same
Chinese rhyme-finals are apparently used indiscriminately for both *e*
and *ë* (but set aside one such case for discussion below, since even
these apparently internally contradictory orthographic examples are
not without a certain amount of illustrative value), we will find that
the following situation obtains for the Middle Chinese rhyme-finals of
the graphs employed as phonograms for writing OJ *e* and *ë* (for the
names of the rhyme-finals and the phonetic reconstructions of the
Middle Chinese finals see Stimson 1966: 31):

OJ *e*	Chinese	*jy*	Middle Chinese	$-^i/j(u)ii$	OJ *ë*	*jie*	*-æi*
	rhyme-	*ma*		$-a$		*hai*	*-əi*
	finals	*jia*		$-(u)\epsilon i$		*huei*	*-uəi*
		jih		$-^i/j(u)\epsilon i$			
		shian		$-^i/j(u)\epsilon(n)$			
			chyi		$-^i/j(u)ei$		

The way in which this Middle Chinese evidence substantiates a
pronunciation as proposed above of the order of *[äⁱ] for OJ *ë* is
particularly clear: Middle Chinese *-æi* and *-əi* are found for OJ *ë* after
the velars, with (understandably enough) the labialized variety *-uəi*
following the labials.

At first glance the Middle Chinese evidence for the pronunciation
of OJ *e* summarized here does not appear to be as uniform or as impressive as that for OJ *ë*, but this situation is more apparent than
real. Leaving aside for the moment the problem of the last item in
the listing above, the rhyme-final *chyi* [560] (that presents special

difficulties and is by the same token of special significance), the only remaining questions are those posed by the rhyme-finals *ma* [4303] and *jia* [594], since the others fit very neatly the earlier speculative formulation of a pronunciation *[ⁱä] for OJ *e*. With both the rhyme-finals *ma* and *jia* we must remember that, in order to understand the modern Mandarin developments of words originally having these finals in Middle Chinese, it is necessary to postulate for as early as the T'ang (and hence exactly relevant to the Old Japanese phonogram orthography) what Karlgren has called '. . . a parasitic *i:* . . . *ka* > *kⁱa*, P[eking] *tśia* ['house']' (Karlgren 1940: 50). Moreover, an exactly parallel 'parasitic palatalization' must also be reckoned with in the modern developments of words originally deriving from the rhyme-final *jia* [594] (ibid., 51).

In other words, at precisely that period in time when the *man'yōgana* phonogram orthography was being actively employed for the notation of OJ *e* and *ë*, those Chinese graphs that were consistently used for OJ *ë* were associated in Chinese with words that in Middle Chinese had a mid-front vowel followed by a final *i̯*-glide, while those graphs that were consistently used for OJ *e* were associated with Middle Chinese words with a medial *i̯*-glide followed by somewhat diverse but phonetically similar vowels. Moreover, it is clear that when in doubt the Japanese scribes assigned the critical role in their selection of a syllable to the location of these *i̯*-glides rather than to the precise quality of the nuclear vowel.

With this understood, we are now in a position to consider the employment of the rhyme-final *chyi* [560] for both the OJ *e* and *ë* categories: since this was Middle Chinese -ⁱ/*j*(*u*)*ei*, its medial -*i̯*- encouraged its use for *e* while its final -*i̯* encouraged its use for *ë*. This explains the fact that graphs going with this rhyme-final *chyi* are found scattered among both the *kō* and *otsu* categories in the Old Japanese written records. For both OJ *e* and *ë*, then, the *man'yōgana* phonogram evidence emphatically substantiates our earlier speculation on their pronunciation as roughly *[ⁱä] and *[äⁱ], respectively.

The *man'yōgana* phonogram evidence for the Old Japanese pronunciation of OJ *i* in terms of the Middle Chinese rhyme-finals is not quite as striking as is that for the pronunciation of OJ *e* and *ë*, but here too it is possible to adduce the evidence of the written records in relation to Middle Chinese phonology in support of the above formulations.

The evidence of the phonograms is presented and summarized in

Wenck (1954: II.54); again, there is a good deal of switching back and forth here between the *kō* and *otsu* categories, and this time the problem is further complicated by the fact that the Chinese rhyme-finals employed as phonograms for OJ *ï* in the Old Japanese texts happen to fall squarely in the middle of what is probably the single most mooted and notoriously difficult to reconstruct segment of all Middle Chinese phonology. But once more, the over-all pattern that influenced the orthographic choices of the Japanese scribes is clearly discernible: the one Middle Chinese rhyme-final that is entirely reserved for the representation of OJ *ï* with no shifting back and forth between *kō* and *otsu* categories or any other anomalies is the rhyme-final *wei* [7061], Middle Chinese *-iəi*, which exactly supports our earlier formulation of a pronunciation of OJ *ï* as *[əⁱ], i.e., some central vocalic nucleus followed by a final *i̯*-glide.

The resulting convergence between the formulation based upon the evidence of internal reconstruction and written records on the one hand, and the evidence of Middle Chinese pronunciation (that, to some degree, must have been one of the underlying factors in the choice of the *man'yōgana* phonograms) on the other, is impressive, all the more so because it brings together two bodies of data arrived at independently. In the process of being brought into association with each other, each body of evidence enhances the other, so that the total value of the findings is considerably greater than the simple sum of the parts involved.

With this enhanced confidence in the formulations (a) pre-OJ *i + a* > OJ /e/, [ⁱä]; (b) pre-OJ *a + i* > OJ /ë/, [äⁱ]; and (c) pre-OJ *ö + i* and/or *u + i* > OJ /ï/, [əⁱ], we may pass on to an inspection of the evidence that it is possible to adduce from the findings of the comparative method, and test whether or not this too can be brought into convergence with these formulations.

We have already noted the importance of the reconstruction of a large corpus of proto-Korean-Japanese roots by Martin (1966). For words involving J *e* (including, we must remember, both OJ *e* and *ë*), Martin reconstructed pKJ **ye* to account for the correspondence of J *e* with K . . . # (Martin 1966: 214, correspondences 16a and 16b). Thus, for J *take*, MK *tay* 'bamboo' he reconstructs pKJ **taxye*, etc. Miller (1967[b]) proposed that it would be possible to take fuller cognizance of the Old Japanese eight-vowel system in these reconstructions by reconstructing instead pKJ **ye* for those cases in which the reflex was OJ *ë*, but pKJ **ywe* for those cases in which the reflex was

OJ *e*. But neither the system of reconstruction proposed in Martin (1966) nor the revisions suggested in Miller (1967[b]) represent the optimal treatment of the data, and both now ought to be substantially revised, particularly in the light of the probable pronunciations for OJ *e* and *ë* suggested above. Furthermore, the revisions of both systems proposed in the present chapter have the added advantage of actually taking fuller account of the Korean data than do either of the two earlier systems.

It is now proposed to reconstruct these correspondences as follows: (a) pKJ **ye* for the correspondence of OJ *e* and MK *i/y* or . . . #, as in Martin (1966); but (b) pKJ **ey* for the correspondence of OJ *ë* and MK *i/y* or . . . #. Not only does such a reconstruction align itself better with what we know about Old Japanese (i.e., **ey* going with OJ /ë/, **[äⁱ]), but it also fits the Korean data more closely, in the sense that it presupposes fewer changes from the postulated proto-Korean-Japanese forms to the actually attested Korean forms than would the original reconstructions of Martin (1966) or their revisions as in Miller (1967[b]); thus, it is easier (in the sense of requiring fewer intermediate forms) to go from pKJ **taxey* 'bamboo' to MK *tay* than it would be to go from pKJ **taxye* (Martin 1966); and it is also easier (again in the same sense) to go from pKJ **jipye* 'house' to MK *cip* than it would be to go from pKJ **jipywe* (Miller 1967[b]). At the same time, we may note the symmetry between the reconstructions proposed in the present paper and the probable pronunciations of OJ *e* and *ë:*

pKJ **ye* > OJ /e/, *[ⁱä]; but pKJ **ey* > OJ /ë/, *[äⁱ].

Reconstructing in this fashion, we arrive at the revised list of proto-Korean-Japanese roots involving OJ *e* and *ë* presented in Table 5.

Further indications of the diachronic structural roles of OJ *e* and *ë* may be gleaned from a recent publication in the field (Ozawa 1968), which brings together a large amount of material of many differing degrees of importance relating to the comparison of Japanese and Mongol. Ozawa collects approximately 230 supposed lexical correspondences between Japanese and Mongol, often bringing together Old Japanese forms (more often than not forms only rarely attested, or even *hapax legomena*) and Middle Mongol forms (again often citing forms that are rarely attested, or even found only once in a single text, as for example in the *Secret History*). (One can only give an approximate total for Ozawa's lexical comparisons because he does not number them serially; and when he does number portions of his list he does not always use the same numbering system consistently throughout the different portions of his own book.) Ozawa's comparisons range from the obvious to the extremely farfetched, and unfortunately in many of his proposed sets of correspondences it is almost impossible to detect any semantic or phonetic similarity. Moreover, he treats each of his comparisons as a separate, special

TABLE 5

Roots involving OJ *e* and *ë*

Martin's Number and Tag-Gloss	Proto-Korean-Japanese (Martin 1966)	OJ (Miller 1967[b])	MK (Martin 1966)	Proposed Reconstruction
7, BAMBOO	*taxye	takë	tay	*taxey
18, BOAT	*pɔnye	Funë	pɔy	*pɔney
56, CROWD	*mur(ye)?	murë	mul, mïli	*murey
147, [2]MOUNTAIN	*myonyex	mine	moy(h)	*myoney(x)
21, BONE	*pYenye ? *penye ?	Fone	sp(y)ëy	. . .
6, BACK	*tsye	se-	ti-	. . .
29, BRUSH	*pudye	Fude ? Fudë ?	put	*pudey ?
45, CLAW	*txumpye	tumë	thop	*txumpey
79, FIELD	*pataxye	Fatakë	path	*pataxey
113, HOUSE	*jipye	iFe	cip	. . .
127, LIQUOR	*swalğye	sakë	suïl	*swalğey
89, FRONT	*alpxye	maFe	alph	. . .
244, TORTOISE	*kampye	kamë	këpup	*kampey
146, [1]MOUNTAIN	*t(x)ákye	takë	thɔk	*t(x)ákey
247, TWO	*turxye	turë	tulh	*turxey

(Note: Superscript [1,2] with glosses refer to root distinctions established in Martin 1966.)

case, and does not even attempt to work out an over-all system of sound-correspondences into which they might all be fitted; hence the most one can say of his effort as an over-all attempt at the comparison of Japanese and Mongol is that every individual item is just as unsatisfactory as every other individual item that he adduces, and that the best in his work is only a little more satisfactory than the worst, because of his failure even to attempt to introduce any over-all order or system into his investigation. For a long, critical review of Ozawa (1968), see Murayama (1969).

Despite all these shortcomings, Ozawa (1968) nevertheless does provide us with a large-scale survey of the gross lexical similarities (and, unfortunately, almost as many nonsimilarities!) between Japanese and Mongol, and it will not be without value for the purposes of the present discussion to glance at the data he has assembled.

Out of the approximately 230 lexical sets that Ozawa cites, only 12 involve Japanese words containing *e*, including both *e* < OJ *e* and *e* < OJ *ë*. Considering the liberal hand with which Ozawa has assembled his materials, this fact is by itself a remarkable statistic. And even this tiny number, 12 out of 230 or so, quickly reduces itself to an even smaller total, because out of those 12, no more than eight may be taken at all seriously as lexical comparisons between Japanese and Mongol.

The following are the lexical comparisons in Ozawa 1968 involving J *e* that do not appear worthy of further comment, because of a lack of (a) phonetic or (b) semantic resemblance:

(a)

Ozawa #13, p. 63, J *ore* 'self', Mo. *öber* 'id.'; but a perfectly satisfactory Altaic etymology for this Japanese form is otherwise available (see below, p. 147).

Ozawa #9, p. 242, J *take-r-u* 'be fierce, brave', Mo. *doɣsin-* 'id.'; even if this etymology were accepted as a tentative point of departure for further study, it would not provide any information about the origin of the J *-e-*, since nothing in the Mongol form appears to correspond to that phoneme; this means that even if the two are in any way related, which seems unlikely in the extreme, the Japanese *-e-* would have to be written off in comparative terms as an echo-vowel. Hence the comparison would be without value for our present purposes.

(b)

Ozawa #40, p. 117, OJ *sume-* 'royal, august', Mo. *süme* 'temple, lamasary'.

Ozawa #41, p. 118, OJ *suwe* 'terminus', Mo. *sübe* 'eye in a needle'.

Ozawa (unnumbered), p. 209, OJ *kömë* 'rice', Mo., Kirg. *kebeg*, Osm. *këpëk* 'bran; scurf; dandruff'. Apart from the semantic problems here, this comparison raises many still unanswered questions; note also that Martin 1966, #276 reconstructs pKJ *$p^i/_u l\H{g}ye$, for the correspondence between MK *pilɔ*, J *Fuke* 'dandruff'.

In Ozawa #7, p. 19, OJ *-kömë* ~ *-kömɨ* 'crowd in', Mo. *qamu-* 'gather together', we have an example of an important though sporadic Old Japanese sound development, with original final OJ *-ɨ* in second syllable position following original OJ *-ö-* in the first syllable of a morpheme shifting to *-ë* or *-e* because of assimilation to the place of articulation of the first-syllable vowel (we shall see below that this particular sporadic assimilatory development is one of the important sources of Old Japanese morpheme-final *-ë/-e*). This means that in this form the Old Japanese allomorph in *-i* is historically the prior one, and that the comparison again, even if correct, tells us nothing about the diachronic comparative origins of J *-e*.

This reduces the 12 cases of J *e* in Ozawa's lexical comparisons by half, and leaves us with a residue of only six out of his some 230 cases to which we must next give serious consideration:

1. Ozawa #43, p. 222, OJ *sime-ru* 'be damp, soaked', Mo. *simed-* 'id.' This probably goes with Martin 1966 #205, pKJ *sə́my-*, MK *simïy-* 'permeate it,' J *som(e)-* 'dye it'; cf. Miller 1967[b] s.v. for OJ *söm(ë)-* 'id.'. The Middle Korean form cited may well show a reflex of the final *i̯*-glide eventually going with OJ *-ë-* *[äi], but before much more can be made out of these etymologies it will first be necessary to untangle the semantic developments and changes involved; 'soak, dampen' is the kind of word that one might expect to be able to reconstruct for an early protolanguage, but 'dye' has reference to a complex operation whose history in Japan is very much involved with the introduction of continental textile technology in the protohistorical period. This makes for difficulties if we attempt to reconstruct the meaning 'dye' for the proto-Korean-Japanese unity. The second meaning must be a later semantic extension or specialization of the first, but until the exact process of meaning-change as well as the history of the technological developments involved have been clarified it is difficult to estimate correctly the significance of the comparison.

2. Ozawa #38, p. 216. OJ *sem-u* 'blame, reproach,' Mo. *čimad-* 'id.'

3. Ozawa #74, p. 160, OJ *yuwe* 'reason, purpose', Mo. *jüi* 'id.'

Both of these appear to be promising comparisons, but in the absence of Altaic etymologies for the Mongol forms cited, for the time being at least they unfortunately throw no light on the origins of the *e* in the Japanese forms.

4. Ozawa #13, p. 27, OJ *mane-* 'numerous', Mo. *meme* 'id.' Unfortunately the Mongol form that Ozawa cites appears to be a lexicographer's ghost, and so the comparison must be abandoned.

5. Ozawa #13, p. 189, OJ *e-ru* 'select, choose', Mo. *ilɣa-* 'separate assort, classify'. Once more our ignorance of the Altaic origins of the Mongol form considerably reduces its value for our immediate pur-

poses, but note that we shall see below that the vowel + *l*-sequence as in M *ilγa-* is not inconsistent with what we shall observe elsewhere concerning one of the possible ultimate sources for OJ *ë*.

6. Ozawa #84, p. 268, OJ *netam-u* 'be jealous, to envy', MMo. *nayida-* 'neidisch, eifersüchtig sein', Mo. *nayidaŋgui* 'Neid', Ev. *nadit-* 'voraussetzen, sich etwas vorstellen oder einbilden, argwöhnen' < *najïdït-* (Poppe 1960: 37, 140, 158). There are, to be sure, a certain number of semantic problems involved in this etymology, and Murayama (1969: 85–86) is correct in pointing out the failings of Ozawa's glosses; but these difficulties are not of sufficient gravity to rule out the over-all importance of the comparison, which is one that, for a change, does actually tell us something about the diachronic comparative origins of the *e* in the Japanese form. As a result this particular lexical correspondence may well be one of the most significant in Ozawa's entire book.

By the time of our earliest Old Japanese written records the contrast between OJ *e* and *ë* had already been leveled out after OJ *n-*, but even in this position it may still be recovered in certain forms by internal reconstruction; thus we may recover OJ *Funë* 'boat', on the basis of its combining-form allomorph J *funa-*, etc., even though the Old Japanese phonograms made no provision for writing an *-ë* following an *n-* in their *kō* and *otsu* orthographic distinctions (Miller 1967: 185 ff.). OJ *netam-u* 'be jealous, envy' is to be derived from OJ *na* 'name' + *itam-u* 'hurt, be painful'; the type of composition involved is one that is not without significant parallels in other Old Japanese locutions (cf. especially, on compounds with *ita-* 'painful' in second position, Miller 1967: 193). This leads us to postulate an earlier pre-OJ *nëtam-u* for this form; but what is of particular significance about this particular item is the fact that apparently this compound itself, as well as the individual forms that comprise it, all go a considerable distance back into the prehistory of both Japanese and Mongol—and by implication, into the common linguistic unity that underlies both—since the Mongol forms that Ozawa cites (1968: 268) display the same lexical elements entering into the same composition, but without the morphophonemic vowel replacement that characterizes the Old Japanese formation. Furthermore (and this makes this particular lexical comparison of singular importance for the prehistory of Japanese), the same formation and the same forms may be traced in Tungus, cf. Ev. *nadit-*. The convergence of the comparative data in this instance with our postulation for the pronunciation of OJ *ë* as *[äⁱ] is borne out to a remarkable extent by the related Altaic forms with their -aᶎï- sequence.

Additional light is thrown on this important etymology by Samuel E. Martin, who points out that 'the *na* of *na-ita-* may have originally been 'face' (cf. K *nach* 'face'), 'name' being a later semantic extension or shortening from *na-mae* 'what is in front of the face' (personal communication, 19 January 1971).

But Altaic sequences of this shape were not the only sources of OJ *ë*; important evidence is also at hand pointing to instances in which this phoneme had its origin in an original sequence of vowel + *l*, where apparently the loss of this postvocalic *l* between the time of proto-Altaic and pre-Old Japanese played a role analogous to that of the final *ᶎ*-glide in the other examples above.

This postulation may be substantiated with one of the most secure of all Altaic etymologies involving Japanese: OJ *kë* 'hair':proto-Altaic *kïl*, Mo. *kilγasun*, MMo. *qïlγasun* 'Haar, Rosshaar, Saite', Chu. *hălăh* < *qïlïq* 'Rosshaar', OT *qïl* 'Haar' (Poppe 1960: 19). We have seen reasons to assume that OJ *ë* was actually [äⁱ]; its final *ᶎ*-glide in OJ *kë* 'hair' would, in the light of this etymology, now appear to preserve a trace of the stem-final *l* of the original Altaic root. This *l* was lost in Japanese, but it did not disappear without leaving its trace, in phonetic terms, in the pronunciation of the Old Japanese vowel phoneme in question—or, in phonemic terms, in the fact that the Old Japanese reflex of this root is *kë* and not **ke*.

With this correspondence in hand we are at once in a somewhat better position to appreciate the importance of another of Ozawa's lexical comparisons, his #13, p. 189, OJ *er-u* 'select, choose,' Mo. *ilγa-* 'separate, assort; classify; select the best', already noted above. Japanese scholars traditionally assign all cases of initial OJ *e-* to *ë*, not *e*. Since there is no contrast between OJ *e* and *ë* in form-initial position the question is not an important one; and moreover, since in all other cases in the language these same scholars elect to write *kō*, not *otsu*, vowels in similar circumstances without contrast (thus, always writing *ne*, *te*, etc., never **në*, **të*, **së*), their choice of the *otsu* vowel *ë* for initial OJ *e-* is more than a little inconsistent. Despite these theoretical objections, however, it is not difficult to understand why the Japanese scholars have generally settled upon this doctrine, since the *man'yōgana* phonograms used for writing initial OJ *e-* fall into the same Chinese rhyme-final classes as those typically used for writing

OJ -ë- elsewhere, notably following the velars and labials (see also above, p. 63).

If we wish to follow their convention in this case and postulate OJ *ër-u for the form in question, it will then appear to follow the pattern of OJ kë 'hair' quite closely, although in the absence of an etymology clarifying the Altaic origins of Mo. ilɣa- the case cannot of course be nearly as convincing. But it may be important to note that Mo. ilɣa- is a secondary verbal formation in -ɣa-, and that the primary root involved is ila- 'vanquish, be excellent'.

We have noted above the evidence available from within Japanese and from inspection of the Old Japanese written records bearing on the pronunciation of OJ *i. We next are entitled to ask what if any light can be thrown on this question from the materials and results of the comparative method. Fortunately, two quite substantial and rather informative etymologies are close at hand:

1. Ozawa #20, p. 76, OJ kï 'fort, stronghold; tomb':Mo. keụid 'lamasery', but in early texts 'dwelling', MMo. geụit 'house, dwelling' (other Mongol cognates in Poppe 1955: 140).

2. Ozawa #21, p. 80, OJ kïri 'fog, mist':K hïli 'be cloudy', pKJ *xayri- (using the revised formulation suggested in the present chapter, and hence rewriting the original pKJ *xyari- reconstructed in Martin 1966: 85). Cf. Mo., MMo. keụ 'wind' (Poppe 1955: 79, 143).

In both these cases, it is significant to note how the OJ *i vocalization correlates in Mongol with a sequence of nuclear vowel + final ụ-glide; the correspondences here are regular, and at the same time they are quite in keeping with our earlier postulation of the pronunciation of OJ *i as [əⁱ]; moreover, they are in significant contrast with the two following etymologies that provide us with evidence on the comparative level for the contrasting phoneme, OJ i:

3. OJ kir- 'cut':pA *kïr-, Mo. kir-ga- 'scheren', Osm. qïr- 'schaben', Ma. giri- 'schneiden', Go. geri- 'ausschneiden' (Poppe 1960: 20, 115), pT *gïrï- (Benzing 1955: 969); these forms are also eventually to be associated with pKJ *kyɔr-, which relates J kir- with K kal-, MK kɔl- 'whet, grind' (Martin 1969: #58).

4. OJ ki- 'wear (clothing, in general)':pA *ked-, Mo. kedüre- 'anziehen, überwerfen', OT käd- 'anziehen'; but here unfortunately a convincing and informative Korean cognate appears to be missing.

Not only are these last two etymologies extremely instructive with respect to the evidence that they provide on the comparative level concerning the simple origin of the Old Japanese vocalism i in contrast with the complex origin of OJ *ï*, as above, but they also incidentally correlate in a striking fashion with the morphological aspects of the Japanese evidence, since they provide for the first time an 'explanation', i.e., a historical account of the origins of the two different Japanese verb inflections represented here, J *kir-, kirimasu* '[I] cut', against J *ki-, kimasu* '[I] wear', though both verbs have identical conclusive forms, *kiru*.

In the case of the verb 'cut', the final *-r-* of the Japanese reflex represents a Japanese inheritance, and preservation, of the original Altaic root-final consonant *$*-r-$. But in the case of the verb 'wear', where the original Altaic root was *$*ked-$, followed by a juncture vowel *-ü-* or *-i-* in the various morphologically more complex descendant forms, as for example in Mongol (see Poppe 1960: 19), the original root-final consonant was the *$*-d-$, which in this morphological position was not inherited in Japanese, i.e., its Japanese reflex in this position is a zero.

In this way, the findings of the comparative method often throw light on more than one problem at the same time, illuminating not only the particular problem area to which our attention was originally directed but at the same time providing insights into other unrelated, but nonetheless important, problems. These etymologies not only help to clarify the historical origin of OJ *i* and the nature of its contrast with OJ *ï*, but they also have something important to show about the earliest stages of the differences that we now observe among the morphological categories of the Japanese verb system.

To be considered along with the above etymologies is still another, although its relation to the four cited immediately above is less obvious at the present time:

5. OJ *k-u-* 'come', < *$*kw-$ (Miller 1967: 322):pA *$*ker-ü-$, Mo. *kerü-* 'wandern, sich umhertreiben', MK *kël/t-*, OT *käz-* 'reizen', Osm. *gäz-* 'sprazieren' (Poppe 1960: 19). Martin 1966: #253, s.v. ²WALK, reconstructs pKJ *$*kař-$, but he is associating the Korean forms with J *kayof-u* 'commute, go back and forth on a regular basis'; and this same proto-Korean-Japanese root must also somehow be associated with Martin's pKJ *$*kaš/l/t-$ (*sic*), which he reconstructs ibid. #252, s.v. ¹WALK, taking account of the same Korean forms but this time involving J *kati* 'a walk; trip on foot'. The Turkish forms show that the original Altaic root must have had root-final *$*-r_2$, and perhaps that is the feature reflected in this rather surprisingly large cluster of cognate forms in both these languages, and above all, in

the almost excessive morphophonemic richness of their finals. Within Japanese, too, the situation is far from simple, since this verb has a variety of stems, including OJ *ke-*, *ki-*, *ku-*, and *kö-*; in view of this multiplicity of forms (most of which are no doubt to be explained as sporadic assimilations of an original root to affixed endings), the verb is a difficult one to account for, particularly at our present state of control of the comparative materials. The comparison does not, as a result, throw much light upon the origins of OJ *i*, or upon the nature of the contrast of that phoneme with OJ *ï*, but it should be kept in mind in connection with the etymologies suggested immediately above, particularly in view of its at least superficial parallelism with some of the structural features of the verbs 'cut' and 'wear'. The **ko-* that Martin (1967: 257) postulates as the proto-Japanese shape for this verb is, like the **kw-* cited above, a result of internal reconstruction, and hence is a reconstructed form of a somewhat different order than those arrived at through the comparative method.

We have noted shortly above a variety of historical linguistic serendipity, in which a search for information on the comparative level relative to the historical origins of the contrast between OJ *i* and OJ *ï* also proved to throw a certain amount of light on the origins of some configurations in Old Japanese verb morphology; a study of the following two etymologies results in a somewhat similar situation:

1. OJ *mi*, MK *mïl* 'water', pKJ **myaldu* (Martin 1966: #257; Miller 1967: id.). Ozawa #63, p. 143 attempts a most involved association of these Japanese and Korean forms with forms in Mongol and other languages, but his formulations in this instance involve so many undemonstrated intermediate stages and undocumented changes that it is probably best not to give them further currency by recapitulating them here; of all his attempts at etymology, those involved with these words for 'water' show Ozawa's ad hoc, unscientific methodology at its least acceptable.

2. OJ *mï* '1st-person pronoun, sg.', pA **bi* 'id.' For details of this etymology see pp. 158 ff. below.

Here we at once notice a parallel with some of the etymologies suggested above, where it appeared that OJ *ï* was a development, at some time in its history, from an earlier combination of the vowel *i* + a *i̯*-glide, or in certain instances, of the combination *i* + *l*, in which circumstances the post-vocalic *l* seemed to have played a role closely analogous to that of the *i̯*-glide. But here we appear at first glance to have exactly the opposite: it was the original form for

'water' that had the post-vocalic *l*—but it is 'water' that had OJ *i*;
while it was the first-person pronoun that had the original *i* vocalism
followed by zero, with neither hint nor possibility of a glide, either *i̡*
or *l*-originated, being involved with its pronunciation—and yet this
is the morpheme that had OJ *ï*. We appear to have found exactly the
opposite of what we might have been expected to be looking out for,
until we recall that there is other independent evidence that has
earlier led to the suggestion that the *kō* and *otsu* labels ought to be
reversed following the Old Japanese labials. The reasons for this suggestion have been summarized by Martin in Miller 1967[b]: 281, n. 8.
We must keep in mind that the *kō* and *otsu* vowel labels are above
everything else philological data based upon the interpretation of the
Old Japanese written records, and upon the patterning of the phonogram graphs in those records. Martin's suggestion is that the interpretation of those records would be more regular and orderly, and
more in keeping with the pattern of the interpretation of the other
segments of those records, if the traditional *kō* and *otsu* distinctions
were reversed following labials. This would mean that OJ *mi* 'water'
would instead become OJ *mï*, and OJ *mï* 1st-person pronoun, sg.'
would instead become OJ *mi*. And with this reversal, carried out because of considerations quite apart from the issues raised by these
two etymologies, we find that the data now fall into an over-all
pattern quite uniform with that already suggested above, namely,
one in which OJ *ï* appears to have resulted from earlier combinations
of vowel + *i̡*-glide or post-vocalic *l*, while OJ *i* appears to have resulted from a single, uncombined *i* vocalization followed only by
zero.

This formulation also provides a clue pointing in the direction of
an eventual solution for one of the most vexing etymological tangles
in the entire Far East, namely the interconnections and relationships
of the various words for 'horse'. Martin 1966: 249 has trenchantly
observed that 'the word is usually assumed to be a borrowing in all
languages, but someone must have had the original horse'. He reconstructs pKJ **mal* to account for K *mal* 'horse' and J *uma* 'id.' This
J *uma* is itself often, perhaps generally, considered to be a loanword
from Chinese, with prothetic *u-* in Japanese, and the many problems
raised by Martin's attempt to associate it directly with the Korean
form are no doubt why he includes the etymology only in his Sup-
plementary List, '. . . about many of which I feel strong doubts'
(ibid., 192). Here we may with profit recall a suggestion made some

time ago by Haguenauer (1956: 242), who proposed that the Japanese form *me* 'horse', which is usually considered to be a so-called *go-on* reading for the Chinese graph *mǎ* 'horse', or, to restate the situation in linguistic rather than purely orthographic terms, to be a rather early loanword from Chinese into Japanese, etymologically has nothing to do with Chinese at all (except of course as Chinese is also involved in the prehistory of the horse in northern Asia). It is difficult not to agree with Haguenauer here, and to conclude with him that in fact J *me* 'horse' has indeed been 'abusivement classé . . . comme **go.on*' (loc. cit.). J *me* must be an old Altaic form; and we note that as the Old Japanese written records are usually read, it is OJ *me*, not OJ **më*. But once again, if we reverse the traditional *kō* and *otsu* labels for the identification of the vocalism of the Old Japanese orthography, as just discussed above, we now have (new) OJ *më* 'horse', going with pKJ **mal*, K *mal*, and providing the same suggestive indication as did OJ *kë* 'hair' for an ultimate origin of the OJ *ë* vocalism in an original vowel + *l* combination.

Since the formulations and statements above might superficially appear to resemble some of the suggestions recently set forth in an attempt at a treatment of the history of J *e* (Lange 1969), it is necessary to make it immediately clear that they have nothing in common with his proposals, which are impossible to reconcile with what we know of the history of the language.

Lange works in terms of an a priori postulation in which the Old Japanese *kō/otsu* distinction between two types of *e* is to be explained by the existence of the following phonological structure: syllables in Old Japanese that, at the time of our written records (the only variety of linguistic evidence with which Lange concerns himself), do not show a contrast between two different types of *e*, had a 'strongly palatalized *e*', while Old Japanese syllables that, at the time of our written records, do show this contrast, had a 'nonpalatalized *e*'. In the changes from Old Japanese to Middle Japanese, the 'nonpalatalized' syllables became palatalized ('the set of syllables lost was the nonpalatalized set'; Lange 1969: 49), so that in Middle Japanese all cases of *e* were his 'palatalized *e*', which then in turn again became 'nonpalatalized' in modern standard Tokyo Japanese.

Quite apart from all the problems in phonetics and phonology, both synchronic and diachronic, that such a postulation presents, Lange's formulation misses the mark in several critical respects. It assumes, without evidence, that the language of the Portuguese romanizations of the late sixteenth and early seventeenth century, in which /se/ is always [še] (just as in modern standard Japanese /si/ is always [ši]), is in a direct line of genetic inheritance from the Old Japanese of the court at Nara, the language that underlies our Old Japanese written records. It also assumes, equally fatally for Lange's thesis, that modern standard Japanese is in a direct line of genetic inheritance from both these two earlier forms of Japanese (i.e., the Middle Japanese of the Portuguese transcriptions and the Old Japanese of Nara), which is manifestly not the case. Rather than focus his attention on the vocalization of the late-fifteenth-century Korean transcriptions of Japanese, which show Korean [-jöi] uniformly for J *e*, both in isolation and following J *k-*, *s-*, *t-*, *n-*, *F-*, *m-*, *r-*, and even *w-* (!), Lange instead centers his argument on the almost surely automatic glide [-i̯] of the Korean equivalents, without even attempting an explanation of the problems presented by the equation, in these transcriptions, of Korean [ö] with Japanese *e*. This equivalence is the point where attention must center in future studies of the problems presented by these Korean-Japanese bilingual materials; but whatever else they may reveal to us about the pronunciation of Korean and Japanese in the fifteenth century, they surely have nothing to tell us about the phonological structure of the language of the Nara court.

We have already stressed, at the beginning of this chapter, the fact that much essential information concerning the special historical role and the structural imperatives of J *e* is preserved within the modern Japanese verb system. Actually, it would be no very great exaggeration to claim that it would be possible to write the history of this vowel from the single fact that in the modern language, verbs of the type J *ka-u* 'buy', *omo-u* 'think', *su-u* 'suck up', *i-u* 'say', etc., never have *-e-* as their base-final vowel, i.e., the vowel here immediately preceding the final *-u* in the forms cited. In this position, we have examples with *-a-*, *-o-*, *-u-*, and *-i-*, as just cited, but never with *-e-*. This is because, as we now can understand, J *-e-* is historically a complex vowel, and if it were to be found in this base-final position, such occurrence would in effect imply a further, more complex morphological structure and one mutually exclusive with the morphological role of a base.

We may also catch a glimpse of the same historical phenomenon as well as the same structural imperatives from still another angle. In Bloch's descriptive treatment of modern Japanese verbs, we find 'vowel verbs' and 'consonant verbs'; the bases of his vowel verbs end in -*e*- or -*i*-, the bases of his consonant verbs end in -*t*-, -*r*-, -*w*-, (**kaw-u* 'buy'), -*s*-, -*k*-, -*g*-, -*b*-, -*m*-, and -*n*- (Bloch 1970: 7–12, where, however, the second table and first paragraph on p. 9 should be moved to p. 10). But as Bloch pointed out elsewhere, J -*i*- may always be taken to be equivalent to /ye/ (Bloch 1970: 7, and n. 8; see also 3, n. 4), so that actually all his vowel verbs would then have bases ending in -*e*- or -*ye*-. But historically his -*e*- verbs also go back to an original underlying -*y*-, so that, essentially and historically, the two classes of verbs both go back to uniform consonant origins, thanks to what might be termed this 'recursive' feature of Japanese historical phonology.

In phonology, still another glimpse of the special historical role of J *e* may be discerned from the fact that among the modern Japanese vowels, it is *e* alone that has no voiceless allophone (Bloch 1970: 136, n. 28). Similarly, the lack of Japanese adjectives in -*e*- points in the same direction (see Martin 1967: 266, n. 29, on the two apparent exceptions to this statement, both of which have conveniently disappeared from the modern language).

A further indication of the special historical nature of J *e* may be detected from the system of permitted metrical irregularities (*jiamari*) in classical Japanese poetry. These rules are a codification by the later poets of examples of metrical irregularity observed in Old Japanese poetic texts; in rough summary, they permit extra syllables in a given line when, but only when, these syllables consist of word-initial *a*-, *i*-, *u*-, and *o*-, but never *e*-. Motoori Norinaga (1730–1801), who first described this system, noted the surprising absence of examples in *e*-, but added that he could not suggest a reason for this lack (cited in Satake 1946: 183–84). Of the cases of metrical irregularity in the *Man'yōshū*, 89 percent actually follow Motoori's rule (data from Satake 1946; but since, unfortunately, he cites and counts together both phonogram and nonphonogram lines, his data are not fully reliable; one may well suspect that a greater percent, perhaps even all, of the phonogram lines follow Motoori's rule). Among this 89 percent, Satake finds 611 examples of metrical irregularity involving *a*- in word-initial, 386 with *o*-, 257 with *i*-, and 150 with *u*-; and he finds none with *e*-. Note that this order is exactly that of (b) in Table 2 above.

The reason why forms with word-initial *e*- did not find a place in this scheme of permitted metrical irregularities in Old Japanese poetry is not hard to establish, given our present knowledge of the history of this phoneme. In the permitted metrical irregularities, words with *a-*, *i-*, *u-*, and *o-* were pronounced in such a fashion that their vowel initials underwent crasis with the final vowel of the preceding form. But OJ *e-* was itself already just such a crasis vowel, and the result of this same process of crasis, so that its pronunciation, in the Old Japanese period, would obviously have inhibited its participation in this scheme. The later poets began simply by imitating the patterns they had observed in the *Man'yōshū* and other Old Japanese poetic texts. They continued by codifying rules evolved from their careful observation of those patterns. As a result, they perpetuated a system of permitted metrical irregularities that had been based upon the pronunciation of Old Japanese, and that was explicable only in terms of that pronunciation, long after the pronunciation had changed beyond all recognition. Nor were the later poets, along with Motoori, any longer in a position to recover the reasons originally underlying the rules that they continued to apply to their poetic composition, because of the structural changes transpiring in the language between the Old Japanese period and their own time.

With this, we have presented all the sources for inherited J *e*, and for OJ *e* and *ë* as well, that it is possible to establish at the present time (see also pp. 153–54, below, for their statement in terms of pA **e*, **ē*, **é*, and **ế*). But not all cases of J *e*, or of OJ *e* and *ë*, are inherited from the Altaic linguistic unity. A certain number, including *e* in many important and common words, have other historical explanations. Some are the result of a sporadic assimilatory process in which earlier and original *i* or *ï* was shifted to *e* or *ë* due to the articulatory pressure of an *o*, *ö*, and *a* in the syllable immediately preceding (the most common case), or in the syllable immediately following (less often observed). Others must be held to have resulted from borrowings from other languages. We shall conclude this chapter with a brief summary of examples of both these possible sources of non-etymological J *e*.

In many important words, J *e* and its earlier sources are the result of a phenomenon of analogic vowel-lowering or centering, in which original *i* or *ï* was altered to become closer to the articulation of *-o-*, *-ö-*, or *-a-* in an adjacent syllable. We have already noted OJ *kömë* as a secondary form deriving from an original *kömï* (p. 68), and numerous other examples can be cited for this same lowering or centering phenomenon. The evidence has been collected in convenient form by Wenck (1959: IV.8, §§ 908.5, 908.6), who gives complete references to the texts in which the forms are found, so that it is not necessary to repeat all the data here. One example (not found in Wenck) will suffice: for original OJ *ti* + *tösi* '1,000 + year(s)', the texts generally have *titöse* '1,000 years', where the final *-e* in *töse* is clearly not etymological but the result of a shift of the original *-i* still seen in J *toshi* 'year' in the direction of the position of articulation of the *-ö-* in the syllable immediately preceding it. It was this analogically altered OJ *töse* that was early generalized to become the ordinary combining form of OJ *tösi* used in counting years, particularly in stating ages (Sanseidō 1967: 494^{c-d}). Otherwise, in order to demonstrate the subtypes of this vowel-lowering or analogic centering phenomenon with which, from time to time, we will have to contend in any account of the historical phonology of Japanese, it is sufficient to cite here the relevant portions of the forms without text references or glosses, since only the forms, and not their meanings, are relevant to the present discussion:

1. with *-o-* or *-ö-* preceding, *-ï* > *-ë:*
   matunökï > *matunökë*
   tumagömï > *tumagömë*
2. similarly, with *-a-* preceding:
   niFunamï > *niFunamë*
   makï > *makë*
3. so also, but with *-i* > *-e:*
   saFi > *saFe*
   kaFiri > *kaFeri*
   titösi > *titöse*
4. and finally, with *-a-* following, *-i-* > *-e-:*
   -kiya- > *-keya*
   -mira- > *-mera-*
   -Fira- > *-Fera-.*

All this makes excellent sense in terms of the pronunciation of OJ *e* and *ë* postulated in the present chapter. When *-o-*, *-ö-*, or *-a-* was found in the syllable immediately preceding, *-ï* was often pronounced in such a fashion that it at first approached, and then eventually fell together with, OJ *ë*, i.e., [äⁱ]. When *-a-* was found in a syllable immediately preceding or immediately following, *-i* was often pronounced in such a fashion that it at first approached, and then eventually fell together with, OJ *e*, i.e., [ⁱä]. From these accidents of pronunciation derive many of the cases of analogic OJ *e* and *ë* that we find in our earliest texts.

Finally, we cannot overlook the possibility of OJ *e* and *ë* appearing in loanwords from other languages, including loans from other Altaic languages. One striking example will suffice. Poppe suggests reconstructing pA **bīle-* to account for Mo. *bile* 'Handgelenk', Mo. *bilečeg* 'Armband', Bur. *behel'ig* 'Ring', Ev. *bīlẹ̄n* 'Handgelenk', Lam. *bīlẹ̄pẹn* 'Armband', OT *biläk* 'Pfote, Hand, Unterarm' (Poppe 1960: 21, 117). This immediately brings to mind OJ *Fire*, the name of several different ceremonial and ornamental badge- or scarf-like objects. The *Fire* was, at different times in the Old Japanese period, a white cloth worn on the shoulder as a kind of phylactery to protect the wearer against demonic possession, as well as during religious ceremonies; it was a white scarf worn by women and ceremonially waved during farewells and in welcoming; and it was a small flag-like cloth device tied to ceremonial and ritual objects, including the phallic-shaped *hoko* (see Nakada 1963: 977[b-c]). Typical texts include *Kojiki* poem 102 (Philippi 1968, no. 103), *Nihon shoki* poem 100, *M* 863, *M* 3243; and in the last sense, *M* 871 (the *kotobagaki*). It is not difficult to see in this word a loan from some continental source, and at the same time to find in this historical explanation for OJ *Fire* the source of its nonetymological final -*e*.

Given this survey of the different sources for modern J *e*, we are finally in a position to understand its various possible historical origins, together with its unique role vis-à-vis the structural imperatives for the history of the language.

Chapter 4

Phonological Evidence

4.1 **d̦-, *ǯ̆-, *č̆-*

It goes without saying that the demonstration of phonological correspondences in matters of precise detail is the essential first step in
any attempt at the recovery of an earlier, but now lost, linguistic
unity; and the linguistic unity represented by Japanese and the other
Altaic languages is no exception to this general dictum. Fortunately,
Poppe's reconstruction of proto-Altaic phonology, particularly in his
Lautlehre (1960), makes it possible for us to focus our attention from
the outset on a small number of particularly critical proto-Altaic
phonemes. These phonemes are all 'critical' in the sense that they
have somewhat complicated and thoroughly distinctive reflexes in

those various Altaic languages on the basis of data from which Poppe was able to achieve his reconstruction of proto-Altaic phonology, and our normal expectation would be that in Japanese too these phonemes would display complicated and distinctive patterning in their attested reflexes. This expectation, as it turns out, is completely justified.

Working along these lines, we will naturally first turn our attention to the problem of determining the Japanese reflexes of the proto-Altaic voiced dental stop initial and, together with it, those of the closely related voiced and voiceless affricate initials. With these solved, we will be in a position to give somewhat less detailed but equally conclusive treatment to the proto-Altaic palatal nasal initial (§ 4.2, below), as well as to the characteristic proto-Altaic palatal liquids (more properly, liquids and vibrants) generally symbolized as *l_2 and *r_2 (§§ 4.3, 4.4), and finally, to the rich proto-Altaic repertory of *e* vowels (§ 4.5). The statement and description of the Japanese reflexes for each of these entities in the proto-Altaic phonological inventory provide a means for recovering just that many more episodes from the otherwise lost history of linguistic events transpiring between the time of the proto-Altaic linguistic unity and our earliest Japanese written records.

Murayama has presented important evidence for an 'Anlautsveränderung' in which pA *d- becomes J y- (Murayama 1962: 108), but a more complete study of the data shows that his relatively simple statement needs (as one might expect) considerable refinement. The Japanese developments of the proto-Altaic initial *d- must be considered together with the developments of initial *ǯ-, with which they have much in common. A reconsideration of all the available evidence shows that in both cases the reflexes of these proto-Altaic phonemes in Japanese were conditioned by whether the syllable in which these phonemes were initial in the parent language had original front or back vocalism in that parent language. This is a finding of capital importance not only for the history of the individual forms involved but for the entire historical phonology of Japanese.

The patterns of development are particularly clear in those cases where the vowel in question was original *u* or *ü*, so that original *du* or *ǯu* > J *tu*, but *dü* or *ǯü* > J *yu*. Parallel developments are somewhat less vividly attested in the cases of original *o* and *ö* in these positions, but even there the over-all pattern is clear, so that it is evident that there too the original front or back vocalism was the principal determining factor for all the Japanese developments.

In the case of original initial *d- or *ǯ- followed by original *a, *é, or *ä, the Japanese developments may be understood only in the light of still further conditioning factors. In these cases the manner of articulation of the consonant immediately following the vowel was the critical factor, so that J t- was the result when an original stop followed one of these vowels, but J y- was the development when an original continuant was found in this position.

These developments are illustrated by the following etymologies:

1.1 pA or pT *d or *ǯ before original *-u- :: OJ tu-.

1. pA *duligān 'warm', Mo. dulaɣan, Ev. dul- 'erwärmen', MTk. ǰiliɣ 'warm' (Poppe 1960: 23, 75) :: J (a)tu- 'be hot', pKJ *(a-)tɔ-, MK tɔs(ɔ)- 'be warm, mild' (Martin 1966: 234, #112).

2. pA *ǯur 'a pair', Ev. ǯūr 'zwei', Ma. ǯuru 'Paar', ǯuwę 'zwei' (Poppe 1960: 28) :: OJ ture 'companion'. Martin (1966: 245, #247) reconstructs pKJ *turxye, on the basis of J tsure and K tul, MK tulh 'two'; on the reasons for preferring the present etymology, and for relating instead both OJ Futa- 'two' and these Korean forms to pKJ *dula, see p. 229 below.

3. pT *ǯuwan 'ten', Ev. ǯān, Ma. ǯuwan (Benzing 1955: 1049) :: OJ töwo (*töwö ?), all 'ten' (Miller 1967: 338).

4. Mo. ǯun 'Sommer', Ev. ǯugañī, Lam. ǯugañ, ǯuwuñi, Ma. ǯuwari, all 'Sommer' (Poppe 1960: 28; Benzing 1955: 1043) :: OJ tuFari 'budding (of flowers, leaves)'.

5. pT *du 'dative suffix' (Benzing 1955: 1031) :: OJ tu 'dative-locative particle'.

1.2 pA or pT *d or *ǯ before original *-o- :: OJ to-.

1. pT *ǯor-, Ev. ǯoromī-, Lam. ǯormī- 'stehlen' (Benzing 1955: 984) :: OJ tor-, Azuma (nonstandard) OJ tör- 'take, hold in the hand', pKJ *twɔr, *tɔr, K tɨl- 'hold in the hand' (Martin 1966: 233, #106; Miller 1967ᵇ: 298–99).

2. pA *dolkin, Mo. dolgijan, Ma. dolčin 'wave (of water)' (Poppe 1956: 210) :: J toro 'quiet pool of water'.

2.1 pA or pT *d or *ǯ before original *-ü- :: OJ yu-.

1. pA *ǯüg-, Mo. ǯüge 'transportieren, fahren', Ev. ǯugū- 'transportieren (auf Schlitten)', Lam. ǯugūt- 'tragen, verladen', Ev. ǯugūwūn 'Tross', OT jük 'Last, Traglast, Gepäck' (Poppe 1960: 28, 111) :: OJ yuki (later yugi, yuge) 'quiver'.

2. pA *dür₂i 'Aussehn', Mo. *düri* 'Aussehn, Form, Gestalt', Ma., Go. *durun*, id., OT *jüz* 'Gesicht' (Poppe 1960: 23, 111) :: OJ *yurö > *yirö > irö* 'color, facial appearance' (Murayama 1962; Miller 1967: 70–73).

3. pA *dür₂-, Mo. *dürü-* < *düre* 'hineinstecken', Ev. *durēki* 'Steigbügel', Chu. *jărana* < *jür₂aɲi*, id. (Poppe 1960: 82, 23) :: OJ *yir- > ir-e-* 'insert', pKJ *dyar-, MK *til-* id. (Martin 1966: 231, #76).

4. pT *ǯülb-, Mo. *ǯügelen* (<*ǯülegen* < *ǯülewen* < *ǯülebèn*) 'weich', Lam. *ǯulbẹr, ǯolbẹχrī* id. (Poppe 1960: 28) :: OJ *yuruF-* 'soften up, loosen'.

5. pT *düli-, Ev. *dul'i-* 'wärmen' (Poppe 1960: 23) :: OJ *yu* 'hot water'.

6. pT *dulī 'Prolativ, Prosekutiv' (Benzing 1955: 1032) :: OJ *yuri* (later *yori*) 'from, then'.

2.2 pA or pT *d or *ǯ before original *-ö- :: OJ *yö-*.

1. pA *dȫ- 'four', Mo. *dörben*, Ma. *duin* < *dügin* < *dȫ-gün*, Ev. *digin* (Poppe 1960: 110), pT *dügün* (Benzing 1955: 1049) :: OJ *yö*, all 'four'.

3. pA or pT *d or *ǯ before original *-a-, *-ä-, or *-è- immediately preceding an original stop (-p, -b, -g) :: OJ *ta-*; immediately preceding an original continuant (-w, -l, or zero) :: OJ *ya-*.

3.1 -a- :

1. pA *ǯab-, Mo. *ǯabi* 'Boot', Ma. *ǯaja* < *ǯawi* 'ein aus Birkenrinde verfertigtes Boot', Ev. *ǯaw* id. (Poppe 1960: 28) :: J *tabi* 'fitted cloth foot covering'.

2. pA *dap-, Mo. *daɣaki* < *dapàkï* 'verfilzte Wolle', Osm. *japaq* 'Fliess, unbearbeitete Wolle' (Poppe 1960: 47) :: J *tawam-* 'bend, twist'.

3. pA *dap-, Mo. *dāgan* (i.e., *da(ga)gan*, cf. MMo. *da'agan*), < *dapàkan* 'zweijähriges Füllen', Osm. *japaq* 'Fohlen' (Poppe 1960: 47) :: J *tawak-* 'sport, play the fool'.

4. pA *dag-, Mo. *daga-* 'folgen', Ev. *daga* 'nahe, neben', OT *jaqïn* 'nahe' (Poppe 1960: 22) :: J *tagai (ni)* 'together, mutually'.

5. pT *ǯapkun 'eight', Ma. *ǯakûn*, Ev. *ǯapkun* (Benzing 1955: 1049) :: J *tako* 'octopus' (Miller 1967: 338; Miller 1967ᵇ: 283 n. 11).

6. pT *daw-, Mo. *daba-* 'über einen Berg steigen', Ma. *daban*

'Übermass', Ev. *dawakịt* 'Bergpass' (Poppe 1960: 23) :: J *yama* 'mountain'.

7. pA *dal_{2}-, Mo. *dalda* 'secret, hidden, secretly', Ma. *dali-* 'to cover, hide' (Poppe 1956: 210) :: OJ *yasirö* 'enclosure for worship of native deities; later, buildings erected within such enclosures'. J. *yarai* 'a palisade, a stockade' may represent the survival of an old doublet, going with original *l against original *l_{2} in *yasirö*.

8. pA *$dalu$-, Mo. *doluɣa* 'lick continuously', Lam. *dal-*, Osm. *jala-* id. (Poppe 1956: 209–10) :: J *yarak-a-s-* 'gobble up, drink off in a hurry (of a delicacy)'.

3.2 -ä- :

9. pT *$\check{g}\ddot{a}g$- 'brennen', Ma. *deiǰi-*, Go. *ǰəgdə-*, Ev. *ǰəgdə-* id. (Benzing 1955: 984) :: J. *tak-* 'burn (something)', pKJ *tax-, MK *thɔ-* id. (Martin 1966: 227, #34).

3.3 -é- :

10. pA *$\check{g}\acute{e}$, Ev. *ǰeǰe* 'Messerschneide', Lam. *ǰej* id., cf. Mo. *ǰebe* 'Pfeilspitze', MMo. *ǰer* 'Waffe' (Poppe 1960: 27) :: J *ya* 'arrow', pKJ *$ja(k)$, K *cak-* 'arrow' (Martin 1966: 208 n. 3).

11. pA *$\check{g}\acute{e}p$-, pT *$\check{g}\ddot{a}p$- 'eat', Ev. *ǰep-*, Lam. *ǰeb-*, Ma. *ǰe-*, all id. (Poppe 1960: 27, 106) :: J *tab-* 'eat', pKJ *cab-, MK *ca(ɔps)-* 'eat' (Martin 1960: 231, #73).

12. pA *$\check{g}\acute{e}m$-, Mo. *ǰeme* 'Aas, Überreste eines von Wölfen zerfleischten Tieres', Ev. *ǰẹmū* 'Hunger, Essenlust' (Poppe 1960: 27, 106) :: J *yabu* 'refuse heap, garbage dump'.

13. pKJ *je 'night', K *cë-* id. (Martin 1966: 237, #155), pT *$dolba$ 'bei Nacht' (with a different vowel grade) (Benzing 1955: 994, 1043) :: OJ *yo-*, *yorö*, *yora*, *ya* 'evening', J *yoru* id. (Miller 1967[b]: 283 n. 11 is probably in error with respect to Mo. *üdeš*).

14. pA *dal-, with the *-o*-grade in Mo. *dolig* 'Sündenbock, Pfand', OT *juluɣ* 'Opfer, Lösegeld' (Poppe 1960: 75, 134), but with the *-a*-grade in J *yar-* 'give', K *tal-* 'give me', pKJ *dar- (Martin 1966: 232, #91).

15. pA *$\check{g}al$-, with the *-a*-grade in Ma. *ǰalan* 'Geschlecht, Generation', MMo. *ǰalga-* 'hinzufügen, aneinanderfügen' (Poppe 1960: 28, 86), but with the *-o*-grade in OJ *yö* 'age, generation, time'.

These statements of regular sound change make it possible for the first time to explain in detail the relationship of the Old Japanese dative-locative particle *tu* to the Old Japanese locative-ablative particles *yu* and *yuri* (later > *yo* and *yori*), as well as to trace the history of the over-all relationship of all these forms to their Altaic prototypes. Again, it is also possible as a result to refine the important but incomplete statements of Murayama on the subject:

Die Suffixe -*yu* und -*yuri* haben lokativische, prosekutivische und ablativische Funktion. Im Altjapanischen wurde -*yu* und -*yuri* beinahe unterschiedlos gebraucht. . . . . Das -*yu* < *-*du* ist mit dem gemeinaltaischen Dativ-Lokativ-Suffix *-*du* ∼ *-*da* (stimmlose Variante *-*tu* ∼ *-*ta*) zu vergleichen. Cf. mongol. Dativ-Lokativ-Suffix -*du*, -*dur-r*, -*da*, tungus. Dativ-Suffix -*da*, türk. Lokativ-Suffix -*da*, mandsch. Lokativ-Suffix -*de*. . . . . Der Prosekutiv hat auch einen engen Zusammenhang mit dem Dativ-Lokativ. Das Tungus. Prosekutiv-Suffix -*dulī* < -*du-lī* ist eine Weiterbildung des Dativs -*du*. Das *-*li* in -*yuri* < *-*du-li* ist mit diesem Prosekutiv-Suffix . . . zu vergleichen (Murayama 1957: 130–31).

Again, on the 'Lokativ (fossile Form)' -*tu*:

Dieses -*tu* kann als eine Variante von -*yu* < *-*du* aufgefasst werden. Das -*tu* war eigentlich eine stimmlose Variante des Lokativ-Suffixes -*yu* < *-*du* cf. tü. *ata-da* 'bei dem Vater', aber *ulus-ta* 'bei dem Volk' (ibid., 131).

What remains to be done is to clarify the phonology of these developments, and in the process relate these forms to the historical phonology of Japanese on the one hand and to that of the original Altaic parent language on the other.

First of all, OJ *tu* is of course as already noted above simply the regular development in Japanese of an original suffixed *du, with which it goes just as J (*a*)*tu*- 'be hot' goes with pA *duligān.

OJ *tu* may be cited from such forms as OJ *ama-tu-kaze* 'wind from heaven', *ama-tu-kamï* 'heavenly god(s)', *oki-tu-kaze* 'offshore wind', *töki-tu-kaze* 'wind (blowing) at time (of high tide)', *nö-tu-tori* 'wild fowl', *soko-tu-iFane* 'rock at the bottom (of the earth)', etc. Shiratori (1937: 72–73) attempts to identify the *tu* in OJ *ama-tu-kaze* with the *si* in OJ *ariFisi*, a word used twice in the *Nihon shoki* to gloss Chinese *nán* (4620) 'south' when referring to specific sites in ancient Korea (and strangely missing from Sanseidō 1967). The word unfortunately does not appear to be recorded in phonograms, but the reading tradition for the texts requires that Chinese *nán* 'south' in these passages be read as OJ *ariFisi* (see Maruyama 1967: 67; the two *Nihon shoki* passages are Suiko 8-year, and Jingō 49-year, 3-month). Shiratori (and the modern Japanese commentators generally, following him) correctly identify this *ariFisi* with K *aph* < MK *alph* 'front; south'; but in addition Shiratori suggests that the final -*si* in the form is somehow 'a particle corresponding to [OJ] *tu* . . .'. (Note also that the

Nihon shoki passages with *ariFisi* are generally read *ariFisi no kara* 'Southern Kara', not *ariFisikara*, as Shiratori has it.) The Japanese reading tradition here preserves what is probably one of the earliest known transcriptions of a Korean word, and it is interesting to note how precisely the Old Japanese form, though pre- served solely by that tradition, coincides with the early Korean pho- nemic configuration. Thus we find OJ *a-* for MK *a-*, OJ *-ri-* for MK *-l̥-*, OJ *-Fi* for MK *-p-*, and finally (and most interesting of all) OJ *-si* for the spirantized final aspiration of MK *-h*. Equally impressive is the correlation of the Korean original with the vocalism of the Old Japanese form, where the uniform *i*-vocalism except in the first syl- lable must be due to the same palatalization of Korean *l* before any consonant that may still be observed in modern Korean; see Martin, Lee, and Chang 1967: xiii. This palatalization must have been why the Old Japanese form has *-ri-* for K *-l*, and also why it follows through consistently from that point on with *-Fi-* and *-si*, rather than electing some other epenthetic vowel in order to render the original consonant complex. Thus it becomes clear that the *-si* of OJ *ariFisi* has nothing to do with OJ *tu*, but rather that it is simply a phonetic reproduction, using the only spirant available in the Old Japanese phonemic in- ventory, of the final spirant of the early Korean form. (I am indebted to my colleague Professor Samuel E. Martin for this interpretation of *ariFisi*, particularly for the explanation of the final *-si* in terms of the Korean aspiration.) Note also that Martin (1966: 232, #89) recon- structs pKJ **alpxye* to account for K *aph*, J *mae* < **ma-aFe* 'front'.

Returning to the simple original suffixed **du* established above, and illustrated by OJ *tu*, we must next consider what took place when original **-li* (or, as shown by Tungus, perhaps **-lï*) was added in the parent language to this **-du*. In this case the final **i* or **ï* of the suf- fixed form resulted in a fronting of the original **u* to **ü*, resulting in **düli* or **dülï*, and it is to this fronted variety of the resulting com- plex form that Old Japanese *yuri* regularly corresponds, just as Ev. *dul'i-* provides evidence for a fronted variety of the original root **dül-*, and this fronted variety goes regularly with Japanese *yu* 'hot water'. Nothing could be more regular, nor could one hope for a more impressive demonstration of the neo-grammarians' hypothesis of regular sound change. Later Japanese *yori* is a sporadically altered form of no particular significance for the relation of Japanese to the other Altaic languages, though it is important for the internal his- torical phonology of Japanese itself.

The replacement of standard Old Japanese -*u*- by nonstandard -*o*-
was a widespread phenomenon in many of the Azuma dialects. A
few unimportant cases of Azuma -*ö*- for standard -*u*- are also found,
but by and large it was not with their -*ö*- but with their -*o*- that these
nonstandard dialects of the Old Japanese period tended to replace
standard OJ -*u*-. Fukuda tabulates sixty cases of the replacement of
standard OJ -*u*- by Azuma -*o*- in the *Man'yōshū* materials, against
only four cases of the replacement of standard OJ -*u*- by Azuma -*ö*-
(Fukuda 1965: 301, and Appendixes Ia and Ib). Apparently this
widespread peculiarity of the Azuma dialects was one of several nonstandard features that from an early period were able to make important and lasting inroads into the domains of the standard language.
This particular process of innovation may still be observed to be in
operation from time to time in Heian texts; for example, in *Tsurezuregusa* § 38 there is a famous case, uniformly attested in the manuscript
tradition, of *madosi* 'is poor, helpless' for standard *madusi* 'id.'; elsewhere this same text has eight cases of standard *madusi*, all of equally
impeccable manuscript authority (Tokieda 1967). Wenck (1959:
IV.5, § 908.1) collects examples of the alternation of *u* and OJ *o*,
with references to other literature (see his Amn. 13, p. 43).

The Azuma dialects with their strong penchant for replacing
standard OJ -*u*- by their own -*o*- were mostly likely responsible for
the development, solely within Japanese itself, of later *yo* and *yori*
from earlier *yu* and *yuri*. The vocalization of Old Japanese *yo* and
yori (not *yö* and *yöri!*) is also important to note in this connection,
since in the main OJ *ö* was the more common of the two vowels and is
attested much more frequently than OJ *o*, so that to find *o* rather
than *ö* in these forms is a valuable clue pointing in the direction of
their correct identification as Azuma innovations in the standard
language.

It remains only to deal with the forms and functions of OJ *yu*,
later *yo*, which in the texts can no longer be kept apart, on semantic
grounds at least, from OJ *yuri* and *yori*. The most attractive explanation for these forms is to be found in such texts as *M* 3396, OJ
më yu 'from, by means of the eyes', and *M* 4054, OJ *kö yo* 'from,
through here'. Both these texts are recorded in phonograms, so that
the Old Japanese readings here are beyond question. If we are also
to admit as linguistic evidence readings based upon the traditional
interpretation and expansion of *kanbun*-texts (a risky business in
most cases), we may also cite *M* 317, OJ *töki yu* 'from the time'.

In each of these cases we must postulate an original *du*, a form that was then fronted in vowel-harmony with the preceding form to which it was suffixed, resulting finally in the forms actually found in the texts, through regular changes along the lines set forth above; thus, in *M* 3396, **më du* > **më-dü* > *më-yu;* in *M* 4054, **kö du* > **kö-dü* > **kö-yu* > *kö-yo;* and in *M* 317, **töki du* > **töki-dü* > *töki-yu.*

The proposed correspondences also make it possible to cast light on the origin and significance for comparative studies of some problems in word formation and the interrelationship of forms within Tungus, by means of reference to parallel and related formations in Japanese, and at the same time to bring a certain degree of order to our understanding of the Korean and Japanese versions of an important set of forms, namely the pair of endoactive and exoactive verbs that go with and were originally formed upon a basic root 'burn'.

It is best to begin by setting forth the Japanese forms in some detail (on endoactive and exoactive pairs in Japanese, see Lewin 1959: 118–22; Miller 1967: 65–66; Kolpakči 1956: 53–54). In the exoactive member of the set, in the generally transitive meanings of 'kindle (a fire), burn (up something)' ('in Brand setzen, anzünden'), we have: a) J *tak-u,* as in *hi o tak-u* 'kindle a fire', *sekitan o taku* 'burn coal'; b) J *yak-u,* as in *ie o yak-u* 'burn a house (down)', *te o yak-u* 'burn, injure one's hand in fire', *tabemono o yak-u* 'roast, grill, broil food', and *setomono o yak-u* 'fire, bake ceramic ware'. Both a) *tak-u* and b) *yak-u* are common both to the modern spoken language and to the written language. In the parallel endoactive member of the set, in the generally intransitive meanings of 'be burning, be in a state of (currently) burning,' or 'be in a state of being or (earlier) having been affected by fire', ('brennen'), we have in the modern spoken language J *yake-ru,* which is paralleled in the written language by J *yak-u,* as in (to cite only spoken language examples) *tabemono ga yaketa* 'the food is done, cooked', *pan wa yoku yakete iru* 'the bread is well baked, or, well toasted'.

Martin has connected these exoactive Japanese forms with Korean through his reconstruction of proto-Korean-Japanese original forms in the following manner: with exoactive a) J *tak-u,* he has associated K *tha-* 'burn (intr.)', both to go with pKJ **táx-* (Martin 1966: 227, #34); with exoactive b) J *yak-u,* he has associated K *tha-* 'burn', both to go with pKJ **dáx-* (ibid., #35). Endoactive J *yak-* (literary) and

yake- (spoken) are not accounted for; and the significant or distinc-
tively marked feature in the original to which all these Korean and
Japanese forms are ultimately to be referred was presumably the
voicing (or unvoicing) of the initial.

Japanese exoactive a) *tak-* goes directly with proto-Tungus *ǰäg-dä-
'brennen', as already stated above (§ 3.2, example 9; see Benzing
1955: 1070); this also is the form that is to be associated with pKJ
*táx- (Martin 1966: #34). The correspondence is regular, with Japa-
nese *ta-* corresponding here to original *ǰ- before -ä- because of the
stop -*g*- immediately following in the same syllable in the original
form. But Japanese exoactive b) *yak-* represents a further morphological accretion to this root, in the same way that the Korean transitive form that Martin involves with his pKJ *dáx- (his #35) is itself
originally a causative < *tha-i-u*. The original causative element in all
these words can be traced ultimately to the Tungus causative formant *-*gi*-, concerning which it must be noted however that 'durch
kombinatorischen Lautwandel in den einzelnen Sprachen meist un-
kenntlich geworden' (Benzing 1955: 1070)—to say the least. One is
reminded by its developments of the Tungus instrumental ending
*ǰi, a morpheme that rather exceptionally turns up in Manchu as *i*
(Benzing 1955: 984, 1035), and one that is as a result not always easy
to distinguish from the causative either in that language or elsewhere
in Tungus. Here as in certain other instances the close parallels to be
observed in obviously independent developments of common or related features in Manchu on the one hand and Japanese on the other
merit future investigation in terms of the original areal relationship
between these two languages. In the present instance, this causative
formant already appears by the time of the original Korean-Japanese
unity simply as the formant *-*i*-, of whose employment in both languages a full account has been given elsewhere (Miller 1967: 65–66).

Here the original suffixation of *-*gi*- > *-*i*- has had the effect of
producing a lenition in the final root consonant of the form in question
(hence, there can be little doubt, the *-*x*- of the proto-Korean-Japanese reconstruction, which appears in both of Martin's forms since
the original proto-Korean-Japanese form reflecting an original stop
in this root cannot be recovered solely on the basis of the Korean and
Japanese evidence). After this lenition, the original final stop no
longer acted like a stop but instead like a continuant, which indeed
it now was; hence, by a regular and even logical progression, Japanese
exoactive b) *yak-*, reflecting this early causative formation, and going

with exoactive a) *tak-* according to regular phonological developments. Meanwhile, the spoken language *yake-* and the literary *yak-*, both endoactive, go with the original unsuffixed **ǯäg-(dä)-*, probably in actual fact without the **-(dä)-* and certainly without any trace of the causative formant **-gi- > *-i-*, to which relationship the most striking testimony possible is provided by the *-e-* vocalization of the modern Japanese spoken form *yake-r-u*: this form has *-e-* because the original root to which it is ultimately related had the **-ä-* vocalization, not the *-a-* vocalization. Thus, original pT **ǯäg-dä-* (probably simplified along the way to become **ǯägä-*) is reflected phoneme for phoneme in modern J *yake-r-u*.

The over-all developments here may best be summarized by giving a sampling of the Tungus data for these formations (Benzing 1955: 1070), thus bringing out the parallels with the Japanese forms in a more striking manner:

	pT	Ma.	Go.	Ev.	K	J
'brennen'	**ǯägdä-*	—	*ǯəgdə-*	*ǯəgdə-*	*tha-*	*yake-r-*
'anzünden'	**ǯägdä-gi-*	*deiǯi-*	*ǯəgǯi-*	*ǯəgdī-*	**tha-i-*	*yak-*;

(cf. *tak-*)

This formulation also clarifies certain difficulties in the historical phonology of the Tungus languages themselves, where there are problems that prove to be best understood in the light of the Japanese connections of the forms involved, when taken together with the sound correspondences set forth above. Benzing (1955: 984, 990) has noted that the Manchu reflexes for initial pT **ǯ-* present certain difficulties: the regular correspondence appears to be Ma. *ǯ-*, but Benzing finds Ma. *d-* 'wenn im Worte *c, ǯ, s* folgen'. This is at once reminiscent of the Japanese reflexes for the original phoneme in question; but of the two examples he gives, one is 'brennen/anzünden' above; and the other may at once be understood as showing Ma. *d-* before a stop immediately following in the same syllable, just as would be expected in Japanese. Benzing reconstructs pT* *ǯüxi-ktä* 'Heidelbeeren' to account for Ma. *duksi*, Go. *ǯusiktə*, Ev. *ǯiktə*, Lam. *gīt*, etc., all presumably to be understood in the same sense as his reconstructed form; to both the reconstruction and the Manchu reflex, however, Benzing adds a query in the form of a question mark (1955: 990). Neither query is necessary; the Ma. *d-* reflex for the original Tungus initial **ǯ-* in Ma. *duksi* 'a fruit resembling the wild grape

(Vitis labrusca)' (Norman 1967: 97), just as for that in Ma. *deiǯi-* 'anzünden', is now seen to be completely regular in terms of the structure of the syllable in which it appears.

The morphological contrast implied in the voiceless/voiced distinction to be observed in the proto-Korean-Japanese forms **táx-* and **dáx-* reconstructed by Martin is also important; it may be taken out of this limited context and related first of all to the larger area of the Tungus evidence, then ultimately to proto-Altaic. The principal difficulty with Martin's reconstruction for these roots is not with the forms themselves, which are undoubtedly correct, but with the semantics of his etymologies, and hence by extension with the semantic values of his reconstructed forms. In his etymology #34, for **táx-*, an intransitive Korean form goes together with an essentially transitive exoactive Japanese form; but in his etymology #35, just the reverse is true, so that for **dáx-* a transitive Korean form now goes together either with the essentially intransitive enodactive Japanese literary *yak-*, spoken *yake-*, or with the exoactive *yak-*, it is not completely clear which. Given this crisscrossing of semantic boundaries, it is difficult to establish any meanings for these reconstructions, correct though they may very well still be as forms, i.e., as simple linear strings of phonemes. But a simple linear string of phonemes is not a linguistic form in the full sense of the term, so long as it remains without its semantic component.

A clue pointing the way out of this maze is fortunately provided by the Tungus forms just cited on the one hand, and by the larger Altaic context on the other, in the form of the etymology connecting Mo. *čaki-* 'Feuer schlagen,' Mo. *čakilgan* 'Blitz', and OT, Osm. *čaq-* 'Feuer schlagen' (Poppe 1960: 26). These forms provide evidence for pA **čak-* parallel with and related to the pT **ǯäg-* with which we have been concerned above. In other words, the original root was not really one form but a set of two, namely the doublet **čak-* ~ **ǯak-*. The first member of this pair goes directly with Mo. *čaki-*, OT *čaq-*, etc., just cited, and also ultimately with J *tak-* (on the sound correspondences for original initial **č-*, see below). All these reflexes agree in semantic value, and the original first member of this pair must accordingly be reconstructed as **čak-* 'set, kindle a fire; burn (it); anzünden'. This first member of the pair is also probably to be assigned the priority both in time and in morphological evolution, since the second member is attested only in an already triply altered shape: (1), voicing of the initial, (2), secondary assimilation of vocalization to the position of articulation of the initial (*-a- > *-ä-), and (3), secondary voicing of the final stop consonant before a secondary derivative suffix *-dä- in Tungus, where it becomes as a result *ǯäg-dä-. Of these three alterations in shape, only the first one noted was significant as a morphological process in derivation; the other two were automatic or sporadic phonetic accommodations without morphological or ultimate historical significance. The second member of the pair goes with forms on the basis of whose meaning we may then postulate its own original semantic value as *ǯak- 'be burning, be on fire; brennen' (cf. J yake-, [literary] yak-), and it is the voicing of the initial rather than the altered vocalization that in all probability must be recognized as the overt feature of phonemic marking to be associated with the semantic differentiation involved in the pair. Note also that the secondary -g- is not only a Tungus innovation but also one that apparently was not of sufficient antiquity to have been inherited by Japanese. Secondary voicings of this variety present many problems in Japanese historical phonology (see Miller 1967[b]: 286 n. 14), and each must be dealt with if and when it appears in the texts; but here the Japanese forms clearly go with the Altaic majority, not with the Tungus minority, as far as the evidence for this particular instance of intervocalic voicing is concerned.

Thus, the original Altaic distinction was, in the briefest possible terms, *čak- 'burn (it)' vs. *ǯak- 'be on fire'. Next, in Tungus, where the root had already acquired a secondary suffix *-dä-, it now underwent a still further accretion in the form of a causative element *-gi-. This had the effect in Tungus of switching the voiced and essentially intransitive forms semantically back over into the domain of the original unvoiced transitive forms; these Tungus apparently had not inherited, and instead it now made these new *ǯäg-dä-gi forms serve in their place and in their function. The Korean and Japanese forms that show a trace of this causative formation go back, in other words, to the voiced rather than to the voiceless member of the original Altaic doublet, and it is possible to sort out the original semantic values of pKT *táx- and *dáx-, even though by the time of the linguistic evidence upon which the reconstruction of these forms must be based, the contamination of the inherited noncausative forms with the also inherited but later and secondary causative forms had fatally obscured the nature and direction of the distinction in Korean and Japanese, when viewed there in isolation from the larger context of their ultimate Altaic relationships.

Another striking piece of evidence of this same variety, also happening to involve remarkably parallel developments in Manchu and Japanese, is afforded by the Manchu aorist participle constructed on the Tungus root *ǯäp- 'essen', aorist *ǯäp-tä; the Manchu form in question is ǯetere < *ǯäp-tä-rī, cf. the Manchu imperative ǯefu, all the forms being based in Manchu on the root ǯe- (Benzing 1955: 982, 999). The parallelism with Japanese here is exact and detailed. The cognate is J *tab-* 'eat' (cf. the etymology in § 3.3, no. 11 above). The vocalism of the second syllable of the modern spoken language forms in *tabe-r-* as well as the morphology of this root in Old and literary Japanese are both to be explained by the vocalism of the original forms underlying the Manchu and other Tungus forms on the one hand and the Japanese forms on the other. In the formations ultimately responsible for the forms that are attested in all these languages there was no original vowel following the final *-p* of the root and preceding any subsequent consonant-initial suffixed element. The *-e-* of the modern Japanese forms (*taberu, tabeta, tabeyō,* etc.), which here goes back to OJ -ë-, is a Japanese innovation, inserted according to the canons of Japanese syllabic structure and morae accounting but nevertheless still in vowel harmony with the original vocalization of the root element *ǯäp-. The striking point is that the evidence for this original vocalism survives in the Japanese verbal morphology even though early in the history of pre-Japanese the vocalism of the root itself was leveled out to its now familiar *tab-* shape, probably through assimilation to the position of articulation of the root-final consonant ('labial attraction').

With respect to that consonant, we have noted earlier that in the case of the root 'burn' Japanese did not inherit what is clearly the Tungus innovation of a voiced final *-g* in that root, agreeing instead with the more widely attested Altaic shape for that root ending in *-k.* In the case of 'eat' the problem is unfortunately rather more complex. This Tungus root has been cited simply as *ǯäp-, but this form is actually something of an oversimplification. It is clear that there was a stop in this position in the root to be reckoned with in proto-Tungus, and it is also clear that the stop in question was a labial, but beyond that the Tungus evidence for voice or lack of voice in this root is extremely difficult to interpret, and we do not have unambiguous evidence from the larger Altaic context available as in the case of 'burn'. Benzing could come up with no more satisfactory solution than to note, under 'Schwund auslautender Konsonanten,' that 'einen alten . . *p-* ⁓ . . *b*-Stamm können wir z.B. im Verbum **ǯäp-* [*sic;* read **ǯ̌äp-*, RAM] 'essen' feststellen' (Benzing 1955: 999); and it is difficult indeed to do more with the Tungus materials than this. Proto-Korean-Japanese **cab-* (Martin 1966: 231, #73) shows that the innovation in voicing in this form, if it actually is an innovation, is at least as old as the Korean-Japanese linguistic unity.

But over and beyond this, the original form underlying the Manchu aorist participle, i.e., pT **ǯ̌äp-tä-rī*, a form that of course has been reconstructed totally without reference to the Japanese data, still impressively correlates with that same Japanese data, morpheme for morpheme and phoneme for phoneme. J *tab-* 'eat' is, in traditional Japanese grammatical terminology, a *shimo nidan* 'lower bi-grade' verb; hence the vowel *-e-* < OJ *-ë-* is the one involved (and to be explained in comparative terms as above) between the root and the perfect ending *-tari*, to make the form *tabetari* 'eaten' (for details on these forms and their meanings, see Lewin 1959: 169–70, and, for the *shimo nidan* verbs, ibid., 115; note also that he cites the form *yaketari* [cf. the discussion of *yak-* above] from the following *Hōjōki* (1212 AD) passage: *kono tabi kugyō no ie jūroku yaketari* 'diesmal waren sechzehn Häuser von Grosswürdenträgern abgebrannt'). Now we are able to 'explain', in the historical-linguistic sense of the word, 'why' J *tab-* is a *shimo nidan* verb, and also 'why' as a *shimo nidan* verb it requires (again in traditional Japanese grammatical terms) the *renyōkei* 'conjunctional form' before *-tari*, i.e., 'why' it inserts the vowel *-e-* in this formation. Note also that the traditional Japanese grammarians' analysis of *-tari* as a contraction of *-te* + *ari* neither affirms nor denies this comparative interpretation; once again, analysis by expansion of contractions, a special variety of internal reconstruction, cannot be maintained against the clear evidence of cognate forms in related languages (see p. 24 above). Whether or not there are grounds for projecting a parallel contraction as a feature in an earlier stage predating Tungus **ǯ̌äp-tä-rī* is a problem raising other questions that would take the discussion here too far afield.

With this statement of the principal reflexes of pA **ǯ̌-* in hand, it becomes possible to identify certain old loanwords in Japanese and the related languages, and to distinguish them from genetically inherited forms with a fair degree of precision. One such set is that involved in the resemblances between MTk. *jüli-* 'rasieren', Osm. *jülü-* 'id.,' Mo. *ǯ̌ülge-* 'abreiben, abschleifen,' and K *cwūl* 'a file, rasp' on the one hand (Ramstedt/Aalto 1957: 148), and J *sor-u* 'shave, cut off,' deverbal in J *kamisori* 'razor' (*kami* 'hair, beard'). Moreover, all these forms are difficult to treat in isolation from J *yasuri* 'a file, rasp' (cf. J *ya* 'arrow', *yari* 'a spear, lance'?). The relation of the Korean and Japanese forms to the words in the other languages is obvious, but because of the phonology it must result from an old borrowing, probably into proto-Korean-Japanese (or, depending upon the history of the technology involved, from proto-Korean-Japanese into the other languages). Facial shaving could hardly have been any more of a concern for the proto-Korean-Japanese than it is a problem for their modern descendants; and it is equally unlikely that they would have had any great need for or familiarity with head shaving until their acquaintance with the canonical requirements of the Buddhist *saṅgha* suddenly made the technique both desirable and important.

Two additional etymologies that have certain problems in common must also be mentioned here, if only in passing, since the difficulties in phonology they present are important for future study, even though they cannot be completely solved at this point. Martin (1966: 246, #265) has compared K *tols* 'anniversary, cycle' with J *tosi* 'year', reconstructing pKJ **tošyi* to account for the correspondences involved. It is tempting, indeed almost inevitable, to extend this comparison to involve MMo., Mo. *žil* 'year' (Poppe 1955: 35, 116), going with Jak. *sïl*, Tkm. *jïl*, and OT *jïl*, all 'id.' (Poppe 1960: 114), and to be referred to an original proto-Altaic form in **-ï-* (Poppe 1960: 113). In this etymology one is troubled, to be sure, by the semantics of the Korean form cited, but this is not by any means an insurmountable obstacle. Much more troublesome are the problems presented by the phonology. In brief, the initial of the Japanese form goes regularly enough with the proto-Korean-Japanese formulation, as well as with the other Altaic data, but the vocalism of the form still presents unsolved problems. Still, the regular correspondence of J *-s-* with pA **-l₂-* in this form gives every indication that the etymology is essentially correct. Closely related are the problems presented by the comparison of Kor. *tol* 'stone', J *isi* 'id.', going together under pKJ **dyoš* (Martin 1966: 243, #224). Chu. *čul*. OT *taš*, all 'id.' show that the original form to which this etymology must be referred was proto-Altaic **tāl₂* (Poppe 1960: 15, 77, 98; the reconstruction **tïla* in Poppe 1956: 206 is not to be maintained), with final **-l₂* going with Turkish *-š*, Korean *-l*, Mongol *-l*, etc. (Poppe 1960: 77). Once again, the regular correspondence of J *-s-* with pA **-l₂-* in this form surely indicates that the etymology is essentially correct, but the correlation of the Japanese initial with the Altaic data presents unsolved problems, even though the Korean-Japanese comparison is unexceptional. Both these etymologies are treated in greater detail below, 'year' as etymology 16 in § 4.3 (b) (pp. 119–20), and 'stone' as etymology 17 (pp. 120–21), where an attempt is made at a partial solution of the problems presented by these initials in terms of early dialect and areal features.

Other important problems remain unsolved with respect to the Japanese reflexes of original *$\check{\jmath}$ when it appeared as a member of a consonant cluster. In the one secure etymology that may be cited as evidence for such an occurrence, Japanese apparently elected to simplify the cluster and in the process lost all trace of evidence for the original *$\check{\jmath}$; thus, pT *$sug\check{\jmath}.nsa$ 'Fisch (südtungusisch), Forelle (nordtungusisch)', Go. *sogdata*, Ev. *sug$\check{\jmath}$anna*, Lam. *hū$\check{\jmath}$anra* (Benzing 1955: 978), J *sakana* 'fish'.

The Japanese reflexes for original pA *$\check{c}$ before *-i- display striking parallels to the Japanese developments of *d and *$\check{\jmath}$, and may conveniently be summarized in the following etymologies:

4.1 pA primary *$\check{c}$ before original *-i- : : OJ *tu-*.

1.   pA *$\check{c}ib\check{\imath}k$, Tk., Uig., Oi., Tat. *$\check{c}ib\ddot{\imath}q$* 'rod' (Poppe 1956: 208) : : OJ *tuwe* 'staff, wand, rod'.

2.   pA *$\check{c}ig$, Tat. *$\check{c}iq$* 'damp, dew', Oi., Tat. *$\check{c}\bar{\imath}$* 'uncooked, raw', Tk. *$\check{c}ig$* 'wet, damp,' Mo. *$\check{c}igig$* 'dampness' (Poppe 1956: 208) : : K *cëc-* < *-k* 'get wet', cf. K *chuk-* 'be damp, moist, wet', J *tuk-e-* 'soak, steep, immerse, pickle', pKJ *cxuk-* (Martin 1966: 230, #60).

3.   pA *$\check{c}\bar{\imath}p$ 'furuncle, pustules', Tk. *$\check{c}iban$*, Mo. *$\check{c}igiqan$* < *$\check{c}i\beta\bar{\imath}qan$* 'furuncle' (Poppe 1956: 208) : : J *tubu* 'grain, lump'; cf. J. *tubaki* 'sputum, saliva'?

4.   pA *$\check{c}\bar{\imath}p\bar{\imath}$ 'filth, sin', Mo. *$\check{c}ibil$* < *$\check{c}\bar{\imath}p\bar{\imath}l$* 'Schmutz, Sünde, Scham, Unreiheit' (>Oi. *$\check{c}ibil$* 'Schmutz') (Poppe 1956: 208, Poppe 1960: 26) : : J *tumi* 'crime, sin'.

5.   pA *$\check{c}imr-$ 'roll, wind up', Tk. *$\check{c}imrin-$* 'roll up the sleeves', Tat., Oi. *$\check{c}irma-$* < *$cimra-$* 'wind, roll up', Mo. *$\check{c}ima-$* 'roll up the sleeves' (Poppe 1956: 208) : : J *tum^a/$_o$r-* 'pile up, accumulate'.

6.   pA *$\check{c}ib\bar{\imath}n$ 'fly', Oi. *$\check{c}imin$*, Chag. *$\check{c}ibin$* 'id.' (Poppe 1956: 208) : : J *tubasa* '(bird's) wing', J *tubame* 'a swallow (bird's name)'.

7.   pA *$\check{c}im-$ 'pinch', Oi. *$\check{c}imc\ddot{\imath}-$* 'pinch', Tk. *$\check{c}imdik$* 'pinching' (Poppe 1956: 208) : : J *tum-* 'pick (something) up', J *tumam-* 'pinch', K *cu^w/$_p$-* 'pick it', pKJ *cump-* (Martin 1967: 238, #164).

8. pA *čïka- 'come out', OT čïq-, Uig., Oi., Tk., Tat. čïq- all 'come out' (Poppe 1956: 208) : : OJ (i)-du-r- 'come out'.

4.2 pA primary *č before original *-a- : : OJ ï̈/ₐ-.

1. pA *čak 'Zeit', MMo., Mo. čaq, OT čaq, Jak. saχ (Poppe 1960: 26) : : MK cëk, K cok, pKJ *cekyi, *cokyi (Martin 1967: 244, ##242, 243), OJ töki, all 'id.' (Miller 1967ᵇ: 294).

2. pA *čak- 'Feuer schlagen,' MMo. čaqï- 'id.', OT, Chag., Osm. čaq-, Jak. saχ-, all 'id.,' (Poppe 1960: 26) : : J tak- 'burn (something)'.

Finally, it is also useful to cite the following additional etymologies, involving the developments of Altaic *t and *d before this same *-i-:

4.3 pA *t before *-i- : : OJ ti-, -du-.

1. pA *tïgïrak, Mo. čigirag < *tïgïrak 'dick, massiv', OT tïγraq 'aktiv, energisch, tätig' (Poppe 1956: 206; 1960: 15) : : J tikara 'strength, force'.

2. pA *tatïg- 'study, learn', Mo. tačija- 'burn with passion, crave for', Ma. tači- 'study, learn,' Ma. tačixijan 'study, doctrine' (Poppe 1956: 206) : : J tadun- 'investigate, study'. Cf. Lam. tatkat- 'tame, train an animal', Lam. tatigā- 'tame, make accustomed' (Poppe 1956: 206), J taduki 'being accustomed, used to (something)'.

4.4 pA *d before *-i- : : OJ yö-.

1. pA *dïrg- 'be happy, gay', Mo. ǰirγa- 'be happy, gay', Chag. ǰïraw 'singer', Kaz. ǰïr 'song' (Poppe 1956: 211) : : OJ yörökö-b- 'rejoice' (Miller 1967ᵇ: 287), K cülkëʷ/ₚ- 'enjoy', pKJ *jɔrɔkeb- (Martin 1966: 231, #75).

Several of these etymologies call for comment. The phoneme-for-phoneme correspondences in the etymology for OJ tuwe 'staff' are impressive, despite the lack of other more representative evidence from elsewhere in the Altaic area. Etymologies 3 and 4 under § 4.1 go together to make up a rather significant set of evidence. It is clear from the forms cited that in J tubu 'grain, lump' the final -u is an 'echo'-vowel added independently in Japanese and hence without significance for the history of the related languages. In this word, the original form ended in a final consonant, represented by pA *-p, and a vowel was added in Japanese following this consonant, in the same position of articulation, in order to conform to the canonical consonant + vowel sequence of the language. But in etymology 4, the final *-i of the original form was itself a secondary element of derivation in the original linguistic unity, ('furuncle, pustules' > 'filth' > 'sin'), and Japanese inherited this entire earlier Altaic formation, including the final vowel, so that the final -*i* of OJ *tumi* 'crime' is not a mere 'echo'-vowel added independently in Japanese but an essential part of the inherited form as well as of the inherited formation. This difference in the levels of historicity of the final vowels in the two Japanese forms, the 'echo' -*u* in *tubu* and the inherited -*i* in *tumi*, no doubt also provides us with the correct explanation for the two differ- ent consonant reflexes that these same two forms present for original proto-Altaic intervocalic *-*p*-, giving J -*b*- in *tubu*, but -*m*- in *tumi*. Time and time again we will have occasion to comment on the wide- spread 'confusion' in Japanese between *m* and *b*, both initial and intervocalic, a situation apparently fully as prevalent in the earlier stages of the language as it is today (see especially p. 49 above and p. 159 below). The problem arises almost every time *m* and *b* forms are discussed. The older written records of the language are of remarkably little help in sorting out the evidence, since they abound in writings that at times almost seem to indicate that -*m*- and -*b*- were in free variation in the language, if only at certain times and places. Here we see one way in which at least a portion of this -*m*- ~ -*b*- variation might have arisen. In etymology 8 the Japanese reflex is apparently a result of the common intervocalic voicing in Japanese (see Miller 1967[b]: 287–88 n. 14).

The most striking problem presented by the eight etymologies summarized above under § 4.1 is that of the J -*u*-. Was this simply the normal, inherited Japanese development of original *-*i*- in these words, or is it rather the result of a secondary assimilation within Japanese? The fact that in six of the eight etymologies the consonant immediate- ly following this vowel is a labial is difficult to overlook in this connec- tion. Surely there is a distinct possibility that the J -*u*- in these cases represents a sporadic but widespread Japanese assimilation to the position of articulation of the following labial, in which case the origi- nal inherited Japanese reflex must have been something else, possibly *-*i*-. But if that is so, then etymology 2, for pA *čig-, and etymology 8, for pA *čika-, become difficult to explain in their turn. Of these two, etymology 8 is in some ways the least satisfactory of the entire body of evidence. The Japanese cognate has preserved no trace of the original velar which appears to have been an integral part of the root, and we are as usual unable to make unambiguous statements about the conditions governing the disappearance of Old Japanese prefixed *i*- (Miller 1967: 201–2, 207). For the time being, it seems best to regard

OJ *tu*- as the normal development for this original sequence **či*-, and best also to withhold judgment on the historicity of the Japanese vocalism vis-à-vis the labials that turn up following it with such suspicious frequency.

The two etymologies cited under § 4.3 present difficulties. Either one of the two is on the surface at least completely unobjectionable, but taken together they probably show that one of them must be fortuitous. The etymology for 'study, learn' turns up the same Japanese -*u*- for original **-ï*- once again, but here with no possibility of secondary assimilation to a labial. This fact, plus the parallel it then offers to other developments, suggests that the etymology for J *tikara* 'strength' may well be a completely fortuitous coincidence; but if so, it is a remarkable one. The single etymology cited under § 4.4 would be of relatively little value were it not for the extraordinary length of the Japanese form involved. This is as a matter of fact one of the most completely convincing Altaic etymologies for any Japanese word that has yet come to light, thanks to the regular progression it presents from the dental initial through to the following -*r*- and finally down to and including the stem-final velar of the original **dïrg*-. As Martin has put it, 'a partial fit that is quite long is better than a short fit that is perfect, for the chance of accidental correspondence goes down with the length of the sequence' (Martin 1966: 191). Here not only is the fit quite long, but it is almost as perfect as could possibly be desired; only the Japanese -*k*- where we might have expected -*g*- mars the otherwise perfect symmetry. Comparison with Korean shows that the third and final -*ö*- of the Japanese form is secondary; it has resulted in part from a leveling of the vocalism in Japanese to a uniform *ö*-vocalism throughout the entire length of the form ('perfect vowel harmony'), and in part from assimilation to the position of articulation of the stem-final labial. That phoneme, the final **-b* of the proto-Korean-Japanese reconstruction, is itself the result of a secondary voicing of OJ -*F*-, a durative morpheme for repeated or continuous action that appears suffixed as an enlargement of the root in a large number of forms, and is also of considerable importance for the history of the Azuma negatives (see p. 265 below). For other examples of this same durative morpheme, cf. OJ *yuruF*- in § 2.1, etymology 4 above (p. 85), and OJ *kayoF*- in § 4.3 below (p. 126). It is interesting to find this evidence for the existence of this durative morpheme on the proto-Korean-Japanese level, where both the morphological accretion and the secondary voicing had already taken place in this form sometime after the separation of proto-Korean-Japanese from the original Altaic linguistic unity, but before the isolation of Japanese and Korean from each other.

Finally, a few special cases in which the Japanese developments of pA *$\check{z}$ are further complicated by other phonological factors require clarification. The following etymology will serve as an introduction to the problem: pA *$\check{z}ir$-, Mo. $\check{z}iru$-, Ma. $niru$- 'zeichnen, malen,' Chu. $\check{s}ir$- < *$j\ddot{i}r$- 'schreiben,' OT jaz- 'schreiben' (Poppe 1960: 28, 115), going with J ni 'cinnabar, ochre, red marking agent', and J nur- < *nir- 'apply paint, lacquer'. The Manchu reflex here is of considerable interest. Its initial n- is the regular development of *$\check{z}$ found when -r- follows immediately in the same syllable in the original root (Poppe 1960: 27), and it is significant to note that once again the Japanese developments have much in common with those in Manchu. To help explain this development on the historical level it is necessary to undertake a short survey of certain parallel phenomena in the related languages, including Japanese.

First of all, it is necessary to postulate a distinctive feature of articulation for certain if not all cases of proto-Altaic intervocalic -r- and -l-, in order to account for some of their developments in the related languages. In Chuvash, for example, r, l, and n go together to form a morphophonemic unity; the locative relational morpheme has one set of allomorphs (-re, -ra) after front (or back) vowel stems and consonant stems except r, l, and n, but another set of allomorphs (-te, -ta) after front (or back) vowel consonant stems in r, l, and n (Krueger 1961: 105 ff; see also Krueger 1962). A parallel and related morphophonemic unity for r, l, and n exists in Tungus (Benzing 1955: 1032). Also in Tungus, original initial *g- appears as initial *η-, i.e., nasalized, when immediately followed in the same syllable by -n- or -l- (Poppe 1960: 24); thus, Mo. gar 'Hand, Arm', Ma. $gala$ 'id.,' MTk. $qari$ 'Oberarm, Elle', but Go. ηala, Ev. $\eta\bar{a}le$, Lam. $\eta\bar{a}l$, all 'Hand', cognate with J $kara$ 'handle' (Miller 1967: 79). The explanation that imposes itself is that at least some cases, perhaps all, of proto-Altaic intervocalic -l- and -r- shared some feature of articulation in common with -n-, and that this common feature of articulation was one that left its most striking evidence in the form of a nasalization of the preceding consonant; hence, that feature of articulation common to all three phonemes in question may most economically be assumed to have been nasalization of the -l- and -r-.

This nasalized pronunciation of -l- and -r- has left other evidence in Japanese. One of the earliest words recorded for Old Japanese (though strangely missing from its proper place in Sanseidō 1967) is *tōri*; this form, as the name of the sculptor of the Śākya bronze trinity in the Kondō of the Hōryū-ji in Nara, appears written in phonograms on the rear of the central nimbus of this image, in the same inscription that dates the work in correspondence with 623 (Lewin 1962: 170; Asano 1963: 72). It is impossible not to associate this name with later Old Japanese *nöri* 'law, specifically the Buddhist *dharma*', and with OT *törü* 'Gesetz', the latter actually used in the Old Turkish translations of Buddhist texts as a correspondence for *dharma* (von Gabain 1960: 343; see ibid. 119 for text examples). Early Old Japanese *töri* must be an early recording of the original form, going exactly with OT *törü*, before the nasal articulation of the intervocalic *-r-* had resulted in *nöri*. Another important etymology involving Old Turkish and Japanese that can be clarified through this feature of Old Japanese pronunciation is that relating OT *torï*, var. *toru* 'rotbraunes' (von Gabain 1950: 343), 'brown (of horses)' (Nadelyayev et al. 1968: 578ᵃ) with J *nori* 'fresh, still undried blood', again with Japanese initial *n-* for an original *t-*. Buddhist Sanskrit *dhāraṇī* generally appears in Japanese as *darani* (probably another example of a direct loan from Indic into Japanese without benefit of a Chinese intermediary; see Miller 1967: 35), but an aberrant form *darari* is attested even as late as a celebrated passage in Chikamatsu's *Nagamachi onna harakiri* (1712): *kenninzi, darari ga naru zo, daratukumai zo* 'the *dhāraṇī* [bell] of the Kennin-ji is sounding—we ought not to dawdle!' (cited and correctly identified in Nakada 1963: 725, though Kindaichi and Kindaichi 1964: 656 are still puzzled by the form). This aberrant *darari* is only to be explained on the basis of a nasalized articulation of the intervocalic *-r-* in the otherwise expected *darani* for *dhāraṇī*; of course in the Chikamatsu passage cited the word is used on two levels, as the name for the bell at the Kennin-ji that was rung to accompany the recitation of a catena of 108 *dhāraṇī*, and at the same time as a sound-imitative evocation of the sound of the bell itself ('. . . booming [with the sound] *darari, darari, darari . . .*'); meanwhile, on still another level, it anticipates the following verb *daratuku* 'to hesitate, dawdle'.

All of this points in the direction of the correct identification of the Japanese cognate for a well-attested Altaic root for 'hear', namely that represented in Ma. *donǯi-* 'hören', Ev. *dōldi-* 'id.,' which has been directly associated with Mo. *duɣul-* 'erfahren, wahrnehmen', and

K *til-* 'hören' (Poppe 1960: 139). Poppe cites this etymology as an example of a 'Schwund des Vokals der mittleren Silbe', as far as the relation of the Mongol forms to Tungus is concerned; and it has already been pointed out that the way in which Manchu here has replaced the internal *-l-*, for which Evenki offers evidence, with its own *-n-* is curiously reminiscent of many of the developments resulting in the syllabic nasal in Japanese (Miller 1967: 214, 371). In this particular word the similarity between the historical processes of linguistic change operative in Manchu on the one hand and in Japanese on the other is more than merely suggestive and not at all fortuitous; they may be considered to be widely separated and independently operative but ultimately related results of an old and identical nasal articulation of the *-l-* in the original root.

The Japanese cognate in question may be traced in OJ *nör-* 'tell, announce', which was also probably the original sense of the widespread Altaic root of which this form is a surviving representative. This Old Japanese form has a secondary initial *n-* due to assimilation to the position of articulation of the originally nasalized intervocalic *-r-* immediately following, which *-r-* of course goes with the *-l-* attested in Tungus. Mo. *duγul-* < **dugūl-* 'erfahren, warhnehmen' (Poppe 160: 139) is best kept historically separate from Ma. *donǯi-*, Ev. *dōldị*, and their more immediately related forms; it goes instead directly with J *tug-* 'announce, tell'. Ma. *donǯi-* 'hören' was originally a causative; the **-di-* that must be reconstructed to account for the second syllable of this form is not difficult to associate with parallel developments of the original Tungus causative morpheme **-gi-*, with **-di-* resulting here in the same manner as that already traced for the root 'burn' (see above, and Benzing 1955: 1070). J *tug-* is original, going directly with the Mongol forms cited, and both its consonantism and vocalism are directly inherited from proto-Altaic. J *nör-* is secondary, going with the Tungus formations and showing a characteristic development of *n-* before *-r-* from *-l-* to replace original *t-*; but once more, in both consonantism and vocalism, it preserves abundant evidence of its intimate relation to the Tungus branch of Altaic. Nor do the semantics of the etymology present any special difficulties. For the developments of J *tug-* 'announce', we may compare J *ki ga tuk-u* 'one perceives, notices (something)'; in Altaic terms, an original **dug-*, as evidenced by the Mongol and Japanese forms, existed in the original linguistic unity in a formation with a secondary affix as **dugul-*. This was then contracted to form an original **dōl-*

(cf. K *til-*). To this a further morphological accretion in the form of the *-di-* development of the original causative *-gi-* took place, to result in the *dōldi-* form to which the Tungus and Japanese forms may directly be related. Semantically, 'tell, announce' plus a causative element resulted in 'have, make someone tell (about something)', which in turn led to 'listen to, (hence), hear'; cf. J *kikasete kudasai* 'tell me about it', lit. 'please cause me to hear about it'. These phonological and semantic developments make it possible to put OJ *nör-* and *tug-* into their proper historical perspective; the key to their relation to the forms in the other languages lies in the original nasal articulation of the internal *-r-* in OJ *nör-* and other early forms.

In these ways, the distinctive Japanese reflexes of pA **d-*, **ž-*, and **č-* provide conclusive evidence for the relation of Japanese to the original Altaic linguistic unity, thanks to the involved detail of the correspondences that Japanese has inherited from that original unity.

4.2 **ñ-*

Sometime still early in the prehistory of proto-Altaic, a major linguistic event began to take place that, by the time it was completed, would radically alter the structure of several of the languages in this family and to a greater or lesser extent bring about changes that would eventually leave discernible traces in all of them. This event involved the proto-Altaic palatal nasal **ñ*, and it can be recovered at least in broad outline by an inspection of the developments of this phoneme in the various Altaic languages.

It is surprisingly difficult to recover any substantial amount of evidence bearing on the prehistory of this pA **ñ*. One is tempted to speculate that sometime early in proto-Altaic an original **n* was automatically palatalized before front vowels, and that the automatic [ñ] allophone resulting from this pronunciation variant later achieved the status of a contrasting phoneme because of the loss of the particular conditioning factor involved, or due to other structural changes, leaving the **n/*ñ* contrast as a new structural feature of the proto-Altaic linguistic community.

But if this was indeed the course of events, all trace of these earlier developments has disappeared from the descendant languages, since by the time of the evidence upon which we base the reconstruction of proto-Altaic, **n* and **ñ* are clearly in contrast before both back and front vowels, thus pA **nap-ti* 'Blatt', contrasting with pA **ñap-ā-* 'kleben, ankleben'; pA **nek-* 'Sklave, Sklavin', contrasting with pA *ñek-* 'verfolgen, hinterher jagen . . .' (Poppe 1960: 37–39 states the reflexes upon which these and other reconstructions of forms with contrasting *n* and *ñ* are based).

Whatever its ultimate origin may have been, the *ñ* of proto-Altaic soon embarked on a course of changes that radically altered the structure of many of the Altaic languages, including Japanese. Its developments in Mongol are striking, even though they are without far-reaching consequences for the history of the other Altaic languages; in Mongol a nonfront vowel following word-initial *ñ* was uniformly assimilated to the position of articulation of this *ñ*, to become pre-Mongol *i* or *ï*, and appearing in the written records uniformly as Mo. *ni-* (Poppe 1960: 36–37), even though in a few forms this sequence then again has undergone secondary assimilatory change, as for example in Mo. *nogoɣan* < *nïgoɣan* < *ñoguɡān* 'grün, das Grün, Gras, Gemüse' (Poppe 1960: 38).

Turkish, on the other hand, preserves evidence on the basis of which we may reconstruct rather different and even spectacular changes in the status of original *ñ* early in the history of proto-Altaic, and therefore it is these changes that are of the most importance for the history of all the Altaic languages, including Japanese. In pre-Turkish, word-initial pA *ñ* shifted to initial *j-*, as also did, at approximately the same time in the history of pre-Turkish, pA *n*; in fact, from the evidence it appears more than likely that it was *ñ* that set off both these changes, and that the shift of *n* > *j* in pre-Turkish is to be explained as resulting from analogy between these two nasal phonemes. In other words, *n* suffered the same fate as *ñ* in pre-Turkish, and both fell together under *j-*; but to say the least they were not without company there, since this same pre-Turkish initial *j-* also had, by this time, become the final resting place of original pA *d-* and *ǯ-*, as well as, of course, *j-* itself.

This striking linguistic event left its most obvious evidence in the Old Turkish lexicon, where as a result of this linguistic change there are no surviving inherited forms in initial *n-* at all, any more than there are any in initial *ñ-*; both initial nasal phonemes were completely wiped out in this set of changes, and *n* and *ñ* survived in Old Turkish only internally in the morpheme or the word, never initially. The only exception was to be OT *nä* 'what?' and forms based on it; but in these the initial nasals can be explained as secondary developments within Old Turkish (see below, p. 195), so that these forms actually are exceptions that provide further proof for the rule. At the particular stage and variety of proto-Altaic to which pre-Turkish is most closely related, neither *n nor *ñ could exist in word-initial position; they survived only internally.

In Korean, n (along with l, for that matter) has not survived in any inherited words before -i- or -y- even in those cases in which the historical orthography (our chief source for Middle Korean) indicates that it once appeared in these positions (Martin, Lee, and Chang 1967: 284[a]; Martin 1968: 91). Thus, K i-, MK ni- 'carry on the head', J ni 'burden, load,' pKJ *ni- (Martin 1966: 227, #33); and along the same lines, showing the characteristic Japanese development for original *ñ, and contrasting it with the Korean developments, cf. K il-, MK nil- 'to rinse, wash out', Go. ñil-uri, Ma. nila-, Olc. ñilu, ñili 'to clean, to rinse' (Ramstedt 1949: 166), going directly with J araF-u 'wash' (Miller 1967: 75). The almost incredibly chaotic situation to which this reduces many of the problems in Korean etymology is well known (for examples see Ramstedt 1949: 165 ff.; Ramstedt/Aalto 1957: 73–77).

With these statements in hand we have the essential facts necessary for understanding the developments in a few important basic lexical items in the Altaic lexicon, and also what is necessary to clarify the developments of these words in Japanese, as well as their forms within Japanese itself. These are words for 'sleep' (also including, and often contaminated with, words for 'forget'), and for 'drink' (again, often involving 'swallow' and 'gulp down').

It is convenient to begin by presenting the Japanese evidence for these words.

For 'sleep', Old Japanese generally employs the 'cognate object' construction 'to sleep a sleep', with OJ i 'sleep' as the noun and OJ n-u 'to sleep' as the verb. The other verb OJ in-u 'to sleep' is an obvious blend-compound that contaminates both these two elements. The noun OJ i 'sleep' is used without the verb n-u only once in the entire Old Japanese corpus, in M 3353, but in this passage this aberrant usage may well be suspected of being a nonstandard Azuma locution (Sanseidō 1967: 64[d]–65[a]). The semantic history of the blend-compound verb in-u 'to sleep' is complicated by the fact that it is homophonous with still another important verb, OJ in-u 'to go, depart', and the competition that apparently existed between these two is of particular linguistic importance since the latter form was also a common circumlocution serving as a euphemism for 'to die'. OJ i 'sleep' may safely be referred to an earlier *yi-, on the basis of OJ imë 'dream', i.e., *i* 'sleep' + *më* 'eye'. OJ *imë* gives J *yume* 'dream', and also appears in nonstandard Azuma as *yumi* 'id.' (*M* 4394); taken together, the evidence of J *yume* and Azuma OJ *yumi* point to initial **yi-* in pre-OJ **yimë* almost without question.

Another important early form involving 'sleep' is OJ *wi-ne-*, generally explained by the later commentators as meaning 'take [someone] along, lead [someone] away and sleep [with them]', but this interpretation is clearly influenced by the fact that the first syllable in the form, OJ *wi-*, is uniformly written in the texts with Chinese *shùai* [5910] 'lead, conduct'; and in many of the early texts (e.g., *Kojiki* poem 8; *M* 3388; *M* 3545), the form is used in contexts in which there seems to be no idea of 'leading' or 'taking along', only of 'sleep'. Hence it is possible to regard the initial syllable of OJ *wi-ne-* as a labial variant of OJ **yi-* 'sleep'.

For 'drink' the Old Japanese evidence is rather less complicated; the verb is OJ *nöm-u* 'drink', and within the Old Japanese corpus itself no 'cognate object' noun correlative is attested. But in the modern language we have J *unomi* 'gulping something down, swallowing something down whole, entire' (often in a figurative sense of being hoodwinked); and from the earliest stages of the language we must not forget that *u* 'cormorant' is also attested—nor that the cormorant is the voracious 'swallower of things entire' par excellence. Historically, OJ *u* 'cormorant' will prove to stand in the same 'cognate object' relationship to OJ *nöm-u* 'drink' as do OJ **yi-*, *wi-* (in OJ *wi-ne-*) to *n-u* 'sleep'.

Inspection of the Altaic data for these same lexical items soon shows that the existence of these paired 'cognate object' forms, *i* and *n-* 'sleep' and *u* and *nöm-* 'drink' in Japanese, is a phenomenon with considerable significance on the comparative level. In Tungus, we find Ev. *um-* 'sich satt trinken', and Ev. *umǯa-* 'trinken', Ma. *omi-* 'trinken', and taking these together with Mo. *umdan* 'Getränk', Poppe (1960: 101) assumes pA **um-* 'drink', with the vowel of the Manchu form to be explained as a sporadic assimilation to the position of articulation of the root-final consonant *-m*; but at the same time, it is both possible and necessary to reconstruct pT **nüm-gä-* 'swallow, drink' on the basis of Ma. *nungge.n-*, Go., Olc. *luŋbe-*, Sol. *niŋə-*, Ev. *nimŋə-*, and other cognate forms (Benzing 1955: 993, where he reconstructs instead **lümgä-*; on the reasons for preferring instead a reconstruction with **n-*, see Murayama 1962: 110).

At the same time, we find pA **um-ga-* 'sleep', demonstrated by Mo.

unta- < **umta-* 'schlafen', *untara* 'erlöschen', *umarta-* 'vergessen', OT *u* 'Schlaf', *unït-* 'vergessen', Ev. *omŋo-* < **umga-*, again apparently with sporadic *o* for *u* because of the following *-m* (Poppe 1960: 100). For proto-Tungus, Benzing (1955: 989) reconstructs **omga-* 'vergessen', and cites Ma. *onggo-*, Gol. *ombo-*, Olc. *oŋbo-*, Sol. *ommo-*, Ev. *omŋo-*, together with other cognate forms in Tungus.

When the Japanese forms cited above are reviewed from the enhanced historical perspective afforded by these Altaic materials, it soon becomes clear that these two separate bodies of evidence reinforce and illuminate each other. Taken together, they demonstrate the nature of the linguistic situation that resulted from the massive structural pressures, noted above, in which both **n* and **ñ* tended to be pushed out of word-initial position and into the interior of the forms in which they had originally appeared, particularly as these structural pressures affected the shapes of these two common, even basic, lexical items. Proto-Tungus **nüm-gä-* goes together with OJ *nöm-* 'drink' (the Tungus form has an additional suffix **-gä-* not represented in Japanese), and both these forms represent the earliest historical stage of this lexical item, before its initial **n* had succumbed to the structural pressures set off by the falling together of **ñ* and **j*, and had as a result itself tended to move from word-initial to word-interior position. Proto-Altaic **um-* 'drink', and the forms going with it, including Mo. *umdan* 'Getränk', Ma. *omi-* 'trinken', and OJ *u* 'cormorant', all represent, by way of contrast, end products resulting from the completion of this structurally motivated shift, in which initial **n-* first moved from its original location, so that **nöm-* > **nüm-* > **ünm* > **um-*, the front vowel of the original form assimilating to the position of articulation of the stem-final *-m* after the assimilation (and encapsulation) of the shifting *n*. OJ *nöm-* 'drink' is valuable for the evidence it preserves for the original, unshifted form of this root; but OJ *u* 'cormorant' and J *unomi* 'gobbling down, drinking down whole' are equally valuable for the evidence they preserve for the secondary, shifted forms.

Much the same appears to be true for 'sleep, forget', with the important difference in this instance that the other Altaic evidence (apart from Japanese) does not preserve evidence for the original nasal initial form of the root. For Altaic without Japanese we can reconstruct only **umga-*; and for Tungus alone we can reconstruct only **omga-*, which however is itself clearly a secondary form going with original **umga-*. The Japanese data cited above, however, when considered in parallel with that for 'drink', indicates that the same situation is responsible for these forms too, with OJ *yi-, or wi- 'sleep' representing the secondary, shifted forms, and OJ n-u representing the original, nasal-initial forms.

It is more difficult, at least at the present state of our knowledge of the problem, to explain the troublesome discrepancy in vocalization between the Japanese forms and the other Altaic lexical evidence in the words for 'sleep, forget'. In the case of 'drink, swallow' the vocalization of all the forms goes together quite precisely, but in 'sleep, forget' there is a wide gulf separating the essentially front, i-/e-vocalization forms shown by the Japanese evidence (cf. J ne-ru 'to sleep', which preserves this feature), and the essentially back, u-/o-vocalization forms of the other Altaic languages. Perhaps one set resulted from an original root 'sleep', the other from an original root 'forget', with these two later becoming hopelessly entangled with one another; but this is nothing more than speculation, and there is not even a hint of a clue, even if this actually were the case, as to which vocalization might have gone with which meaning. The only significant data that can, at present, be brought to bear on this problem is that of the Korean forms; Martin (1966: 235, #124) has compared K $nu^w/_p$- with J ne-, in terms of pKJ *nup-, and notes also the existence of Ryūkyū forms for this word with initial n- and root-final -p-. Apparently the critical point in the development of the Japanese vocalism for this word is to be located at some point in time subsequent to the establishment of the Peninsular and Pelagic linguistic unity.

Given the disappointingly uniform nature of the Turkish developments, in which both *n and *ñ fell together under the same ubiquitous *j that independently subsumed so many other portions of Altaic phonology, we expect (and indeed find) but little significant evidence for the development of these forms in that branch of Altaic. An exception is, perhaps, Chuvash, which has a verb ĕš- 'trinken', but another verb Chu. săt- 'verschlingen', and an important noun/verb set, Chu. šĭvăr- 'schlafen', but ăyăx and ĭyxă, both 'Schlaf'. The last two nouns cited are obviously related to one another by simple metathesis; and one is tempted to look one step further back into the history of the language and ask if they might not also both be related to the verb šĭvăr- in terms of the two different developments of pA *j- in Chuvash that depended on the front- or back-vocalism of the vowel immediately following (see below, p. 206). Certain details remain obscure, but at least this approach would open the possibility of relating the Chuvash words for 'sleep; to sleep' both to each other, and to earlier Altaic forms in initial *ñ. With 'drink' the evidence is even less substantial, but the initial of *šăt-* could also point in the same direction of an original *ñ-, and one wonders if with *ĕš-* we do not have once again to reckon with a metathesis within pre-Chuvash, < *šĕ- ?

In Japanese, the far-reaching structural changes in the prehistory of Altaic that were set off by the shift of initial *ñ > *j left their mark in many other words over and above the small set of basic lexical items just considered; in particular, these changes may be traced in the form of sets of related forms within Japanese involving cognate words with zero-consonant, i.e., vowel initials, with *n*- initials, and with *y*- initials (examples in Haguenauer 1956: 299-300, 349). The over-all direction of these changes and the general patterning of the forms resulting from them are just barely perceptible, and many unsolved problems remain in the evidence, tending to confuse and obscure the exact nature of the original historical events. Still, here as often in linguistic history, the wonder is not that there are problems and anomalies in the resulting patterns, but rather that, given the immense time-depth of the changes involved, the direction of the original structural shifts can still be recovered at all.

This Japanese evidence may be arranged under the following by no means totally exclusive headings:

(1) doublets in which one member has zero-consonant, i.e., vowel-initial, and the other member has *n*- initial.

(2) doublets in which one member has *n*- initial, and the other member has *y*-initial.

The over-all pattern that is discernible in the case of these doublets of both varieties is for the vowel-initial words to have *a*-, *o*-, or *u*-, while the *n*- initial words tend to have this *n*- followed by *-i-* or *-e-* in the preponderance of the cases, though *no-* and *yo-*, as well as *ya-*, also occur. Thus, the general pattern that may be abstracted from this evidence is that original Altaic initial *ñ disappeared in Japanese before those Altaic vowels that gave J *a*, *o*, and *u*, but shifted to *n*- and survived as such in those cases where it was found before those original vowels that eventually gave J *i* and *e*. We may contrast this pattern with that shown by the Turkish evidence, with its complete annihilation of initial *ñ and *n alike; with that of the Mongol evidence, with its preservation of original initial *ñ but only in the guise of

*n; and with that of Korean, with its selective disappearance of *ñ
and *n alike before -i- and -y-. The Japanese developments share
features in common with each of these other patterns of change but
maintain their own distinctive individuality to the end.

Evidence relating these Japanese doublets to Altaic etymologies
involving *ñ has already been presented in considerable detail (Miller
1967: 74–75), and there is no need to repeat it here, except in summary form, although the addition of more Korean evidence than it
was possible to cite earlier may be useful, together with a few additional etymologies.

As an example of the doublets of type 1, above, the following may
be cited: J oso-i 'be slow', against J noro-i 'be slow-moving, sluggish';
Martin (1966: 241, #203) reconstructs both pKJ *nór- and *nós- to
accommodate the -s- and -r- in the Japanese forms; but in Altaic
terms, this is merely a classic instance of the Japanese reflexes of pA
*l_2 on the one hand, and pA *l on the other (see below, p. 122), and
need not occasion the reconstruction of two different allomorphs for
this word.

Another more involved, and hence more instructive, example of the
same type of doublet is the following: J ok-u 'place, put (something
down)', against J noke-ru 'leave, finish'; Martin (1966: 239, #175)
compares K noh- 'put aside, finish' and reconstructs pKJ *nox- to
account for the two forms. Unfortunately, this set cannot be completely separated from another word, which involves it as a doublet
of type 2 above, J yoke-ru 'avoid'; nor does this etymological tangle
stop there, for in Tungus we find pT *nā̆- 'hinlegen, hintun' (Benzing
1955: 986; all the Tungus languages he cites have the reflex for this
uniformly as nə̄-). But with this form in hand, we also find it difficult
to disassociate K $nu^w/_p$-, J ne-ru 'lie down, sleep', pKJ *nup- (Martin
1966: 235, #124), which has already claimed our attention above—and
so we have come full circle! It would be difficult to find a better example of what, in etymology, constitutes an embarrassment of riches.

The Altaic evidence for doublets in Japanese with a- (rarely u-,
or ya-) in one member and ni-, ne-, also yo- in the other has already
been presented (Miller 1967: 74–75); thus, going together with pA
*ñag- 'Eiter, Rotz' (Poppe 1960: 38), we have, on the one hand, J
-aka 'dirt (rubbed off on a well-handled object)', but on the other
hand, still another doublet in the form of J yogos-u 'soil, make (something) dirty', and nigor-u 'get muddy, dirty'. Martin (1966: 230,

#66) understandably avoids coming to grips with the highly involved relationships connecting all these words.

One final additional etymology conforming to this general over-all pattern of developments may be cited; this is J *ase* 'sweat', going directly with pTg **niǎ-* 'schwitzen', Ma. *nei*, Go. *ne.saŋgi* 'Schweiss' (Benzing 1955: 974; note that there are problems in the vocalization of certain of the Tungus reflexes for this root). The Japanese form has no etymology forthcoming within Japanese; this plus the fact that the final *-se* element of J *ase* is represented in all the Tungus cognates provides impressive indication for its ultimate relationship to these forms.

A hasty reviewer has remarked that in the attempt to relate OJ *niFi-* 'new, fresh', and also OJ *niwa-* 'id.' with Altaic (Miller 1967: 74–75) 'all we are comparing is *ni-* and *a-* from Proto-Altaic **ñï-* and **ña-*' (Chew 1969: 204), but this careless, superficial approach to a serious problem need not delay us for long. Had the reviewer taken the trouble to study the etymology with a little more care—or had he been interested enough to consult the Altaic reflexes upon which the reconstruction is based—he would have found such forms as Ma. *ñowaŋǧān* 'das Grün, grün', (Poppe 1960: 38), in which the labials of OJ *niFi-* and OJ *niwa-* are immediately reflected. The problems of the field are already quite great enough without being added to by such hasty, uninformed critical attempts as this.

The Japanese role in this early Altaic linguistic event involving these wholesale shifts of the nasals is also probably mirrored, in some way or other, in one of the most curious (and still virtually unexplained) anomalies within the entire Old Japanese corpus, namely the apparent replacement of early OJ *oyazi* 'the same' with later OJ *onazi* 'id.', the second of these forms of course being the starting point for the modern word also. OJ *oyazi* is attested in *M* 3464, 3978, 4006, and 4154, and also, most interestingly, in an inscription found on a wooden slip excavated from the site of the Nara palace buildings and dated in correspondence with A.D. 746 (Sanseidō 1967: 152[c-d])—one of the very few instances where an important aberrant linguistic form from the early history of Japanese may be verified by epigraphical evidence apart from literary sources. One of the *Man'yoshū* citations of *oyazi* is from a nonstandard Azuma poem; the other three are from the *œuvre* of Ōtomo Yakamochi (718?–785), who often employed archaic forms for their literary effect, and might very well have been doing so in this case. For once, the Azuma dialects do not seem to have anything very important to contribute either to the problem of the *oyazi/onazi* doublet, or to the entire history of the Altaic nasals in Japanese; surprisingly enough, no instances of Azuma replacement of standard OJ *n* by nonstandard *y*, or of the opposite phenomenon, are noted (Fukuda 1965: passim). The nearest one approaches to this in the Azuma materials is the single case of a dissimilation of two successive labial nasals *m . . . m m . . . y* in *M* 4427, which has *mayusuFi* 'true binding' for a presumably original *mamusuFi. Somehow, the existence of OJ *oyazi* beside OJ *onazi* must point to an early stage of the language in which even noninitial, intervocalic -*n*- had somehow become involved in the fate of *ñ, and involved also with its disappearance from initial position in Japanese words with *a* and *o* vocalization.

To sum up, the Japanese evidence bearing on pA *ñ and *n in the prehistory of Altaic is complex and far from completely under control, but what we know of it does fit in quite well with the over-all outlines of what we are able to learn of the fate of these sounds from the evidence preserved in the other Altaic languages. Most important of all, perhaps, are the indications that may be observed here for different developments within Japanese for original *ñ depending on the front (-*i*-, -*e*-) or back (typically -*a*-, also -*u*- and -*o*-) vocalism that originally followed this phoneme; in this respect, the developments of pA *ñ within Japanese clearly conform to an over-all pattern of linguistic change that has significant parallels elsewhere in the history both of Japanese and of the other related languages.

4.3 **l$_2$*

A brief summation of the Japanese reflexes for pA *l, **l$_2$*, *r and **r$_2$* has been attempted earlier (Miller 1967: 71–72); but it erred seriously in the direction of oversimplification, and the entire problem requires a complete reinvestigation of the relevant data.

The statement was made earlier that Japanese corresponds with its *r* to pA **l$_2$* (Miller 1967: 72), but no etymologies were given to substantiate this claim—and with good reason, since the statement proves to be false. A few pages later (op. cit., 75) a single example of a Japanese reflex for pA **l$_2$* was belatedly cited, comparing J *yawaraka* 'soft, delicate' with OT *yïmšaq, yumšaq* 'gentle, weak', and presenting OJ -*r*- as the reflex for pA *-*l$_2$*-; but this etymology, as we shall see below, represents a case of a special development within Japanese due to a particular phonemic environment and does not as a result illustrate the normal development of pA *l_2* in Japanese. The Japanese reflexes for pA *r_2* are also rather more involved than the simple J *r* proposed in 1967 would suggest, and these are also treated in some detail below (§ 4.4). For the purposes of the present chapter, however, J *r* is still taken as the only as well as the normal development of pA *r_2* despite the more precise findings now available and presented immediately below. This rather arbitrary treatment has been elected for two main reasons. First, it greatly simplifies the presentation of the already complex data necessary for the present chapter, without doing any major violence to the facts, since J *r* was still the most common reflex of *r_2*, and the other development, J *t*, appears to have been quite limited in its occurrences. Second, this treatment reflects to some extent the relative degree of security of the two different sets of data; for pA *l_2* we have a large number of extremely secure etymologies that can leave no doubt remaining as to the accuracy of the formulation, but for pA *r_2* the data are severely limited in scope, with a necessarily consequent diminution of authority for the proposed statements of historical change that can be made. These considerations have led to the present decision to treat pA *r_2*, for the purposes of the present chapter only, as if its only reflex in Japanese were *r*; § 4.4 below will supply the available evidence for those instances where this turns out not actually to have been the case. As we will see below, the Korean reflexes for all four original Altaic liquids are extremely diverse and in many respects still cannot yet be summarized in a systematic fashion; this arbitrary treatment of *r_2* also somewhat facilitates handling the Korean evidence in its present unsatisfactory state of formulation.

The overwhelming evidence of the lexical correspondences makes it clear that pA *l_2* normally appears in Japanese as -*s*-. Since neither *l* nor *l_2* ever occurred in syllable-initial in proto-Altaic, all Japanese evidence for either is of course also found in noninitial position. The following etymologies may be offered in substantiation of this revised statement; they are presented here in three groups, arranged as follows: (a) etymologies in which both the phonetic and the semantic correspondences are exact and precise enough so as to leave virtually no room for reasonable doubt about their relevance as evidence for the proposed sound law; (b) etymologies involving either a semantic or phonetic discrepancy, so that while they still are considered to be important as evidence, they are nevertheless best considered apart from the former group of etymologies; finally, (c) etymologies presenting serious problems, either in semantic or phonetic relationship, or in both, and therefore cited merely for the sake of completeness; etymologies of this last group are frankly speculative and do not play a part in the historical phonology formulation proposed in the present chapter.

(a)

1. pA *dal_2i-, Mo. *dalda* 'heimlich, verborgen', MMo. *dalda* 'Schirm, Schutz', Ma. *dali*- 'verdecken, die Sicht verdecken, verbergen, verheimlichen', Ev. *dal*- 'bedecken', OT *yašur*- 'verdecken, verheimlichen' (Poppe 1960: 77, cf. Poppe 1956: 210) :: OJ *yasi-rö* 'enclosure for worship of native deities; later, buildings erected within that enclosure'. OJ *-rö* is a spatial-locative suffix, cf. OJ *tökö-rö* 'place'.

2. pA *(ta)-bl_2g-, Mo. *taulai*, MMo. *tawlai* < *tablai* 'Hase', OT *tabïšɣan*, Osm. *tavšan* 'id.' (Poppe 1960: 44, 77) :: OJ *wusagi* > *usagi* 'id.' (the original initial *w-, going with pA -*b-, is further attested by nonstandard OJ *wosagi* in *M* 3529; the sequence w + u did not occur in standard Old Japanese by the time of our texts). Ōtsuki (1932: 1.382[b-c]) attempts to relate J *usagi* to Skt. *śaśa(ka)*, but surely there is little to be said in favor of such speculation; in addition, he brings into the discussion an 'Old Korean' word, the ancient Peninsular form *wū-ssū-hán* (see immediately below), which he glosses in *kana* as *wo-sa-ga-mu*, presumably for *wosagam*, and cites from Kanazawa Shōzaburō, the pioneer student of the Korean-Japanese linguistic unity (see Miller 1967: 62). In the ancient pre-Japanese fragments from the Korean peninsula (the so-called Koguryŏ fragments of Murayama 1962[b] and Lee 1963), the word for 'rabbit' is written *wū-ssū-hán* [7166, 5574, 2017] in Chinese phonograms. This writing would represent Middle Chinese *·uo-si̯e-ɣậm, 'rabbit' for this ancient Peninsular variety of pre-Old Japanese. Murayama (1962[b]: 6, 7, 9) reconstructs *wusigam, and suggests a comparison with Turkish *tawišɣan*, but does not go any further into the problem. Lee (1963: 102) reconstructs *osagam, but contents himself with remarking that 'here we find a great similarity with AJ [*sic*—for OJ] *usagi*'. The entire etymology is an important one, and the form preserved in the 'Koguryŏ' fragments is of particular value for tracing the details involved in its history. The Japanese reflex appears to have neglected the initial (prefixed?) pA *ta-; it would not be difficult, though speculative, to associate this element with J *ta* 'field', later specialized as 'paddy', but also used as a prefix in Japanese in the sense of 'wild, untamed', as in J *tasigi* 'a snipe', etc. Whatever its origins, this *ta-* is

unrepresented in the Japanese reflex, which however reproduces the remainder of the original inherited Altaic form with impressive correspondence in matters of precise detail, so that the original phoneme sequence *-bl_2g- (on which shape see Poppe 1960: 89) may be traced, step by step, in the Japanese form. We shall see shortly below that the normal expectation for the vowel immediately following the Japanese reflex of pA *l_2 as -s- is J -i-; but at first it appears that this expectation is violated in the word for 'rabbit', unless we invoke what would seem to be a completely ad hoc metathesis from an original *usiga > usagi. But the 'Koguryŏ' form shows that such a metathesis is far from being ad hoc, since the form preserved in these ancient fragments has exactly the expected vocalism, with original -i- after J -s- going with pA *l_2, and -a- in the following syllable; in the course of the history of this word in Japanese, the two vowels have simply interchanged positions relative to the consonants. The initial *w- indicated by the Azuma form of M 3529 is also supported by the 'Koguryŏ' form, so that we may with confidence write *wusiga as the oldest configuration that may, at present at least, be recovered for the Japanese word for 'rabbit'. We may also note the existence of the (truncated?) form J u 'rabbit' (in the special context of the animal cycle); this form makes it at least possible that the oldest original root that may be traced here is simply pA *b- plus an automatic syllabic-nuclear vowel, and that the remainder of the Altaic form consists of various historical layers of suffixal accretions on both sides of this root element. Still, it must be kept in mind that in the Japanese animal-cycle names, we must probably reckon with truncated forms in the special context of listing (thus, J ne ushi tora u . . . 'rat' [for nezumi], 'ox', 'tiger', 'rabbit' . . .), so that the evidence provided by this form is of questionable importance for historical purposes. Menges (1968: 97) has suggested that the final -š, -šγan, and -lai of the various Altaic words for 'rabbit' are all suffixal materials, with different suffixes appearing in the different languages, and that for this reason the word may not properly be cited as an example of pA *l_2, since the -š- of the Turkish forms does not go directly (and etymologically) with the -l- of the Mongol form. But the basis upon which he has made this morphological division is unclear, and it does not appear to be necessary to go to this extreme in treating the form, which remains as satisfactory an example for pA *l_2 as any other. The same word, with the prefixed ta- in place, with the labial element following, and with internal -l-, is preserved in Chinese transcription for the language of the Khitan Liao dynasty (907–1125); it appears as *ťáo-lĭ* [6156, 3857], i.e., **tauli*, in the fourteenth-century canonical history of the dynasty (Wittfogel and Fêng 1949: 270 and n. 156; Menges 1968ᶜ: 53). The different treatments of pA $*l_2$, with *-l-* in the Khitan Liao form, but *-s-* in the 'Koguryŏ' form, are of great importance, showing as they do that the ancient Peninsular forms already went closely together with Japanese, while the continental Liao forms, of much later date, went instead in the direction of the Mongol-Tungus developments. All these early forms, which happen to be particularly well preserved in the various sources, can be employed to throw additional light on Japanese historical phonology, once the correct association of J *-s-* with pA $*l_2$ has been made.

3. pA $*äl_2$-, Mo. *ele-* 'sich durchreiben, sich abnutzen', *elesün* 'Sand' (Resultat des Zerreibens), < $*el_2$-, Chu. *al-* 'pflügen, eggen', Osm. *äš-* 'kratzen, rudern' (Poppe 1960: 78) :: J *usu* 'a mortar', *usu-i* 'thin', *us-* in *ussuri* 'thinly, faintly'.

4. pA $*bal_2$-, Tk. *baš* 'Kopf', Chu. *puś* 'Kopf, Anfang', Go. *balča*, *balža* 'Kopf, Gesicht,' K *mëli* 'Kopf' (Ramstedt/Aalto 1957: 109) :: OJ *Fasi-ra* 'main pillar, support of a building'; with suffix *-ra*, cf. *-rö* in etymology 1 above. The Korean form presents difficulties, since Martin does not reconstruct a proto-Korean-Japanese phoneme for the correspondence of K *m*, J *F* (Martin 1966: 200–201). If the Chuvash form is not a borrowing, its *-ś* is to be explained as a special development, within Chuvash, of the consonant sequence $*-l_2č$- seen in the Tungus forms cited.

5. pA $*sal_2$-, Tk. *šaš-* 'in Verlegenheit sein, den Verstand verlieren', Osm. *šašqïn* 'verwirrt', Mo. *šali-* 'unmöglich sein, verpfuschen' (Ramstedt/Aalto 1957: 109) :: J *sasi-* in *sasitukae* 'hindrance, impediment', *sasitukaer-u* 'be hindered, impeded, interrupted', *sasitukaenai* 'may, can, be warrantable'.

6. pA $*kol_2$-, Tk. *qoš* 'Paar', Mo. *qoli-dqa-* 'vergleichen', *qolba-* 'zusammenbinden, vereinigen' (Ramstedt/Aalto 1957: 109) :: J *kos-u* 'follow after, come along with from behind'.

7. pA $*tabl_2i$-, Tk., Chag. *taïš-* 'laufen', Mo. *tauli-* 'laufen, springen' (Ramstedt/Aalto 1957: 109) :: OJ *taFasir-u* 'run', attested in *M* 2312, where it is written with the semantograms for 'hand' (to be taken here as going with OJ *ta-*, the combining form of OJ *të* 'hand') plus the semantogram for 'run', though 'hand' can hardly have anything to do with the sense, so that *ta-* must simply be a prefixed element, as shown also by the Altaic comparison. With OJ *Fasir-u* 'run', without this

prefixed element, cf. MTk. *äš-* 'traben', Bur. *eli-* 'fliegen, eilen', Tg.
hęli-nče- 'eilen' (Ramstedt/Aalto 1957: 110), a form apparently also
with proto-Altaic *-l₂-*. On the apparent discrepancies in the initials
in these forms see the discussion of words for 'foot', 'walk', and 'run',
p. 144 below.

8. pA *ul₂-*, Tk. *uš* 'feucht', Mo. *ulum* 'Sumpf', Tg. *ulu-p-* 'wässerig
werden' (Ramstedt/Aalto 1957: 110) :: OJ *usiFo* 'tide', incorporating
OJ *siFo* 'salt; tide' (< *usi* + *siFo* ?).

9. pA *kul₂*, Tk. *quš* 'haarlose Stelle (am Pferde)', Mo. *qol-, qol-ga-*
'wund schaben' (Ramstedt/Aalto 1957: 110) :: J *kosur-u* 'rub, chafe
the skin'; cf. the related form, with *-a-* vowel grade, J *kasa* 'scab;
slough; the pox'.

10. pA *bel₂*, Tk. *beš* 'fünf' (cf. Benzing 1959: 694), Chu. *pillěk*,
pilěk, Kirg. *bilek* 'Handwurzel', Lam. *bilan* 'id.' (Ramstedt/Aalto
1957: 109) :: OJ *Fusa* 'handful'.

(b)

11. pA *kol₂-*, Mo., MMo. *qoli-* 'mischen, vermischen', MTk.,
Osm. *qoš* 'hinzufügen, beimischen' (Poppe 1960: 78; Ramstedt/Aalto
1957: 109) :: J *kos-u* 'filter, strain', pKJ *keš-*, K *kĕli-* 'id.'

12. pA *sil₂*, Mo. *šilügüsün*, Kh. *šülūs*, Bur. *šülüheŋ*, Ma. *silun*
'Luchs' (Poppe 1960: 78) :: OJ *sisi* 'wild animal', J *inosisi* 'wild boar'.

13. pA *sil₂*, Tk. *säš, šiš* 'Bratspiess, *šišliq* 'am Spiess begratenes
Fleisch', Tg. *sila-* 'am Spiess braten, *silawūn* 'Spiess' (Ramstedt/Aalto
1957: 108) :: OJ *sisi* 'flesh, meat (as food)', pKJ *syɔš*, MK *sɔlh* 'id.'
But cf. also J *sas-u* 'to pierce, stick into, insert'?

14. pA *til₂-* Tk. *tiš*, Mo. *čili-ji-* 'anschwellen' (Ramstedt/Aalto
1957: 108) :: J *tusi-m-u* 'to have discoloration appear on the skin (as
in the bruises from a beating)'. The pA *ti-* :: J *tu-* correspondence is
regular.

15. pA *pil₂-*, Tk., Chag. *piši-* 'buttern, umrühren', Mo. *büli-*
'buttern, umrühren, quirlen (den Kumiss im Ledersack)' (Ramstedt/
Aalto 1957: 108) :: OJ *FisiFo* 'a liquid, made from barley and soy
beans, mixed, fermented, and salted, and used as a pickling vehicle for
vegetables'. Cf. *M* 3829.

16. pKJ *tošyi*, eventually going with (but not directly cognate
with) pA *ǯil₂-*, Mo. *ǯil* 'Jahr', OT *jaš* 'Lebensalter', Chu. *śul* 'id.'
(Poppe 1960: 113–14; Ramstedt/Aalto 1957: 110), proto-Tk. *yāš*
(Benzing 1959: 694) :: J *tosi* 'year; age', K *tols* 'anniversary, cycle'.
The initial of the Japanese form relates directly and regularly to the
initial of the proto-Korean-Japanese reconstruction, and goes together

with the proto-Altaic initial, even though the correspondence in vowels leaves problems. But the correspondence here for proto-Altaic *-l₂- is what is of immediate concern, and that is regular.

17. pKJ *dyoš*, eventually going with (but again, as in the case of the etymology immediately above, apparently not directly cognate with) pA *tāl₂*, Mo. *čilaɣun*, Chu. *čul*, OT *taš*, Jak. *tās* 'Stein' (Poppe 1960: 77; Ramstedt/Aalto 1957: 108) :: OJ *yisi* > *isi*, K *tol* < MK *tolh*, pKJ *dyoš* (Martin 1966: 243, #224). pA *t*- before pA -*ā*- would normally yield J *t*-, not *y*-; but pA *d*- before pA -*ā*- would normally yield J *ya*-. The Japanese form must go back to an earlier form with a voiced dental stop, as in pKJ *dyoš*; and here this stop developed in Japanese according to the general rule for voiced dental stops and affricates before pA -*ü*- and -*ö*-, i.e., before front vocalism, no doubt because of the medial -*y*- in the proto-Korean-Japanese form. The precise formulation of the relation of this *dyoš* to pA *tāl₂*, however, presents many problems still awaiting solution. Poppe (1960: 13) has noted 'sporadic' Turkish reflexes in *d* for pA *t*, notably in the south-western areas; and Tuvak (~Tuak) *daš* 'Stein' and other allied 'eastern' forms that may be cited from 'Krimosmanisch' (Doerfer 1959: 275) are certainly relevant here. Not only are earlier forms in initial *d*- necessary to account for the Japanese and Korean data, but they are also necessary to account for such Tungus forms as Go. *ǯolo* (Menges 1968: 201), Ev. *ǯolo*, and Lam. *ǯol*. Poppe (1960: 77) gives these last two Tungus forms following Bur. *šuluŋ*, relating them to the various Mongol forms he cites with the notation '>'; does he intend to indicate by this device that he regards these Tungus forms as loans from Mongol? It is more likely to prove to be significant that these *d*- forms from the Crimea are 'eastern' within that West Turkish area. One can postulate that within the earliest Altaic linguistic community there were *t*- dialect forms in the west and *d*- dialect forms in the east for the word 'stone' (note, however, that this is simply a historical-descriptive statement and not an 'explanation' for this phenomenon, since we do not yet have a clue as to the origin of this *t*-/*d*- doublet). With the gradual break-up of the original Altaic linguistic community, the eastern *d*- forms naturally were the ones inherited in proto-Tungus and proto-Korean-Japanese, as the evidence from these languages shows clearly; but these same *d*- forms also persisted to a certain extent even in other parts of the later, more widespread Altaic area, as witness the Crimean forms in *d*-, which are 'eastern' within that area because *d*- forms for this word persisted in

being 'eastern' rather than 'western' in their over-all geographic orientation even after the radical population displacements and whole-sale migrations that eventually shifted the various subgroups of Altaic speakers far from their original locus.

(c)

18. pA *kal_2ba-, Mo. *qalbaga*, MMo. *qalbuga*, Chag. *qašuq*. Osm. *wašïq* 'Löffel' (Poppe 1960: 78) :: OJ *kasiFa* 'container for liquids'. The homonymous forms OJ *kasi* 'oak (Quercus myrsinae-folia)' and OJ *kasiFa* 'oak leaves (specialized for Q. dentata)', are surely to be kept separate from this form, though to be sure all three have become hopelessly confused in the exegetical traditions of some of the early texts, with rather amusing results. Thus we are asked to believe that OJ *kasiFa*, as the traditional school-reading for a semantogram in a passage in the second book of the *Kojiki*, § 2.102 as numbered by Philippi, refers to oak leaves, even though the context makes it abundantly clear that a container for liquids, specifically, the im-perial wine, is meant (see the text edition of Kurano Genji in NKBT 1.245 [1958]). Philippi (1968: 279) translates '. . . take the oak [-leaf cup containing] the great wine and give it to the crown prince . . .', and adds as his footnote 3, the following: 'It appears [*sic*] that oak leaves were folded or sewn together and used as wine-cups at ancient banquets.' It would be interesting to know exactly how it is imagined that this remarkable feat of technology might have been accomplished. Of course, 'oak leaves' here has nothing to do with the case at all; the word in question is simply OJ *kasiFa* 'container for liquids'. This is also the word involved in the ancient guild designation *kasiFade-nö-oFotömöbe*, with which Mills struggles unsuccessfully in several places (1954: 113–33). On some of the problems involved with these words see also Miller 1967[b]: 190–91; Martin (1966: 237–38, #156) recon-structs pKJ *$kašyi$, going with K *kal* 'oak'.

19. pA *il_2-, Tk. *iš* 'Arbeit, Sache', MTk. *iš, iš* 'id.', Mo. *üile*, Ma. *weile* 'Arbeit, Handarbeit' (Ramstedt/Aalto 1957: 109) :: J *$i/_asar-u$* 'catch fish'.

20. pA *al_2-, Tk. *aš* 'Essen, Speise', K *al* 'Same, Korn, Getreide', Mo. *ali-sun* 'Spreu' (Ramstedt/Aalto 1957: 109) :: J *e-sa* 'food (for animals, spec. birds)', but this form is most likely from earlier *we-, so that the initial causes difficulties; apart from this, the etymology ap-pears to cast some light on the possible origin of the comparatively rare Japanese initial *e-* in this form, as perhaps resulting from an earlier *$\ddot{a}i_{\lambda}$ < *ai_{λ} < *al.

These etymologies make it possible to summarize the over-all scheme of the Japanese, Korean, and proto-Korean-Japanese reflexes for the proto-Altaic liquids:

pA	Tk.	Chu.	Mo.	Tg.	pKJ	K	J
*r	r	r	r	r	*r(x)	l(h)	r

For the proto-Korean-Japanese and Korean reflexes, cf. pKJ *t(w)ɔr, K *til*, OJ *tör-* 'take', Tg. *ǯor-* (Benzing 1955: 984); pKJ *turxye, MK *tulh*, 'two', J *ture* 'companion', pA *ǯur-* (Poppe 1960: 28); J *aru, are* 'that one', pA *är*, Mo., MMo. *ere* 'Mann', Chu. *ar* 'id.', OT *är* 'Mann, Gatte' (Poppe 1960: 79). Additional examples of this correspondence in Miller 1967: 71 § (2).

pA	Tk.	Chu.	Mo.	Tg.	pKJ	K	J
$*r_2$	z	r	r	r	*r	l	r, t

For the proto-Korean-Japanese and Korean reflexes, cf. pKJ *dyar, K *til*, OJ *yir-* > *ir-* 'insert', pA $*dür_2-$ (Poppe 1960: 82, 23); J *ore* '(one's)self', pA $*ör_2$, Mo., MMo. *örö, öre* 'das Innere, Herzader', Chu. *var* 'Mitte, Tal', OT *öz* 'selbst' (Poppe 1960: 81). Additional examples of this correspondence in Miller 1967: 72, and p. 148 below, for the conditions in which J *t* appears rather than J *r*.

pA	Tk.	Chu.	Mo.	Tg.	pKJ	K	J
*l	l	l	l	l	*r	l	r

The proto-Korean-Japanese and Korean reflexes are illustrated by pKJ *dar-, K *tal-*, OJ *yar-* 'give', pA *dal-*, but appearing with the -*o*-grade (i.e., pA *dol-*) in Mo. *doli-* 'freikaufen, Lösegeld bezahlen', OT *yuluγ* 'Opfer, Kösegeld' (Poppe 1960: 75). Additional examples of this correspondence are to be found in Miller 1967: 71 § (1).

pA	Tk.	Chu.	Mo.	Tg.	pKJ	K	J
$*l_2$	š	l	l	l	*š	l(s, h)	s(i)

The proto-Korean-Japanese and Korean reflexes for this original proto-Altaic phoneme are established by etymologies (5) 'meat', (11) 'filter (it)', and (16) 'year, age' presented immediately above.

The above sets of correspondences hold true for those cases where the phonemes in question were found in the original language in inter-vocalic position, or following a vowel and preceding zero; but the same correspondences are not necessarily true in those cases, which did occur, in which one of these phonemes appeared as an element in a consonant cluster. In such cases other reflexes may be expected; these of course complicate the correspondences, but at the same time they are difficult to systematize because such combinations are attested in too few a number of cases to permit satisfactory generalization.

Thus, J *kak-u* 'scratch' appears to go with K *kïlk-* 'id.,' both attesting to pKJ **kalk-* (Martin 1966: 240, #189), and this in turn must go with pA **kar₂-*, Mo. *qar-u-* 'graben, kratzen', Chu. *xïr-*, OT *gaz-* (Poppe 1960: 17).

This provides a clue toward the clarification of the problem presented by the single example of a Japanese reflex for pA **l₂* cited earlier, namely J *-r-* in *yawaraka* 'smoothly', apparently corresponding to Tk. *-š-*, and eventually to **l₂*, in OT *yïmšaq* 'weich', going with proto-Altaic **ńïm-* (Poppe 1960: 38, 114; Miller 1967: 75). Here the Japanese reflex, which earlier had appeared to be the rule, now clearly shows itself to be the exception instead and to be exceptional precisely because of its environmental location in the word in question, i.e., as a part of the consonant cluster **-ml₂-* in the original inherited form that underlies these later changed forms. The second *-a-* coming between the *-w-* and the *-r-* in J *yawaraka* is a secondary development; the original form in question here had instead a consonant cluster consisting of the nasal labial *-m-* followed directly by the liquid *-*l₂-*. Under these environmental circumstances, just as in the case of the forms for 'scratch' cited earlier in connection with **-r₂-*, the Japanese reflex is anomalous, rather than being the norm.

Another way in which to present these same developments would be to call attention to the fact that in the case of *yïmšaq* :: *yawaraka* we have the Japanese reflex that we would have expected for original **-l-* rather than *-s-*, the one that we would have expected for original **-l₂-*. Whatever may be said of original **l₂* as against original **l*, it is certainly beyond argument that the former was a palatalized or fronted variety of the latter, and also that the former differed from the latter principally in terms of this feature of palatalization. It is not difficult to imagine that when originally palatalized **l₂* occurred together with original *-m-* in a consonant cluster, the **l₂* tended to lose its characteristic (and distinguishing) feature of palatalization. In other words, **l₂* fell together with **l* in this environment, and as a result it shows the same reflex in Japanese in this form that we would expect for original **l*.

At first glance it might appear that etymology number 2 suggested above for 'rabbit' tends to contradict this postulation, since that form also apparently had an original **-bl₂-* cluster. But that such a parallel is only apparent, not real, is demonstrated by the fact that in the

Japanese reflex, as we have already seen, we have evidence for another original form *without* the initial **ta-* element that the Altaic cognates generally display, so that originally the cluster of **-b-* and **l₂* was not internal, but rather initial, in this morpheme. In other words, it was not a cluster at all but a sequence of initial **b-* followed by an original vowel (original, at any rate, insofar as the Japanese reflex is concerned), and this in turn was followed by **l₂* (cf. also the *-i-* vowel in OT *tabïšɣan* in this connection). This original **b* + vowel sequence

FIGURE 3

The Liquids from Proto-Altaic to Korean and Japanese

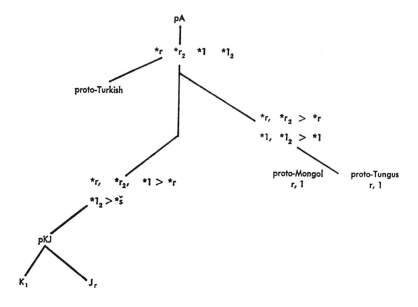

was the source of the older Japanese **wu-*, with the result that the Japanese reflex here for **-l₂-* is the normal and expected one, i.e., J *-s-*. Another apparent anomaly to be explained along essentially similar lines is that presented by etymology number 7 for 'run', where once again the original form brought **b* and **l₂* together, but where the Japanese development apparently segmented its inheritance of this form in such a way as to preserve an unassimilated variety of original **l₂*.

The above summary also permits us to make a few important observations on the nature of the relationship of Japanese and Korean to proto-Tungus on the one hand, and to proto-Altaic on the other; these may be conveniently summarized in Figure 3.

In other words, the full proto-Altaic repertory of four distinctive, contrasting liquid phonemes is preserved solely in proto-Turkish, thanks to the surviving differentiation there between common Turkish *l* and *r* on the one hand and *š* and *z* on the other with Chuvash *l* and *r*, according to the well-known pattern of distribution for these correspondences within Turkish. This four-way contrast was simplified early in the history of the Altaic languages, with proto-Mongol and proto-Tungus and their surviving binary *r/l* contrast representing one variety of this simplification and proto-Korean-Japanese and its distinctive collapsing of the original quadripartite contrast as set forth above representing another. The proto-Korean-Japanese developments were along the same general lines as those in proto-Mongol and proto-Tungus, but they were not identical; and it is necessary, at least on the basis of this evidence from the liquids, to posit a separation of proto-Korean-Japanese from the common proto-Altaic unity different from and independent of the separation (or better, perhaps, the separations?) of proto-Mongol and proto-Tungus from that same unity.

The above summation is somewhat simplified and may by that token obscure a number of points of detail that still remain to be clarified. Martin reconstructs not only proto-Korean-Japanese **r* and **š*, but also **l* and **ř* (Martin 1966: 210–11), according to the following correspondences:

pKJ	K	J
*-l-	l	t
*-ld-	l	d
*-l	l	#
*-l + C(-)	l + C	C
*-lg-	lk	g
*-lǧ	l	k
*-r(-)	l	y

We have already inspected one of these correspondences above, in our consideration of pKJ **kalk-*, K *kïlk-*, J *kak-* 'scratch', forms going with proto-Altaic **-r₂-*, and have noted that the phonological difficulties in this etymology are most likely due to the appearance of the original Altaic liquid **r₂* in this form as one member of a consonant cluster. In this same connection we have also to note the set of related forms pKJ **kaš-/*kal-/*kat-* that Martin (1966: 245, #252) must reconstruct to account for K *kël/t-* 'walk', going with J *kasi, kati* 'walking', and note also that these most likely also go with the original

*-r₂- of Mo. *kerü*- 'windern, sich umhertreiben', OT *käz*- 'reisen', Osm. *gäz*- 'spazieren', etc. (Poppe 1960: 19). Another case in which pKJ **l* appears to go with original **r₂* is pA **ñār₂*, Chu. *šur* 'Frühling', OT *jaz* 'id.', if this can indeed be connected with K *nyälïm* 'summer'. As noted earlier, for the purposes of the present chapter only we are treating all cases of original pA **r₂* as if their normal Japanese development were always J *r*; but here we depart from that convention for the moment to note that **r₂* in this environment turns up as J *t*, since the cognate form is J *natu* 'summer'. (Martin 1966: 243, #230 reconstructs pKJ **nYalɔm* to accommodate the etymology.)

The unfortunate fact is that, apart from these few cases, evidence from the other Altaic languages throws little or no light upon the ultimate etymologies of any of the other words for which Martin reconstructs his pKJ **l*, either alone or in its various combinations with other consonants, or upon words with his pKJ **ř*. From the large number of cases in which his pKJ **l* appears in consonant clusters, and from its behavior in those few instances in which we can at least partially clarify the history of its development with evidence provided by the other Altaic languages, it appears that his pKJ **l* might well have ultimately been a special environmental or positional allophone of another phoneme, most likely his pKJ **r*.

His pKJ **ř* is if anything even more difficult to interpret on the broader comparative level; about all that can be said concerning this phoneme is that it participates in the embarrassingly rich morphophonemic variety of the root 'walk', where in addition to pKJ **kal-/*kat-/*kaš*- to account for J *kati, kasi*, Martin also reconstructs still a fourth form, pKJ **kař*-, to account for J *kay-oF*- 'go back and forth (regularly)'.

Without further evidence and additional Altaic etymologies, it is difficult to detect any pattern in all this, and also all but impossible to relate pKJ **l* and pKJ **ř* to the over-all system proposed above to account for the proto-Korean-Japanese reflexes of the original proto-Altaic liquids. It is surely preferable first of all to work with what is clear and overt, rather than to neglect the evident because of difficulties occasioned by a scattering of difficult, contradictory, and perhaps even anomalous forms.

But these difficulties may also have a certain amount of linguistic significance of and by themselves: the situation may well appear to be this obscure because our investigation has caught it, as it were, in a moment of transition, so that it is those shifts that were in the course

of transpiring within the data at precisely that point in time revealed
to us by our investigation that are the principal obscuring factors. The
fact that Martin finds it necessary to reconstruct *four* related but
different morphemes for 'walk'—pKJ **kaš-*, **kal-*, **kat-*, and **kař-*,
with final pKJ **š*, **l*, **t*, and **ř*—is most likely not purely a fortuitous
coincidence: we cannot but recall in this connection that there were
four related but different and contrasting liquids in proto-Altaic. It
may well be that this particular root, because of borrowings and other
analogical changes within the common Altaic area that we are now
most understandably by and large incapable of recovering, has preserved, or at least reflects in some way or other, the more complex
phonology of the original proto-Altaic liquids than does the bulk of
the Korean-Japanese lexical evidence. Certainly the bulk of that
evidence, i.e., the evidence for an original Korean-Japanese linguistic
unity, argues in the direction of the filiation suggested in the graphic
representation above, in which proto-Korean-Japanese separated
from proto-Altaic after a point in time at which original **r*, **r_2*, and
*l had all fallen together under pKJ **r*, which however then still
contrasted with original pA **l_2* > pKJ **š*. The correspondences noted
above in which pKJ **l* appears to go with original **r_2* may well represent an intermediate stage within the separation of proto-Korean-
Japanese from proto-Altaic, in which there were three distinctive,
contrasting liquids, pKJ **r*, **š*, and **l*, i.e., one more (**l*) than the two
for which the bulk of the lexical data provides evidence, but one less
than the original four of proto-Altaic out of which the system grew.

It is possible to discern the broad outlines of at least one of the
processes of linguistic change by which these simplifications took
place in the history of the various words involved in etymology 13
above, going with pA **sïl_2-*. Fortunately for words going with this
original form we have Pelliot's celebrated study 'Širolɣa—Širalga',
which makes clear some of the enormously complicated interrelationships and associations, many of them due to borrowing and reborrowing throughout the Altaic area, in addition to (and further complicated by) genetic inheritance; see especially Pelliot (1944: 107, 108,
n. 2, and 109, n. 1).

What apparently happened in the case of this word was something
along the following lines. The original linguistic unity had one root
of the shape **sir-* for 'pointed stake,' later specialized in the sense of
'spit for roasting meat'; another originally separate root with which
however this soon became contaminated in the different languages,

for obvious reasons, was **sil-* 'to roast, cook meat'. Alongside these two, there was also the semantically, if not etymologically, related **sïl₂-* just noted. In Mongol, both 'spit' and 'to roast' ended up with -*r*-, while in Tungus both ended up with -*l*- (Pelliot 1944: 109, n. 1).

The sweeping simplifications in the four original Altaic liquids that resulted, more or less independently to be sure, in the reduced number of contrasts that have survived in Mongol, Tungus, and Korean-Japanese were most likely significantly accelerated more than once in the history of all these languages by far-reaching semantic contaminations of this same type, operating among forms closely related in both sound and meaning. Pelliot's magisterial study of the whole vast range of problems centering upon this single group of words throughout the Altaic area fortunately puts us in the possession of data for this one case that in many other instances we do not yet possess; and it helps us, at least partially, to dispel some of the obscurities surrounding these forms and their developments, while reminding us that there is probably at least as much that still remains to be uncovered in the case of almost every one of the etymologies suggested above. Furthermore, and over and above the phonological and semantic considerations that have been our principal concern up to this point, this set of words reminds us that there are also important morphophonemic aspects to all these problems.

Proto-Altaic **l₂* was, as already observed above, most likely a palatalized variety of pA **l*. Martin's pKJ **š*, which as we have also seen appears to be the principal reflex of pA **l₂* in proto-Korean-Japanese, was reconstructed by him totally independently from the evidence presented in the present paper; yet the correlation of the presumed articulatory characteristics of this unit, reconstructed element in a postulated protolanguage though it be, is impressive. In this connection, the next problem that logically follows is to investigate what if any traces of the articulatory feature of palatalization may be detected in the Japanese evidence.

These traces may be most strikingly detected in the articulatory position of the vowel immediately following the Japanese -*s*- reflex, since in almost every case it is evident from the etymologies that this vowel is not an inherited feature of vocalization but instead has appeared in the Japanese cognate as a semiautomatic feature, the phonetic shape of which has been largely (or completely) determined by the original palatal articulation of the immediately preceding pA **l₂* > J -*s*-.

We have considered above a total of 17 etymologies in groups (a) and (b) as the basis for our theoretical formulations; the three etymologies in group (c) are too frankly speculative to serve as a basis for generalization. From among these 17 etymologies, we note at once that the Japanese cognate suggested has not only -*s*- but the sequence -*s* + *i*- in a total of 11 of these 17 cases, an impressive majority of the available evidence. These are etymologies 1, 4, 5, 7, 8, 12, 13, 14, 15, 16, and 17. (Note that even in etymology 18, which is one of the group (c) etymologies and hence not counted in the totals here, the same -*s* + *i*- sequence appears.) It is clearly evident from this data that the original palatal nature of pA *l_2 not only persisted into the proto-Korean-Japanese unity (as witness pKJ *$\check{s}$), but also that it survived well into pre-Japanese, following the separation of Korean and Japanese.

This accounts for 11 out of a total of 17 cases; what then of the remaining six cases? In three of them, verbs are involved, and since the Japanese reflex of pA *l_2 appears here as root-final -*s*- in these verb stems, it is not difficult to understand why in two of these cases, etymologies 6 and 11, its original articulatory nature has been obscured by subsequent morphological accretions within the verbal morphology. In etymology 9 the same situation appears to hold true even though in this case a morphological enlargement has been added to the original verb stem (thus, **kos-* + -*ur*-), though we note that in 14, where we have another case of verb stem with enlargement (**tusi* + *m*-), the addition of the enlargement apparently did not inhibit the display of the original palatalization in the form of the Japanese -*s* + *i* sequence. This leaves only three cases, 2, 3, and 10, without an immediate and obvious explanation. There is no trace of the original palatal articulation in 3 and 10. But in 2, as we have seen immediately above, the happy circumstance of the preservation of the old Peninsular ('Koguryŏ') form **wusiga* shows us that the attested Japanese forms have undergone a metathesis of the -*i*- and -*a*-, and that here too -*i*- following J -*s*- from pA *l_2 represents the original ordering of the phonemes in question. And so this form too becomes an instance of the classical 'exception that proves the rule'.

Each time we successfully recover otherwise lost evidence for an event in the earlier history of a language—or put more simply, each time that we formulate a sound law—we may properly expect that our statements will also provide historical explanations for other phenomena over and above those to account for which they were originally written. The statements for the Japanese reflex of pA $*l_2$ are no exception. They also make it possible to provide historical explanations for several other problems in the history of Japanese that might otherwise continue to be without solutions. Two of the most important of these are summarized briefly below—the skewed distribution of the allophones for OJ /s/, and certain interrelationships between 'endoactive' and 'exoactive' verbs.

This formulation of the Japanese reflex of pA $*l_2$ provides us for the first time with a clue to the origin of the rather unusual distribution of allophones for the Old Japanese /s/ phoneme. According to the usual theories of Old Japanese pronunciation and phonology, OJ /s/ was [tˢ] before /a u o ö/, but [s] before /i e/ (Miller 1967: 192–93; 202). This is a rather surprising pattern of distribution for allophones, but given the palatal nature of pA $*l_2$, as well as its normal development in Japanese as -s- followed by a front vowel, we are now well on our way to understanding how this somewhat skewed distribution probably arose. The original pattern was no doubt a completely regular one, with OJ /s/ pronounced as [tˢ] before all the Old Japanese vowels before which it occurred. In other words, at this stage of the language it is actually incorrect even to speak of an /s/ phoneme; it was rather a /tˢ/ phoneme. The phone [s] existed in this earliest stage of the language only as the normal Japanese inheritance of pA $*l_2$; it was always immediately followed by a front vowel, and hence was itself probably palatalized in pronunciation. But it was through the Japanese development of pA $*l_2$ as [s] that this phone found its way into the phonetic inventory of the language in the first place, and originally the [s] phone had nothing at all to do with the /tˢ/ phoneme. This [s] pronunciation, always before OJ -i or -e, was then analogically imitated in the pronunciation pattern for the OJ /s/, i.e., /tˢ/ phoneme, where it soon replaced the earlier uniform [tˢ] pronunciation before OJ /i e/, to give the skewed distribution of allophones found in the texts. Similarly, OJ /z/ was [dᶻ] before /a u o ö/, but [z] before OJ /i e/, and here too a similar analogical remodeling of pronunciation took place. The cases in Azuma texts where standard OJ /ti/ is written as [si] (Miller 1967: 166) provide indirect but important documentary evidence for the process of pronunciation change postulated.

With J -s- established as the normal Japanese reflex of pA $*l_2$, it also becomes possible for the first time to throw a certain amount of light from the level of comparative grammar on the origin and development of one of the most characteristic, perplexing, and anomalous segments of Japanese verbal morphology.

The distinction between 'endoactive' (or, 'intransitive') and 'exoactive (or 'transitive', 'factitive') verbs is an important morphological and semantic dichotomy in modern Japanese and has been a feature of the language from the time of the earliest periods known to us from the texts. Some insights into the origin of this dichotomy provided by comparison with related languages, particularly with Tungus, have been discussed earlier (p. 90), but the most important evidence from the comparative method has had to wait for the formulation of the Japanese reflex of pA *l_2, since this original phoneme provides the clue to the correct solution of much of this puzzling segment of Japanese verbal morphology.

Setting aside those verbs for which the endoactive and exoactive forms are homonymous (Lewin's 1, Typ a), we have the following three principal patterns of internal relationship between the two categories (1 = Lewin's 1. Typ b; 2 = Lewin's 2; 3 = Lewin's 3):

Endoactive	Exoactive
1. (a) *nor-u* 'ride (on a vehicle)'	*nos-u* 'carry (something on a vehicle), give (something) a ride'
nar-u 'become'	*nas-u* 'do, make'
kaer-u 'return'	*kaes-u* 'bring, send (something) back'
(b) *nokor-u* 'remain, stay behind'	*nokos-u* 'retain, keep behind'
(c) *kiy-u* 'disappear'	*kes-u* 'extinguish'
2. *ugok-u* '(something) moves'	*ugokas-u* 'move, shift (something)'
ak-u '(something) is open'	*akas-u* 'open, disclose (something)'
3. *fusagar-u* '(something) is in the way'	*fusag-u* 'stop up, block (something)'

As Haguenauer (1956: 332–33) has perceptively pointed out, the essential historical problem inherent in this body of forms is in actual fact located only in our group 1.a (and, by implication, also in our group 1.c); in the other cases the sets of forms are clearly the result of secondary and tertiary formations or enlargements going upon original verbal roots that remain unchanged and whose identity survives despite the complex processes of suffixation that they have undergone;

thus, *nokos-u* goes back to an original root *nok-* (cf. pKJ **nox-*, Martin 1966: 239, #175), plus a vocalic-juncture element *-o-*, followed in turn by the formants *-r* + *u/-s* + *u*. In the case of verbs belonging to our groups 2 and 3 above, similar processes of affixation have been operative, in slightly different ways but along the same general lines, so that these sets too present no particular problems.

It is only in sets of the type *nor-u/nos-u* (and hence by extension also *kiy-u/kes-u*) that the historical problem exists, for these forms cannot possibly be analyzed as resulting from the addition of suffixal formants or enlargements of the roots; in these forms, instead, something happens that is completely anomalous as far as Japanese morphology is concerned—the endoactive vs. exoactive distinction is marked in these sets of forms by variation of the final consonant of the root itself (*-r-*, *-y-/-s-*). The problem is such an important one, and the forms involved are so extremely distinctive within the morphological system of Japanese, that it is surprising in the extreme to realize that no particular effort appears to have been made by Japanese scholars to work out a solution for the historical conundrum that they present (cf. Haguenauer 1956: 334).

The formulation for the Japanese reflex of proto-Altaic *$*l_2$ proposed in the present chapter makes it possible to explain the historical origin of this distinctive and anomalous variation of the root-final consonants in Japanese endoactive/exoactive sets of the *nor-u/nos-u* variety for the first time. It now becomes possible to approach the question on the historical level, where the anomalies observed in the synchronic materials will be found to reduce themselves to an underlying, earlier, and regular pattern.

Before entering upon the details of this demonstration, it is necessary to arrange the Japanese materials in as orderly a fashion as possible and to bring together the relevant data, separating it from those items that are of less immediate application to the immediate problem. Haguenauer (loc. cit.) has done a genuine service toward the solution of this problem by suggesting that there is more than one layer of sets among the Japanese forms at issue, and that it is possible (as already noted above) to localize the problem within a particular group of sets, i.e., that group in which the *-r-*, *-y-//-s-* alternation takes place with respect to the original final consonant of the root itself; but unfortunately he then goes on to ignore this important principle in his own arrangement of the forms, so that complex, secondary formations of the type of *kaeru/kaesu* < **kaF* + *e* + *$^r/_s$* + *u*, and

naoru/naosu < **naF* + *o* + *ʳ/ₛu*, and the like, all end up in his
analysis alongside the truly relevant simplex forms of the *nor-u/nos-u*
type. Among the many forms in Haguenauer's lists that are clearly
irrelevant to our problem only the set *tōru* 'pass through'/*tōsu* 'put
(it) through' presents any problem; but this set too is almost surely to
be deleted, for the reason that if the etymon in question here is an
original Japanese root, the word is then a case of **taF* + *o* + *ʳ/ₛu*,
and hence not relevant; or in the (more likely) case that it is an old
Chinese loanword < **taŭ* < **t'uŋ*, (6638), it all the more clearly has
nothing of significance to add to our knowledge of the origin of a
Japanese morphological device.

Adhering to Haguenauer's principles, then, but largely ignoring his
results, we may instead draw up the following list of Japanese forms
that are genuinely relevant to the root variation anomaly under discussion. The first 14 items in the following list are sets of forms about
the interrelationship of which there can be little question; items 15
through 18 are frankly speculative and probably do not add anything
of importance to the discussion (in which they play no part after this
point), but they are included here to make the list as complete as
possible. Taken as a body of data, these two lists (items 1 through 14
and items 15 through 18) appear to be an exhaustive inventory of the
Japanese data that may be cited in relation to this problem:

1. *tar-u* 'suffice', *tas-u* 'make (something) sufficient'.
2. *wor-u* 'be, exist', *wos-u* 'rule over, command'.
3. *kar-u* 'borrow', *kas-u* 'lend'.
4. *nor-u* 'ride', *nos-u* 'transport (something)'.
5. *nar-u* 'become', *nas-u* 'make, do'.
6. *a-maru* 'be in excess', *mas-u* 'increase, multiply'.
7. *nir-u* 'resemble', *nis-u* 'imitate, copy'.
8. *Fur-u* 'fall down (specifically of rain, snow)', *Fus-u* 'place, lay
   (something) face down, prone'.
9. *Fer-u* 'diminish, decline, pass (of time)', *Fes-u* 'diminish, cut
   down, back (something)'. Cf. OJ *mer-u*, doublet with *Fer-u*.
10. *mir-u* 'see', *mis-u* 'show'.
11. *yur-u* 'move; move accompanied by a sound', *yus-u* 'pluck, play a
    stringed instrument'.
12. *yor-u* 'approach', *yos-u* 'bring into proximity'.
13. *kir-u* 'wear clothing', *kis-u* 'clothe (someone)'. Cf. OJ *kes-u*,
    doublet with *kis-u*.
14. *Fir-u* 'dry up', *Fos-u* 'desiccate (something)'.

15. *ur-u* 'sell', *us-u* 'loose'.
16. *or-u* 'weave textiles', *os-u* 'press down'.
17. *sar-u* 'leave', *sas-u* 'stop'.
18. *Fir-u* 'let go, let be', *Fis-u* 'crush'.

A clue to the coordination of this data with Altaic is presented in Martin's reconstruction of proto-Korean-Japanese, where, it is important to note, it was reached entirely independently of the materials presented in the present paper. Under his item #185 Martin (1966: 240) wrote, in connection with J *nor-u/nos-u*, of the possibility of reconstructing 'the derivative suffixes as a polarity marker in proto-Korean-Japanese: *-š-/-r-* on the basis of CARRY and RIDE.' He added, 'we are not always sure that one or the other of these phonemes [i.e., *š/r*] is not basic to a particular pair of words in spite of the many cases where both are to be treated as suffixes.'

The above list provides a core of evidence for those cases in which these phonemes are clearly *not* to be treated as suffixes, and it is precisely in those cases where they are, in Martin's terms, 'basic to a particular pair of words', i.e., represent an original alternation of root-final consonants, that they are the most informative for the history of the language.

What we have, in effect, in the above lists, notably in items 1 through 14, is a surviving unified body of data going very far back into the prehistory of Japanese and preserving in its root-final alternation a very old, and inherited, morphological device that may be traced in parallel, and cognate, roots in proto-Altaic.

First of all, if the formulation suggested above is correct, a possible proto-Altaic original for each of the Japanese pairs cited above would be a set of roots in which the alternation in the final consonant consisted in one member having pA *l, giving OJ *-r-*, and the other member having pA *l_2, giving OJ *-s-*. (The correlation of this formulation with Martin's proto-Korean-Japanese reconstruction is obvious.) But is it possible to verify this hypothesis from Altaic data outside Korean, and if so, to what extent?

Fortunately, we find that for at least a few important items on our list of Japanese forms, we are able to detect precisely this same predicted proto-Altaic variation between *l and *l_2 in cognate roots. The most striking evidence relates to J *tar-u*, *tas-u*, with which we may immediately compare OT *tol-* 'voll sein, füllen', against OT *toš-* 'füllen, vollständig machen'. The Turkish forms have the *o*-grade of the original a/o (OJ $\ddot{o}$) ablaut variation; otherwise there are no difficulties of any kind, either in the phonology or in the semantics of the comparison, and the morphological correspondences in items of detail is most striking:

	pA $*t^a/o^l$- (endoactive)	pA $*t^a/o^l{}_2$- (exoactive)
OT	*tol-*	*toš-*
OJ	*tar-*	*tas-*

The correspondences in different items of detail exhibited by these forms alone would probably be sufficient to demonstrate the genetic relationship of Japanese to Old Turkish, and by extension to the Altaic languages in general, even if no other evidence were forthcoming on this entire problem, so striking are their correlations on the several independent levels of phonology, morphology, and semantics.

A feeling for the close relationship of the two verbs OT *tol-* and OT *toš-* must have persisted among the users of the language for some time, since we find that these two verbs go together in one of the characteristic synonym-collocations that distinguish the literature of the Old Turkish translations of Buddhist texts from the Chinese. The synonym-collocation OT *tol-* . . . *toš-* may be cited from the Old Turkish version of the Chinese *Suvarṇaprabhāsa;* Nadelyayev et al. (1968) cite it once from *Suv.* 118_{16} (loc. cit., 572^b), once from *Suv.* 118_{14} (loc. cit., 18^a), either because of a lapsus in their citations or because of parallel passages in the original text. Whatever the case, the persistence of the Old Turkish synonym-collocation *tol-* . . . *toš-* in this and similar texts provides concrete evidence for the continued association of these two related forms on the part of the Old Turkish translators.

Another equally striking set of correlations between this same morphological phenomenon both in Old Japanese and in the Old Turkish materials as well is provided by a comparison of OJ *wor-u* 'be, exist' and OJ *wos-u* 'rule over, command' with OT *bol-* 'be, become', against the semantic value of OT **boš-* '*rule, direct' in OT *bošɣur-* 'to organize, form', OT *bošɣur-* 'teach, give advice, make suggestions', and OT *bošɣut* 'Unterweisung'. We have already discussed the involved relationship between Japanese and Turkish forms for 'to be' in some detail (pp. 37–38 above); this further data adds additional value to these associations. Once again the correspondences in matters of detail are so precise that only the genetic inheritance of an original feature can provide a reasonable explanation.

Altaic evidence may also be brought into the discussion of the above Japanese data in a few other cases, and though in these instances it generally is not as striking as the Turkish evidence just cited, nevertheless it does point in the direction of an earlier *l (rather than, for example, pA *r or *r₂), and hence fits into the over-all formulation proposed. Thus, for J *kar-u* 'borrow', *kas-u* 'lend', we may cite pA *kal-, Mo. *qaltas* 'Teil, Fragment', Ev. *kaltakat* 'entzwei, in Stücke', K *kali-* 'teilen, entzweischneiden' (Poppe 1960: 17), which represents a root-final case of pA *l (Poppe 1960: 75, 85). For J *nor-u*, *nos-u* we may tentatively suggest OT *yäl-* 'reiten, traben' (Miller 1967: 77), again demonstrating (if this etymology is correct) that the original root was pA *l and not pA *r. For J *nar-u, nas-u* it is difficult to locate relevant data; if the Japanese forms somehow involve contractions of the order *ni + *aru, then perhaps OT *ol-* 'is, are', is relevant; and Martin (1966: 226) has in this connection cited Chukchi *nel*, Koryak *nal* 'become', for whatever significance these forms might eventually prove to have; at the very least, they too show original *l and not *r. For J [a]mar-u, mas-u, one is reminded of the use of OJ *amari* in the formation of the higher numerals in the Old Japanese numeral system, thus *misotiamariFutatu* '32' (*misoti* '30', *Futatu* '2'; see Miller 1967: 337), and perhaps the comparison may be made with Ev. *hələk*, Lam. *hulək* 'darüber hinaus, überschüssig' (cf. Ma. *fulu* 'viel, zu viel', Go. *puliə* 'zu viel'), employed in similar and probably genetically related ways in the Tungus numerals (Benzing 1955: 1050, § 116). Again, whatever else may be said for or against this comparison, at the very least it shows original *l rather than original *r. But at present, it is difficult to go beyond these few suggestive indications from the Altaic materials; and there are other still unexplained cases, such as that of J *kir-u, kis-u*, in which the Altaic materials appear to show neither *l nor *r, but original *d: Mo. *kedüre-* 'anziehen, überwerfen', OT *käd-* 'id.' (Poppe 1960: 19). (Could this in some way be related to the anomalous vocalization of the OJ doublet-form *kes-u* already noted above?) All these cases remain to be explained, but they do not necessarily contradict the formulation proposed herein for those other cases in which the Altaic originals clearly have *l and *l₂.

One further correlation of this formulation with proto-Korean-Japanese is possible, in terms of the important and well-documented endoactive/exoactive formant pKJ *i (Miller 1967: 65–66); this becomes particularly relevant when we recall that pA $*l_2$ is to be taken in general as a palatalized variety of pA $*l$, i.e., $*l + i/į > *l_2$. Thus,

	$*t^a/_o l$-	$*t^a/_o l + i- > *t^a/_o l_2$-
OT	tol-	toš-
OJ	tar-	tas-, *etc.*

This leads us naturally to a brief consideration of those cases in Old Turkish itself in which OT š and *l* have a morphological relationship that, while it cannot be explained within the Turkish materials alone, becomes regular and transparent in the light of this comparative evidence presently under consideration:

(a) OT *balï* 'verwundet', but *baš* 'Wunde'.

(b) OT *il-*, *yil-* 'anhängen, angreifen', but *iš* 'Tat, Geschäft, Unternehmen, Dienst'.

(c) OT *qïl-*, 'tun, ausführen, wirken, zu etwas machen', doublet with *qïš-* 'id.'

Within Japanese itself, it is impossible to explain the relationship of *nor-u* to *nos-u*; within Turkish itself, it is impossible to explain the relationship of *tol-* to *toš-*, just as it is impossible to explain the internal relationship in the three sets just cited. But taken all together, not as discrete, isolated items but as part of a larger morphological phenomenon, and viewed in terms of the broader Altaic horizon to which they may all be related, it is possible to discern the underlying (and inherited) patterns responsible for the otherwise totally anomalous forms of the attested languages.

Most strikingly, and having particular relevance to the particular problem of verbal morphology under consideration here, the same formulation brings together two important Old Turkish verbal morphological elements, the 'reflexive and/or passive' OT -*l*- (von Gabain 1950: 80, § 156; Tekin 1968: 115, § 3.114.4), and the 'reciprocal and/or frequentative' OT -*š*- (von Gabain 1950: 82, § 164; Tekin 1968: 117, § 3.114.9). The relationship of these elements to the formulation suggested here ($*l : *l_2 ::$ OT $l : š ::$ OJ $r : s$) is obvious.

A description of the function of this OT -*š*- in the verbal morphology of that language is, however, so reminiscent of the problems involved in the description of the proto-Korean-Japanese endoactive/exoactive formant $*i$ (Miller 1967: 65–66), that it is worth citing at length:

Die Wechselseitigkeit besteht in Aktivität der einen Seite und Passivität der anderen Seite; das -š- kann also angewendet werden, wenn man darauf Wert legt zu betonen, dass einer ruft, und zugleich ein anderer gerufen wird. Es können aber auch beide Beteiligten aktiv tätig sein (von Gabain 1950: 82, §164).

If all this sounds very much like a description of the similar phenomenon in proto-Korean-Japanese and Old Japanese, there is a reason for the similarity: the phenomena look so much alike because they are historically related, i.e., they are the same phenomenon.

In his purely synchronic description of modern Japanese, Bloch summarized the derivation patterns for this segment of the verb morphology in the following general terms:

Many intransitive verbs are distinguished from root-related forms or derived from underlying words by a morpheme that contains (or consists of) the phoneme *r*; many transitive verbs are similarly distinguished or derived by a morpheme that contains (or consists of) the phoneme *s* (Bloch 1970: 98).

It is no very great overstatement to say that from this single descriptive statement alone it would have been possible, by internal reconstruction, to postulate an original phoneme playing the same role in pre-Japanese that pA *l_2 may now be demonstrated to have done with respect to the Japanese relationship to the other Altaic languages· From this statement also, it should have been possible long ago to see the special relationship that obtains between J *r* and J *s*, and to have speculated that both would historically stand in some special relationship to each other. Especially when taken together with our present findings concerning the role of pA *l_2 in the origin of the enodactive/ exoactive verbal dichotomy in Japanese, Bloch's summation of the descriptive facts is of great importance both for its content and for its place in the history of Japanese studies.

One small residue of forms remains for treatment, that of division 1 c in our classification above, represented by the sets J *kiy-u* 'disappear' against *kes-u* 'extinguish', and J *moy-u* 'be on fire, be burning' against *mos-u* 'burn, set fire to (something)'. It is not difficult to fit these forms into the over-all formulation proposed in the present paper, since it is evident that the original root-final consonant in these words must have been -*y*-, so that the original roots were, in the two cases cited, *$k^i/_ey$*- and *moy*- (the vowel variation in the former root remains unexplained; the normal expectation, in view of our knowledge of the prehistory of the Japanese vowel system, would be to hold that the -*i*- vocalization in this root is original, and that the -*e*- is a later, secondary development, but the problem requires further study). What happened in the original language in the case of this set of residue forms must have been something along the following lines: *l was added to form the original exoactive construction, thus *kiy- + -l-, *moy- + -l-; coming as it did here immediately following the root-final -y-, this *l suffix was then palatalized in these residue cases just as, in the other main body of the data, it was palatalized by the subsequent addition of the original proto-Korean-Japanese endoactive/exoactive formant *i following the same *l (*l + -i- > *l_2), so that these roots too turned up *l_2 > -s- in the Japanese exoactive, eventually resulting in *$k^i/_e y$- + *-l- > *kes-, *moy- + *-l- > *mos-, etc.

We should also note that the Japanese evidence in this small residue of forms does not necessarily rule out the possibility of a further suffixation, even in these cases, of the same proto-Korean-Japanese endoactive/exoactive formant *i following the *l (thus, *moy- + *-l- + *-i-, which would have yielded an identical mos-); given the original root-final -y- of these forms, the reflex in Japanese would have been the same, i.e., J -s-, with or without this final layer of suffixation.

It is also important to note that the modern standard-language colloquial equivalents of the exoactive members of these nor-u/nos-u sets generally preserve evidence of the original palatal nature of this formation, and of the original palatal articulation of the proto-Altaic *l_2 out of which they have evolved, in the form of the -e- vocalization upon which many of them are constructed in the modern spoken language of Tokyo; thus, equivalent to the nos-u member of the old nor-u/nos-u set, we find J $nose$-ru, in the same meanings; with mis-u of old mir-u/mis-u, we find J $mise$-ru; with yos-u of yor-u/yos-u, we find $yose$-ru, etc. Our historical formulation for the Japanese reflexes of proto-Altaic *l_2 and our findings concerning the role of this phoneme in the original verbal morphology make it possible to 'explain' (in the historical sense) *why* these particular verbs belong to this -e-ru morphological set in modern spoken Japanese; this evidence is of a part with that cited above on the relative frequency of J -i- following J -s- from original *l_2.

Finally, we must note that there are still unsolved cases in which Ryūkyū -s- apparently corresponds to J -r-; is it significant, in view of the materials presented herein, that one notable case for this correspondence occurs before -i, in Shuri $kibusi$, J $kemuri$ 'smoke' (Miller 1967: 84–85)? The phenomenon deserves further investigation.

Haguenauer (1956: 332–33) cites a set of Ryūkyū forms that at first glance appear to be of extreme importance for the study of this problem, R *tūruŋ* going with J *tōru*, but R *tūsiŋ* going with J *tōsu*. Unfortunately, as we have already seen, the set J *tōru, tōsu* is most likely not relevant to the discussion, for either of two very likely reasons; and furthermore, it appears that the Ryūkyū forms Haguenauer cites, which appear to demonstrate a highly significant variation with -*r*- before -*u*- but -*s*- before -*i*- in related forms, are little more than misprints, since the *Okinawago jiten* (Kokuritsu kokugo kenkyūjo 1963: s.v.) does not appear to know them at all, at least for the standard Shuri language, where the set going with J *tōru, tōsu* is Shuri *tuu(r)juⁿ, tuus(j)uⁿ*. But had Haguenauer's forms been correct, or if they could be substantiated from reliable sources, they would have considerable importance for the problem here considered.

This formulation of the Japanese reflex for pA $*l_2$ also helps to clear up a number of problems in etymology and mutual relationships among words within Japanese itself; a few brief illustrations of the help it provides in this connection will be informative.

1. J *sizuwa* 'cantle (upwardly projecting rear part of a saddle)' apparently goes back to MJ *siduwa* 'id.'; cf. J *maewa* 'saddlebow'. The word does not appear to be attested before Middle Japanese, but it must be far older; certainly the object to which it has reference is of considerable antiquity in Japan. The earliest *kana* spellings for the word that are recorded in the lexical sources (e.g., Ōtsuki 1933: 2.666ᵃ) are no later than the first part of the thirteenth century and come from a time when earlier [dᶻu] and [zu] had both fallen together; hence the *kana* spelling *siduwa* might equally well stand for either *siduwa* [sidᶻuwa] or *sizuwa*. Given the contrast between *maewa* and *sizuwa*, we are tempted to see in *sizuwa* some form of J *siri* 'buttocks, rear end', also appearing in OJ *usirö* 'rear, behind'. J *siri* goes with pA $*sil$ (Miller 1967: 71; Poppe 1960: 31). In J *siri* the final -*i* is an automatic epenthetic vowel added in Japanese in 'vowel harmony' with the previous -*i*-. J *sizuwa* has resulted from the final consonant in pA $*sil$ being palatalized by the addition of a 'connective vowel' $*-i-$ (cf. the 'connective vowels' of Old Turkish, Tekin 1968: 63–65), followed in turn by -*Fa* 'band, ring'. The addition of the $*-i-$ 'connective vowel' had the result of shifting the final original pA $*l$ in this word to pA $*l_2$; and this regularly gave J -*s*-, here subsequently voiced in intervocalic position; finally, the $*-i-$ was shifted to -*u*- ('labial attraction') before the following -*Fa* > -*wa*, thus giving $*sil_2-i-Fa$ >

sisiFa > *sizuwa*, this last underlying the attested MJ *siduwa* of the texts, as well as J *sizuwa*. Without the correct formulation of the Japanese reflex of pA *l_2, it is not possible to relate J *sizuwa* and J *siri*. The usual etymologies (e.g., Ōtsuki, loc. cit.) are unsatisfactory; they attempt to relate J *sizuwa* to OJ *sid-u* 'lower, drop down'. The semantics of such an explanation do not fit; the part of the saddle concerned is to the rear of the rider, not under him. The etymology involving pA *l_2 is strengthened by the form MJ *siriwa*, cited by Nakada (1963: 594[c]); he also cites an interesting compound form in the same sense, MJ *sirituwa*, but with no indication of text source, and since this form is apparently unknown to all the other lexical sources, it must be suspect, a lexicographer's ghost.

2. We have already noted above the phonological problem posed by R *kibusi* alongside of and cognate with J *kemuri* 'smoke'. The chance that this correspondence may conceal a trace of pA *l_2 is considerably enhanced by the further existence, beside these nouns, of J *kusub-u* 'to smoke, fumigate (something)'. Obviously a syllabic metathesis has operated here sometime in the history of these words, along the same lines as that in J *atarashii* 'new' beside J *arata ni* 'anew'; but it is difficult to ascertain whether the noun or the verb preserves the original order. Assuming for the sake of argument that the syllabic order in the noun is original, then the verb *kusub-u* goes back to earlier *kubus-u*, and this form, beside J *kemuri*, R *kibusi*, strongly points in the direction of an earlier *l_2. In fact, simply within the paradigm represented by the noun J *kemuri* 'smoke' beside the verb J *kusub-u*, it is possible by internal reconstruction to catch a glimpse of a pattern of historical phonological development of the same general order as that here postulated for pA *l_2 in Japanese.

3. In much the same way, a fair number of doublets in Japanese become more readily comprehensible in terms of the Japanese reflex of pA *l_2. Here we may note such sets as J *yappari* beside J *yappasi* 'yes, certainly', noting also in this doublet the characteristic final *-i* vowel following the *-r-* ∼ *-s-* alternation. A similar doublet from proto-Korean-Japanese is that reconstructed by Martin (1966: 241, #203) for 'slow', with both pKJ *$nɔr$-* and pKJ *$nɔs$-*; with the first of these two reconstructed forms goes J *noro-* 'be slow moving, sluggish', with the second, J *oso-* 'be slow'. All this too can best be brought into order in terms of the proto-Korean-Japanese and Japanese developments of pA *l_2.

The over-all congruity of the above presentation with the analysis of Pritsak 1964 will be immediately apparent. The Japanese evidence too leads us to the same conclusion as that of his magisterial study, namely that the long mooted problem of the Turkish 'rhotacism/lambdacism' in relation to the other Altaic languages is neither a phonetic nor a phonological problem—it is essentially (and historically always was) a morphophonemic problem (loc. cit., 344).

It remains to note that Japanese preserves at least one example of Pritsak's $X = \check{c} < $ *ti, in late OJ *kokoti* (*kököti?*) 'feeling, spirits, emotion', a word apparently not attested in the Old Japanese corpus proper but common in texts from early Heian on. The form of course must be considered together with OJ *kökörö* 'heart, spirit', cognate with OT *kököz* 'Brust', and the forms going together with that word (Miller 1967: 72; Miller 1967[b]: 295 and n. 18). The key form which helps us to connect all the scattered members of this set of related etymons is the *hapax legomenon* of *M* 4390, where the text (in nonstandard, i.e., Azuma Old Japanese) has quite clearly and unequivocally *kököri* for standard OJ *kökörö*. The form *kököti* is generally regarded by Japanese lexicographers as somehow resulting from a contraction of the final element of *kokoromoti* 'feeling, spirit, mental attitude', < *kokoro* + *moti*-, deverbal nominative formation in -*i* from J *mot-u* 'have, hold, possess'. It now seems rather more likely that in J *kokoti* we have to deal instead with the semantic specialization of a form that goes, according to Pritsak's formulation, quite regularly with his $X = \check{c} < $ *ti, with an expected simplification within Japanese, which has never allowed consonant clusters, of the original *$l + $ *$ti > $ *ti.

This by no means exhausts either the data available from nor the problems presented by the Japanese evidence relating to the Altaic liquids, or even that relating to pA *l_2, though it points in the direction of the solution of the principal problems that the Japanese materials offer. In the category of unsolved residue calling for future detailed consideration, the following forms may also be mentioned.

(a) The Japanese materials, and proto-Korean-Japanese, may very possibly have valuable clues to offer on the question of the *δ that some scholars think it necessary to introduce into a discussion of the history of the Altaic liquids in Turkish (cf. Benzing 1959: 693–94 and the literature cited there). The key word for this *δ is the common Altaic term for 'foot', often reconstructed as pA *$pa\delta ak$, and often also used as a key to the classification of the Turkish languages (Poppe 1965: 34). The Japanese lexical data here is plentiful and important.

J *aruku* 'to walk' is the result of a later contamination of several different earlier forms, and therefore it is not immediately relevant for comparative purposes; instead we must work with OJ *ayumu* 'to walk', and late OJ or early MJ *ariku* 'id.', this last form attested only in glosses for the Old Japanese period but not actually appearing in texts before the Heian. For 'foot' there is OJ *asi* as a free form, with a combining form OJ *a-* (though OJ *a* 'foot' does appear once as a free form in *M* 3387).

The most important correlations are those that may immediately be made among these rich Japanese lexical materials. The Japanese forms in initial *a-*, including OJ *asi-*, OJ *a-*, OJ *ayumu*, and late OJ *ariku*, are all examples of the well-attested phenomenon of underarticulation of a labial initial consonant (cf. J *watakushi*, J *atakushi*, etc.); the fully articulated labial initial is attested in OJ *Fasiru* 'to run'. The second-syllable vocalism of J *aruku* has resulted from contamination between OJ *ayumu* and late OJ *ariku*, a process of sporadic change greatly encouraged by the fact that these two forms in *-ku* are no doubt etymologically to be understood as **asi* 'foot' + **duku* 'go'; for the vocalism cf. the modern doublet J *yuku* ∼ **yiku* > *iku* 'go'.

In other words, the *-r-* in *ariku*, *aruku* appears to have been the result of an earlier coming together of *-s-* + *-*d-* > *-y-*; and this fact, plus the alternation of *-s-/-r-* in J *asi* beside J *ariku* immediately points in the direction of an earlier pA **l₂* having been involved somewhere in the history of this word.

Now Benzing (1955: 992–93) has pointed out that in proto-Tungus it is precisely in those instances where pT **l* and pT **r* come together with another consonant immediately following that it often becomes difficult to distinguish between *l* and *r* from the evidence provided by the reflexes in the various languages; and to illustrate this difficulty, he cites the following proto-Tungus reconstructions:

1. pT **palan* '(Fuss-)Boden'.

2. pT **palgan* '(Fuss-)Sohle'.

3. pT **pargan* 'bei den Schneeschuhen ein aufgeklebtes Stück Birkenrinde, worauf der Fuss steht'.

4. pT **paliŋa* 'Handfläche'.

On the other hand, all the forms that may be cited from Turkish show two important phenomena; one has an immediate parallel in the Japanese evidence (underarticulation of labial initial consonant, hence initial *a-*), the other in the Tungus evidence (**r*—more exactly, **r₂*—

rather than $*l$, i.e., $*l_2$; hence Chu. *ura*, Xaqas (Abaqan) *azaq* 'foot', with the normal correspondence of Chu. *r*, other Turkish $z < *r_2$). For Middle Turkish, Kāšɣarī has *aδāq* 'foot'. All these Turkish forms contain an old collective suffix $*-ak$ (Pritsak 1964: 349), and so for proto-Turkish we are left with an original $*uza- < *ur_2a-$, with the initial $*u-$ preserving the trace of the initial labial consonant that has otherwise disappeared in this underarticulated form; hence, $*ur_2a-$ may safely be referred to a still earlier $*par_2a-$ 'foot'.

This pTk. $*par_2a-$ may now be directly related to the forms underlying pT $*parg-$ (the third of Benzing's reconstructions, above); and at the same time the Korean and Japanese evidence will provide us with an earlier $*pal_2g-$ that may be directly related to the forms underlying pT $*palg-$ (the second of Benzing's reconstructions).

For proto-Korean-Japanese Martin (1966: 232, #87) has reconstructed pKJ $*vašyi$ on the basis of J *asi*, K *pal*; but his pKJ $*v-$ does not actually recover an original initial phoneme of the Korean-Japanese linguistic unity; rather it merely serves, in this and the other forms in which it has been reconstructed by Martin, to symbolize instances of the sporadic Japanese underarticulation of initial labial consonants. Hence it is more satisfactory in many respects to reinterpret this reconstruction as pKJ $*pašyi$, on the basis of OJ *Fasiru* 'to run'. (Cf. also the forms cited above under etymology 7, p. 119.) With this, we are immediately able to make a further significant association between this pKJ $*pašyi$ and pKJ $*palǧyi$, reconstructed by Martin to account for OJ *Faki* 'shin' and K *pal* 'foot' (on the forms and the shape of the reconstruction, see Miller 1967[b]: 289). With pKJ $*pašyi$ beside pKJ $*palǧyi$, we are at once clearly in the presence of an original pA $*pal_2-$ form, and this must be the same $*pal_2-$ that we have earlier reconstructed on the basis of OJ *asi* 'foot' beside *ariku*, *aruku* 'to walk'. The 'confusion' here between original $*r_2$ and $*l_2$ is of the same variety (and for the same reason) as the 'confusion' between pT $*r$ and $*l$ observed by Benzing: 'In Verbindung mit anderen Konsonanten ergeben sich beim $*l$, mehr noch beim $*r$, Lautveränderungen der Konsonantengruppe, die eine endgültige Beurteilung des jeweiligen Falles sehr erschweren. Hierzu kommen Fälle des Schwankens zwischen $l \sim r$ . . .' (1955: 992). Out of this also grows our basic uncertainty about whether $*r$ or $*l$ (and each in either of its two varieties) is to be reconstructed, an uncertainty that can only be contained by reconstructing, with Benzing, multiple earlier forms for Tungus, and in the light of the data presented here, parallel multiple earlier forms also for proto-Korean-Japanese.

Japanese also provides a clue to the origin of the underarticulation of the labial initial, both as it is observed in Japanese and as it is observed in Turkish. This indication is in the form of the location of the Japanese pitch accent. J *así* 'foot', *hasíru* 'to run', and in particular J *hagí* 'shin', but OJ *Faki* 'id.' provide evidence for assigning this set of words to an early sound-change within Japanese in which the location of the pitch accent immediately following the -*k*- correlated with the eventual voicing of this -*k*- > -*g*-, thus making it possible to relate OJ *Faki* 'shin' directly and regularly with J *hagí* 'id.' (Miller 1967[b]: 286, n. 14). Projecting this situation back in time from the proto-Korean-Japanese linguistic unity, we may postulate that a similar situation obtained in the proto-Altaic linguistic unity, and that it was the position of some sort of suprasegmental feature of pitch, stress, or tone on the second syllable in all these forms that initially set off the underarticulation that has characterized the history of the first syllable in these words.

Since proto-Turkish preserves this second-syllable consonant in positions where its development was not complicated by occurring with another consonant immediately following, we may safely assume that the proto-Altaic root for 'foot' was *par_2-, with various suffixal materials. But when the pA *r_2 in this word came together with a following consonant—pT *g, pKJ *$\check{g}$, or *y, for example—it apparently shifted in certain cases to pA *l_2, and it is the variety of the root with this *l_2 that is attested in Japanese and Korean as well as in certain of the Tungus forms. But thanks to the Japanese evidence in particular, it is possible to relate all the developments attested in the later languages to prior forms in various stages of the earlier linguistic unities without any necessity for setting up a proto-Turkish or a proto-Altaic phoneme *δ.

(b) So also with the words for 'star', where we have pM *$podun$, MMo. *hodun*, etc. (Poppe 1955: 54, 97, and passim); but where Pelliot (1944: 100, n. 1) has shown that it is not possible simply to dismiss OT *yultuz*, *yulduz* 'id.' from any discussion of the history of these forms, much as one might like to; cf. also Chu. *šăltăr* 'star, planet'. Again, the problem is clearly one of the special developments of an original liquid followed by a stop. With that information in hand, one next must naturally turn to K *pyël* J *Fosi*, pKJ *$pYešyi$ (Martin 1966: 243, #220), and proto-Tungus *$x\bar{o}sïkta$ 'id.' (Benzing 1955: 991). It is also difficult to disassociate these words for 'star' from K *pul*, OJ *Fï* 'fire' (i.e., 'star' < 'little [?]' + 'fire'?), pKJ *$pyal$

(Martin 1966: 232, #82), or pKJ **pywal* (Miller 1967[b]: 296), and
hence also eventually going with pA **pula* attested in Mo. *ula*, MMo.
hula, Mongr. *fula* 'Feuerschwamm', Ma. *fulaqčan* 'ein kleiner Beutel
für den Feuerschwamm' ('a bag for carrying a flint', Norman 1967:
137), Ev. *hula* 'Feuerschwamm' (Poppe 1960: 12). The importance of
the Japanese form for the Tungus materials has already been noted
by Menges (1968: 54–55); now we are able to go one step further and
at least make a tentative suggestion that all these forms, including
the Japanese, are somehow involved not only with each other but also
with the history of the Altaic liquids.

(c) Within Turkish alone, it is hardly possible to disassociate OT
qadïr 'grimmig, hart' and OT *qadïz* 'Zimmt (their finals, by the way,
to be explained by an **r/*r₂* variation essentially of the same morphophonemic origin as the **l/*l₂* variation that we have been discussing
above). With these forms go also OT *qadɣur-* 'sich sorgen' and OT
qadɣu 'Trauer, Leid', cognate with Chu. *xĕrxü* 'bitter' (cf. Poppe
1924: 777). Poppe (1960: 53) puts OT *qadɣu* together with Mo.
qadu- 'mähen, schneiden'; the obvious Japanese cognate is the adjective stem *kara-* 'acrid, salty, hot (of taste); bitter (of experience)'.

(d) The history of words for 'water' is equally as vexing in Japanese
as it generally proves to be in all the Altaic languages. Martin reconstructs pKJ **myaldu*, going with K *mïl*, J *midu* (1966: 246, #257), and
one cannot but note the suggestive similarities in both form and
meaning between this reconstruction and Old Hungarian *gimilc* <
*ži.milč 'Frucht, Obst' (Pritsak 1964: 343, § 2.52). The association
would be compelling even without prior knowledge of the modern
descriptive expression for fresh fruit J *mizugasi*, lit. 'water sweets,
confections' (where *gasi* < *kasi* is a Chinese loanword).

All these forms no doubt hold concealed many more important
facts yet to be revealed about the precise history of the relationship of
Japanese to the other Altaic languages; in the meantime, our present
findings on the developments of pA **l₂* in Japanese do much to clarify
the relationship of Japanese to the other Altaic languages.

4.4 **r₂*

Just as with pA **l₂*, so also in the case of pA **r₂*, more deliberate consideration of the data shows that the Japanese reflexes are actually
somewhat more involved than was thought to be the case earlier
(e.g., Miller 1967: 72).

The most usual and widespread Japanese reflex for pA **r₂* is, obviously, OJ *r*, and there is no lack of supporting etymologies for this statement. A few of the most familiar ones are presented below in briefest possible fashion; further details about most of these will be found elsewhere in the present work.

1. pA *dür₂e- 'hineinstecken' :: pKJ *dyar- :: OJ *yir > ir- 'insert' (Poppe 1960: 82; Martin 1966: 231, #76).

2. pA *dür₂i 'Aussehen, Gesicht' :: OJ *irö* 'color, facial expression' (Poppe 1960: 82; Miller 1967: 70 ff.).

3. pA *kökür₂ 'breasts', :: OJ *kökörö* 'heart' (Miller 1967: 72).

4. pA *atir₂ 'wildes, unbebautes Land, brach liegendes Land' :: OJ *atira* 'place over there' (Poppe 1960: 82).

5. pA *küber₂- 'stolz, prahlerisch, Prahler' :: MJ *kubar-u* 'to assign rank, to order' (Poppe 1960: 82).

6. pA *ör₂ 'das Innere, selbst' :: OJ *ore, onöre* 'I, myself' (Poppe 1960: 81).

7. pA *ar₂, shown in OT *azu* 'oder' :: J *arui wa* 'or, rather'.

These and several other parallel etymologies that could also be cited substantiate the earlier formulation of OJ *r* as the principal reflex of pA *r₂.

The following etymologies, however, form an important residue of forms that do not appear to follow this regular development:

8. pA *ñār₂- 'frisch, neugeboren; Frühling; Sommer' :: pKJ *nYalɔm :: OJ *natu* 'summer' (Poppe 1960: 81; Martin 1966: 243, #230).

9. pA *bïr₂- '*one' in Mo. *biraɣu* 'Kalb zwischen einem und zwei Jahren', Chu. *păru*, Osm. *buzaɣï* 'zweijähriges Kalb' :: OJ *Fito-* 'one' (cf. OJ *Futa-* 'two') (Poppe 1960: 21, 81 and passim).

10. pA *pür₂- 'in kleine Stücke schneiden, zerreissen' :: OJ *Fod-ök-u* 'take apart, dismember' (Poppe 1960: 12, 111, 132).

11. pA *-mar₂-, aorist negative suffix :: J *-mad- > -maz- (cf. below, p. 275).

This residue of forms cannot simply be ignored. Its evidence indicates that in addition to the normal and principal Japanese reflex of pA *r₂ as OJ *r*, there was another reflex for this same original phoneme that was rather less common and hence is now more difficult to document, but one that was quite as regular a development as the more common one.

The clue to the pattern that determined these developments in pre-Old Japanese appears to lie in the manner of articulation of the initial phoneme in the roots cited. In etymologies (1) through (7), above, the roots uniformly have stop consonants in proto-Altaic. At first glance (6) and (7) appear to be exceptions to this statement, but these roots may also be subsumed under the same statement when we recall that their vowel-initial is most likely equivalent to an automatic initial glottal stop articulation (cf. Hattori's similar analysis of the apparent vowel-initial syllables in Japanese, summarized in Miller 1967: 191), so that these etymologies too fit into the same pattern as that established by etymologies (1) through (5). In other words, OJ r was the normal reflex of pA $*r_2$ when it occurred immediately following a stop consonant in proto-Altaic as well as in pre-Old Japanese; and open (i.e., vowel-initial) syllables for the purposes of this development at least functioned in the same way as syllables with stop-consonant initials, due no doubt to their own automatic glottal-stop initials. This rule obtains both for roots of the most general consonant + vowel + consonant shape, as well as in the fairly rare cases (see etymology [3] above) where the root was of somewhat longer configuration.

This contrasts clearly with the pattern presented by etymologies (8) through (11); here the proto-Altaic initial was a continuant, rather than a stop, consonant ($*\tilde{n}$- in [8], $*m$- in [11]), or a proto-Altaic stop initial ($*b$-, $*p$-) that became a continuant (OJ F) early in the history of pre-Old Japanese ($*b$- in [9], $*p$- in [10]). In these cases, where the consonant immediately preceding pA $*r_2$ was a continuant rather than a stop for the purposes of the Japanese developments, the Japanese reflex has -t- or -d-, the alternation between the voiceless and the voiced varieties being of course a problem of subsequent developments solely within Japanese, and without significance on the comparative level.

Therefore we must modify our former statement on the Japanese reflexes of pA $*r_2$ to include OJ t (or d) as well as OJ r.

A few additional etymologies must be considered, in order to round out the treatment.

In the first place, it is obvious that the new formulation reached immediately above holds true only in cases in which pA $*r_2$ was intervocalic, and did not occur in immediate proximity to any other consonant. (It goes without saying that pA $*r_2$ was never initial.) When pA $*r_2$ occurred as one member of a consonant cluster, other developments appear to have taken place, but we are not always able to predict the manner in which these changes will appear. OJ r appears to be the only reflex attested for these occurrences of pA $*r_2$ in clusters with other consonants, but there is also evidence that in certain other, still undefined circumstances, the Japanese reflex was simply a zero.

Thus, for pA *kar_2k- 'graben, kratzen', we have pKJ *$kalk$-, but J *kak-u* 'scratch, engrave, write' (Poppe 1960: 17, 82, 95; Martin 1967: 240, #189). Here Japanese appears to respond to pA *r_2 simply with a zero. But beside pA *pur_2t- 'lang', there is OJ *Furu-* 'old' (Murayama 1962: 111), where Japanese appears to respond to the same phoneme, under the same conditions of clustering with another consonant, with OJ *r*. (Martin 1967: 235, #129 attempts to relate the Turkish and other cognates of pA *pur_2t- to J *oy-* 'age', through pKJ *$oř(a)$-, in an etymology that is probably best abandoned since it does not take notice of the original stop consonant in the Altaic root involved.) All this requires further study, but more examples of the phenomenon than are now at hand will be necessary before any more precise formulation can be attempted. In general, the Korean reflexes of pA *r_2, both when taken by themselves and particularly when considered together with the Japanese evidence, must at present be admitted to be far from an orderly solution. It is not possible, given the present data, to make regular statements about the developments of pA *r_2 either in Korean or in proto-Korean-Japanese. The problem is an important one and urgently requires further study; but it does not in and of itself reflect either upon the patterning or upon the significance of the Japanese reflexes presented herein.

An apparent exception to the above formulation for OJ *r* and *t* as reflexes of pA *r_2 is provided by pA *ser_2-, under which rubric Poppe (1960: 82 and passim) subsumes a surprisingly wide variety of Altaic forms: Mo. *seri-* 'wach werden, nüchtern sein', Mo. *sere-* 'erwachen', MMo. *sere-* 'zweifeln, argwöhnen, etwas merken', MMo. *seri-* 'merken, wissen', Ev. *sele-* 'erwachen, wach werden', Chag. *säz-* 'fühlen', OT *säzik* 'Zweifel'. This root has been connected with OJ *sir-u* 'to know' (Murayama 1962: 111, and following him, Miller 1967: 72), but on more careful consideration it seems all but impossible to reconcile the striking semantic divergence among the Altaic forms that Poppe brings together in his etymology, and surely impossible to bring the resulting Altaic root (if it is historically valid in the first place) into a cognate relationship with OJ *sir-u* 'to know'. The etymology, particularly its Japanese component, is best abandoned, and hence it throws no light on the Japanese reflexes of pA *r_2. For the same word, Martin (1967: 234, #121) reconstructs pKJ *$syɔr$-.

Another overt similarity that it is probably best to regard as due to an old loanword rather than as a genetically inherited form is that represented by OT *äz-* 'engrave, scratch', and OJ *wer-u* 'id.' It is interesting, perhaps even significant, to note that in both languages the word appears to have been specialized early in the sense of 'engrave, inscribe an inscription on stone'. Thus, the Old Turkish form may be cited from the phrase *bän äzip b[itī]dim* 'I scratched and inscribed these inscriptions', from the envoi (South, line 2) to the Kül čor inscription (Tekin 1968: 258, 295, a text that is curiously missing from Nadelyayev et al. 1968: 192); while the Old Japanese appears in OJ *werituk-u* in the *Bussokuseki* inscription poem 3. But the two words can hardly be genetic inheritances from an earlier common form; against such a theory we have the evidence of the initial *w-* of the Japanese form, unrepresented in the Turkish, as well as the *-e-* of the Japanese, here going together 'all too well' (on the level of gross, superficial phonetic similarities) with the Turkish. As we have seen above, OJ *e* and *ë* are historically complex vowels, and their representations in the other Altaic languages are by no means as simple as an equation of OT *äz-* with OJ *wer-u* would seem to indicate. These phonological considerations, plus the strangely similar semantic specialization of both forms in both languages—together with the fact that it would be difficult to believe that the engraving of monumental inscriptions on stone is something that goes as far back as the Altaic linguistic community—all these considerations incline us instead to see here an old loanword, probably into Japanese from some Turkish language. But it is to be particularly noted that if a Turkish form was here borrowed into Japanese it must have come from one of the early Chuvash-like languages in which pA *r_2* was represented by *-r-*, hence the *-r-* of OJ *wer-u*, and not from any language that had undergone developments allied to those that produced the *-z-* of OT *äz-* (cf. Chu. *xïr-* 'scrape, shave'?). Even though OJ *wer-u* 'engrave, scratch' is to be related to Altaic as a loanword, and not as a genetically inherited form, it still can be explained only in terms of some earlier original now lost, an original *$är_2$-* that can be recovered only through our understanding of the sound laws relating Altaic to Turkish on the one hand and to Japanese on the other, rather than as a direct loan from the single form attested in our Old Turkish texts.

Finally, we may note a word of great importance for the Altaic relationship of Korean, and one that in addition also includes a further example of pA *r_2*; unfortunately, the Japanese reflex for this form shows no correspondence for the morpheme in which the phoneme in question appears, and therefore once more casts no light on the immediate problem. This is pA *$agur_2$* 'Lippe', going with K *akali*, *akuli* < *ak_2li* 'jaw', on the basis of pKJ *ag_2*, *agu* (Martin 1967: 234, #119), though the contamination in form and meaning of words for 'jaw' and 'mouth' with one another in both Korean and Japanese has rendered the precise relation of the Japanese evidence to the Korean extremely difficult to judge (Miller 1967[b]: 289, #119).

The form is of great importance for the relationship of Korean to the other Altaic languages because it preserves pA *r_2* in its usual morphological role as an ancient dual-plural suffix. K *akali*, *akuli* preserves an important survival of this once widespread morphological device, but unfortunately, this element does not appear to have survived in any attested Japanese form that might be directly related to this root. Pröhle (1916/17: 180) cited J *agota* and *agoto* in an attempt to relate J *ago* and its related forms to Finno-ugric; J *agota* is a West Japan dialect form for *ago* (Ōtsuki 1932: 1.40[a]); but *agoto* cannot be verified. What little is known of the history of these words is brought together by Maeda (1970: 79–80), but too many intermediate steps in their development remain unknown. Perhaps the *-ta* in J *agota* might somehow be related to this problem, but to do so at the present state of our knowledge would make necessary still another rule, by which the suffix *r_2* in this word was treated differently from the usual developments of *r_2* in Japanese, thus giving *-t-* here instead of the *-r-* that we would expect from its position immediately following a stop consonant in the previous syllable. This would be a completely ad hoc formulation, raising more additional problems than it would solve, and one that would moreover still leave the final *-a* of *agota* unexplained.

The lack of a cognate Japanese form and our inability to explain the *-ta* of the West Japan dialect form *agota* on the comparative level are a pity, for if there were such a form, or if we could include *agota* in our present formulation, it would help to complete the evidence for what is otherwise a root quite well represented in Altaic, particularly in Turkish: Chu. *šăvar* 'Mund', Tkm. *aγïz* 'Mund', Jak. *uos* 'Lippe' (Poppe 1960: 131; it is difficult to understand what Mo. *aγur* 'Dampf, Zorn', also cited by Poppe, has to do with this etymology on the semantic level, though of course the phonology fits in well). But the form that above all we would like to be able to verify, i.e., a Japanese reflex going directly with K *akali* 'jaw' (and hence ultimately also with pA *$agur_2$-) is apparently missing.

We have already noted above that the Japanese reflexes of pA *l_2 help to explain the possible origins of the characteristic and skewed allophone distribution for OJ */s/. With pA *r_2 almost the reverse is true; here, we may gain an understanding of some of the reasons underlying the curiously skewed Japanese reflexes for this original Altaic phoneme from a consideration of, for example, the different morphemes (or allomorphs?) that Martin finds it necessary to reconstruct for proto-Korean-Japanese 'walk'—forms that end in *-š, *-l, *-t, and *-ř (Martin 1966: 245). In this complex formulation, *-š and *-l are now easily subsumed under the Japanese reflexes for pA *l_2, while *-t and *-ř fit together equally neatly under the Japanese reflexes for pA *r_2. The over-all historical correlations thus assumed take on added significance when we recall that Martin's proto-Korean-Japanese reconstructions are, of course, completely independent of the formulation for the Japanese reflexes for pA *l_2 and *r_2 in the present work.

All in all, the existence of a great number of similarities in purely lexical items between Korean and Japanese, together with the strange absence of any comparable amount of similarities in purely grammatical features (apart from general similarities of syntactic order and structuring, all too general to be of utility for historical purposes), has been a continuing embarrassment to the comparativist. Since Martin's reconstruction of proto-Korean-Japanese is based on 'lexical evidence', not on 'grammatical evidence', it has still left open the remote possibility that even the forms with which he dealt in 1966 were nothing but a very old layer of loanwords.

The evidence on the Korean and Japanese reflexes for pA *l_2 and *r_2 presented here do much to make that possibility even more remote, now so remote in fact that it need no longer be considered seriously. Even though much remains to be done in refining the formulation of the Korean reflexes for pA *l_2 and *r_2, the Japanese reflexes are now well enough understood, and well enough correlated with the Korean evidence, to add a further element of security to our conclusion regarding the genetic relationship between these two languages, as well as to that regarding their common relationship to Altaic. Loanwords, even of great antiquity, are all but ruled out thanks to the phonetic variety of the reflexes that have been established. Attested forms cannot explain all the similarities; this can only be done through reconstructed forms, and these reconstructions have meaning and reality only so long as we maintain our present conclusions about the relationship of Japanese and Korean to each other, and eventually also to the original Altaic linguistic unity.

4.5 *e, *é, *ē, *ē̇

The Japanese reflexes for pA *e (= *ä) and pA *é are summarized below, since it is more convenient to treat these developments as part of the system in which pA *č, *ǰ̌, *d and allied phonemes may be traced in the Japanese materials. In each case, the normal Japanese reflex is a; thus, for pT *ǰäg, J tak- 'burn something' (cf. 3.2, #9, p. 86 above), and for pA *ǰé, J ya 'arrow' (cf. 3.3, #10, ibid.).

The data relating Japanese to the Altaic long vowels *ē and *ē̇ remain to be set forth in detail, since they are important to an understanding of the over-all fate of the Altaic vocalization in the Japanese area. All the Altaic data cited immediately below are drawn from Poppe 1960: 106 unless otherwise noted.

1. pA *ē.

1. Mo., MMo. ere 'Mann', Chu. ar < *är 'Mann' :: J are 'that one', ore 'I (vulgar)'.

2. Mo. gerel 'Licht, Strahl', Mo., MMo. geji- 'hell werden', Mo. gegen < *gēgegēn 'Hell, leuchtend', Ma. gere- 'hell werden', Ev. ŋērī 'Licht', Ev. nērīpču 'hell', Lam. ŋērīl- 'hell werden', pT *ŋäri- (Benzing 1955: 969) :: J kagayak-u 'sparkle, shine brightly'.

3. Mo. keb 'Form, Model', Kalm. keb 'id.', Tkm. gäp 'Vogelscheuche' :: OJ kaFa 'leather'.

4. Mo. gelme- 'erschreckt sein', Ev. ŋēlē- 'erschreckt', pT *ŋälä- (Benzing 1955: 985) :: J kar-u 'urge, spur on, inspire'.

2. pA *ē̇.

5. Mo. bel 'Taille', belkegüsün 'Lenden, Hüftengegend, d. Hintere', Chu. pilĕk 'Mitte des Leibes', Tkm. bīl 'Taille' :: OJ Fara 'stomach', K pä, MK pǝy, pKJ *párya (Martin 1966: 243, #223).

6. pA *ǰép-, J tab- 'eat', cf. 3.3, #11, p. 86 above.

7. Mo. erte 'früh', Chu. ir 'id.', Tkm. īr 'id.' :: J ari- in ariake 'dawn, daybreak'. The first element in this Japanese synonym-compound is commonly taken as if it were ari-, stem of ar-u 'to have, be', but this is a folk-etymology based upon the Chinese characters generally used to write the word in Japanese orthography.

8. Mo., MMo. *del* 'Mähne', Ev. *dẹlin*, Ma. *delun*, Chu. *śilxe* < *dẹlkei*, OT *jil*, all 'Mähne' :: J *eri* 'collar, neck-line'.

This last etymology shows an additional subvariety of Japanese reflex for original *ẹ́*; at first glance it appears to be anomalous, but actually it fits quite regularly into the over-all patterning in terms of which the vocalization of Japanese may be related to the vocalization of the earliest stages of Altaic. The initial *d-* in this word has, of course, undergone its customary treatment as initial *j-* (i.e., -*i̯-*) in the course of the development from Altaic into Japanese; and following this initial, the original Japanese *-a-* that we would expect in this word has in its turn been assimilated to the position of articulation of this initial *j-*, resulting in the form *eri*. The intermediate stages most likely followed something resembling the following sequence: *dẹl-* > *jāl-* > *jēl-* > J *yeri* > *eri*.

In this way, what at first glance appears to be an exception actually turns out to follow quite closely the predicted treatment in Japanese. We also may note that in this case, even in such a form as *eri*, where J *e* appears to go with an Altaic *e* vowel, the facts of the historical developments underlying the form are somewhat different. The similarity between the two vowels in question is here only superficial, since the J *e* in *eri* is the result of a complicated process of development totally within Japanese, after its separation from Altaic, and so it is only accidental that the attested Japanese form resembles its Altaic prototype as closely as it does.

Quite apart from this Japanese evidence, the structural status within proto-Altaic of the vowels reconstructed as *ẹ́* and *ẹ̄* urgently requires more detailed formulation. Poppe has suggested that it might perhaps be best not to regard his *ẹ́* as an independent phonemic unit in proto-Altaic (Poppe 1960: § 84, 105); and his *ẹ̄* certainly appears to have been a conditioned variant of his *ē*, at least at certain times and places within the Altaic linguistic unity (Poppe 1960: § 85, 105). Our inability to recover either the long or short variety of *ẹ́* in unstressed syllables (Poppe 1960: § 100, 124 ff.) is both suspicious and at the same time suggestive of a possible direction for further study in this problem. In the course of that study, the Japanese evidence for the existence, nature, and structural role of both these vowels will have to be considered.

Chapter 5

Lexical Evidence

5.1 Pronouns

The correspondences in details of form and meaning among the pronouns in Old Turkish, Chuvash, Mongol, and Tungus are of an order and degree of complexity that cannot possibly be held to be the result either of borrowing or of chance (Poppe 1965: 193–94; Kotwicz 1936); by the same token, these correspondences provide one of the most striking demonstrations of the genetic relationship of these languages to each other through their descent from the earlier common unity we call proto-Altaic. These correspondences may even be regarded as diagnostic for certain general problems of relationship within the Altaic languages, so that if the pronoun system of a given language may be demonstrated to preserve any appreciable portion of the arbitrary formal structuring that distinguishes the pronoun systems of already well-established Altaic languages, then that language too may with confidence be assigned a place somewhere within the line of descent from proto-Altaic. The present chapter attempts to make this demonstration for Japanese, with particular attention to Old Japanese, the language of the eighth century, and further attempts to demonstrate that the configuration of the Japanese pronoun system is such that the relationship of Japanese to the Altaic languages, and its common descent together with them from proto-Altaic, can no longer be questioned.

The most striking single feature of the proto-Altaic pronoun paradigms, and that of the most significance for comparison and the working out of genetic relationships, was a morphological dichotomy in the singular between forms for nominatives and forms for the oblique cases. Different stems were involved, so distinct from one another that they provide an extremely reliable diachronic index.

The original proto-Altaic pronoun paradigm may be reconstructed in the following shapes (Poppe 1965: 193–94):

	Sg.	Pl.
1-p.	nom. *bi*, oblique *män*	nom. and oblique *bir*
2-p.	nom. *si*, oblique *sän*	nom. and oblique *sir*
3-p.	nom. *i*, oblique *än*	nom. and oblique *ir*

The major reflexes of this original system are exhibited in Table 6, which brings together pronoun paradigms from some of the Altaic languages of particularly great historical importance.

An inspection of this data makes clear the principal courses of development that the Altaic pronouns have undergone in the various languages. Turkish generalized the oblique stems *män* and *sän*, and these then replaced the original nominative stems that had been distinctive forms in proto-Altaic, as the evidence from the other languages shows. But even in Turkish it is still possible to trace the nominative stem, without the final -*n*, as for example in the possessive suffix of the 3-p. -*i* < *i* 'he', cf. Tk. *ev-i* 'his house', nom., but -*in* < *in*, with the oblique stem, in all oblique forms, thus Tk. *ev-in-de* 'in his house'. So also in Mongol, where *i* 'he' must be reconstructed, while *inu* 'his' has the -*n*- stem; but in Manchu the nominative stem *i* 'he' is found, beside the oblique stem in *ini* gen., and *inde*, dat.-loc.

TABLE 6

The Altaic Pronouns

Proto-Altaic nom./oblique		Old Turkish	Chuvash	Proto-Mongol
sg. 1-p.	*bi/*män-	b[ä]n¹/ban-²∽bin-³	epĕ/man-	*bi/*min-⁶, *nama-⁷,⁹
2-p.	*si/*sän-	s[ä]n/san-∽sin-	esĕ/san-	*(ti)⁸ > *či/*čin-⁶, *čima-⁷
3-p.	*i/*än-	(ol,/an-)⁴	(văl/un-∽an-⁵)	*i/*in-⁶, *ima-⁷
pl. 1-p.	*bir	biz	epir/pir-	[incl.] *bida/ *bidan- [excl.] *ba/*man-
2-p.	*sir	siz	esir/sir-	*ta/*tan-
3-p.	*ir	(olar)⁴	(vĕ-/vĕ-)	*a/*an-

¹ m[ä]n, 'gewöhnlich', min, 'einmal . . .'
² m[ä]n-, 'ungewöhnlich'
³ min-, 'meist'
⁴ 'jener'
⁵ with dative only
⁶ genitives in proto-Mongol
⁷ other oblique cases in proto-Mongol
⁸ pre-Mongol
⁹ origin not clear, great profusion of forms here for proto-Mongol dat.-loc.

TABLE 6—*Continued*

Proto-Tungus¹		Manchu	Lamut	Old Japanese³
*bi/min-		bi/min-	bi/min-	mĭ/wan-u⁴
*si/sin-		si/sin-	hi/hin-	si⁵/sön-e⁶
*i/in-		i/in-	(noŋan/noŋăn-²)	aⁿ/r-, oⁿ/r-, onör-e
*mün-ti	[or] ---?---	muse	mut	wa-, war-e [incl., hence -e//*-i-]
*büä		be/men-	bu/mun-	mar-ö, war-ö⁷ [excl., hence -ö//*-a-]
*süa	*su/*sun-	suwe/suwen-	hu/hun-	na-, nar-e ta-, tar-e
*ti	---?---	(če/čen-)	(noŋartan/ noŋar . . . tan-²)	---?---

¹ after Benzing (1955:1056), but revised in details.
² cf. *ŋuga > Ma. gûwa 'anderer, einer, man'?
³ arranged in part to demonstrate ultimate Altaic origins cf forms.
⁴ M 3476, M 4358
⁵ M 904, Nihon shoki poem 80
⁶ Kojiki poem 11
⁷ M 4343

Let us first of all see which Japanese forms may be cited, and to what extent they preserve traces of the original Altaic paradigm.

1. OJ *mï*, 1-p., sg., may be cited from a wide variety of texts, embracing virtually the entire history of the language. Examples: *M* 903 (dated in the text in correspondence with A.D. 725), . . . *mï ni wa aredö* 'though I am . . .'; *Makura no sōshi* (early eleventh century), 4. 43 *kore wa mi no tame ni mo hito no tame ni mo* 'this [is] both for my sake and for the sake of other[s]'; *Shin kokin wakashū* (early thirteenth century), *omohi iru mi wa* 'I [subject] who am deeply in love' (Lewin 1965: 167, n. 82); *Hōjōki* (A.D. 1212), *mi no tame ni* 'für sich selbst' (Lewin 1965: 241, n. 43); *Kyōgen, midomo* 'we' (Nakada 1963: 831); *Osome Hisamatsu ukina no yomiuri* (early nineteenth-century Kabuki text), *mi mo kimoti wo warūitasita wai no* 'mir wurde ganz sonderbar zumute' (Lewin 1965: 366, n. 34). As a kind of royal plural, the form *mimï* is also attested, as for example in the *Senmyō* edict of A.D. 749, *mimï aFetamawazu are* 'Wir selbst (sie) nicht zur Ausführung bringen (können)' (Lewin 1965: 35, n. 41). The word *mimï* is found, written in phonograms, in one of the earliest Japanese inscriptions, the bronze text accompanying and documenting the supposed origins of the celebrated Yakushi image in the Hōryū-ji, Nara (Sanseidō 1967: 696ᶜ). This text is internally dated in correspondence with A.D. 607, which would make it of impressive antiquity, but unfortunately the most recent Japanese scholarship has begun to cast serious doubt upon its authenticity (Asano 1963: 78).

The traditional interpretation of this form *mimï* as containing the honorific prefix allomorph *mi* + *mï* 'body' is clearly wide of the mark, since the honorific *mi* would be semantically out of place in a first-person form, even in the special context of royal proclamations and pronouncements. The pronominal form *mi* may also be abstracted from J *mizukara* 'by, through one's self', which consists of *mi* < OJ *mï* 'I' + the Old Japanese genitive allomorph *tu* + *kara* 'relationship, kinship'; the sense of J *mizukara* may also partly be the result of semantic contamination of this *kara* with a (probably) unrelated *kara* 'because'. OJ *mï* 'body' has also often been confused with its homophone OJ *mï* 'I' by the lexicographers, even apart from the misleading traditional exegesis of the royal *mimï* noted above; but OJ *mï* 'body' goes with Korean *mom* 'id.' and is to be associated with pKJ **myom* (Martin 1966: 226, #19).

OJ *mï* 'I' preserves the original Altaic nominative form for the first-person pronoun, without the final -*n* element. Unfortunately, these words immediately involve us in the history of the Altaic labials in Japanese, and as we have already noted above, this happens to be one of the most perplexing portions of the entire Altaic-Japanese comparative phonology. OJ *F* appears to be the normal correspondence for pA **b*, while OJ *m* generally goes with pA **m*, but the origin (or origins) of OJ *w* is another and still largely unsolved problem.

2. OJ *si*, 2-p. (see Yamada 1954: 75–76). This form may be cited from *M* 904, *si ga katarakëba* 'because you say'; another early occurrence is in the *Nihon shoki* song 80, *si ga nakeba* 'if you are not [here]'. The Old Japanese form seems curiously restricted to conditional or contingent constructions, but this limitation does not appear to have any significance outside of Japanese. At any rate, this important if rare Old Japanese lexical item preserves the original Altaic nominative form for the second-person singular pronoun.

In order to trace the original Altaic oblique stems for the first- and second-person pronouns, as well as their original plural forms in Japanese, it is necessary first of all to take account of certain developments that took place, probably independently, in different parts of the Altaic domain at different times, but that had an over-all pattern and hence produced fairly uniform end products. The Japanese developments were one part of these changes, and so they too are most easily understood when presented against the perspective of their general Altaic background.

First of all, just as Turkish generalized the oblique stems and used them to replace the original nominative forms, so also did Old Japanese, with the immediate and most striking result that OJ *mï* and OJ *si* can be cited only from a relatively few survivals in the oldest levels of the texts. This is particularly true in the case of the excessively rare OJ *si*. Otherwise the expanding vitality of the oblique forms soon wiped away virtually all traces of the nominatives from our Japanese materials. The same was true of the plurals; these too were generalized very early in the Japanese area, where they obliterated virtually all traces of the original and old singulars.

The Old Japanese forms showing the closest degree of analogy to the Altaic oblique stems for the first-person singular may be cited from the nonstandard Old Japanese materials preserved in the so-called Azuma portions of the *Man'yōshū* (see Miller 1967: 163–71). In *M* 3476, which is in nonstandard Old Japanese, we have *wanu* in the line *wanu ni koFu namo* '[my love] must long for me'; the form goes with the Altaic oblique stem. *M* 4358 also has a case of *wanu*, where it is interesting to note that the usual paraphrase and translation into the modern language renders it as J *watakushi ni*, i.e., in the sense of an oblique case. The initial correspondence of OJ *w-* with proto-Altaic **m-*, like that mentioned above in the case of OJ *mï*, proto-Altaic **bi*, requires further study.

For the second-person we have evidence for the original Altaic oblique stem in an occasional form to be found in some of the early texts. But by the time of our earliest written records it is clear that the meaning had already shifted in the direction of a deictic, in what was only one aspect of a larger, even more far-reaching development of which we shall see more below (pp. 173 ff.). This shift of original pronoun to deictic begins early in Japanese, where it helps to accelerate the eventual total obliteration of the original Altaic pronominal paradigm.

In *Kojiki* poem 11 the text has *söne ga mötö* 'its root'; but already by the time of the parallel text for this poem in the *Nihon shoki* poem 13, this same expression appears as *sönö ga mötö*, a collocation that points clearly in the direction of much later developments. (The modern spoken language would have either *sono moto*, or *sore no moto*; the later classical language would have *so ga moto*, or, with the modern spoken language, *sono moto*.) The preservation of the original final *-n* in the *Kojiki* form *söne* is a precious survival, preserving evidence for the structure of the original paradigm.

At this point we are now able to parallel the original Altaic paradigm for the first two persons from the Old Japanese materials as follows:

	Altaic	OJ
1-p.	**bi/*män*	*mï/wanu*
2-p.	**si/*sän*	*si/söne*

From this it is at once apparent that the final vowels in the Old Japanese reflexes of the original oblique forms for the pronouns are neither original nor etymological. Here as elsewhere in comparisons of Japanese with Altaic, when final vowels in the Japanese forms are not represented in the other forms with which they are being compared, we must assume that the Japanese vowels in question are later, epenthetic accretions, or what might be termed 'echo-vowels'. These epenthetic vowels were selected in pre-Old Japanese in accordance with certain rules of vowel combination in successive syllables, a system that continued to be operative down to the time of the large-scale Chinese loans into Japanese, where, for example, it determined that one would have -*u* after -*o*- in *koku* 'country', but -*i* after -*e*- in *teki* 'enemy', etc. This system of epenthetic vowel selection cannot now be recovered in all its details, but in general terms it operated as a set of 'vowel harmony' limitations on vowel occurrences, so that, in the Old Japanese pronoun paradigm above, we find -*u* after -*a*- but -*e* after -*ö*-.

Closely related to the Old Japanese first-person forms in this paradigm are the most common first-person forms in the bulk of the Old Japanese texts, namely *wa*, *a*, and *ware*, all for first-person and completely undifferentiated with respect to number.

The immediate Altaic analogue for OJ *wa* is the Mongol first-person inclusive plural *ba*; this is a nominative form, going together with an oblique *man-*, which in turn is closely parallel to OJ *wanu*. OJ *a* is best explained as an early allegro allomorph, in free variation with *wa*, to which it is directly related through the same under-articulation of initial labials that in the modern spoken language underlies such sets as female speaker's *atasi*, var. *atak[U]si*, alongside male speaker's *watasi*, var. *watak[U]si*, all 'I' (see also Wenck 1959: IV.209, Anm. 43.) The ultimate etymological relation of the first syllable in these modern forms to the Old Japanese morpheme in question is problematical but not completely to be ruled out.

What evidence, if any, can be detected in the texts that might ultimately throw light upon the exact nature of the historical relationship between *a* and *are* on the one hand and *wa* and *ware* on the other? Yamada Yoshio (1873–1958), the great scholar of Japanese historical grammar, devoted an important section of his monumental *Naracho bunpo shi* (1954) to the question, and the answer at which he arrived there is the one commonly presented in the handbooks and schoolbooks of Japanese grammar today. Yamada concluded that the *a* and *are* forms are original and older, and that the *wa* and *ware* forms are later, secondary developments from original *a* and *are*. Since this historical interpretation of the evidence appears to run directly counter to the comparative evidence presented here, and since it also appears to contradict the evidence from the modern language, his case (Yamada 1954: 55–57) must be inspected in detail.

Yamada's argumentation is based upon three points, but unfortunately in none of these has he made any attempt to correlate his theories on the historical priority or secondary origin of these forms with the actual appearances of the forms themselves in datable texts. The texts he cites and their dates provide no basis for assigning historical priority to either the *a*, *are* set or to the *wa*, *ware* set. Both sets appear in the earliest Old Japanese texts and continue to be in active use throughout the Old Japanese period; so if we are to arrive at a theory of chronological priority at all, it apparently cannot be on this basis. The history of the texts, here as so often, will not give us the history of the forms.

Yamada argues instead in three different directions, as follows: first, that the *a*, *are* forms must be taken as earlier than the original sources for the *wa*, *ware* forms because in the texts *a* enters into such compounds as *agi* 'my lord', *ago* 'my child', and *ase* 'my elder brother', whereas *wa* does not enter into such compounds. He argues that this compounding (actually and more exactly, it is rather a special type of contraction) is a good index for determining the older forms; the argument is that this compounding found its way into the texts only after it had been well established in the language, and it was more deeply entrenched for the (according to Yamada) older *a*, *are* forms than for the newer (again, according to Yamada) *wa*, *ware* forms.

At first this may appear to be a convincing argument, but it will not hold up under closer scrutiny. Compounds of the same variety are well attested for *waga*, and in fact Yamada himself devotes two pages of this same historical grammar of Old Japanese (1954: 42–44) to listing their numerous examples. They include both *wakiFe* and *wagiFe* for *waga iFe* 'my house', *wagimo* for *waga imo* 'my love', and (a very common case, with 19 examples in Yamada's grammar!) *wagimoko* for *waga imoko* 'my love [+intimate suffix]'. Yamada has clearly slanted his argument in favor of his own ultimate conclusions by implying that all the early compounds are with *a* and none with *aga*, and also (if only by further implication), that all the other early compounds are with *waga*, and none with *wa*. But it is far more consistent with what we know about the language to analyze the contraction-compound *agi* as resulting from *aga* + *ki*, than to regard it, as Yamada does, simply as resulting from *a* + *ki* (in any case, the example is a poor one, since the morpheme *ki* is a unique constituent in this compound, and the connection that the traditional exegesis makes between this *ki* and the first syllable of *kimi* 'lord' is a morpheme identification without any real basis at all, except in the traditions of the schools). The same is true (but mercifully this time without the troublesome complication of the morpheme identification of unique constituents) for *ago*, where it is far more satisfactory to postulate an original *aga* + *ko* and as a result at the same time be able to explain the voicing of the -*g*- in this form than it is to refer it to an original *a* + *ko*, as Yamada does. The third form he cites, *ase*, proves nothing one way or the other, since the traditional exegesis of the schools analyzing this form as containing the morpheme *se* 'elder brother' is totally irrelevant to the oldest texts in which it can be cited, as for example *Kojiki* song 104, where *ase wo* is used as a meaningless line-filler in verse (of the 'hey-nonny-nonny' variety). So the argument from this very special kind of compounding, which is Yamada's chief reason for postulating a chronological priority of *a*, *are* over *wa, ware*, simply cannot be maintained.

Yamada's second point is a simple statistical one. In the Old Japanese corpus he finds 271 secure citations (i.e., words actually recorded in the texts in phonograms, not merely postulated from semantic or rebus writings in Chinese characters) of *wa, ware* against 132 similarly secure citations of *a, are*. (Yamada's insistence upon restricting his citations to forms securely attested in phonograms is one of the strong points of his work, in refreshing contrast with so much other Japanese scholarship that uncritically mixes the evidence of phonogram texts with that of the always partly arbitrary traditional 'readings' of semantic or rebus writings.) Having already reached the conclusion, on the basis of the supposed evidence from compounding, that the *wa, ware* forms are historically later developments, Yamada then uses this statistical evidence (or better, this simple arithmetical data) to argue for the 'greater vigor' of the new, intrusive *wa, ware* forms as against the declining popularity of the earlier *a, are* forms.

But if this statistical evidence is approached without any a priori bias in favor of one historical explanation or the other, it serves far better to substantiate the secondary development of the *a, are* forms as simple underarticulated allegro forms based upon *wa, ware*, and hence to point in the direction of the same conclusion as the comparative evidence also indicates. Statistically *wa, ware* is the preponderant set of forms throughout the Old Japanese corpus, but enough instances of *a, are* are also recorded to make it clear that the allegro pronunciation phenomenon that resulted in this second set of forms was also both old and important. Yamada presents his data in a very simple form, giving only the total number of citations for all the texts, and presenting no information on the relation of these totals to various datable portions of the Old Japanese corpus; but even apart from this methodological difficulty, to agree with Yamada's argument that, in effect, the set of forms most commonly recorded throughout the Old Japanese corpus must be the late innovation, is simply to twist the available data so that it will not immediately contradict his earlier conclusion already reached on the basis of the supposed evidence from compounding.

Yamada's third argument can be disposed of most quickly of the three. He argues that the evidence of extremely old place names (e.g., Abiko, Ata, Aduma, AgaFa) points to the historical priority of *a*, *are*, since there are no place names in *wa-* of equal antiquity. This might be an important variety of argument, if the essential elements as he presents them were literally true, but unfortunately for Yamada the only basis we have for morpheme identification in all these ancient place names is that provided by the script, which uses Chinese characters to make morpheme identifications, but from the point of view of historical linguistics this is totally irrelevant. Abiko is written 'my grandson', Ata 'my paddy-field', Aduma 'my wife', and AgaFa 'my river'. Many of these morpheme identifications embodied in the traditional use of Chinese characters for writing proper names are extremely old in Japan, and they have often generated literary and aesthetic associations of great importance in the culture. Some of these identifications are as old as the eighth-century *Fudoki* texts that preserve them in the contexts of ancient folklore and mythology out of which they grew; but in the absence of other evidence (and Yamada cites none) they remain without linguistic significance.

We simply do not 'know' that the *a-* of *abiko*, *ata*, *aduma*, etc., is the same morpheme as the *a* of the pronoun set *a*, *are*, going with *wa*, *ware*. There is no way for us to 'know' this, and no way to verify a theory to that effect. They might have been the same, of course; but they might also not have been. The morpheme identification involved may neither be demonstrated nor refuted; and so any argument wholly based upon it, as is Yamada's, cannot successfully be maintained. Morpheme identification, by which in the present context is meant historical identity, is the essential link between Yamada's data and his conclusions based upon that data, and here that essential link is missing and at the same time impossible to restore. So this third argument too proves to collapse, and it is impossible as a result for us to accept Yamada's over-all conclusion that *a*, *are* are prior to *wa*, *ware*. The comparative evidence points in exactly the opposite direction, and nothing in the Old Japanese texts contradicts this opposite conclusion; in fact, the statistical data, meager as they are, support it; and hence as a result on all scores we are justified in treating *wa*, *ware* as the earlier and original set of forms within Old Japanese and *a*, *are* as the later, secondary developments.

The importance of restricting any consideration of the Old Japanese first-person pronouns to texts in which the forms in question are recorded in phonograms is strikingly demonstrated by Satake (1946: 185–89). (Regretfully, Satake himself makes uncritical use of both phonogram texts and traditional semantic and rebus 'readings' as if all these varieties and levels of texts were of equal authority for the history of the language.) Satake is concerned, in his study, with instances of real or apparent metrical irregularity (*ji-amari*) in the *Man'yōshū*, and the way in which the *Man'yōshū* poems appear to differ from Motoori's formulation for such metrical irregularity, Motoori's principal statement being that the phenomenon was limited to lines in which morphemes with vowel-initial (i.e., zero consonant) *a*, *i*, *u*, or *o* occur (see p. 78 above for further details on metrical irregularity and Satake's study). Following Motoori's formulations, we would expect that all cases of apparent metrical irregularity in the *Man'yōshū* containing inter alia the first-person pronoun would have *a*, *are*, not *wa*, *ware*. Satake has found 170 lines in the *Man'yōshū* that apparently do not follow Motoori's formulation; of those lines from among this total that do contain examples of first-person pronouns, in the nonphonogram texts, there are 22 cases with *waga* and 15 cases with *ware*; but in the phonogram texts, all the apparent metrically irregular lines with first-person pronoun have either *are* or *aga*, for a total of 9 cases. In other words, the phonogram texts follow Motoori's formulation perfectly. This makes it very clear how often the traditional school readings of the nonphonogram portions of the *Man'yōshū* must diverge from the original Old Japanese original underlying this text, and how important it is, in any historical linguistic investigation, to restrict ourselves to the data of the phonograms. Here even considering the nonphonogram evidence at once involves us in a fatal circularity; the nonphonogram lines are held to be metrically irregular, and violate Motoori's formulation, but this is simply because the school tradition by which they are read with *wa*- rather than with *a*-pronoun forms is wrong.

The origin of the final -*re* element in OJ *ware* involves a complicated but extremely interesting and important set of relationships. Ultimately it is to be explained by a convergence within Old Japanese of what were originally several distinct forms in the earlier Altaic linguistic community. It also involves certain significant aspects of the relationship of the nonstandard Azuma dialects to standard Old Japanese.

We must recall, first of all, that Old Japanese *r* had at least four possible origins with respect to proto-Altaic. OJ *r* is the normal Japanese reflex for pA *l_1, and for certain special cases of pA *l_2 (for which however the more general Japanese reflex was OJ *s*); OJ *r* is also the normal reflex for both pA *r_1 and pA *r_2, although *r_2 was also under certain circumstances represented by OJ *t* (the details for these correspondences have already been presented above, pp. 114–53). But all the Japanese reflexes described earlier and just summarized above are only those for the standard language of the Nara and Kyoto area; otherwise in the Azuma dialects the texts often have nonstandard OJ -*n*- corresponding to standard OJ -*r*-, and hence falling together with OJ -*n*- from several other sources, notably from proto-Altaic *n*, as well as from proto-Altaic *ñ* before certain vowels (cf. pp. 111–14 above).

For example, in *M* 3476, already cited above, we have nonstandard *kona* for standard *kora* 'lover, sweetheart'; *nuganaFe-* for *nagaraFe-* 'fleeting by', and -*namo* for -*ramu* 'how'. The existence of these forms gave rise to the traditional exegesis of the Japanese schools for the form *wanu* 'I' in this same text as being another case of this same -*n*-/-*r*- correspondence, but as we have seen above, the form *wanu* is best explained in historical and comparative terms along other lines.

This sporadic representation of standard OJ -*r*- by Azuma -*n*- had major implications for the subsequent history of many important forms in the language, as did several other Azuma aberrations. The nonstandard Old Japanese dialects for which the Azuma portions of the *Man'yōshū* provide our major body of textual evidence played a part in the development of the modern standard language. It is always necessary to keep in mind, in any discussion of Japanese historical linguistics, that the modern standard language is essentially an 'Eastern' Japanese dialect, as was Old Japanese Azuma, while standard Old Japanese (and the modern nonstandard dialects of the Nara-Kyoto area) was a 'Western' dialect. For example, another case that might be cited illustrating the long-range importance of these nonstandard Old Japanese dialects is provided by the modern standard-language verbal negatives in -*nai*; these forms appear to descend more or less directly from Azuma forms rather than from any of the verbal negative forms attested in standard Old Japanese texts (see Miller 1967: 169; also p. 258 below).

In the case of the pronouns, this -*r*-/-*n*- correspondence was particularly important, because it involved a proto-Altaic dual-plural suffix *-*r*₂ that in other languages gave the Old Turkish -*z* and the Chuvash -*r* plurals. In Old Turkish this particular suffix survives only in a small set of forms that appear to be old duals, for example OT *köküz* 'Brust', *köz* 'Auge', and *tiz* 'Knie', and significantly also in the pronominal plurals *biz* 'wir' and *siz* 'ihr'.

In Old Japanese, too, this suffix may be traced in certain ancient duals, as for example in the important early aberrant form OJ *kököri* 'heart' for standard OJ *kökörö* in *M* 4390, a word that, phoneme for phoneme, goes together with OT *köküz* in a very impressive fashion. This Old Japanese *kököri*, with final OJ -*ri* representing the old dual suffix, was subsequently altered in the course of its development in two different directions. In one set of late Old Japanese dialects its vocalism was leveled under -*e*- (or perhaps first under -*ë*- and then later -*e*-), to give the form *kekere*, attested for example as an eastern dialect form in the *Kokin wakashū*, a poetical anthology of A.D. 905–922 (see Miller 1967: 166, 369). This form *kekere* in turn reminds us of the fairly common cases in Old Japanese texts where nonstandard Azuma -*ë*- (later > -*e*-) corresponds to standard Old Japanese -*ö*-, as for example in *këtöba* for *kötöba* 'word', and *mëti*- for *moti* (<*möti*- ?) 'holding' (Fukuda 1965: 253, 328).

The other variety of change in this form was less spectacular but equally important. The final vowel of earlier *kököri* was simply assimilated to the vocalization of the first two syllables, resulting in the familiar *kökörö* of the bulk of the Old Japanese corpus, and ultimately too in the familiar modern *kokoro*. In Old Japanese *kököri* the final -*i* is essentially epenthetic in origin, but its quality (-*i*, and not, for example, -*a* or -*u*) is a reflex of the palatal quality of the original proto-Altaic *-*r*₂; in other words, the final vowel of the Japanese form is -*i* because the original form in the Altaic linguistic community had *-*r*₂.

At the same time that distinctions of this kind between the nonstandard Azuma and the standard Nara-Kyoto Old Japanese dialects were being leveled out, the oblique forms of the pronoun were being generalized in Old Japanese for all uses, as also happened (most probably independently, though some degree of areal influence cannot be ruled out) in Old Turkish. Japanese singular oblique forms in original -*n*- were easily contaminated with plural forms with original -*r*- because of the large number of cases in Japanese in which non-standard Old Japanese -*n*- corresponded to standard Old Japanese -*r*-; and once this process was well under way, there was nothing to prevent the complete leveling of original forms from -*n*- and -*r*- under Old Japanese -*r*-, with Old Japanese *ware* the final result.

The final -*e*- of *ware* was, as already noted, nonetymological and completely epenthetic in origin, like the final -*i* of early Old Japanese *kököri* 'heart' and its later developments ($>$ -*e* $>$ -*ö*), but also just as in the case of the final vowels of all these forms, its quality too (-*e*, not for example -*a* or -*o*) still preserves evidence for the palatal nature of the proto-Altaic suffix *-r_2.

The relationship of unattested **wari*, the form that would be expected as a regular development from an earlier form with final pA *-r_2, to the attested *ware* of our texts, is of course easily understood in terms of the widespread vowel-lowering phenomenon of Old Japanese, already described above (pp. 79 ff.). In the case of these particular lexical items, it seems more than likely that the shift of original final OJ **-i* in the pronoun paradigm originated in forms with -*ö*- in the first syllable, *köre* and *söre*, and that from these it was analogically extended to those other forms with the ablaut-related vowel -*a*- in the first syllable, thus ultimately resulting in *kare, tare, idure, nare, are,* and the like, as well as of course in *ware*.

One major problem of the Old Japanese pronoun paradigm can be solved only by means of comparison with the related languages. This is the relationship of the pronoun forms in final -*re* to the shorter but parallel forms without this ending. Most of the Japanese handbooks and dictionaries do not even allude to the problem, leaving the casual reader with the impression either that the question does not exist or that it has long since been solved; but neither conclusion could be further from the truth. Yamada has several scattered notes on the problem throughout his chapter on the personal pronouns (1954: 22–97; see for example 37–38 and 49–50), and most of the secondary handbooks base themselves upon Yamada's work in all their statements concerning the Old Japanese pronouns; but the data as he presents them are difficult to summarize, and his suggested explanation for the reasons underlying the distribution of the two sets of forms is so tentative and speculative that it can hardly be called an explanation at all.

The most useful parts of Yamada's study of this problem are his succinct tabular statements for the occurrences of both members of each pair of forms, but in his presentation this has been somewhat unnecessarily obscured by the inclusion of nondistinctive syntactic elements. Least satisfactory is his attempt to assign the over-all pattern of alternation to 'phonetic causes'. In the case of *a* and *are*, for example, he concludes by saying that in his opinion the alternations in the texts 'must have resulted from some mutual [process of] development and decay on the level of pronunciation (*seichō no ue ni te*), so that originally [*a* and *are*] were one morpheme (*ichigo*), which then was split up because of the exigencies of pronunciation (*seichōjō no hitsuyō yori*)' (Yamada 1954: 38). Similarly vague statements are made elsewhere in his chapter on the personal pronouns concerning other pairs with and without -*re*; in these too he suggests some underlying phonetic explanation, but can offer nothing more concrete.

The over-all pattern in the use of forms with and without final -*re* in the Old Japanese corpus is, however, not too difficult to detect if we focus our attention upon those occurrences that appear to be critical in the sense that they do distinguish forms with -*re* from those without this ending, and do not allow our statements to be unduly complicated by including accounts of the perhaps equally important but for our present purpose nondistinctive occurrences, where it is clear that by the time of the bulk of the Old Japanese corpus the two sets were already in free variation. In other words, going through Yamada's summation of the actual occurrences of the two sets in the Old Japanese texts, we will find that the pattern is quite clear for *wa* as against *ware* (1954: 54), for *a* as against *are* (1954: 37), and for *na* as against *nare* (1954: 64), as well as for *kö* and *köre* (1954: 70), *sö* and *söre* (1954: 75), *ta* and *tare* (1954: 84), and *itu* and *idure* (1954: 91); only *ka* as against *kare* does not seem to present a regular pattern, but this may be more apparent than real, and due only to a scarcity of material.

The pattern that the materials collected in Yamada's grammar reveals may be summed up as follows: in each case, the Old Japanese form without final -*re* enters into composition, and may be followed by the particle *ga*, while the forms with the final -*re* do not enter into composition, and are not followed by the particle *ga*. It is at once clear that these distinctive features of occurrence, one on the level of composition, the other on the level of syntax, correlate precisely with what comparison with the related languages has already told us concerning the historical origin of this -*re* element. This -*re* derives, as we have seen, from (among other converging sources) an inherited proto-Altaic dual-plural suffix. This means that the Old Japanese pronouns (*wa, a*, etc.) when they appear without the final -*re* element represented bare root forms, and hence it is only natural that it should be these root forms, and not those with -*re*, that should enter into composition. At the same time, another of the sources for this final -*re* is, as we have also seen, to be traced to the original Altaic oblique morphemes in the pronoun paradigm. This fact finds its reflex in the Old Japanese patterns of occurrence when the set of pronoun forms with -*re* is not used with the particle *ga*, while the set of forms without -*re* is on the contrary followed with *ga*. The members of the bare root set, i.e., those forms without -*re*, had no inherited Altaic suffix, and hence were free in Old Japanese to assume an additional new suffix or enclitic element. The other set, those forms ending in -*re*, already had an inherited Altaic suffix firmly fixed in place; and even in those cases where the -*re* was instead an inheritance from the original oblique morphemes of the pronoun paradigm, it had even by the time of early Old Japanese completely fallen together in Japanese with those forms where -*re* was a remnant of the proto-Altaic dual-plural suffix. In both cases, as a result, the prior presence of an inherited Altaic suffixal element was apparently sufficient to inhibit the syntactic employment of the form together with a particle *ga*. In this way, comparison with the related languages can demonstrate an original underlying order in the otherwise largely inexplicable distribution of these forms in the Old Japanese texts. The comparative method is hence able to recover structure and patterning even in this area of the language where, because of massive changes and shifts, these original features of order had been rendered so obscure as to be beyond the grasp of the purely descriptive student of the texts.

In its ordering of these suffixal elements in the personal pronouns Old Japanese was following the inherited Altaic pattern of ordering for the plurals of all substantives, in which the bare root was followed directly by plural morphemes, which then were followed in turn by the case endings (which last correspond to the Old Japanese enclitic particles.) This ordering is seen in OJ *söre ga*, 2d-p. gen., where *sö*- is the root, -*re* corresponds to the Altaic plural morpheme, and is in turn followed by the particle *ga*. Cf. also *köre nö*, in the *Bussokuseki* inscription poems 10 and 20. This construction has its exact formal correspondence in OT *siziŋ*, 2d-p. pl. gen., and Chu.

sirĕn, id. In the nouns only Chuvash has changed this inherited order, so that it has the plural morpheme in word-final position, following any other suffixes, but in the pronoun even Chuvash still has the older inherited order for these elements (Krueger 1961: 95, 133). So firmly attached to the root did the plural morphemes become in Old Turkish that later pleonastic plurals with an additional plural morpheme *-lar* are common in the texts: OT *sizlär*, 2d-p. pl. nom., *sizlärniŋ*, id., gen., etc. This persistent and apparently indissoluble adhesion of the plural ending to the root in Old Turkish reminds us of and is to a very large extent parallel to the equally firm adhesion of the *-re* to the root elements in the Old Japanese pronouns.

In related forms in the other Altaic languages, and particularly in Tungus, this same suffix *-re* proved to be of extraordinary vitality, and can be seen gradually to have expanded its area of domination (see Kotwicz 1936: 66). A clear indication of this vitality of the suffix *-re* is to be observed on the proto-Mongol level, where we have **ene* 'this' but **tere* 'that' for the nominatives, with **egün* and **tegün* for the oblique stems, respectively. As Poppe expresses it, 'the final *e* in *ene* and *tere* is a deictic element. The element *-n-* occurs in all pronouns, . . . The element *-r-* in *te-r-e* cannot be explained by the facts of Mongolian linguistics alone. It occurs, however, as an element in the demonstrative pronouns in Manchu-Tungus languages, cf. Ma. *ere* 'this', Tung. (Solon) *ri* 'this', and Ma. *tere* 'that' . . . (Poppe 1955: 225). In other words, we can observe the steady expansion and generalization of this suffix *-re* throughout the Altaic linguistic domain, apart from Turkish, with the process eventually carried to its fullest extent in Tungus and Japanese.

In Japanese, where the suffix ceased very early to be separable, all sense of its inherited dual-plural meaning was soon lost sight of, this last process being considerably accelerated, as we have seen above, by the phonetic contamination of oblique forms in *-n(-)* with the forms in *-r(-)*. With the plural sense gone, Old Japanese, like Old Turkish, was then able to indulge in the luxury of pleonastic plurals; in Japanese these would be of the *köre-ra*, *söre-ra* variety, for which forms the Old Turkish pleonastic plurals in *-lar* again provide close and significant parallels.

Also probably pleonastic is the rare Japanese familiar inclusive first-person pronoun *wanami*, not attested earlier than the mid-sixteenth-century lexicon *Unpo irohashū* (1547–48), but surviving at least into the nineteenth century; it appears in the *Hachikenden*

(1814–1841) of Takizawa Bakin (1767–1848) (Nakada 1963: 1186ᵇ). The form *wanami* most likely involves the now-familiar first-person *wa-*, followed by a vowel-harmony alternant of the referent particle *no* > *na*, and this followed in turn by a suffixed personal element parallel to (and ultimately cognate with) the suffixed *-m* for first-person singular noun possession in Old Turkish (Tekin 1968: 122, § 3.212). But apart from this important relic form *wanami*, Japanese does not appear to preserve other evidence of morphological formations parallel to the Turkish noun possession structures.

The Altaic origins of the second-person set OJ *na, nare,* as well as the other secondary derived Japanese forms that ultimately go together with this set, are somewhat less clear than for the first-person forms. The obvious direction in which to look for such origins is that provided by pM **ta,* 2d-p. pl., and its oblique stem pM **tan-* (Poppe 1955: 218). It is not necessary to recapitulate here the double origin for the OJ *-re* ending, which would account for the finals in this comparison; but the initials do raise serious, and still partly unsolved, difficulties. The clue must lie in the sporadic change of Old Japanese initial *t-* to *n-* under certain special phonetic circumstances, typically when the phoneme *-r-* was found immediately following in the same morpheme; the evidence for the widespread influence of this analogic shift on the Old Japanese lexicon has already been presented above (pp. 102 ff.). For these second-person forms, the necessary phonetic conditions are fully met; original **ta(n)-*, a shape that might normally have been expected to have resulted in Japanese *ta, tare,* has apparently instead given OJ *na, nare.* But the problem is further complicated by the existence of the Old Japanese interrogatives *ta, tare* 'who?'. It would be quite possible to involve these forms too in the etymology but considerations of the interrogatives taken as a whole, and concern also for economy of historical statement, make it more satisfactory to regard the interrogatives *ta, tare* as independent forms, unrelated either to the Altaic second-person or to its somewhat aberrant Japanese reflex (see p. 189 below).

Against original pA **ti* > **či* for 2d-p. sg. and **ta* for 3d-p. pl., Shirongol has *č'i,* 3d-p. sg., and *t'a,* 2d-p. sg. (Kotwicz 1936: 17). The later portions of the Old Japanese corpus have several examples of pronoun-equivalent periphrases for second-person originating in compounds of the first-person combining morpheme *wa-* plus a noun head, thus *wa-nusi* 'my master', *wa-dono* < *wa-nö-tono* 'my lord', *wa-bito* < *wa-nö-Fitö* 'my man' (Murayama 1950: 44). Even in eighth-century texts OJ *wakë* is found as a deprecatory second-person (*M* 1460, *M* 1461; in both these poems the form is written in the text proper with Chinese logographs meaning 'mean knave', but in *M* 1460 this is also glossed in phonograms as Old Japanese *wakë* in an appended note of the same date as the text). The etymology of OJ *wakë* is disputed. Ōno Susumu (1957 [= *M* 1]: 362, gloss to *M* 552; cf. Ōno 1959 [= *M* 2]: 294) attempts to relate it to the adjective *waka-* 'young, immature'; cf. Sanseidō 1967: 816^d. The traditional etymology instead relates this initial *wa-* element to the *wa-* first-person morpheme (Murayama 1950: 44; Yamada 1954: 96). If the traditional morpheme identification is correct, the form *wakë* is parallel in structure and semantic drift to *wa-nusi* and the others cited above; at any rate, a considerable amount of wavering in the meaning of *wakë* between first-person and second-person is evident in the Old Japanese texts. Yamada (1954: 96) held that the form was originally a second-person that had been shifted to first-person uses in the Old Japanese period.

This inevitably confronts us with one of the most perplexing problems in the entire history of the pronoun forms in Japanese, and indeed in all the Altaic languages, namely the shifting back and forth in semantic category from one person to another which such forms appear to have undergone from time to time—and sometimes even more than once during their history. Common to all these examples of semantic interchange between first-person and second-person are two sociolinguistic elements—the self-deprecatory employment of a pejorative second-person in the resultant sense of a humble first-person; and the converse employment of a humble, self-deprecatory first-person in the sense of a particularly pejorative second-person. Unfortunately these two main currents of semantic shift have crossed and recrossed each other so many times throughout the history of the languages involved that it is now all but impossible to recover any original, over-all pattern underlying these changes, which appear to have taken place independently in the different languages at different times.

These problems in semantic shift become especially critical when we attempt to study the set of forms represented by OJ *onö* 'myself, one's self', OJ *ore* 'you (deprecatory)', and OJ *onöre* 'myself, one's self'. In the texts, OJ *onö* is clearly a bare stem form, since it rarely appears without some following particle, usually *ga*, or in composition (OJ *onödukara* 'by one's self', etc.), or in the reduplicative *onöonö* 'every, all'. OJ *ore* is a comparatively rare form in the texts, where it appears to be limited to its use in glossing second-person pronouns in Japanese versions of Chinese texts (Sanseidō 1967: 169ᵇ). In all the later forms of the language, it is best known as a vulgar, first-person singular, and as such it survives down to the modern standard language. OJ *onöre* survives in the sense of 'my self', although in the standard language this form is probably a borrowing from the literary language. It is important to note that the old deprecatory second-person usages by no means disappear from the texts, even after the Old Japanese period; cf. the Middle Japanese examples in the *Konjaku monogatari* (Lewin 1965: 119, n. 49a), and the Kyōgen *Iroha* (Lewin 1965: 261). Yamada (1954: 96–97) argued that, in parallel with what he held to be true for OJ *wakë*, the second-person uses of *ore* were original and the first-person uses secondary developments.

Unfortunately, comparison with cognate forms in other languages shows that the actual course of the historical developments was probably rather different from the impression that, together with Yamada, we might gain solely from an inspection of the Japanese materials. Old Turkish has *ol* 'that, he, they' as well as the reflexive pronoun *öz* 'own, self; he'. Either might be compared with OJ *ore*, and ultimately also with OJ *onö* and *onöre*. Unfortunately a satisfactory Altaic etymology for OT *ol* appears to be lacking, but OT *öz* goes directly with an important group of cognate forms, including Mo., MMo. *örö*, var. *öre* 'das Innere, Herzader', Ev. *ur* 'Tiermagen', Lam. *ur* 'Magen, Bauch', Chu. *var* < **ör* 'Mitte, Tal' (Poppe 1960: 81, 109, 126). If we assign OJ *ore* and its related forms to this same etymology (and nothing argues against such an assignment, either from the point of view of phonology or from that of semantics), it would appear that the reflexive meaning 'self' was the original one for all these words, and that their employment as second-person forms represents later developments. In other words, what limited comparative evidence there is available appears to indicate that in these words the reflexive meaning was original and central, rather than any personal reference, either first or second, and that the course of historical development was one that saw the specialization of this originally reflexive meaning toward one or the other of the persons, sometimes in one direction, at other times in another, rather than the general drift from second- to first-person that Yamada and the other Japanese scholars following him have formulated. The other Old Turkish reflexive is *käntü* (von Gabain 1950: 102, § 201), which goes directly with the Japanese deictic *kanata* 'that direction, place over there';

we must compare the other parallel Japanese forms *sonata* and *anata*, both original deictics that are later specialized for use as pronoun surrogates (p. 201 below).

In Old Turkish *ol* 'that' is also employed as a third-person pronoun, and in such usages this form has an unusual oblique stem *an-*, so that the accusative of *ol* is *anï*, dative-locative *aŋar*, locative-ablative *anta*, etc. (von Gabain 1950: 94, § 190; Tekin 1968: 140, § 3.222). This nominative/oblique stem variation is totally anomalous in terms of Turkish alone, but immediately falls into place when viewed against the perspective of the Japanese comparative evidence, with *ore, onö*, and *onöre*, already discussed, to be considered against the remote deictics *ano, are* 'that (over there)'. The key to the relationship of all these forms is of course the *a/o* ablaut variation in the original language, the variation typically represented by OJ *a/ö*, and here this makes it possible to bring the *ol/an-* stem variation into a meaningful association with OJ *ore/an-*, the comparison revealing exact correspondences both in forms and in their meanings.

Another apparent example which may be cited from the comparative materials in support of a shift from second-person to first-person (or perhaps, with equally effective reasoning, the other way around), is OJ *namuti*, MJ *namudi*, J *nanji* 'you' (this last form in the modern language is a borrowing from literary Japanese). One is tempted to compare this with the dative-locative oblique stem pM **namadur* (Poppe 1955: 209) and to see in the comparison another example of a second- to first-person shift (if the Japanese represents the original semantic state of affairs), or of a first- to second-person shift (if the Mongol data preserves the original meaning). But the prior element in all these Japanese forms is surely to be identified simply with the same element already discussed in OJ *na, nare*, and hence it goes in some way or other with pM **ta*, and hence also the traditional Japanese etymology for *namuti*, etc., as containing *na* + OJ *muti* 'esteemed, honorable', is probably (for once) worth taking at face value.

Despite the unsolved problems that they present, these examples of semantic change in both directions between first-person and second-person, as well as back and forth between these forms and the reflexives, do make it possible to bring into the general Altaic relationship at this point the otherwise difficult Korean set *na* 'I' and *në* 'you'. Their association with several different Old Japanese forms is an old one (Ōno Susumu 1957: 181; Doi Tadao et al. 1961: 42). One difficulty surrounding the problem has been that different scholars have attempted to relate these Korean forms to a rather bewilderingly diverse assortment of Japanese forms—principally to OJ *ana*, which is unfortunately not a pronoun at all but an exclamatory particle, and also to OJ *onö* 'one's self, myself'; but which Old Japanese form goes with K *na* and which goes with K *në* has never been satisfactorily determined.

Equally obscure is the fate of the initial syllable in the Old Japanese forms most commonly suggested as cognates. The derivational process relating K *na* 'I' and K *në* 'you' within Korean itself is at present impossible to relate to an inherited Altaic pattern, but apart from this difficulty the set clearly goes somehow or other with the OJ *na, nare* set for the second-person.

Another important aspect of semantic change that must be kept in mind in any consideration of the pronouns in the Altaic languages (including Japanese) is that of the exclusive and inclusive categories. It is difficult to refer this distinction to the time of the proto-Altaic linguistic unity because it is not sufficiently well represented in a wide enough variety of the later, related languages to allow us to reconstruct it with complete confidence as an early feature for the entire group; but nevertheless it is sufficiently well documented in a number of the descendant languages for it to have been an areal feature common to at least a considerable portion of the original proto-Altaic community.

The exclusive/inclusive contrast in the pronouns is particularly well represented in Mongol and Tungus, and certain traces of it may also be detected in the Old Japanese materials. But except for the evidence that it left in the phonological shape of certain Old Japanese forms, it had ceased to be of any importance in the language before the time of our earliest Japanese texts. In Mongol and Tungus, however, it proved to be a distinction of considerably greater vitality, and has survived there to the present day. Perhaps this distinction was an early innovation in that geographical segment or early dialect area within proto-Altaic to which Mongol, Tungus, and Old Japanese relate most directly, and out of which eventually developed proto-Eastern Altaic; or perhaps (and somewhat less likely) it was a later innovation in proto-Northern and Peninsular Altaic, and was imitated from there by the closely related and contiguous proto-Mongol.

In proto-Mongol this distinction existed for the first-person plural, where the exclusive form was **ba* and the inclusive form was **bida*; the oblique stems were **man-* and **bidan-*, respectively. While the distinction has not been preserved in all the related languages, Written Mongol, Middle Mongol, Monguor, Khalkha, and Kalmuck all have full declensions of both the exclusive and the inclusive pronouns, while Dagur, Mogol, Urdus, and Buriat all preserve some, even if less complete, traces of the original system. In other languages where the full system is not preserved, the oblique cases of the exclusive pronoun have taken the place of the oblique cases of the inclusive pronoun (Poppe 1955: 215). This direction of drift in the analogic changes resulting from the break-up of the exclusive-inclusive system as a whole should be kept in mind in connection with the Old Japanese developments, as will be explained in greater detail below.

In Tungus the evidence for this distinction is particularly clear. It is necessary to reconstruct both the exclusive *büä and the inclusive *mün.ti for proto-Tungus (Benzing 1955: 108). Manchu has *bi*, 1st-p. sg., oblique stems *min-, mim-; be*, 1st-p. pl., exclusive, oblique stems *men-, mem-; muse*, 1st-p. pl., inclusive. Evenki has, for the same forms in the same order, *bi, min-; by, myn-*; and *mit* (Ikegami 1955: 474–75).

By the time of the Japanese texts, the semantic dimension of this original distinction (if indeed it was original) has completely disappeared, and all that remains is a certain amount of suggestive phonetic data. We may first of all cite, in this connection, the striking variation in initials between one of the older relic forms for the first-person pronoun, OJ *marö*, in *Kojiki* poem 48 (with an identical form in the parallel text in *Nihon shoki* poem 39), beside OJ *warö*, in the same sense, in *M* 4343. OJ *marö* later becomes a common element used in second position in aristocratic given names.

But their initials are not the only features of these forms that provide evidence reminiscent of the exclusive-inclusive distinction. The final epenthetic vowels in these forms also, particularly the final -*ö* of *marö*, preserve valuable clues by means of which the original vowel differences marking the exclusive-inclusive distinction (exclusive: *-a-*; inclusive: *-i-*) may also be traced to a certain extent in the Japanese materials, despite the fact that in their first syllables all the Japanese forms had leveled out this earlier distinction in vocalization under a uniform OJ -*a-* well before the time of the earliest of our texts.

OJ *marö* and OJ *wanu* go together with the probably original exclusive forms, with the inherited vocalism *-a-* in their first syllables. To both forms the final epenthetic -*ö* and -*u*, respectively, were added in 'vowel harmony' with this original -*a-* vocalism. Semantically also,

something of the sense of the original exclusive category is perhaps
preserved in the first-person singular sense of OJ *marö*; and also perhaps in its later use as an element in given names (a typically 'first-
person' and characteristically 'singular exclusive' context, to be sure);
but apart from this the semantic differences marking these forms did
not prove to be nearly as durable in Japanese as did their phonetic
shapes.

In OJ *ware*, meanwhile, the quality of the final epenthetic *-e* was
also determined, as we have seen, by several separate historical considerations that can be traced in considerable detail on the comparative level; but among these we may also note the requirements of the
same 'vowel harmony' phenomenon, due to the fact that in the forms
ultimately underlying OJ *ware*, there was once an original front vowel
in the first (and only) inherited syllable, parallel with the original
-i- vocalism of the earlier inclusive category. And semantically,
these inherited inclusives naturally provided the most natural point
of departure possible for the later developments of the Japanese
forms. Hence we may say that, in these pronoun forms, even though
the final vowels are completely epenthetic and nonetymological, they
still provide valuable indications of the earlier shapes, as well as of the
earlier meanings, of the forms to which they have become attached in
Japanese.

5.2 Interrogatives

The Japanese interrogatives are a fertile field for Altaic comparison—
so rich a field, in fact, that it is possible, even at our present state of
information on the precise relationships of Japanese to the other
Altaic languages, to account for the details and historical origins of
virtually all the Japanese forms belonging to this set in terms of cognate forms in the other related languages. We shall see that, although
evidence from throughout the entire Altaic area is of value in recovering the history of the Japanese interrogatives, it is Turkish and
Tungus that provide the most important data while Mongol is the
least useful.

If we classify the Old Japanese interrogatives along purely formal
lines, we can at once identify three main groups of forms: those involving a general, nonspecific prefixed interrogative element OJ *i-*;
those based on the morpheme *nani;* and a closed set consisting of the
two forms *ta, tare*. The first of these three groups is by far the largest;
the other two are disproportionately small, particularly since the

third consists only of the two forms just cited for the purpose of identifying the group.

The historical treatment of the Japanese interrogatives that follows takes as its point of departure this purely formal division, but otherwise the treatment under each of these major categories has been arranged so that the historical and comparative significance of the forms involved may be approached most conveniently and economically. As is often true, it is not until we have a succinct but compendious arrangement of the Old Japanese data at our disposal that the historical and comparative evidence may be fitted into the problem in a meaningful fashion; and as is also often true, in the case of the interrogatives, once again the more usual presentations of the forms in the grammars and other handbooks of earlier forms of Japanese, where they are arranged solely in terms of semantic categories, will not serve our purposes here; hence the necessity for the arrangement of forms as well as for the order of the treatment below.

OJ *i-* functioned as a general, nonspecific interrogative prefixed formant in Old Japanese, where it appeared in two primary formations (OJ *itu* 'when', OJ *ika* 'what?') as well as in a variety of complex secondary formations (OJ *iku-tu* 'how many?', OJ *idu-ku* 'where?', etc.). Among these complex formations it is necessary further to distinguish two principal subgroups: those in which the inner layer of the secondary formation is OJ *iku-*, which was a combining-form of OJ *ika*, and related to it by an anomalous vowel alteration in which -*a*- has become -*u*-; and those in which the inner layer of the secondary formation is OJ *idu-*, which consists of OJ *i-* plus an original Altaic locative formant -*du*-. Forms involving OJ *idu-* are to be distinguished historically from those involving OJ *ika* in its combining form as OJ *iku-* because *idu-* exists only as a secondary bound form, in contrast with *iku-*, which has its ultimate origins in the free primary formation *ika*. (For the apparent exception of OJ *idu* (or *itu*) in *M* 3549, see the discussion below, p. 184 and p. 187.)

Since OJ *i-* was a bound morpheme there is no need to consider cases in which it appeared in isolation: no such cases occur. We may accordingly begin our discussion with the two primary formations in which it appeared, OJ *itu* 'when?' and OJ *ika* 'what?'.

1. The first of these is clearly to be analyzed as a compound of *i-* with -*tu*, which was a combining form of OJ **tö* 'when, if . . .' This latter form must be postulated as the ultimate source of the modern clause particle *to* of similar meaning (Bloch 1970: 46). In the com-

pound formation OJ *itu*, this original *tö* appears with the anomalous vowel alteration *ö* > *u*, which has parallels throughout the interrogative paradigm. The importance of these anomalous vowel alterations, which resulted in an almost uniform -*u*- vocalism in second syllable position throughout the entire range of the interrogatives, has already been noted above, and will again be of importance to the discussion below in the consideration of the combining form *iku*- in which original *ika* appears in several important secondary formations.

The *tö* involved in this compound cannot be cited as a free form from Old Japanese texts, but it is common enough from Heian on; see the citations in Lewin 1959: 85, § 109 (it is one of the *setsuzoku-joshi* of the modern Japanese grammarians).

Martin (1966: 238, #169) has commented upon this *to* (i.e., OJ *tö*) as follows: 'it is unclear whether this is to be regarded as a shortening of *toki* 'time when [i.e., OJ *töki*] or of *tokoro* 'place' [OJ *tökörö*]'; he reconstructs both pKJ *cekyi* and *cokyi* to account for, on the one hand, MK *cëk*, J *toki*, and on the other, K *cok-cok* 'every time that . . .' and J *tokidoki* 'sometimes', reduplicating J *toki* 'time when' (Martin 1966: 244, ##242, 243). OJ *töki* 'time when' must be related to Mo. *čag*, OT *čaq*, both 'Zeit', and their cognates in the various Altaic languages (Poppe 1960: 26; see also above, p. 99). The shorter form OJ *tö* appears to have been the underlying root in OJ *töki*, entering into one kind of composition in *töki* and into another in *itu*.

The second of these forms, OJ *ika* 'what?' is of importance both as a form in its own right and also because it is the original form underlying several secondary formations in its combining form *iku*-. It too is to be analyzed in a fashion completely parallel to that employed for *itu*, i.e., as composition involving *i*- with a following element -*ka*, but with the difference in this instance that the second element -*ka*, unlike the second element -*tu* in *itu*, is not so easily identified with any underlying or free form appearing elsewhere in the language. It would be tempting to attempt to identify it with the question sentence particle *ka* (Bloch 1970: 44), for example, but this would be an over-facile identification that would immediately have to be ruled out by even a cursory consideration of the over-all syntactic roles of the forms involved. Ramstedt/Aalto (1952: 78) collects important comparative evidence on this sentence particle, among others, and there is little more that needs to be said on the subject. (The present study limits itself, it should be noted, to free interrogatives and does not further concern itself with enclitics or sentence particles.) It is better to consider the -*ka* involved in *ika* to be a unique constituent appearing only in this compound, and not attempt further to identify it within Japanese; it is also probably best not to attempt to identify it with the Turkish interrogatives deriving from earlier **qa* and related forms (see p. 191 below).

The Old Japanese interrogative *ika* is, of course, very richly attested in the texts, in a wide variety of syntactic structures too great to permit summation here; and it is from one of these typical structures, that in which it appears as a part of the collocation *ika ni ka* (where the second *ka* is the indefinite referent particle *ka;* see Bloch 1970: 54), that modern J *ikaga* 'how?' has developed (Miller 1967: 217; Lewin 1965: 157, n. 83).

2. All other forms in which the generalized interrogative OJ *i-* appears are secondary and complex, since they contain two different morphological layers of suffixal materials. Some of the forms here involve OJ *i-* plus the originally locative -*du*- (p. 87 above) > OJ *idu-* as their inner layer; in the others OJ *ika*, the simplex form already discussed above, appears in a combining form with anomalously altered vocalization as *iku-* as the inner layer of a number of important forms.

OJ *idu-* is a secondary formation, but is itself a bound form, and appears only as an inner layer in further morphological structures, notably OJ *idu-ku* 'where (of place)?', *idu-ti* 'where (of direction)?', and *idu-re* 'which (of two different things or choices)?'.

OJ *idu-ku* underlies J *doko* 'where?'; the modern form has preserved the same semantic specification that its ancestor form had in the earlier stages of the language, while OJ *idu-ti* underlies both J *dotti* and J *dotira* 'which way?', the modern forms again closely maintaining the original semantic differentiation among these interrogatives of place. The double -*tt*- in J *dotti* is probably another example of the expressive or emphatic consonant gemination that has long characterized the Edo dialects out of which the modern standard language has grown (see Miller 1967: 154).

The suffix -*ra* in J *dotira* is an important modern survival of an old Altaic locative suffix -*ra*. With it may be compared the Old Turkish 'Direktiv-Endung' -*ra/-rä*, as seen for example in OT *tašra* 'outward, on the outside', *öŋrä* 'ahead, in the front, in the east, eastward', *kisrä* 'backward, later, westward, after' (other Old Turkish citations in von Gabain 1959: 31); cognate with this same form is the Chuvash locative -*ra/-re* (Benzing 1959: 723–24; Krueger 1961: 105); and the same morpheme may also be traced in a few forms in Mongol and Tungus (Kotwicz 1936: 56–67). Compare also MTk. *qayra* 'whither?' (Mansuroğlu 1959: 93). The Japanese reflexes for this morpheme in *idure* > *izure* and *dotira* complete the evidence for the early distribution of this ancient locative formant throughout the original Altaic linguistic unity.

It would also be tempting to associate the suffixal *-ku* in OJ *idu-ku* with the similar suffixal element in OJ *kökö* 'here, this place'; we note also that Martin (1966: 244, #240) reconstructs pKJ *$k\acute{o}$, *ko 'this' on the basis of K *ki, ko* 'that (near you)', J *ko-re* 'this'. In other words, one is led to suspect that *kökö* was originally *kö* 'this' + *kö* '*place', and also that *idu-ku* was originally *idu-kö* 'what place?'. If this identification is historically correct, it might also possibly provide a clue to the ultimate impetus under which the final syllable of the modern form was altered to *-o;* in other words, a still earlier but unattested *idu-kö* underlies OJ *idu-ku*, and in *idu-ku*, the vocalization of the final suffixal syllable has been altered from earlier *$\ddot{o}$ to the attested *u* under the obvious influence of the preceding *-u-* of *-du-*. But the semantic associations due to its ultimate origin in the same morpheme that appears in the final syllable of *kö-kö*, plus the general pressure exerted by the deictic paradigm in general, later resulted in its subsequent remodeling (which by this time was actually not a remodeling but rather a restoration!) back from *u* to *o* again, in J *doko*. The same explanation would then hold true for the final-syllable vocalization in J *izuko* 'where?', a recent borrowing into the spoken language of a literary form that preserves the configuration and sense of original OJ *idu-ku*, but that also shows the restoration of the vocalization of the original locative element *-kö* in its last syllable. On the history of these forms, some material is available in Wenck (1959: 4.64 and ibid. 65, n. 3) and Lewin (1965: 96, n. 48, *izuku* in the *Utsuo monogatari;* ibid. 113, n. 9, *izuko* in the *Tsutsumi chūnagon monogatari*). But as is usually the case in Japanese historical linguistics, we lack the most essential tool for any comprehensive study of the problem, namely a complete monographic treatment of the forms bringing together in one place the materials preserved in texts, manuscripts, and editions of various dates. Until such studies are undertaken it is both difficult and risky to generalize on the history of the forms involved.

The suffixal *-ti* of OJ *idu-ti*, seen both as the final element in J *dotti* and as the inner suffixal layer in J *dotira*, is more of a puzzle; this element appears to have no secure Altaic connections.

The Old Japanese corpus also includes several sporadic occurrences of other interrogatives of place. These do not survive into the later stages of the language, but they are nevertheless extremely valuable for the evidence they supply for what appears to have been rather free derivational activity involving the basic locative-interrogative OJ *idu-*, together with a variety of suffixal elements.

The following are the principal examples of these sporadic forms for locative-interrogatives that may be cited from the texts:

idusi, M 3474, appears to have been the nonstandard Azuma dialect equivalent for standard OJ *iduti*. On the replacement of standard OJ *t* by Azuma *s*, see Miller 1967: 166. Japanese scholars customarily treat the phenomenon as resulting from an affricated pronunciation of standard OJ *ti* as [tˢi], [tˢï], etc. It seems clear from the texts that at least by the time of the Azuma poems in the *Man'yōshū*, the standard-language form *iduti* had also been borrowed into Azuma, where it then continued to exist in competition with original Azuma *idusi* (Sanseidō 1967: 82ᵈ). There can be little question that this kind of complex borrowing back and forth between standard and nonstandard varieties of Old Japanese must ultimately be held responsible for many of the linguistic developments for which we can detect a certain amount of evidence in our materials but whose precise details will probably never be completely recovered.

iduFe, M 88 and *M* 4195, does not seem ever to have attracted scholarly attention as an Azuma feature; at any rate, it has not survived in the history of the language. Note that the Old Japanese vocalism of the final syllable was *-Fe*, not **Fë*.

idura, M 3689, is a unique and instructive example of the same basic locative-interrogative element, this time compounded with the well-attested Altaic locative-directional suffix *-ra*. On the form in the later literature, and with different meanings, see Lewin 1965: 113, n. 9; Nakada 1963: 98.

In addition to these sporadic forms themselves the Old Japanese texts also provide several clues to the prehistory of all the interrogatives in *idu-* within Japanese itself, i.e., in pre-Old Japanese. The evidence of the texts indicates that although these interrogatives are apparently generally attested with medially voiced *-d-* (and are almost universally so written in *kana* or otherwise transcribed), they ultimately must be referred to earlier pre-Japanese forms with voiceless *-t-* instead, and that as a result all these forms can be traced back to originals of the general shape **itu*. This evidence is of two sorts.

First, there is the evidence of the orthography in a few passages in the Old Japanese texts, though this is in part ambiguous, since these passages employ a phonogram unfortunately used both for OJ *tu* and for OJ *du*, notably the Chinese graph *tòu* (6478) 'bean'. Since this graph is used as a *man'yōgana* phonogram for both *tu* and *du*, it is impossible to determine whether the scribe intended *itu* or *idu* when it appears in any given passage as a portion of the writing for the interrogative in question. Unfortunately, modern Japanese editors and grammarians have not been at all consistent in rendering such phonogram orthographies into modern Japanese script in the course of preparing their editions and commentaries. Thus, to take the single unique example where the Old Japanese corpus appears to have preserved the interrogative of place in its simplex forms, OJ *idu* (or, OJ *itu*) in *M* 3549, Yamada (1954: 91) reads the passage OJ *itu*, but Sanseidō (1967: 81ᵇ) reads it *idu;* the text has Chinese *ī-tòu* (2936, 6478) 'that' + 'bean'.

A further glance at a few of Yamada's citations will show how utterly irresponsible modern Japanese scholarship has been on this point. We shall limit ourselves here to citations involving OJ *idu* (or *itu*) written with Chinese *ī* (2936) 'that' followed either by Chinese *tòu* (6478) 'bean' or Chinese *tū* (6500) 'capital, metropolis'. While Chinese *tòu* is a common phonogram in the Old Japanese corpus for either OJ *tu* or *du*, Chinese *tū* is a common phonogram only for Old Japanese *tu*. Even so, it is impossible to determine any underlying principle at all in Yamada's readings for *man'yōgana* writings involving these phonograms, as the following sampling shows (all citations from Yamada 1954). On p. 90, the combination of graphs *ī-tòu* occurs five times, and each time it has been read as OJ *idu;* but on p. 91, immediately following, the same combination of graphs is read as OJ *itu* (in *M* 3549!). On p. 89, the combination of graphs *ī-tū* is read ten times as OJ *itu*, but immediately following this same combination is read once on p. 90 and twice on p. 92, as OJ *idu*. One is forced to the regretful conclusion that Yamada first decided what the Old Japanese form was 'supposed to be', and then wrote it that way, but in the process simply ignored the precise nature of the phonetic evidence provided by the *man'yōgana*. And his practice in this, far from being unusual or idiosyncratic, is the common one among most Japanese scholars. (Yamada once writes *iture* [1954: 25] in *kana* for *idure;* but judging from the rest of his treatment of this form together with the other Old Japanese interrogatives [ibid., 81–94], this single instance of *iture* in his grammar is probably nothing more than a printing error.)

When the phonogram in question is ambiguous, as is the case with Chinese *tòu* 'bean' used in the texts for both OJ *tu* and *du*, all that we can do is either to maintain this ambiguity in every instance in our transcription, employing for that purpose some special sign or character ($^t/_d$, ᴅ, or the like), or else normalize our transcription on the basis of later attested forms in the language, where in this case we always have forms with -*d*-, never forms with -*t*-; and such normalization is the course that has been adopted, except as otherwise noted, throughout the present study. What must be avoided at all cost is the whimsical switching back and forth between one form and another in which Japanese scholars and their editions indulge, in utter disregard of the plain evidence of the texts.

To sum up, then, the evidence of the phonogram texts in the Old Japanese corpus, ambiguous though it sometimes is, and distorted though it has been by Japanese scholarship, shows us this, and nothing more or less—namely that *it would be possible* to postulate still earlier forms in OJ **itu* underlying all the later, attested forms for the interrogatives in OJ *idu*.

And there the matter would have to remain, were it not for the second variety of independent evidence that fortunately is also available, and that provides far less ambiguous evidence for the previous existence of these forms in OJ **itu*. We will see shortly below (p. 193) how these Japanese interrogatives are to be referred, thanks to the data put at our disposal by the comparative method, to proto-Tungus forms of the shape **xa.i + dū*, among other forms in the related languages. The proto-Tungus vowel system made the expected distinction between front and back vocalism, with proto-Tungus front **ä, i, ö*, and *ü* contrasting as a set with proto-Tungus back **a, ï, o, u* (Benzing 1955: 967–73). In the diphthongal combination **-a.i*- in the proto-Tungus interrogative **xa.i*-, there was no contrast between front **i* and back **ï*, i.e., the original contrast had been neutralized in this position sometime earlier in the prehistory of Tungus. But it is clear from other evidence that the -*i*- vowel here derives from an earlier back **ï*, and that **xa.i*- represents in fact a later development of earlier **xa.gï* (Benzing 1955: 1062). This means, in effect, that the diphthongal combination **-a.i*- in the proto-Tungus interrogative morpheme **xa.i*- operated within the morphophonemic system of the protolanguage as a back rather than as a front vocalic stem.

This being the case, when the proto-Tungus locative case morpheme *-dū* was affixed to this interrogative stem, this locative morpheme would then also have to appear with back vocalism *u* rather than with front vocalism *ü*, given the requirements and patterns of vowel harmony. Now we know from other considerations (p. 84 above) that it was precisely in those cases where *-d-* originally fell before original back *-u-* that the combination of the two resulted in Japanese *tu* (while the same combination of original *-d-* coming before original front *ü* resulted instead in Japanese *yu*). For this reason, we should regularly expect, in terms of the historical phonology concerned, to have OJ *tu* in these interrogative forms at some early state in their history—and this quite apart from the unfortunately ambiguous evidence of the *man'yōgana* phonograms. The OJ *idu-* interrogatives are most likely to be traced to still earlier, pre-OJ *itu-* interrogatives; and these forms in *itu* not only explain some of the wavering in the phonogram transcriptions in the Old Japanese texts, but far more importantly, they substantiate (and are themselves substantiated by) certain of the basic sound laws by which the phonology of earlier stages of Japanese has been shown to reflect the original and basic dichotomy in Altaic phonology between stems with front and stems with back vocalism.

With this information in hand, we are now in a position to return to a more careful inspection of some of the problems posed by the text of *M* 3549, where we may now with confidence read the word written there with Chinese *īt-tòu* as OJ *idu*, meanwhile understanding that an earlier pre-OJ *itu* probably lies behind this form, according to the materials and arguments set forth immediately above. The poem in question is, once more, an Azuma dialect piece, and hence the Sanseidō editors, for example, suggest (1967: 81ᵇ) that the use of the simplex interrogative *idu* (or *itu*) for 'where?' was an Azuma feature, to which the standard language corresponded with OJ *iduku*. This is an appealing line of argumentation, partly since it would imply that the Azuma dialects maintained a form that was somewhat earlier (because it was somewhat less involved derivationally) than did the central standard language; and also that this earlier (because simpler) form had been driven out, or at any rate replaced, in the standard language by a complex form in which the original interrogative element *itu* > *idu* had been extended by an additional morpheme, originally *-kö* > *-ku* '*place', to result finally in the well-known *iduku*.

Finally, we ought also to note that, by an amazing though of course totally fortuitous coincidence, this same text, *M* 3549, the only one in which this simplex OJ *idu* (or *itu*) is used for the interrogative 'where?', happens also to employ this form in the collocation *idu-yu* 'from whence?', and that in this text OJ *yu* is the same locative-dative particle with whose relation to earlier forms in the cognate languages we have been concerned in detail above (p. 84). Here we have clearly to deal with the result of a generalization, in other contexts as well, of the Japanese form resulting originally from a vowel-harmony fronted variety of the original *du > *$dü$ that, as we have seen above, then resulted in the *yu* 'from' of our early Old Japanese texts.

Among the other Old Japanese interrogatives, OJ *idu-re*, which underlies J *dore* 'which?', deserves special attention. Beside *dore* the modern language also has *izure*, in the same sense; but the latter form, like *izuko*, is again a recent borrowing from the literary language into the modern colloquial. The suffixal element in OJ *idu-re* is of special interest, particularly since it survives in both the modern forms J *dore* and the literary borrowing *izure*. The origin of this -*re* in the old Altaic dual-plural suffix, and its development in these interrogative forms along parallel lines with its development in the pronouns (p. 165 above), at once explains the sense of OJ *idu-re*, J *dore*, as interrogatives of discrimination between, typically, two alternatives.

OJ *iku-ra* 'how much?' is a complex secondary formation that has survived unchanged both in configuration and sense into the modern language; it consists of *iku-*, the combining form of *ika*, plus the same Altaic dual-plural suffix as above, this time in the vowel-harmony form -*ra*. The shape of the dual-plural suffix here is of particular importance, since its -*a* vowel preserves evidence for an earlier *ika-ra stage, before the anomalous alteration of the second-syllable vowel to -*u*-. OJ *iku-tu* 'how many?' also goes closely with the modern form of identical configuration and sense; here the suffixal element -*tu* is to be identified with the similar element found as suffix throughout the Old Japanese numeral system (Miller 1967: 337–38).

3. The second major group of Old Japanese interrogatives is that involving the primary interrogative OJ *nani*. This is a free form that appears as an interrogative in its own right, as well as a form that can also be isolated from a number of contracted forms that appear in the early texts. Some of the contracted forms have survived, along with *nani* itself, into the modern language.

The earliest stages of the language appear to have distinguished those interrogatives involving or based upon *ika* from those related to *nani* along the following general semantic lines: the interrogatives in *ika* were used for 'how?' questions, and for questions on the progress of a matter (i.e., 'how?' something had transpired, or 'how?' it had happened), as well as for questions relating to state and condition, means, and method—all essentially part of the general 'how?' semantic range—while the interrogatives with *nani* were used for questions relating to cause, reason, or objective—all part of a general 'what?' or 'why?' semantic range (Sanseidō 1967: 527[d]).

The modern usage of J *nani* need not be commented upon here in detail, except to note the later development of the contracted allomorph J *nan*, which now appears in regular morphophonemic alternation with *nani*, the original full form appearing in all contexts except before an immediately following form-initial *t-*, *d-*, and *n-*, where the newer and shorter *nan* is now used (Bloch 1970: 33). The form *nan* thus provides an additional and instructive example of the generation of the Japanese syllabic nasal *-n* from an earlier *-ni* sequence (Miller 1967: 215).

In the early texts the most important of the contracted interrogatives involving original OJ *nani* are OJ *nado* and OJ *nasö* (later *nazö* and *nazo*), all 'why?'. OJ *nado* is a contraction of *nani* with a following particle *to*, and is generally employed preceding a verbal, with some animate actor overtly mentioned or implied; OJ *nasö* and its later developments with the expected intervocalic voicing of *-s-* > *-z-* are generally found without the actor element, preceding an adjectival or adverbial expression (Sanseidō 1967: 526[c]). All these forms are contractions of *nani* with a following particle OJ *sö*, which particle itself generally later becomes *zö* > *zo* in all its occurrences. As a result of this most Japanese editors, both in their texts and their lexical aids, have too often lumped together all possible cases of this interrogative contraction under a uniform OJ *nazö*, *nazo*, thus even Sandeisō 1967: 523[b], where the only rubric is *nazo*, but where under this single entry one will find the passage from *M* 3684 in which the text unmistakably has the form OJ *nasö* written in phonograms.

The familiar modern form J *naze* 'why?' does not appear to have an immediate progenitor registered in the Old Japanese texts, but an allegro allomorph, with a characteristic underarticulated initial, to which J *naze* may be related, does occur in the nonstandard Azuma corpus, with OJ *aze* registered in *M* 3461 and *M* 3513. On the basis of this Azuma *aze* 'why?', we may with safety also postulate the existence of the full form **naze*, which however did not find its way into the texts.

All these forms are contractions along the same lines as the developments responsible for the creation of the OJ *nasö*, *nazö*, and *nazo* forms, but with -*ë* for -*ö*, a typical Azuma feature whose importance in explaining other forms in the history of Japanese we have already noted (Miller 1967: 166–67). Once again, it would appear from this additional evidence that it was often the nonstandard Azuma language of the Old Japanese period that provided the ultimate and direct ancestors for many of the modern forms with which we are most familiar, rather than the prestige dialect of central, standard Old Japanese.

4. Finally, we must note briefly the forms OJ *ta*, *tare*, (and secondary *tasö*), all 'who?', the second of which goes directly with J *dare* 'who?'. This set is of course valuable chiefly for the evidence it preserves for a pair of forms, one without, the other with the original Altaic dual-plural suffix that survives here and elsewhere in the language as J -*re* (p. 165); but apart from this fact, the set is not of any great importance for our present purposes, since it proves to have almost no other relevance for the Altaic relationship of Japanese.

OJ *ta* is most common in syntactic structures involving an immediately following possessive particle *ga*. OJ *tare* is used freely in several other contexts with a large variety of grammatical particles following it, except generally the possessive *ga* (Sanseidō 1967:408[c], 451[a]; Yamada 1957: 82).

OJ *tasö* appears to be known in the texts only in the set-phrase or literary cliché OJ *tasökare* 'who is he, that one?', thus in *M* 2240 and *M* 2545. From an early time this collocation also takes on the additional meaning of 'twilight', i.e., that time of day at which it becomes impossible clearly to distinguish a person's features in the waning light of the setting sun, and hence difficult to determine 'who he is'. Eventually, and from Middle Japanese on, the form means only 'twilight'; the modern language has J *tasogare*, but the Portuguese bilingual sources for Middle Japanese still register *tasokare*, with unvoiced intervocalic -*k*- (Sanseidō 1967: 419[d]). Old Japanese also has at least a single instance of *ka Fa tare* 'who is that?' in *M* 4384. Presumably the *sö* involved in OJ *tasö* is again the familiar Old Japanese grammatical particle of identical shape, which later generally becomes *zö*.

Finally, we may note that the voiced initial of J *dare* is without any question the result of an analogic remodeling of the original *t-* initial of OJ *tare*, which took place here because of the presence of so many other interrogative forms with initial *d-* (J *dore, donata, dō,* etc.); meanwhile, as a recent loan into the modern colloquial from the literary language, there is also J *tare* 'who?', which coexists with J *dare* as a specialized form with formal and literary connotations.

Altaic cognates for certain of the suffixal elements appearing in the Japanese interrogatives have already been noted immediately above in the course of the descriptive and morphological treatment of the forms themselves; now it remains to see what comparison with the other Altaic languages can tell us about the ultimate origins of the remaining root morphemes seen in these forms. We shall see that this comparison also provides striking evidence for an original linguistic unity that Japanese once shared with the other Altaic languages. Ultimately, the Japanese interrogative roots *i-* and *nani* can both be connected with quite secure Altaic sources; but the *ta, tare* 'who?' interrogatives remain isolated and are apparently Japanese innovations.

The clue to reconstructing the developments that resulted in the Japanese interrogatives lies in the proto-Altaic interrogative root **jā-*, which appeared together with various suffixal elements in the original protolanguage in such secondary formations as **jāg-, *jān-,* and **jādu,* and probably also in still other related shapes. It is impossible to make precise semantic identifications for each of these secondary forms in the original language, but some idea of the way in which these original formations are attested in the various Altaic languages may be gained from the following rearrangement of some of Poppe's etymologies (Poppe 1960: 32, 33; Poppe 1955: 229–31); in the examples below, the primary morphological division follows the morpheme **jā-,* while **-g-, *-n-,* etc., as written here all go etymologically with the following morpheme:

pA **jā,* in **jāg-,* Mo. *jaγun* 'what?'
    in **jān-,* Mo. *jambar,* MMo. *jan* 'what kind of, what sort of?'
    in **jām-,* Ev. *ēma* 'id.'
    in **jādu,* Ev. *ēdu,* Lam. *jādu* 'why?', Go. *xaidu* 'where?'.

It will be noticed at once that the above data involves Mongol and Tungus exclusively; Turkish (Chuvash excepted) tends in large measure to stand apart from the other Altaic languages as far as the interrogatives are concerned, and in point of fact Japanese proves to preserve more total evidence for the state of affairs in the original linguistic unity in this particular lexical area than does Turkish (again, apart from Chuvash). Turkish has an interrogative root **qa-*, which appears with secondary suffixal elements as **qan-* and **qal-*, but as we have already noted above, it is hardly possible to relate this root either to Altaic or to Japanese. An important exception is the Turkish interrogative root **nä(n)-*, which goes together with Japanese and is of great value in explaining some of the Japanese forms; but, as usual in the Altaic languages, Turkish has in addition its own innovating forms for 'who?', OT *kim*, Chu. *kam* 'who?'.

To understand the nature of the over-all relationship of the Japanese interrogatives to the Altaic materials it is first necessary briefly to consider an important development that must have begun to be operative within Altaic sometime before the final separation of proto-Tungus and proto-Peninsular and Pelagic from the original linguistic unity. This was a typical example of an areal linguistic change, and provided the raw materials, as it were, for later contrastive differences in features that were eventually to distinguish sharply some of the major Altaic divisions, once the geographical dimension of the original linguistic unity had begun to be violated by the increasingly powerful centrifugal drifts that drew the various groups further and further away from their original geographical locus with its more or less homogeneous linguistic unity.

The best attested (and for that reason we must also necessarily conclude the most widespread) type of interrogative in the original proto-Altaic linguistic unity consisted of various secondary formations resulting from suffixation onto the original interrogative root pA **jā-*; of this there can be little doubt. But early in the history of the Altaic linguistic community, and before the geographical and linguistic separation of proto-Tungus and proto-Peninsular and Pelagic from the other languages, i.e., more or less at the time of the proto-Northern and Peninsular Altaic unity, this root itself subdivided into two different varieties, one continuing the original proto-Altaic shape unchanged as **jā-* and its related forms, the other showing an early Northern and Peninsular innovation as a root **xa-* (**xā-* ?); and it was this second form that next served as the root morpheme in numerous secondary and tertiary formations in the Northern and Peninsular languages.

The precise phonological or morphophonological circumstances under which this early Northern and Peninsular innovation **xa-* for the Altaic interrogative arose cannot be recovered at this stage of our knowledge. Perhaps the factors that gave rise to this development will never be completely understood. One would suspect that this new root in *xa- initially arose as an automatically conditioned pronunciation variant of the old original root in *$j\bar{a}$-, perhaps under some circumstances of assimilatory or dissimilatory pronunciation affecting the initial *j- in terms of an immediately following (and probably also a suffixed) consonant. But whatever the conditions responsible for the, at first automatic, change of pronunciation of this initial *j- to *x-, it is clear that at some later, intermediate stage the conditioning factors originally responsible for this variant pronunciation (i.e., 'responsible' in the sense of 'regularly correlating with it') were themselves removed, or for some reason at least disappeared from the language, leaving the now no longer automatic variant established as a new, different, and contrasting form that would in turn be inherited by much of Northern and Peninsular Altaic, and hence would also be of particular importance for the history of Tungus on the one hand and for that of Japanese on the other.

In other words, from the point of view of the Altaic languages in general, and also from the point of view of what we can recover of their earliest phonology and lexicon, these Northern and Peninsular interrogatives in *xa- are the result of an early innovation, and hence they are without value on the comparative level for the history of the earliest stages of proto-Altaic itself (thus agreeing with the position of Poppe 1960: 32, § 21); but when we consider the history of the later subdivisions of proto-Altaic, it is not possible to comprehend all the forms in the various related languages under a single, original, and undiscriminated interrogative root *$j\bar{a}$-, with the result that in this sense it is also necessary to take full cognizance of those subsequent developments that involved this innovating root *xa- (as does Benzing 1955: 989–91 and 1062–63). Hence, although it might appear that Poppe and Benzing differ strikingly in their approaches to the problems in reconstruction that the Altaic interrogatives in general present (and the interrogative forms happen to monopolize the Altaic lexical material providing examples for reflexes of pA *j-), actually their two approaches to the problem are complementary; and when these two approaches are taken together from a slightly more extended historical perspective, they provide precisely that information about the early history of the Altaic languages essential for clarifying the sources of the Japanese forms.

This becomes even clearer when we inspect some of the Tungus forms in detail, since these are the particular interrogatives, within Altaic, with which the Japanese evidence goes most directly. Following Benzing's formulations (1955: 1062–63), original Tungus *xa- (if not, with Poppe, pA *jā-) regularly developed into initial ī- in the interrogatives. Particularly important for comparison with the Japanese forms are Sol., Ev. īdū 'where?' (dat.), īlə̄ 'where' (loc.), and Lam. īdū 'where?' (dat.) and īlə̄ 'where?' (loc.). Both the development of the innovating Northern and Peninsular interrogative root *xa- > ī- and the suffixation with the proto-Tungus dative marker *-du that these forms show have important and obvious parallels in the Japanese materials. Along with Tungus, Japanese in these words further changed the pronunciation of the innovating Northern and Peninsular *xa- in still other directions, to result in Tungus ī-, OJ i-. Also along with Tungus, Japanese formed a number of interrogatives by means of a secondary formation in which an original proto-Tungus locative element -du was compounded with this resulting initial ī-/i-, so that Sol., Ev. īdū and OJ idu, *idu-kö > idu-ku, as well as OJ idu-re, etc., all go together in the closest possible fashion. These interrogative forms provide evidence for earlier common phonological development and innovation, as well as for earlier common morphological processes shared by Tungus and Japanese. The evidence could not be plainer in its indication that the Japanese forms must be the result of a significantly long period of common association of proto-Japanese in a linguistic community together with proto-Tungus, since in these interrogatives the Tungus developments in points of precise detail so closely resemble those in Japanese.

Japanese does not preserve any forms that provide parallels for the Tungus interrogative locatives of the īlə̄ type, nor does it offer forms that, like Udh. jələ, Negd., Ev. ēlā, and Lam. jālā, all 'where?', might show that the original, noninnovating Altaic interrogative root *jā- also, in certain circumstances, survived unchanged despite the competition of the Northern and Peninsular areal developments. Nor does Japanese preserve evidence providing parallels for what might be termed 'earlier' innovating forms, of the type of Go. xaidu 'where?'. Rather, all the Japanese evidence points to what might be termed 'later' innovating forms, of the type of Ev. īdū. (The labels 'earlier' and 'later' are applied here on the basis of the amount of gross linguistic change displayed in the subsequent treatment, within Tungus and allied forms such as Japanese, of the innovating morpheme *xa-, forms of that shape being taken as 'earlier', but forms involving sub-sequent changes in shape, such as *ī/i-*, being considered 'later'.)

The importance for the history of Japanese of such forms as Go. *hadu*, Olc., Udh., Negd. *adi*, Ev., Lam. *adĭ*, pT **xa-dū*, all 'how much?', beside the words going with the extension of this form, i.e., pT **xadū.rā* 'more times', such as Go. *hadora*, Ev. *adīrā*, Lam. *adīrā-dā*, etc. (Benzing 1955: 1062), is obvious, and requires no further comment; of course they are to be considered together with such forms as OJ *idure, ikura*, and the like, with which they are closely connected.

The second Japanese interrogative root for which Altaic evidence is forthcoming is OJ *nani* 'what?'. This form goes directly with OT *nä* 'what?', which latter word is itself to be referred to **nän-*, on the basis of the equative case form OT *nänčä* 'so much'. The Old Turkish equative suffix is *-ča/-čä* (Tekin 1968: 136; von Gabain 1950: 89), and the internal *-n-* in OT *nänčä* is to be explained as an original morpheme-final phoneme that disappeared in the isolation form OT *nä* < **nän-*, but that survived in at least the equative, and probably also in the form (genitive?) OT *neŋ* 'any, whatever, whatsoever' (Tekin 1968: 356; Nadelyayev et al. 1969: 358). Elsewhere in the paradigm of forms constructed by adding suffixal elements to OT *nä(n)-*, e.g., *näkä* 'why?', *näčä* 'how?, somehow', *nämän* 'how?', *nälük* 'why then?', etc. (von Gabain 1950: 100, § 195), this morpheme-final *-n* was eventually leveled out, virtually to disappear by the time of our Old Turkish texts, except in the equative *nänčä*.

Thus, OT *nä* 'what?' goes back, on the basis of the evidence of *nänčä* (and perhaps also *neŋ*), to an earlier **nän-*, and it is this earlier **nän-* that is to be connected directly with OJ *nani*. The comparison is made all the more secure by the nature of the final vowel in the Old Japanese form *nani*; the *-i* of *nani* may now be explained as being due to the fact that the original Altaic root to which the word goes back, along with OT *nä* and its kin, had the *ä*-vocalism, not the *a*-vocalism, and hence it called for a final epenthetic *-i* in Japanese according to the general vowel harmony requirements determining the selection of such nonetymological, morpheme-final vowels added in Japanese. We may also recall the evidence, cited above (p. 79), pointing to the fact that in such words as J *kore, sore*, etc., and their earlier forms, the final epenthetic vowel was an original **-i* that was later leveled out to become the *-e* now familiar from the modern language, though some important traces of earlier **-i* in these forms do survive in the texts. But in the interrogative *nani*, the original quality of the nonetymological final epenthetic vowel has been maintained unchanged throughout the history of Japanese. OJ *nani* and J *nani* both go directly with OT *nä*, and they both end in -*i* because Old Turkish has *nä*, not **na*, for 'what?'. Because of the number of precise historical correlations in matters of exact detail that this etymology provides, it has historical importance over and above its obvious value for explaining the origin of one of the principal Japanese interrogative forms.

This being so, we are also entitled to ask one further question about these forms, namely whether or not they might possibly have some relation to those just treated above; in other words, is it possible to relate the proto-Altaic form underlying OT *nä*, at one geographical extreme of the Altaic linguistic community, and OJ *nani* at the other extreme, with the proto-Altaic interrogative **jä* that, as we have already seen, underlies such forms as pT **xa-*, Tungus *ī-*, and OJ *i-*? The demonstration of such further relationships among these forms turns out not only to be possible but extremely probable.

The initial clue to the course of the historical developments here is the fact that, within the lexicon of Old Turkish, words with initial *n-* are extremely rare. The historical importance of this fact has already been explored in detail above (p. 106); for our purposes here, it is sufficient to note that if we inspect those few Old Turkish words that do appear with this initial, we find that they consist entirely of forms deriving from two sources: the one, loanwords from foreign languages (e.g., OT *nom* < Sgd. *nwm* 'Lehre, Gesetz, Religion, Lehrtext'; OT *nikay* < Skt. *nikāya* 'Schule', etc.), the other, the interrogative OT *nä* 'what?' and its derivatives (Tekin 1968: 82, Pritsak 1963: 33; for the fullest inventory of Old Turkish forms with initial *n-*, Nadelyayev et al. 1969: 354–61). This striking statistical evidence for the lexicon of the language must mean either that the Old Turkish interrogative *nä* and its kin are also loanwords or that these forms are somehow the result of anomalous and sporadic changes within Old Turkish itself. Since there is no likely candidate forthcoming for the role of the foreign prototype form that it would be necessary to identify if we were to attempt to explain this anomalous phonological situation within the Old Turkish lexicon as resulting from a wholesale borrowing of the *nä*-interrogatives, we are compelled to opt for the second alternative.

In so doing, we are actually following up the explanation suggested many years ago by Ramstedt (1915/16: 67; repeated in Ramstedt/

Aalto 1952: 77), who attempted to find in the nasal initial of OT *nä*
and its kin the result of a sporadic assimilation of the original initial
*j- to the nasal articulation of the internal *-n-* in such secondary
derivative forms as OT *näŋ* and OT **näniŋ* (this last form cited by
Ramstedt in 1915/16 and repeated in 1952, although I am unable to
verify it from any other source). The Old Turkish equative *nänčä*,
which Ramstedt does not cite in this connection, would of course provide another excellent phonological context for the generation of this
sporadic assimilatory development.

The ultimate starting point for the developments thus assumed to
have taken place would be, once again, the original Altaic interrogative root **jā-*, in the form of its secondary derivative formation in *-n-*,
thus **jān-*. Sometime in the prehistory of the Altaic linguistic community this root, with its suffixed *-n-* already in place, must have
undergone two sporadic changes: one, a shortening of the stem vowel;
the other, an assimilation of the position of articulation of this now
shortened stem vowel to that of the original initial **j-*, so that the
resultant altered form was now of the shape **jän-*. Finally, this already much altered morpheme underwent still another sporadic
change, this time an assimilatory accommodation of the pronunciation
of the initial to the position of articulation of the now root-final consonant, to result finally in **nän-*, the same form we have already
found it both possible and necessary to reconstruct on the basis of the
evidence in Old Turkish on the one hand and Old Japanese on the
other.

Since this now considerably altered form **nän-* was not only inherited by Old Turkish at one geographical extreme of the Altaic
linguistic area but also by Old Japanese at the other, these sporadic
assimilatory changes must have taken place within the earliest stages
of proto-Altaic and must also have been completed before the breaking
off of proto-Western Altaic from the proto-Eastern branch; we may
also conclude that at the time these changes were being accomplished,
the forebears of the later Japanese linguistic community must have
been existing in close symbiotic proximity with the forebears of the
later Turkish linguistic community, to permit areal sharing of these
unique sporadic developments in the interrogatives. No doubt also the
assimilatory replacement of original **j-* by later secondary **n-* in the
interrogatives was enhanced and facilitated if not actually accelerated
by the fact that original Altaic **j-* fell together with the Turkish
developments of original **n-* and **ñ-* (as well as with the Turkish de-

velopments of original **ǯ-* and **d-*) early in the prehistory of proto-Western Altaic (Poppe 1960: 32). When we recall that the regular reflex for original Altaic **ñ-* is also OT *j-* (Poppe 1960: 36), we are considerably aided in our understanding of the complex milieu of linguistic change in which the remodeling of the interrogative **jän-* > **nän-* was accomplished (see also p. 106 above).

Given the great importance of OT *nä* for the history of the Japanese interrogatives, it is only natural that we also at least ask the question of whether or not, again in parallel with Old Turkish, the simplex form OJ **na* ever actually occurs as an interrogative in the corpus of Old Japanese. Yamada (1954: 86–87) is of the opinion that it does. He states that this simplex form 'is seen to some extent' (*tashō miyuru nari*) in the texts, but the two examples that he is able to cite do not actually support even this very cautious statement. *M* 3430, his first citation, has the simplex interrogative *na* only if a variant of the usually accepted text be read; but reading the text here, as usual, with *yösi*, rather than with **na si*, is not only sounder on textual grounds but also fits in better with the over-all sense of the poem itself. The only other passage that Yamada is able to cite as an example of the supposed simplex OJ **na* is *M* 3684, *na sö kököFa/inönerayenu mo* 'why am I unable to sleep to this extent?'. But here it is clear that we do not actually have the simplex interrogative **na* followed by a particle *sö*, but instead nothing more than another case of OJ *nasö* 'why?', the contracted form that we have already noted above. The form in *M* 3684 is unusual only in that it shows a voiceless variant, with *-s-*, where most other instances, and the later forms in the language, uniformly have voiced *-z-*; but this is its only interest for us, and it does not constitute a valid example of a simplex interrogative OJ **na*. Nor do the usual lexicographical sources and handbooks of Old Japanese offer any other convincing examples of this form.

We can only conclude, as a result, that it is neither historically nor etymologically correct to consider (as does Yamada 1954: 86–87 and the traditional Japanese grammarians generally), that OJ *nani* itself is ultimately a compound of a simplex OJ **na* plus a following particle *ni*. This explanation makes sense only in terms of Japanese taken alone and in isolation—and indeed, as an explanation it is necessary only when Japanese is considered solely in terms of itself; but then in neither of these two circumstances is the conclusion that it embodies actually supported by the evidence of the texts, and hence it is better abandoned. OJ *nani* is not a compound form, but the normal and expected development within Old Japanese of the same original Altaic interrogative that otherwise gave OT *nä;* and the Japanese form goes directly with the combining form OT **nän-* that must be reconstructed in order to account for the behavior of OT *nä* in its own derivational paradigm.

We have already noted above from time to time, when the information appeared to be particularly pertinent to the discussion, a few of the developments of the Old Japanese interrogatives in modern Japanese and also a few of the changes responsible for the shapes that these forms have now assumed in the modern language. Two over-all sets of developments must initially be considered as responsible for most of the linguistic changes to be observed in this lexical area; they are, of course, first, the loss of earlier prefixed OJ *i-*, which in the case of all interrogatives of the *idu-*pattern then left the originally internal *-d-* remaining in form-initial position; second, the remodeling of other forms in original initial *t-*, notably OJ *tare* 'who?', to conform to the now almost universally prevalent paradigmatic pattern of initial *d-* throughout the interrogatives, to give J *dare*. But within these two broad areas of change, there are many other features of detail that are of importance for the history of Japanese. For example, J *dō* 'how?' (cf. J *dō site* 'id.', J *dōmo* 'indeed, anyway') can easily be seen to have resulted from the emphatic vowel lengthening of a modern interrogative root **do* abstracted from such forms as *dore, doko, dotira,* etc. This vowel lengthening is to be compared with the emphatic consonant gemination already noted in *dotti* vs. *dotira;* in other words, the *ō* of *dō* is both morphologically and historically (as well as phonologically) *oo*. But above everything else, it is the pitch configuration and pitch patterns of the modern interrogatives that distinguish these forms within the Tokyo standard language.

The interrogatives of the modern spoken language are distinguished not only by their distribution vis-à-vis the syntactic structures of the language, but also by the fact that all the forms that constitute this set have, in modern Tokyo, a high pitch on their initial syllable (J *dáre, dónata, dóre, dóko, dótira, dótti, dóo; íkura, íkutu, ítu; náni, náze*). The single striking exception to this pattern is J *ikága* 'how?' (Bloch 1970: 56). In any case where we have a single anomaly of this kind appearing within an otherwise homogeneous body of linguistic material, or where we have a single exception of this sort disturbing an otherwise uniform paradigm, it is generally possible to locate valuable clues for the recovery of earlier stages in the history of the language, in terms of the technique commonly designated as 'internal reconstruction' (see Miller 1967: 184–89, and the literature cited ibid. 370). In this respect, the Japanese interrogatives prove to be no exception.

We will immediately recall that all the modern interrogatives in initial *d-* (thus, *dáre, dóre, dótira,* etc.) may be demonstrated, as above, to have derived from earlier Japanese forms that were simplified in the course of their development through the loss of their earlier first syllable, OJ *i-*. (Many instances of OJ *i-* may be demonstrated to derive from earlier **yi-*; such may or may not also have been the case with the interrogative OJ *i-* here under discussion, but the problem is not of particular relevance to the present consideration.) We do not at present understand very well the circumstances under which this, and other similar instances of prefixed OJ *i-*, was lost in the course of the history of the language (see Miller 1967: 201–2); but in the case of the interrogatives at least it certainly appears as if internal reconstruction, based on the data supplied by a study of the position of the modern Tokyo pitch, reveals some if not all of the factors that were operative.

McCawley (1968: 192) summarizes a general, important historical 'rule', i.e., an event in the history of the Japanese pitch, in the following terms: 'The Tookyoo type of accent developed from a system of the Kyooto type by a shift of accent one syllable to the right' (see also ibid. 196, 199). McCawley has stated this rule, i.e., recovered the evidence that this historical event took place, through a combination of the comparison of data from the modern dialects with the internal reconstruction technique. His results do much to clarify our understanding of the developments that transpired within the Japanese interrogative paradigm.

What happened in the course of the history of the interrogatives must have been something along the following lines: when McCawley's shift of the high pitch one syllable to the right took place, resulting in the present-day modern Tokyo forms, the old prefixed initial *i-* was not only suddenly minus the high pitch that it had once carried at a still earlier stage of the language (**i-du-re*), but now it also found itself one syllable removed from the new peak of pitch prominence. As a result this initial considerably diminished in acoustical importance, so much so that it was soon reduced to zero; in other words, earlier **i-du-re* > **i-dú-re* in McCawley's shift, and this then finally resulted in J *dóre*. At this point in the history of the interrogative paradigm, it remained only for the initial of *tare* 'who?' to be analogically remodeled to conform to the now-all-but-uniform initial *d-* appearing throughout the interrogative paradigm, resulting in J *dáre.* The first-syllable pitch on this form is also, like its initial phoneme, surely the result of analogical pressures exerted on the earlier form by the existence of the other set (*dóko, dóre, dótira,* etc.).

We cannot suggest a plausible reason why this shift in the location of the high pitch did not also take place in the course of the historical development of the forms underlying J *íkura, íkutu,* and *ítu,* but with these forms at least two points are abundantly clear: the shift did *not* take place, and hence these modern forms still have the high pitch on their initial syllable (in this sense conforming to the 'classical Kyōto type' of pitch distribution); and it is also precisely in these cases where the pitch location was not shifted (for reasons that still remain obscure) that the earlier OJ *i-* prefix has survived in modern Tokyo, in contrast with its fate in the pitch-shifted set *dóre, dóko, dótira,* etc.

Perhaps it was the earlier form underlying J *ítu* that provided the effective stimulus for the retention of the high pitch on the first syllable in this subset of interrogative forms; after all, *i-tu* is, as we have seen above, a somewhat special type of compound within the interrogative system, consisting as it does of the original interrogative morpheme OJ *i-* in composition with a combining form or allomorph based on OJ *tö* 'time when'. There is no other interrogative in the system consisting of precisely this same type of composition, and so perhaps McCawley's pitch-location shift was inhibited in this form by reason of the unique nature of its composition. But it would be easy to overstress this point, and the tentative suggestion just advanced will not bear undue emphasis.

We must note that the pitch location also was not shifted in the forms underlying J *náni* and *náze,* which as a result constitute still another minor subset within the interrogatives, maintaining their original Kyōto, i.e., historically non-Tokyo, pitch location. If the suggestion made above toward an explanation for the priority of the pitch location on the form underlying J *ítu* is valid, then perhaps the *náni, náze* subset escaped McCawley's pitch shift thanks to the influence, within the over-all interrogative paradigm, of the forms of the *ítu, íkutu,* and *íkura* type, but the point, once again, should not be pressed.

At any rate, and whatever the ultimate reason for the retention of the high pitch on the first syllable in these two subsets of forms may originally have been (and we must remember that several different factors may actually have been operative simultaneously), it is clear that the retention of the high pitch on the first syllable correlates with the preservation of original prefixed *i-*; and it is also clear that in those forms that did undergo the shift of pitch location, this same original prefixed *i-* was lost. The correlation is as significant for the history of Japanese as it is elegant in the demonstration it provides for one of the ways in which internal reconstruction can, on occasion, throw light on the history of linguistic change.

One thoroughly anomalous form among the modern interrogatives still remains to be accounted for—J *ikága* 'how?', with its second syllable bearing the high pitch. The form appears to have undergone McCawley's historic pitch shift from the 'classical Kyōto type' to the normal Tokyo type of pitch configuration; but under these circumstances its preservation of the prefixed *i-* is anomalous. Perhaps this is a transition form, midway, as it were, between the unshifted forms of the *ítu, íkutu* type, and the shifted forms, with loss of *i-*, of the *dóre, dóko, dótira* type; but if so, the reasons for its preservation in this particular shape remain obscure. J *ikága* goes back to an earlier sequence of *ika* plus the sentence particles *ni* and *ka*, as *ika ni ka*, and perhaps the pitch location in J *ikága* is not, in actual historical fact, the result of McCawley's pitch-location shift, but rather a prosodic result of the syntactic collocation of an original **ika* with an immediately following particle sequence . . . *ni ka;* if so, J *ikága* might very well then be an example of the anomalous form that is, in reality, the exception that proves the rule.

Together with this consideration of these modern forms we should also note briefly the etymology of J *dónata* 'who?', which despite its present meaning is both historically and semantically an interrogative of direction. The initial element *do-* is the same modern abstracted interrogative root noted above in the consideration of *dō (dóo);* the final element *-nata* is the same morpheme that is seen in a large set of other pronominal surrogates generated out of expressions of directional circumlocution, thus MJ *sonata* '(lit.) that [middle-distance] direction', i.e., 'you', and the most common word for second-person in the modern language, J *anata*, in which we have *a-* 'that over there' + *-nata*.

The Ryūkyū interrogative forms are, with one important exception, largely comprehensible in terms of Old Japanese; the only exception is R *maa* 'where?', which appears to be a Ryūkyū innovation. Otherwise these forms go closely with their Japanese cognates; thus, R *nuu*

($<$ *noo* $<$ **nayu*) translates J *nani* 'what?'; R *taa* and *taru* go with J *ta, tare* $>$ *dare* 'who?'; and R *²içi* goes with J *itu* 'when?'. Of special interest is the Ryūkyū dichotomy between literary interrogative forms with initial R *²i-*, and cognate colloquial forms from which this suffix (continuing OJ *i-*) has disappeared. Thus, literary R *²ica* goes with and translates J *ika* 'how?', but the parallel form in colloquial Ryūkyū is *caa*, with combining forms based on R *ca-*, typically as in colloquial R *canutuci* 'when?', which incorporates R *tuci* 'time when', the cognate of J *toki* 'id.' Cf. literary R *²içi* 'when?'. The structure of R *canutuci* 'when?' is closely parallel to that conjectured above for OJ *itu* $<$ **i-tö*, i.e., the interrogative prefix plus a combining-form of OJ *töki* 'time when'. (All Ryūkyū forms cited from Kokuritsu kokugo kenkyūjo 1963, passim; cf. ibid. p. 38, for the literary interrogatives contrasted with the colloquial forms and for their Japanese cognates.)

Whenever we deal with Turkish materials on the level of Altaic comparison and historical grammar, it is always necessary to pay particular attention to the evidence that may happen to be preserved in Chuvash, in many ways perhaps the most valuable of all the Turkish languages for historical purposes because of the light it often throws on complex problems of interrelationship among the various languages of this family. The interrogatives prove to be no exception to this general rule.

Benzing presents more or less convincing etymologies for several of the Chuvash interrogatives, but adds that there are also other interrogatives in this language that do not easily lend themselves to analysis; in this category he specifically mentions Chu. *ăšta* 'where?', and *ăštan* 'whence?' (1959: 736). One attempt has been made at proposing an etymology for these words; this would see in them contractions of **xai šĕrta* and **xai šĕrten* 'what land, country,' along the following lines: **xai šĕrte* $>$ *xaišărta* $>$ *xăišta* $>$ *xăšta* $>$ *ăšta*, and **xai šĕrten* $>$ *xăišărtan* $>$ *xăšartan* $>$ *xăštan* $>$ *ăštan* (Yegorov 1964: 44). In nonstandard Chuvash dialects the variant forms *xăšta* and *kăšta*, as well as *xăštan* and *kăštan*, are also attested for this same interrogative *ăšta* of the standard language (Yegorov loc. cit.), and while this fact does help to explain why such an etymology might have been proposed, the implied historical explanation is nevertheless not very satisfactory, mainly for two reasons—first, it makes use, for its prior element, of a form **xai*, which is not actually a part of the interrogative system of Chuvash (though Benzing [1959: 736] invokes Uig.

qayï-si to explain Chu. *xăsĕ* 'which?'), and hence, if the explanation is
to hold at all, it must somehow involve the additional complication of
a loanword or other type of borrowing phenomenon; second, it suggests that we are able to identify the supposedly contracted morpheme *šĕr* 'land, country' simply because of the survival of its initial
-*š*- as the first medial consonant in the supposed contraction *ăšta*.
This -*š*-, after all, would be the only visible, overt connection between
the forms invoked in Yegorov's etymology and the Chuvash interrogative at issue, and as such it simply is not a substantial enough
feature upon which to base an etymology. Explaining Chu. *ăšta* as a
contraction of **xai šĕr* cannot be maintained, and we must look elsewhere for an explanation of the origin of this form.

Ramstedt long ago attempted an Altaic etymology that would have
related these Chuvash interrogatives of place to an earlier form **jada*
(1915/16: 67; 1922: 34). This was a perceptive suggestion that, as we
shall see shortly below, by and large pointed in the right direction; but
unfortunately he was working with an abbreviated Chuvash form, an
allegro allomorph that he cites as Chu. *šta* (an error carried over intact
a generation later in Ramstedt/Aalto 1952: 77). As a result of this
faulty lexical data Ramstedt was unable to go any further in his
analysis of the form; otherwise, given his productive and imaginative
insight, it seems more than likely that he would have succeeded in
solving the etymological puzzle presented by *ăšta*.

Fortunately, this Chuvash interrogative happens to preserve within
itself the necessary clues for its own solution, and it happens also to
provide a veritable textbook case for demonstrating how the findings
of internal reconstruction may be brought into correlation with data
uncovered by the comparative method, to provide finally a rather
complete historical explanation for the form in question.

The first steps are along the lines of internal reconstruction, seeing
what we are able to learn of the prior history of *ăšta* (and *ăštan*)
within Chuvash by simple inspection of the forms themselves. We begin by recognizing that the final -*ta* of *ăšta* and the final -*tan* of *ăštan*
are both suffixes that appear in the shapes -*ta*, -*tan* only when they are
added following back vowel consonant stems in final -*l*, -*n*, -*r*; otherwise and in other environments and circumstances of suffixation these
suffixes have other, strikingly different shapes, notably -*ra*, -*re*, and
-*te*, among other forms (the full statements will be found in Krueger
1961: 105–6; Benzing 1959: 724–25). This identification of these final
elements both as suffixes and also as these particular suffixes is based

primarily upon the meanings of the forms involved. The suffix that appears as -*ta* after back vowel consonant stems in final -*l*, -*n*, and -*r* and is here identified as final in *ăšta* is the locative relational morpheme 'used in the function of indicating the place where something is or where an action takes place'; the suffix that appears as -*tan* under similar circumstances and is here identified in *ăštan* is the ablative relational morpheme, 'used in the general meaning of English "from," or "out of, owing to, because of" ' (Krueger 1961: 105, 106). These meanings fit in precisely with the meanings of *ăšta* and *ăštan*, and are the basis for the preliminary morpheme identification that, in turn, is the point of departure for our internal reconstruction of these forms.

This identification having been made, we may then make our first reconstruction of a prior form on the basis of this identification and assume that the attested forms *ăšta* and *ăštan* were preceded at some point in their history by earlier forms *ăšCta* and *ăšCtan*, where *-C- may have been *-l-, *-n-, or *-r-. This assumption is based on the observed fact that the suffixes in these words are -*ta* and -*tan*, not one of the other shapes possible for these morphemes; but internal reconstruction does not tell us which of the three possibilities, *l*, *n*, or *r*, should be selected in filling the slot just reconstructed above simply as *-C-. Were we in the possession of no additional information about the history of these forms, and if we knew nothing else about the history of the Altaic interrogatives in general, it would be difficult to go beyond this solely by means of internal reconstruction; but fortunately this is not the case, and we are able, at this point in the discussion, to draw upon the resources of comparison with other languages in order to select the *n* alternant, and to reconstruct therefore *ăšnta* and *ăšntan* as prior forms underlying those actually attested in Chuvash. Our reason for selecting *n* rather than *l* or *r* will become clear in the discussion below; all that need be made clear at this point is that this choice is determined by historical considerations, on the basis of evidence from comparison with other related languages, and hence is, at this point, on a different level from the methods and findings of internal reconstruction.

We now assume, therefore, that at some earlier time in the history of Chuvash than our present texts the form *ăšnta* became *ăšta* and the form *ăšntan* became *ăštan*, and also that we may therefore continue our internal reconstruction further back into the history of the language, this time taking as our second point of departure these reconstructed forms. At no stage in its history known to us does Chuvash admit of sequences of three consonants of the order *šnt*, which we have however reconstructed in these two forms (cf. 'Table of Consonant Clusters', Krueger 1961: 85). We must therefore re-interpret these reconstructed forms in terms of the permitted sequences of consonants in the language and assume that our reinterpreted reconstructions in turn result in still earlier forms from the internal history of Chuvash.

At this point several different alternative solutions are, of course, possible, but we elect what is in effect the simplest of these (the simplest, because it reduces the triple *šnt cluster to a permissible double cluster by removing the first of the three—this being essentially a 'simpler' step than would be removing instead either the second or third, because it is the most proximate, i.e., the 'nearest' solution). We assume therefore, that *ăšnta and *ăšntan were the result of a metathesis in which, at some still earlier stage in the history of the language, the š and ă interchanged their positions, and that as a result those still earlier forms involved were *šănta and *šăntan.

Too often, to invoke metathesis in an etymological discussion of this kind seems to be little more than an involved admission of defeat, leaving one with the uneasy feeling that the phenomenon has been introduced only because no other way could be found out of a historical puzzle—in short, that as a historical explanation, metathesis generally is no explanation at all. In the present instance, however, there is rather more to be said for metathesis than is usually the case, in the form of two different but interlocking sets of evidence. First, there is the evidence for the phenomenon of metathesis itself in Chuvash: 'mundartlich nicht selten, in der Schriftsprache hauptsächlich bei k + Sibilant > Sibilant + k, z.B. *-mah-šăn > -maškăn . . . '(für zu tun >) um zu . . .' (Benzing 1959: 710, 740). Therefore we are hardly invoking an arbitrary deus ex machina when we suggest that we have to deal here with a metathesis during the course of the history of the Chuvash interrogative forms with which we are particularly concerned in this discussion, all the more so since it is š that we have concluded was the consonant principally involved in this conjectured metathesis. Of course, this still does not fulfill all the requirements for Benzing's archetypal (*hauptsächlich*) Chuvash metathesis, since we have in our conjectured metathesis only the sibilant element, and apparently no k; but we approach fulfillment of this condition too with our second variety of evidence, that preserved by an extremely important Chuvash correlative set, both members of which are clearly related to the interrogatives at issue. This is the set Chu. *kăštan . . . šanta*, which appears in the following fashion in a text cited in Ašmarin (1919: 4.122): *kayăksem vara, kăštan kilně, šanta kayaššě,* translated 'die Vögel nun, von wo sie gekommen sind, dorthin gehen sie' by Benzing (1959: 736). This extremely valuable text provides several different elements of the substantial evidence necessary to advance our argument: it shows that our reconstruction **šănta* has the parallel of an actual attested form, closely resembling it in both form and meaning, i.e., the *šanta* of this text; and at the same time, in the *kăštan* of this text, it provides another attested form that shows that the prime conditions for a metathesis in Chuvash, namely the combination of a sibilant and *k*, probably did occur in this same morpheme in certain Chuvash dialects at certain times in the history of the interrogatives.

With this evidence in hand, we may proceed to work with our reconstructed form **šănta* with confidence, first removing the suffixal element *-ta*, and then asking what Altaic connections outside of Chuvash in particular and Turkish in general it is possible to suggest for the remaining interrogative root **šăn-*, which we have thus been able both to reconstruct and to isolate.

We will wish to begin, of course, with a consideration of the possible Altaic origins of the initial *š* in this reconstructed form, an essential first step toward an understanding of the ultimate relationships of this form to others from among the various cognate languages, including Japanese.

The usual statements in the handbooks identify Chuvash initial *š* as the normal reflex of proto-Turkish **j-* (thus, Benzing 1959: 710; Krueger 1961: 62; cf. also Poppe 1960: 27 and passim). The formulation goes back to Poppe 1925: 30–31, § 16, and Poppe 1926: 75–76, and hence is one of the older scientific statements of sound correspondences in the entire Altaic field. But a closer inspection of the evidence reveals that this classic statement requires considerable refinement, and that Chuvash *š* is not the only normal, regular reflex of proto-Turkish **j-*, which instead actually appears in Chuvash sometimes as initial *š* and sometimes as initial *y*, each of these two different Chuvash reflexes appearing under conditions that can be stated quite precisely.

a. Chu. *y-* :: pTK **j-* before original proto-Altaic front vowels (keeping in mind always that pTK **j-* derives from a rich variety of historical sources, including pA **j-*, **d-*, **n-*, **ń-*, and **ǯ-*, the last four of which fell together with **j-* early in the history of pre-Turkish).

   1. Chu. *yĕp* 'needle' :: Mo. *ǯebe* 'Pfeilspitze', Mo. *ǯegün* 'Nadel',

Kh. *ǯü* 'id.', Ev. *ǯeje* 'Messerschneide', Chag. *ignä* < **jignä* 'Nadel' (Poppe 1960: 27).

2. Chu. *yĕner* 'saddle', *yĕnerčĕk* 'id.' :: Mo. *nemüre-* 'bedecken, ein Kleidungsstück überwefen', *nemürge* 'Bedeckung, Mantel', MMo. *nemürge* 'Filzmantel', Ev. *nĕmęlē-* 'satteln' (Poppe 1960: 37–38). Note that Poppe adds the important note, to this etymology, 'wenn dieses Wort kein sekundäres *n-* aufweist und nicht auf mo. *emegel*, kh. *emēl* 'Sattel' zurückgeht'; all these words are without doubt interrelated in one fashion or another, due to borrowing and reborrowing of the artifact concerned, but the sound correspondences for the initial *n-* forms and the Chuvash forms cited are all regular, and there is no reason to regard any of them as secondary developments.

3. Chu. *yĕkĕt* 'young man, youngster' :: Mo., MMo. *nekün* 'Sklave, Sklavin', Ev. *nękūn* 'jüngerer Bruder od. jüngere Schwester', Ma. *nexu* 'Sklavin' (Poppe 1960: 38).

4. Chu. *yĕkĕr* 'pair, couple', *yĕkreš* 'twins' :: Ev. *ǯūktē* 'beide', Mo., Mmo. *ǯirin* 'zwei', Mo. *ǯitüger* 'zweite Frau', Ma. *ǯuru* 'Paar' (Poppe 1960: 28). Tungus, notably the Evenki form cited, shows the medial velar consonant of the Chuvash cognate; the Mongol forms demonstrate the original front vocalism of this stem, which appears as part of a variety of extremely complicated morphological structures in the various languages.

5. Chu. *yĕkelĕ* 'acorn' :: Mo. *ǯigde* 'Brustbeere', Ew. *ǯiktę* 'Beere', Oi. *jīläk* 'Beere' (Poppe 1960: 28). Poppe includes Chu. *s̆irla* 'Beere' in this etymology, but to do so it is necessary to suppose an intermediate form that he reconstructs as **jigdläk;* in this reconstruction, the internal cluster **-gdl-* is, in effect, simply a gleaning of all the consonants appearing in this position in any of the various forms brought together in his etymology, the **g* and the **d* picked up from the Mongol and Evenki, and the **l* from the Chuvash, while the *-r-* of the Chuvash form is more or less ignored. But Leb. *jigläk* 'Erdbeere' shows precisely the same internal consonantal configuration as does the Chuvash cognate proposed here.

6. Chu. *yărana* 'stirrup' :: Mo. *dürüge* 'Steigbügel', Sol. *duręŋki,* 'id.' (Poppe 1960: 23, where he also includes this same Chuvash form, accounting for it by an intermediate **jüräŋä*, but not commenting on the development of the initial).

7. Chu. *yălkăs* 'burn, blaze brightly' :: Mo. *nölüge* 'Flamme', Ev. *nul-* 'Feuer machen', Lam. *nulul-* 'flammen', *nurī* 'Flamme' (Poppe 1960: 38). Poppe (loc. cit.) also includes K *nul-* 'brennen' in this

etymology, but probably this word is better kept apart. Martin (1966: 240, ##187, 188) attempts to associate K *nulï-* 'be brown, yellow' either with J *nuru-i* 'be tepid,' i.e., pKJ **nur(u)-*, or with J *niy(e)-* 'get cooked', i.e., pKJ **nyŏř-*. It is clear that all these words involve extremely complex semantic problems and probably also, as a result, blends and contaminations of one (perhaps cognate) root with another; but none of this affects the Chuvash etymology proposed here.

8. Chu. *yăm-yăm xura* 'coal-black' (*xura* 'black') : : Mo. *negüresün* < **newüresün* 'Kohle', Ma. *nemuri* 'Kohlengrube' (Poppe 1960: 38).

9. Chu. *yăvăš* 'sanft, sanftmütig' : : Mo. *ǯügelen* 'weich', Kh. *ǯ̌ölwör* 'weichlich, recht weich', Lam. *ǯulbẹr* 'weich' (Poppe 1960: 28). This root had an original **ȫ*, shown by the Chuvash cognate in which *-ăvă-* is one of the regular developments in that language of this original front long vowel (Poppe 1960: 107).

We note in these etymologies that in (1) through (5) the Chuvash development is initial Chu. *yĕ-*; in (6) through (9) it is Chu. *yă-*; in other words, while in the first five examples the Chuvash form has *y-* followed by the front reduced vowel, in the remainder it has the same initial *y-* followed instead by the back reduced vowel. Since these first nine etymologies illustrate the over-all pattern for the developments in front vowel stems, those examples with the front reduced vowel *-ĕ-* are quite expected; but we must look for some explanation for those cases where instead we have the back reduced vowel *-ă-*. Such an explanation is close at hand in the case of etymologies (6), (8), and (9), where the occurrence of full back vowels in the rest of the word (6), or of a labial consonant in the immediate vicinity of the reduced vowel in question (8) and (9), provided an obvious impetus for the shift from original front reduced to secondary back reduced vocalism. In this connection, only (7) remains obscure.

b. Chu. *š-* : : pTk **j-* before original proto-Altaic back vowels (again keeping in mind the diverse possible Altaic origins for pTk **j-*).

10. Chu. *šula-* 'lecken' : : Mo. *doulγa-* 'lecken', Ev. *dala-* 'belecken', Lam. *dal-* 'id.' (Poppe 1960: 74).

11. Chu. *šul* 'Lebensalter' : : OT *jaš* 'frisch, grün, jung, Lebensalter', Mo., MMo. *nilqa* 'klein, jung, frisch, unvernünftig' (Poppe 1960: 77). Poppe (loc. cit.) also cites K *nalkẹt* 'roh, ungekocht' as part of this etymology; Martin (1966: 232, s.v. #95) suggests the possi-

bility of a connection between K *nal* 'raw' and J *nama* 'raw'; again the problem, which is complex, posed by these Peninsular and Pelagic forms does not affect the Chuvash etymology.

12. Chu. *śul* 'Träne', :: Mo., MMo. *nilbusun*, OT *jaš*, all 'id.' (Poppe 1960: 39, 154).

13. Chu. *śuran* 'zu Fuss', :: OT *jadaγ* 'Fussgänger', Mo. *jada-* 'nicht können, nicht imstande sein, Not leiden', MMo. *jada'u* 'schwach' (Poppe 1960: 32, 154).

14. Chu. *śulśă* 'leaf' :: MTk. *jaburγaq*, Chag. *japraq* 'id.', Mo. *nabčin* 'Blätter', Ev. *naptama* 'flach, eben' (Poppe 1960: 154). Note that Poppe (loc. cit.) has this Chuvash form incorrectly with front vocalism as *śülźɛ*; for the correct form with back vocalism as written here, cf. Paasonen 1908: 141; Krueger 1961: 232; and Yegorov 1964: 217.

15. Chu. *śir-* 'schreiben' :: Mo. *ǯiru-* < *ǯĭr-u-* 'zeichen', OT *jaz-* 'schreiben', Ma. *niru-* 'zeichen, malen' (Poppe 1960: 28).

16. Chu. *śăm* 'Wolle' :: Mo. *noγosun*, Ma. *nuŋgari* 'id.', Go. *ńóŋokto* 'Weidenkätzchen' (Poppe 1960: 73).

17. Chu. *śăban* 'Furunkel' :: Mo. *čigiqan* < *čĭpĭkan* 'Geschwür, Furunkel', Chag. *čĭpqan*, Tkm. *čĭban* 'Furunkel' (Poppe 1960: 26).

18. Chu. *śăvar* 'Mund' :: Mo. *aγur* < *agŭr* 'Dampf, Zorn', Tkm. *aγïz* < *aγŭr₂* 'Mund', Jak. *uos* 'Lippe' (Poppe 1960: 131). Poppe's etymology (loc. cit.) also involves K *akali/akuli*, MK *akwi* 'mouth'; Martin (1966: 234, #119) has connected these forms with J *ago* 'jaw', in terms of pKJ *agɔ, *agu. But it is a little difficult to see precisely how the Chuvash form fits in with Poppe's etymology, there being no overt source in any of the attested forms for the original pTk *j- that would in this instance result in Chu. *ś-*; therefore the etymology has been included here simply for the sake of completeness. On the Japanese and Korean cognates for these forms see pp. 151–52 above.

c. But in addition to the two statements (a) and (b) above, it must also be noted that Chu. *ś-* regularly resulted when pTk *j- was found before original *-e- or *-ė-, long or short in either case, all of which acted in this respect like *back* instead of *front* vowels. Here the Chuvash development was regularly Chu. *śi-* for original combinations of pTk *j- plus either the long or the short variety of either of these original *-e- vowels.

19. Chu. *śi-* 'essen' :: Mo. *ǯeme* 'Wolfsfrass, Aas', Ma. *ǯe-* 'essen', Ev. *ǯew-, ǯep-* 'aufessen', *ǯepte* 'Speise' < *-ė- (Poppe 1960: 106).

20. Chu. *šilĕ* 'Euter' : : Mo. *deleŋ*, Ma. *delen*, Lam. *dẹlŋa*, all 'id.' < *-e-* (Poppe 1960: 126).

21. Chu. *šilxe* 'Mähne' : : Mo., MMo. *del*, Ma. *delun*, Ev. *dẹ̄lin*, OT *jil* (*jĕl*), all 'id.' < -*ė̄-* (Poppe 1960: 106).

Examples of original *-e-*, long and short, contrasting under these circumstances with original *-ė-*, also of both varieties, are suspiciously missing from the Altaic materials; behind this probably lies a clue to the situation at a somewhat earlier stage of the original linguistic unity, in which there was only one undifferentiated phoneme *e*, variant conditioned pronunciations of which later achieved the status of contrasting phonemes due to other linguistic changes elsewhere in the system, resulting in the *e*/*ė* contrast of the bulk of the Altaic materials. We are also reminded by this situation of the case of the Japanese reflexes for *d* or *ǯ* before original *-a-*, *-ä-*, or *-e-*, where, as we have already noted, these three vowels determined uniform developments in Japanese (p. 85 above).

d. Other cases of Chu. *y-* are clearly the result of the automatic development, in the history of pre-Chuvash, of a yodicized glide-onset to an original zero-initial high vowel, either front or back; thus we find Chu. *jĕr* 'Spur, Streifen' : : Mo. *ir* 'Schneide', Bur. *ermeg* 'Rand, scharfe Kante', OT *iz* 'Spur' (Poppe 1960: 81) (cf. J *eri* 'collar, edge of neck opening of a garment' ?), from original *-i-*; and Chu. *jăran* 'Furche' : : Mo. *iraɣa* 'Spur, Furche, Spur auf dem Wasser', Ma. *irun*, with original *īr₂an* (Poppe loc. cit.). But with other vowels, the Chuvash forms have preserved the original zero-initial, thus Chu. *ir* 'früh, Morgen' : : Mo. *erte* 'früh', from *ē* (Poppe 1960: 106); Chu. *ar* 'Mann', from *ār* (loc. cit.); and Chu. *atte* 'Vater', from *etike* (Poppe 1960: 103). These examples incidentally throw further doubt on etymology 18 above, in which the initial of the Chuvash form seems to be without any overt origin in the supposedly related forms.

e. A residue, in the form of one important exception to the above formulations, remains to be commented upon. This is the problem presented by the relationship of Chu. *šĕr* 'hundred' to OT *yüz* 'id.' We would, of course, according to the above statements, expect instead Chu. *yĕr* for this form, and hence we must ask if it is possible to suggest reasons that might have been responsible for upsetting the regular sound correspondences in this particular case. If *šĕr* : : *yüz* were to be accepted as a regular correspondence, we would have to abandon instead the large amount of evidence presented above that points in the opposite direction, simply in order to salvage this single example; and important as the word involved is, we are not justified in disregarding the clear evidence of regular developments in all the other forms already cited simply in order to accommodate this single form. Chu. *šĕr* :: OT *yüz* therefore, must be the exception, rather than the rule, and we must next attempt to find at least some plausible explanation for how this exception may possibly have arisen. The exception will, however, remain an exception, with or without such a reason, no matter how plausible it may be; nor would the lack of a plausible reason make it any more or less of an exception. Our ability or inability to suggest what might possibly have happened in this particular case to interfere with the regular sound developments has no essential or direct relationship to the formulation of the historical phonological developments one way or the other. But fortunately, in this particular case, a very likely explanation for the observed forms, and their departures from the sound laws, happens to be forthcoming.

The correspondence Chu. *-r* :: Tk. *-z* in the word for '100' immediately shows that the original final consonant in this word was pA *r_2 (Poppe 1960: 81, and above, p. 122); and it is this essentially front, palatal phoneme *r_2 that appears to have been responsible for the analogic shifting of an original back *-u-* vocalism in this word to the front *-ü-* vocalism now common in most of the attested Turkish forms. It is significant that unshifted, back *-u-* versions of this word have also persisted in at least a few varieties of Turkish. We may with confidence cite modern Uigur *yuz* '100' (Pritsak 1959: 547); and Yegorov (1964: 211) gives other cognate forms with *-u-* rather than *-ü-* (though his etymological glosses do not, in general, inspire our confidence in the accuracy of the forms that he cites; in this case, for example, in the same line of type he includes two different Qara-qalpaq forms for '100', one with *-ü-*, the other with *-u-*! The correct Qara-qalpaq form appears to be *džüs*, Wurm 1951: 565). The old Volga-Bulgarian inscriptions write the word for '100' with Arabic *jiim + w + r*. Benzing (1959[b]: 692, 693) uniformly vocalizes this as *$\text{*}ğür$*, but since Arabic initial *jiim* is used in these inscriptions in words with both back and front vocalism, there is no overt reason why the form in question might not just as well have been *$\text{*}ğur$* in these early, pre-Chuvash inscriptions also. In fact, Poppe so transcribed it in his original, classic treatment of Chuvash historical phonology, where he wrote the form as *ǰur* (1925: 31). The use of Arabic *ǰīm* to write the initial deriving from earlier pTk **ǰ-* that later, as just described above, became Chu. *š-* in certain environments and Chu. *y-* in others, is uniform throughout the old Volga-Bulgarian inscription corpus (Benzing 1959[b]: 693). It is difficult to interpret this orthographic evidence with any great confidence or precision; Arabic *ǰīm* here may have been intended to represent the affricate [dž-] or the spirant [ž-]; at any rate, the sound in question was almost surely voiced, and this in turn reminds us of Poppe's original suggestion, in his first attempts at a formulation of the Chuvash reflexes for pTk **ǰ-*, that the Chuvash representations in *š-* were in effect a devoicing, in pre-Chuvash, of an original **dž-*, phonetically intermediate between the original **ǰ-* from which it had developed and the *š-* that he found in Chuvash (Poppe 1926: 75–76, § 18, where he now, however, writes *džür;* cf. Menges 1947: 35).

To sum up our hypothesis on the causes probably underlying this aberrant correspondence Chu. *šer* :: OT *yüz* '100', the earliest form that we are able to recover for this word is pA **dūr₂* '100' (the reason for reconstructing an Altaic **d-* rather than an original **ǰ-* initial in this form will become clear below). This, the oldest form that can be reconstructed for '100' in this language family, left direct traces in forms surviving in a few of the Turkish languages, typical of which are modern Uig. *yuz*, with the original front vocalism. It was from this ancient shape, with its original, unaltered vocalism, that the Chuvash reflex directly derives, showing as it does the regular development of Chu. *š-* rather than *y-* because of the back vocalism original in this root. But early in the history of Turkish (but significantly, *after* the establishment of the Chuvash form in question), the front, palatal **r₂* that was final in this word caused the vowel to be shifted from back to front, leading directly thereafter to OT *yüz*, and also to all the other forms with *-ü-* commonly attested throughout Turkish. Old Volga-Bulgarian *ǧwr* in Arabic script may very well stand for the old unshifted **ǧur*, with *ǧ*, Arabic *ǰīm*, writing either [dž-] or [ž-].

Once again, this particular explanation may seem to be a little less ad hoc if we are able to cite a parallel development in another unrelated, but phonetically very similar, word, which fortunately we are able to do. The form in question is one of the elements of the common Altaic lexicon for which we have available on the comparative level what are, in many ways, some of the richest materials that can be recovered anywhere in the area, namely those forms going with pA *dür₂i* 'Aussehen, Form, Gestalt, Figur, Gesicht'. On the reconstruction of this form, and its cognates in the various languages, cf. Poppe (1960: 23) for the initial, ibid. (82) for *r₂*; ibid. (135, 138) on *-i;* and ibid. (111) on the first-syllable vowel *ü*. Note that Poppe (1960: 111) reconstructs this first syllable as short *ü*, as written here, and adds, 'Die Länge im Jakutischen muss sekundärer Herkunft sein' (the Jakut cognate *süs* 'Stirn' would otherwise and normally indicate an original long vowel); but earlier and in different contexts Poppe had reconstructed an original long *ü* in this form expressly for the purpose of accommodating the Jakut reflex (Poppe 1959: 674). The problem cannot be resolved at this point, but fortunately it has no direct bearing on the present discussion.

The Japanese reflex of pA *dür₂i* is OJ *irö* 'color, facial expression'; on this form and its phonological relation to its Altaic cognates, cf. Miller 1967: 70–73. Today J *iro* is common not only in the sense of 'color, facial expression' but also meaning 'sexuality, sexual activity', and the historical connection between these two apparently rather disparate areas of meaning is worth a moment's consideration. One is tempted to assign the meanings of 'sexuality, sexual activity' in Japanese to an extension of semantic range under the influence of the Chinese script; the logograph *sè* (5445) is used, in Chinese, to write two homophonous (and/or etymologically connected?) words, ¹*sè* 'color' and ²*sè* 'sexuality'. It seems quite natural to assign the parallel semantic configuration of J *iro*, which in all its meanings is normally written with the same Chinese graph *sè* (5445), to the influence of Chinese upon Japanese (thus, Miller 1967: 293). But more careful consideration of the Japanese lexical evidence, and also a study of the comparative Altaic data, shows that this is probably an oversimplification. Old Japanese has *irö* in the sense of 'color, hue', but also already with adumbrations of its future semantic range in the collocation *irö ni idu* 'to show [romantic, conjugal emotion] in one's facial expression', as for example in *M* 301 and *M* 3560 (this last text has *irö ni dete* in phonograms, obviously contracted from *iro ni [i]dete*). Ōtsuki (1932: 1.367ᵈ) indulges himself in a thoroughly engaging even though absurd attempt at an etymological explanation of the 'sexuality' semantic value of J *iro* by deriving it from *iroka* 'women's facial makeup'. Much more to the point is his comment that the meaning is established from Middle Japanese of the Heian romances on, a statement that is substantiated by the citations he collects.

On the comparative Altaic level, it is clear that this same meaning of 'sexuality, sexual activity' can also be traced, in the form of Chu. *yerške* 'liebhaber, geliebte; konkubine' (Paasonen 1908: 23), in which *-ške* is a diminutive suffix (Benzing 1959: 717). Ašmarin (1929: 4.285) lists the same form, and includes the following text-example: *văl tatax tapănnă, tet, ančax yereyman ăna văl* 'id efficere non potuit, ut cum femina coiret' (loc. cit., 281). Sirotkin (1961: 95) registers *yerkĕn*, in the same senses as Paasonen's *yerške*. We can only conclude, from this Altaic evidence as well as from the early Japanese lexical evidence, that both the semantic areas 'color, facial expression' and 'sexuality, sexual activity' were associated with pA *$d\ddot{u}r_2i$*, and that all these meanings, as well as the form itself, are part of the Altaic inheritance for this morpheme in Japanese. The congruence of semantic areas in the case of Chinese *sè* is either sheer coincidence, which does not appear likely, or else an instance of interlingual areal calque developing at some period far too remote ever to be recovered. Chu. *yer-* in *yerške* and allied forms continues both the original Altaic form for this word, with its front vocalism giving the Chuvash initial *y-*, and one of its original Altaic meanings. At the same time, it is also possible to detect other traces of this same Altaic root in still another Chuvash word, this time Chu. *săr* 'Farbe', together with which we should also probably consider Chu. *sară* 'yellow, fair, beautiful'. The initial in Chu. *săr* is, of course, still another problem, and it would seem reasonable to suspect this form of being a loan into Chuvash from some language in which earlier *š* < *$*j$-*, etc., has regularly been shifted to *s* (cf. the Jakut developments summarized in Poppe [1959: 678] for examples of this type of linguistic situation within Turkish, without attempting to identify Jakut as the actual source of this particular borrowing). If this can be accepted, then the original *$*š$* underlying the initial of Chu. *săr* is still an aberrant development, since original *$*d$-* before *$*\ddot{u}$*, long or short, should have given Chu. *y-* (and, we may safely assume, so also in the nearby language from which Chuvash may have borrowed this form in the first place), as in Chu. *yer-*. But here again, the form contained *$*r_2$*, which may once more be suspected of having brought about an analogical shift from a still earlier original back *-u-* vocalism, the stage responsible for the Chuvash form, to the *-ü-* vocalism that we reconstruct on the basis of the Altaic materials *apart from* Chuvash.

Among the several other important problems that the Altaic words for '100' present (few of which can be treated here in detail), perhaps the most interesting is that of their possible relationship to the words for '10'. In Tungus we may reconstruct pTg *$\check{z}uwan$ '10' (Benzing 1955: 1049), which goes closely with OJ *töwö* '10' (Miller 1967: 338). If we postulate *d- rather than *$\check{z}$- as the initial of the earliest re-coverable form for '10', *$duwan$, and remove the final suffix *-wan from this form, replacing it with the dual-plural index *-r_2 (i.e., OT -z, etc.), we can then reconstruct pA *$d\bar{u}$-r_2 '100', semantically and morphologically 'tens', and taking us back to a point extremely close to the shape of the original earliest form for '100' in Altaic that we were able to recover above. Ramstedt attempted to involve K *cul* 'line, rope, string of things' with his etymology for '100' (1949: 43), but this surely cannot be maintained; the form goes instead directly with J *turu* 'id.' (Martin 1966: 243, #226). Nor should the partial overt resemblance between pTg *$\check{z}uwan$ '10' and pM *$\check{z}a\gamma un$ '100' (Poppe 1955: 248) probably be considered to be significant for the history of either of these forms.

At last, then, we are in a position to relate the Chuvash interroga-tive *$\check{s}\breve{a}n$- to forms of similar meaning and shape in the other Altaic languages, including Japanese; *$\check{s}\breve{a}n$- goes regularly with pA *$j\bar{a}n$-, the original Altaic interrogative as reconstructed by Poppe (1960: 32). The initial correspondences are normal; the Chuvash vowel is the back reduced -$\breve{a}$-, here for original *-$\bar{a}$-, but appearing as the reduced vowel because of the full -a- vowel in the second syllable of the attested form Chu. *ăšta* (cf. Benzing 1959: 703). The correspondences of the morpheme-final consonant *-n are also unexceptionable. We may also note that there is an exact parallel between these forms and the correspondences in another phonetically similar but totally unrelated root, pA *$ju\eta$ 'Wolle', Chu. *šăm*, Mo. *noγosun*, Ma. *nuŋgari*, etc., al-ready cited above (see Poppe 1960: 73).

From this we may conclude that the forms anterior to Chu. *ăšta* must have been established in pre-Turkish before the development of the characteristic Turkish variant for the interrogative morpheme, with secondary front vocalization, as *$j\ddot{a}n$- (with the vowel long or short), which underlies, as we have seen above, both OT *nä* and OJ *nani*. Chu. *ăšta* clearly points to the earlier, preassimilatory back vocalism of the original Altaic root in *-$\bar{a}$-, just as the Old Turkish and Old Japanese forms point with equal clarity to the later version of this root in which the vocalization has been assimilated to the place of articulation of the initial *j- of the form.

But by a curious coincidence it is also possible to trace this secondary **jän-* in Chuvash, in the form of Chu. *yeple* 'what sort of; how?; thus'. The initial and first-syllable vowel of this form are both precisely what we would expect as normal developments of an earlier **jä-* sequence; the ending in *-le* can be explained by a glance at some of the case forms of the other interrogatives, notably *měnle* 'how?', and *měnli* 'what sort?' < *měnle* (see Benzing 1959: 737). Only the internal *-p-* of *yeple* remains unexplained; perhaps it is to be referred to a sporadic development, in this particular environment, of the labial final of pA **jā-ma* 'what sort?' (Poppe 1960: 32).

This confronts us, finally, with Chu. *měn* 'what?', the last of the three Chuvash interrogatives upon whose origins we may throw at least some degree of light by comparison with the other Altaic materials, including the Japanese. Benzing has speculated about the etymology of this form in the following laconic terms: '*měn* (< **min?*, vg. osm. Fragepartikel *mi* ?)' (1959: 736); but a more fruitful source of a possible etymology exists, in the form of J *mono* 'thing, something'. We may concern ourselves first of all with the phonology, then with the semantics, of this comparison.

In the area of phonology, there is nothing remarkable to comment upon, and no particular problems present themselves. OJ has *monö*, and there appear to be no unambiguous phonogram texts dating from that earlier period in which the language distinguished between *o* and *ö* following *m-* (Sanseidō 1967: 743c); but since Old Japanese *o* and *ö* did not occur in the same morpheme (Miller 1967: 197), it is probably safe enough to write OJ **mönö*, since the *ö*-vocalization of the final syllable of the form is secure from our knowledge of the written records. Chu. *měn* would be the normal development of an earlier **mön-*; we may compare Chu. *věler-* 'töten' < **öl-ür-* (Benzing 1959: 706–7), going with pA **-ö-*, cf. Mo. *ötel-* 'alt werden', *ötegü* 'alt, Greis', MMo. *ötegüs* 'die Ältesten' (Poppe 1960: 108). With this same root Murayama Shichirō (1962: 110) has convincingly compared OJ *ötöröF-u* 'grow old, become decrepit', where the final *-F-u* is a durative base-enlarging suffix.

Semantically the comparison is of great interest. J *mono* is of course best known simply as a word for 'thing, something', and it may be difficult at first to see in the semantic range of the present-day word any trace of the original interrogative sense that this comparison would imply. In earlier texts, however, and in certain set expressions that the literary language has preserved intact (some of which have, in turn, been borrowed from it into the modern language), there are ample traces of the original interrogative sense of J *mono*. This comes out perhaps most clearly, for example, in passages such as one in the *Izumi Shikibu Nikki* (NKBT ed., p. 440), where we have *mono no eda* 'a certain branch, some kind of branch or other'. But this word is nothing more or less than the same essentially (and originally) interrogative *mono* that appears in such famous set-expressions as OJ *monökanasiki* 'somewhat, somehow or other sad' (e.g., M 723, M 4141); these are the *mono* + adjectival structures that the modern Japanese grammarians, significantly, paraphrase as '*nañ to naku* . . . [adjective] . . . *de aru*' (see Nakada 1963: 1002ᵇ). As such, they have provided Japanese literary aestheticism with one of its most notable devices. Motoori Norinaga's (1730–1801) employment of the cliché *mono no aware* as an epitome for all Japanese classical literature is too well known for further detailed comment here; it will be sufficient, to make the point necessary for this proposed etymology, to cite briefly a recent attempt at an English paraphrase of Motoori's commentary on *mono no aware:*

Mono literally means "thing(s)"; so *mono no aware* would mean "a deep feeling over things." [but note that, significantly, it does not!—RAM]. Norinaga explains the meaning of "things": "*mono*," he says, "is a word which is added when one speaks in broad terms." *Mono*, in other words, generalizes the meaning of *aware* . . . (Ueda 1967: 200).

Motoori knew his texts, and the language in which they were written; he knew that *mono* in *mono no aware* had almost nothing to do with *mono* 'things', and certainly nothing at all to do with *mono* 'person' (begging the question of the relationship, if any, between these two). He detected its earlier, basically interrogative sense from the survivals of this meaning in certain passages in the early texts, and from the more important survivals in a handful of literary and aesthetic clichés. For him, he makes it clear, *mono no aware* had nothing to do with 'things'; it was rather a feeling or sensibility (*aware*) modified by 'some, certain, some . . . or other' (*mono*).

To this same semantic area may also be assigned the well-known Heian expression *mono no ke* 'evil, unclean, inauspicious spirits', originating in a taboo-avoidance circumlocution meaning roughly 'some spirit (*ke*) or other'.

The historical relationship between the interrogatives and the indefinites in Japanese is a complex problem upon which we cannot enter here, although of course even the brief consideration of the various historical meanings of *mono* above inevitably brings it to our attention. In the modern language, and generally throughout the history of Japanese, the interrogatives become indefinites with the addition of further interrogative layers, either in syntax or composition, so that we have J *nani* 'what?', but *nani ka* 'something'; and J *itu* 'when?' but *itu ka* 'sometime, whenever'. The various semantic and comparative problems that this situation involves have been discussed in considerable detail by Haguenauer (1956: 587–98), and while his treatment is both inconclusive and discursive, it will nevertheless serve as a useful point of departure for any future treatment of this extremely involved topic. We will content ourselves here by noting the fact that the Japanese grammarians, out of consideration for this special feature of the interrogatives, actually list all these forms in their grammars not as interrogatives at all but rather as 'indefinites' (*futeishō*); in other words, for the Japanese grammarians, the indefinite senses and employment of these forms are primary, while their interrogative meanings and uses are all secondary (cf. Lewin 1959: 53, 98).

Finally, there is the problem of the Korean evidence, which in the case of the interrogatives is particularly disappointing. Martin does not treat these forms at all in his attempt at a reconstruction of the proto-Korean-Japanese lexicon, probably because they are, in his sense of the terms, 'grammar' and not 'lexicon' (though this does not prevent him from including items such as K . . . *to*, J . . . *do*, 'although', 1966: 225, #4). Whatever his reasons, we unfortunately do not have the benefit of the light his study of these forms would surely have cast upon the problem. K *muës* 'what?' probably involves an encapsulation of K *kës* 'thing', which in turn goes together with J *koto* 'id.' (Martin 1966: 244, #239, pKJ **kes*). Perhaps this points in the direction of J *mono* 'thing, something', taken in its interrogative uses as noted above. In K *ënce* 'when?' and K *ëtä* 'where?' the initial *ën-*, *ë-* element may possibly go together with the original Old Japanese interrogative *i-*, since K *ë* does in a few cases apparently correspond to J *i;* note that for this correspondence Martin reconstructs pKJ **yi* (1966: 213, #15c). But beyond this it is difficult to go; and we must regretfully conclude that the Peninsular evidence casts very little light indeed upon the relation of the Japanese interrogatives to those in other Altaic languages.

5.3 Numerals

The Old Japanese pronouns and interrogatives, as we have seen above, preserve exceptionally valuable materials for Altaic reconstruction. At the same time that the comparison of these Japanese forms with those in the other Altaic languages helps us to recover many of the historical events ultimately responsible for the presently attested forms in all these languages, it also irrefutably establishes the genetic relationship of Japanese to the original Altaic linguistic community.

The Altaic numerals present another and strikingly different kind of problem. They are not a particularly rewarding area for the activities of the comparative linguist, who in surveying the evidence is more than once tempted to conclude that they were especially devised to try both his patience and his ingenuity. In fact, so great are the problems that this portion of the Altaic lexicon presents to the comparativist that they have on occasion been advanced as grounds for abandoning all attempts to recover proto-Altaic. This extreme position (of which Kotwicz 1929/30 is the classic example) need not concern us further here, even though it is not difficult to understand how investigators have, from time to time, been tempted to adopt it (see the discussions in Benzing 1953: 9, Poppe 1954: 465, Lee 1963: 99, and Poppe 1965: 134).

That there has been widespread borrowing of numerals in all possible directions among all these languages at many different times and in several different places is the first and most obvious conclusion to be drawn from even a cursory inspection of the evidence. The words for '4' offer the most complete representation of a uniform, original numeral root throughout the Altaic languages, including Japanese, and hence this numeral is more securely established for the original common linguistic unity than is any other single element in the numeral system. But even in the case of '4', it is evident that the Turkish forms, while ultimately related, are not direct genetic inheritances from proto-Altaic, since a regular genetic relationship would have given, instead of the actual attested forms, an Old Turkish form with initial *j-*, and a Chuvash form with initial *š-* (Poppe 1960: 110; Ramstedt/Aalto 1952: 62) or *y-* (see also above, p. 206). But Ramstedt's attempt (loc. cit.) to bring Korean into line with the rest of the Altaic forms is not successful. He cites Korean *turi* as meaning '4', but the form means '2 [people]'; and his so-called North Korean citations *ndujin*, etc., simply give orthographic expression to the optional, automatic, and nonsignificant *-d-* off-glide

TABLE 7

The Altaic Numerals

	Old Turkish (Orkhon)	Chuvash	Written Mongol	Dagur	Proto-Tungus	Manchu	Old Japanese	Korean (Middle Korean)
1	bir	pĕr	niken > nigen	neke	ämün	eme	Fitö-tu	hana (hɔnah)
2	iki (eki)	ikĕ	qoyar¹	hoire²	žör	žuwe	Futa-tu	tul (tulh)
3	üč	višĕ	γurban	guarebe	ilan	ilan	mi-tu	sëy(s) ~ sëk (sëyh)
4	tört	tăvată	dörben	durube	dügün	duin	yö-tu	nëy(s) ~ nëk (nëyh)
5	biš	pilĕk	tabun	taau	tuñga	sunža	itu-tu	tas(ŏs) (tasos)
6	altï	ultă	žirγuγan	jireuoo	ñöñün	ninggun	mu-tu	yŏs(ŏs) (yĕsĭs)
7	yiti (yeti)	šičĕ	doloγan	doloo	nadan	nadan	nana-tu	ilkop (nilkup)
8	säkiz	sakăr	nayman	naime	žapkun	žakûn	ya-tu	yĕtëlp (yĕtĭlp)
9	toquz	tăxăr	yisün	ise	xüjägün	uyun	kökönö-tu	ahop (ahop)
10	on	vună	arban	harebe	žuwan	žuwan	töwo (*töwö?)	yĕl (yĕlh)

¹ cf. ǯirin 'two [women]'

² cf. ǯiee 'the second'

TABLE 7—Continued

	Proto-Altaic	Old Turkish	Proto-Mongol	Proto-Tungus	Proto-KJ	Old Japanese	Korean
1	*bir- (*bīr₂-?)	bir	--	--	*pil-ó-	Fitö-	pilos
2	*dir₂- > *ǰir₂-	--	*ǰir-	*ǰör	*dul	Futa-²	tul
3	--	--	(*γu-)¹	--	--	//mi-//³	--
4	*dör-	[tört]	*dör-	*du-	--	yö-	--
5	*ta- (?)	--	*ta-	*tu-	*t-?-	i-tu-	ta-s(ës)
6	--	--	((*ǰir '2' + *γu '3'))	[*ñöŋ-]	--	//mu-//	--
7	--	--	*dal-	[*nada-]	--	nana-	--
8	*de-(*dä-)	((säkiz '10,2'?))	--	*ǯa	--	ya-	--
9	--	--	--	((*γu '3' + *γu + -n))	--	((kökönö-))	--
10	--	--	--	*ǯuw-	--	*töwö	--

¹ Cf. OJ and Tungus '9', and Proto-Mongol '6'.
² Remodeled from *yuta-.
³ But cf. Chuvash *viśĕ* '3', etc.?

Key:
[ ]   loanwords
( )   not cognate with Old Japanese
(( ))   compound numerals
// //   no secure Altaic connections

pronunciation normal for every initial *n-* in Korean, so that the only completely accurate Korean form that he cites in this entire passage is *nĕj*, i.e., the equivalent in his transcription of our *nëy(s)* ~ *nëk;* and this form cannot be brought into any meaningful association with the general and original Altaic word for '4'.

It is easy to speculate concerning some of the causes ultimately underlying this widespread phenomenon of borrowing in the Altaic numerals—easy, even though the exercise is not particularly fruitful. Numerals easily become attached in various complex fashions to systems of religious belief and superstition. Even in modern times the Japanese avoidance of certain numeral forms in particular contexts, and the rationalization of these practices of avoidance and substitution in terms of other 'unlucky' or 'inauspicious' homophonous forms is a well-known phenomenon. The principle is the same, even though in modern Japanese it usually concerns the avoidance of certain Chinese loanword numerals and their replacement with original and native Japanese lexical elements.

Thus, if we are incautious enough to ask a modern Japanese 'why' the current term for the fourth hour of the day interrupts an otherwise regular series of Chinese loanword numerals (*ichiji* '1:00', *niji* '2:00', *sanji* '3:00', *goji* '5:00', etc.) and combines the native Japanese numeral for '4' with the Chinese loanword *ji* 'hour of the day', resulting in *yoji* '4:00', we will almost surely be told that this happens 'because' the Chinese loanword *shi* '4' is unlucky since it is a homophone with the Chinese loanword morpheme *shi* 'death', and because any expression of time involving *shi* '4' would hence sound extremely inauspicious: 'we say *yoji*, not *shiji, because *shiji would sound like (or, mean) "death hour".' But all this does not prevent April from being *shigatsu*, even though we might well imagine that an entire 'death month' would, if anything, be even less auspicious and even more to be avoided than a mere 'death hour'. In most recent times, we know for a fact that *shi* '4' and *shichi* '7' have tended to be replaced by native Japanese *yo* and *nana*, respectively, in telephone conversations simply because the poor acoustic quality and unsatisfactory frequency response of the average Japanese telephone instrument tend to scramble both these numerals with each other, and with *hachi* '8' as well. Purely practical acoustic considerations have led to these common numeral substitutions in modern times; and anciently also, one has probably to look to equally 'practical' considerations of prosody and taste for the ultimate explanation of most of these substitution phenomena, even though this means abandoning many charming fables of rationalization. (It remains only to add that the modern Chinese, at least, make no inauspicious association between *ssù* '4' and *ssŭ* 'death'; of course, the forms are not, and never have been, homophones in Chinese.)

It is not difficult to imagine substitution processes of this kind being repeated over and over again throughout the long history of close contacts among the many Altaic languages, the raw materials for such avoidance-replacement always being close at hand in the form of lexical loans from geographically nearby and often genetically closely related languages. Even though the precise twists and turns of these borrowings and replacements can probably never be completely reconstructed, the modern Japanese evidence shows some of the ways in which they must have happened; and we have the older evidence of the Altaic numerals themselves to prove that these borrowings did as a matter of fact take place many times in the past. But it is neither necessary nor desirable to attempt to push our speculation on this score much beyond these general statements.

Even though the relationships among the numerals in the Altaic languages, including Japanese, have often been very much disturbed and sometimes almost completely obscured in certain of their details by this long-standing process of interlingual borrowing, it is still possible to detect many extremely old patterns in the evidence that these languages preserve, and it is also possible to identify some of the older numerals, in the sense of those numerals for which the evidence surviving in the different languages is particularly well preserved. In the process we can throw some light on the origins of the Japanese numerals as well; at the same time, the Japanese numerals can be shown to have preserved certain features sometimes lost in other branches of Altaic. All this will in its turn help to reconstruct the general course of change in still other areas that without the Japanese evidence would have to remain beyond recovery.

In this same connection, it is important to notice that the Altaic numerals, including those of Japanese, provide excellent evidence showing that numerals in many, if not most, languages are in no way 'basic', in the sense of being particularly resistant to or inhibiting of borrowing. The concept that numerals are somehow a part of a 'basic' stratum of vocabulary, and that they are less susceptible to borrowing than other segments of the lexicon, has its origins in Indo-European studies; but it is plainly mistaken as well as misleading when taken over bodily and applied to the study of languages in other parts of the world, particularly in the Far East. The Chinese numerals have been borrowed into many other languages—Japanese and Thai are both excellent cases in point; and there is additional evidence from as far afield as Dravidian (Emeneau 1957), all pointing in the same direction. Numerals in this part of the world seem fully as likely to undergo borrowing as are any other sets of linguistic forms; and it is clear that they are in no sense of the term 'basic vocabulary'.

The best documented phenomenon for which evidence is forthcoming from among the Altaic numerals is one that may be termed PAIRING. In this, forms adjacent to one another in the numeral paradigm show partial phonetic similarity, to be explained historically as the result of analogic imitation or intraparadigm remodeling. This phenomenon of pairing may be observed in Indo-European ('4' and '5', according to some theories, and '7' and '8' in certain Greek dialects), but while it was in operation in those languages from time to time, it was never a particularly important process in Indo-European. In Altaic, on the other hand, pairing is the single most important phenomenon for a full understanding of the historical developments in the numerals. In Japanese in particular, pairing was eventually to be employed to a considerable degree, and the phenomenon provides, together with an inherited Altaic ablaut derivational device, the historical explanation on one level or the other for all the lower numerals from '1' to '8', with the exception of '5' and '7'.

Though pairing was a generalized Altaic phenomenon, it operated in the numeral systems of the different languages at different times and in different, independent ways. Perhaps as a derivational device pairing was diffused throughout the original common Altaic area, before much of the later geographical separation of the different dialects and languages had taken place. At any rate, it is the key to understanding much of the historical development of the numerals in Altaic.

Pairing shows itself, for example, in Old Turkish *altï* '6', and *yiti* '7'; the suffix *-tï/-ti* is unique, in the Old Turkish numerals, to this pair; or, for another example from Old Turkish, in *säkiz* '8', and *toquz* '9' where again the suffix (the old dual-plural) is unique, among the lower numerals, to this pair. (In Chuvash, which is an *-r* language, this same pairing feature survives, thus Chu. *sakăr* '8', and *tăxăr* '9'.) In Korean pairing is extensive and important: K *sëy(s)* '3' and *nëy(s)* '4' are one such pair, and K *tas(ës)* '5' and *yës(ës)* '6' are another.

Old Turkish continues pairing into the decades in a most striking fashion, so that it has *qïrq* '40' and *ilig* '50', but as another distinct pair *altmïš* '60' and *yitmïš* '70', and what is in effect still another separate pair, this time compounding with *on* '10', for the two remaining, *säkiz on* '80', and *toquz on* '90'.

In these cases it generally is not possible to identify with confidence the prior member of each, i.e., the member of the pair that served as the analogical model for the remodeling of the other member. Once pairing has operated both members are identical, and one is indistinguishable from the other for historical purposes. A few unimportant exceptions to this general statement occur. If in fact, as has been suggested (Ramstedt/Aalto 1952: 64), OT *säkiz* '8' somehow preserves the remains of a contraction in which *iki* '2' has earlier been encapsulated (and as we shall see below, in the consideration of Korean '7', '8', and '9', such encapsulations were by no means unknown in Altaic), then the *-z* is more likely to have been original in '8' and analogically imitated from there into '9', since this would fit better with its role as the old dual-plural suffix. In other words, it seems more likely that this ending would have originated in a form encapsulating the word for '2' and subsequently have been imitated from this form to make up the other member of the pair, rather than the other way around.

In addition to the inherited set of numerals, modern Japanese of course has another set of numerals borrowed from Chinese; in this borrowed set pairing has operated in certain nonstandard Western Japanese dialects, which have *hichi* '7' beside standard *shichi* '7', because of the initial of the following *hachi* '8' (Lehmann 1962:12). Here of course the member of the pair originating the analogic shift is clearly marked. But generally no clues exist pointing to priority for either member in a pair.

It is quite easy to observe in Table 7 how in some of the Altaic languages this pairing went on to spread to other numbers adjacent to the original pairs, and eventually swept through the entire numeral paradigm. It appears to have been particularly popular in proto-Eastern Altaic, to judge from the evidence, and within this Altaic group, the proto-Mongol and proto-Peninsular branches pushed the phenomenon even further than did proto-Tungus. In proto-Tungus a pair distinguished by *-ün/-un* may be observed in '8' and '9'; it appears then to have spread, at least in part, from this pair back up the paradigm (cf. proto-Tungus '7', and '6', and '4', '3'). In Mongol, the process was pushed to completion, so that all the lower numerals have one form or another of this same suffix. In Mongol an interesting and historically significant differentiation may be noted in the words for '2': *qoyar* '2' does not have this suffix, generalized, as we have seen, from an original *-n* pairing somewhere in the paradigm; but it is precisely this same word *qoyar* '2' that is the more recent of the Mongol words for '2'; and the older word *ǰirin* '2 (of women)', Dagur *jiee* 'the second', does appear with the generalized *-n*. We know that *ǰirin* is older than *qoyar* because it is *ǰirin* for which we have the most widespread Altaic evidence, rather than for the relatively isolated *qoyar*. Inspection of the paradigm shows that *ǰirin* dates from the time of the generalization of the *-n* throughout the Mongol paradigm, while the specialization of this form in Written Mongol as a feminine dual, and in other special senses in other Mongol languages, as well as its replacement as the ordinary numeral for '2' by *qoyar*, must post-date this same generalization.

With this process clarified we are now for the first time in a position to understand the way in which the suffix *-tu* was generalized through-out the Old Japanese numeral paradigm. In Mongol and Tungus the parallel generalization of the *-n* extended even to '10'; Benzing (1955: 1049) suggests an analysis of all the proto-Tungus numerals as com-pounds with a final element *-gun/-guan*, and this appears to have been the original form of the proto-Tungus generalized numeral suffix. But Japanese stopped one step short of Mongol and Tungus, and hence Old Japanese '10' does not have a final *-tu;* but otherwise Old Japanese too ended up with virtually complete generalization of a numeral suffix.

The question of which pair, and also of which individual member of that pair, it was from which this suffix *-tu* began its progress toward generalization throughout the Old Japanese paradigm is not an easy one to answer with any degree of confidence. In the Old Japanese decades, the suffixal element for '10' is *-so-ti*. The final *-ti* in the decades is a generalized suffix, similar to *-tu* in the lower numerals, its *-i* vowel to be explained by considerations of vowel harmony operating with the preceding *-o-* (cf. J *futsuka* '20th day [of the month]', but *hatachi* '20 years [old]'; the complete statements for re-lating these forms to Old Japanese would take us too far afield, but the vowel-harmony alternation in the element *-tsu-* ∼ *-chi-*, i.e.,

/tu/ ∼ /ti/, is immediately evident). Japanese scholars (e.g., Ōno 1955: 276–77, 296) often try to associate this *-so-t-* in the Old Japanese decades with K *son* 'hand', but there is neither necessity nor justification for this improbable hypothesis. The form is simply an allomorph of OJ *töwo* (or **töwö*) '10', with internal *-s-* for *t-* in composition; for an analagous *t-/-s-* variation in another form, see Miller 1967: 194. Since the final epenthetic vowel of OJ *-tu* (in the lower numerals) and OJ *-ti* (in the decades) was determined by vowel-harmony with respect to the preceding syllable, what is left to deal with in both cases is simply a generalized suffix OJ *-t-*. Since this is the final phoneme of OT *tört* '4', and also since '4' has the most widespread evidence in common Altaic of any of the numerals, it would not be out of place to assign its origin to some pre-Old Japanese form of the word for '4'. For its initial pairing in pre-Old Japanese, there are two possibilities, '3' or '5'. The first of these seems the more likely, partly again because of the form of OT *üč* '3' (cf. *otuz* '30'), and partly also because of the geminate consonant cluster surviving in modern Japanese *mittsu* '3'. From this pair the *-t-*, with the addition of the final epenthetic vowel necessary according to the requirements of Old Japanese phonology, was eventually generalized throughout the lower numerals, and, with the addition of a different final vowel, throughout the decades also.

Second only in importance to this phenomenon of pairing and the secondary generalization of various elements that resulted from it was the derivation of numerals in patterns of BINARY PROGRESSION characterized by regular vowel alternation in otherwise similar forms, either according to secondarily imitated patterns of vowel variation, or independently developed in one or more of the descendant languages.

It is difficult to know whether or not to assign this phenomenon of numeral derivation by means of binary progression to proto-Altaic. Unfortunately the critical clue as to whether or not such an attribution is correct appears to have disappeared. Old Turkish does not continue the inherited Altaic numerals either for '2' or for '8'; in both cases the original Altaic forms have been replaced by Turkish innovations (see above for a hypothesis about OT *säkiz* '8'; OT *iki*, Chu. *ikĕ* '2' is a Turkish innovation that utilized the common Altaic word for 'twins', cf. Mo. *ikire*, Ev. *igire* (a loan from Mongol?), Chu. *yăkăr*, Azerbaijan *äkiz*, all 'twins' (Poppe 1960: 105). The most likely place to look for evidence on the existence of the phenomenon of binary progression in proto-Altaic is in the sequence '2' :: '4' :: '8';

but Turkish has borrowed, not inherited, the original Altaic form for
'4', and since it has in addition innovated on its own initiative for its
forms for '2' and '8', it provides no evidence for or against the original
existence of this phenomenon in the Turkish branch of Altaic. But
elsewhere throughout this linguistic community we can detect clear
traces of the operation of this derivational device, so it is surely to be
assigned at least to the original unity represented by Mongol, Tungus,
Korean, and Japanese, or in other words, to proto-Eastern Altaic.

The original '2' : : '4' : : '8' progression is attested in these languages in the following fashion. The word '4' is the best attested, but
at least for descriptive purposes (and also perhaps historically) it is
more convenient to take the only slightly less well-attested '2' as the
starting point for the discussion, particularly since this word demonstrates the Japanese reflexes of an important proto-Altaic consonant,
and incidentally provides important evidence for establishing many
additional lexical connections between Japanese and other languages.

This consonant is proto-Altaic initial *ǰ-, which had two origins
not always easy to distinguish from each other. One was an original
Altaic *ǰ, the other a secondary *ǰ resulting from the palatalization
and affricatization of earlier Altaic *d before i/ï, or apparently at
certain times in the prehistory of Altaic, before other front vowels
also (Poppe 1960: 27). It is the second of these two varieties of initial
*ǰ- that is of immediate concern in the etymologies for the numbers
'2', '4', and '8'. The other original Altaic root for which the later
descendant languages provide the most evidence is pA *dir$_2$ '2'; in
this form early in the prehistory of Altaic the original initial *d- was
changed before the following -i- to become *ǰir$_2$-. The source of this
particular case of *ǰ in an original unpalatalized, unaffricated *d may
be established from the other members of the '2' : : '4' : : '8' binary
progression, and also from the Korean reflex, which preserves the unshifted initial, though in Korean it now appears before a secondary
development in vocalization. This secondary proto-Altaic *ǰir$_2$- appears in Mongol as ǰirin (cf. the other cognates for this form, and
documentation on its semantic specialization in the various Mongol
languages, notably as a feminine dual, in Poppe 1955: 243–44; Poppe
1960: 28). In Tungus it developed an -ö- vocalization in a regular
change, thus giving such forms as Evenki ǰūr and Manchu ǰuwe, but
for proto-Tungus we must reconstruct an earlier form with a front
vocalization, proto-Tungus *ǰör (Benzing 1955: 1049), and it is this
original (and Altaic) front vocalization that is one of the most im-

portant clues for tracing the developments in this and the immediately related forms, namely '4' and '8'. Note that Tungus inherited the shifted $*d > *\check{\jmath}$, showing that this change in the pronunciation of the initial took place before original -i- prior to the development of the Tungus vocalization, which is secondary. A parallel change in vocalization was either inherited or imitated in Korean, but in either case the Korean initial shows that this form was inherited or imitated before the shift $*d > *\check{\jmath}$.

This etymology, of course, is primarily contingent upon the statements for the Old Japanese regular correspondences for original pA $*d$ and $*\check{\jmath}$ before original Altaic front and back vowels as already set forth in some detail above (p. 84 ff.), and it is not necessary to recapitulate those statements here. These regular correspondences imply that, in the case of '2', since the word had an original front vocalization, we would expect a Japanese form with initial $*y$-; but what we have instead is OJ *Futa*. It is not difficult to speculate that the initial of this attested Old Japanese form simply represents another instance of pairing, and that the *F* of *Futa* has been imitated from the initial of the previous member of the paradigm. Since the final -r- of the original Altaic form for '2' clearly goes back to the old dual suffix pA $*r_2$, a Japanese reflex in -t-, as in the attested OJ *Futa*, or the regularly expected but unattested $*yuta$, would imply that the Japanese developments are to be related to an intermediate stage in which $*\check{\jmath}$ or its subsequent developments in this root was a continuant, not a stop (see p. 148 ff. above).

Here we must pause to take reluctant issue with one of the etymologies proposed by Martin (1966: 245, #247), who reconstructs pKJ $*tur\chi ye$ '2' on the basis of K *tul* and J *tsure* 'companion'. The etymology and reconstruction are at best only of Martin's category III, 'those with perfect (or very good) fit but with meanings that are somewhat divergent'. By recognizing the operation of pairing and analogic sound-change in this word, and the imitation of the initial of '1' in the Old Japanese word for '2', it becomes possible to replace Martin's category III etymology with what would then be one of his category I, '. . . of equivalent meaning with perfect fit, such that each correspondence of each pair "checks out" when we complete the comparisons'. For '2' we may therefore reconstruct the form pKJ $*dula$. All the sound correspondences involved in this reconstruction, as well as the semantics, are perfectly regular, so that we have $*d :: K\ t :: J\ y$ (but J y has been replaced in this word by F through pairing with '1');

-u- :: K *-u-* :: J *-u-*; *. . . l* :: K *-l* :: J *-t-*; and *. . . (C)a* :: K # :: J epenthetic *-a*.

Martin (1967: 238, #157) has associated OJ *Fitö-* with K *pilos* 'beginning', reconstructing pKJ **piló(su)*. This would in turn go together regularly with OT *bir* and its related forms. Other languages have replaced this numeral with a variety of innovations (with pT **ämün*, Ma. *emu* '1', cf. J *omo* 'paramount', OJ *omo*, Azuma *amo* 'mother'?), but given this remarkable correspondence between Turkish at the one extreme of the Altaic area and Japanese and Korean at the other (even though Korean later specialized its old inherited word for '1' in the sense of 'beginning', and replaced it in the numeral system with an innovation), it is quite safe to refer the original term reflected in OT *bir*, pKJ **piló(su)*, and OJ *Fitö*, all '1', to the common Altaic unity. And it was this old, original Altaic word for '1' that, as we have just seen, was responsible, through pairing, for the initial of OJ *Futa-* '2', a form that otherwise goes exactly and regularly with the even more widespread Altaic form for '2', **dir₂*, reflected in all of the descendant languages with the exception of those of the Turkish branch, where it was replaced with an innovation. Otherwise '2' proves to be remarkably uniform throughout Altaic, including Japanese.

Recognition of the importance of developments resulting from pairing also makes it possible to clarify, in large measure, the detailed sequence of earlier forms underlying Japanese '1' and '2'. We have already noted pA **bïr₂-*, tentatively glossed as '*one', in a set of compounds attesting the earlier existence of pA **bïr₂agù* 'calf in its second year' (see p. 147 above, and Poppe 1960: 21, 60, 81, 131, 146, 147; note that Poppe gives the Osmanli cognate as *buzaγï* on 21 and 81, but otherwise uniformly as *bïzaγï*; Alderson and İz (1959: 47) know only *buzaǧı* 'sucking-calf'). Together with this form, it is of course necessary to consider pA **bir* '1', and while the ultimate connection between these two forms is in part obscure, there can be little doubt that they go closely together. In the sequence of pre-Japanese developments, **bir* '1' and **dir₂* '2' first of all went together, in pairing, to result in **bir₂* (cf. **bïr₂-* above) and **dir₂*; next there developed in pre-Japanese the intermediate forms **Fir₂* and **yur₂*, with the vocalism of this last form possibly related in some way to the vowel of pA **ǯur* 'a pair'; and finally, these intermediate forms were again paired to result in **Fir₂* and **Fur₂*, these last going directly with the attested OJ *Fitö* '1' and OJ *Futa* '2'. (I am indebted to a personal communication from John C. Street, dated 23 March 1970, for portions of this theory.)

Original *dir*₂ '2' also served as the point of departure for the generation of both '4' and '8' by binary progression through vowel alternation, and the evidence for this operation is so widespread throughout Altaic that the process must be attributed to the proto-Altaic linguistic community. For '4' Turkish has, as already noted, replaced its original inheritance by borrowing a related form from some other language, but otherwise '4' is regular throughout all the languages except Korean: original pA *dō- gave OJ *yö-* '4', and, with the addition of different derivational suffixes in different languages, this same form was also directly responsible for the Mongol and Tungus developments. Then, in one further stage of this same process of binary progression through vowel alternation, utilizing this time the ablaut set that we can with most confidence attribute to the proto-Altaic unity, i.e., the alternation -ö- ∼ -a-, '8' is to be related to '4' (and to '2') through the form *de- (=dä-), again regularly resulting in OJ *ya-* '8', as well as in the Tungus forms, where pT *ǰapkun*, Ma *ǰakûn* '8', show by their initials both the original Altaic *d- and its secondary development before the front -ä-. Korean has an ingenious innovation for '8' (see below), as does probably also Turkish (on which, see above); and Mongol *nayman* remains an isolated and still unexplained innovation. But the importance of OJ *ya-* '8' for Altaic numeral relationships, and its integral connection with the Altaic numeral system through its association with '2' and '4', are clear.

So far we have considered Old Japanese '1', '2', '4', and '8', and have been able to establish etymologies relating all these numerals to the original common Altaic linguistic unity. One additional Old Japanese numeral is susceptible to this treatment, namely '10', a numeral that incidentally also illustrates the second development of Altaic *d and *ǰ before back vowels, where it regularly results in Japanese *t-* ('4' and '8' illustrate the first development).

The word for '10' hardly ever occurs written in phonograms in the Old Japanese corpus, where it is almost always recorded instead with the Chinese logograph *shih* (5807) '10'. A rare exception is provided by the phonogram orthography *töwo* in the collocation *töwo ka* 'ten days' in *Kojiki* poem 26 (see below, p. 235), a citation that is curiously missing from among those in Sanseidō (1967: 511b), which lists nothing but logograph writings for the word '10'. This single phonogram text, however, renders unnecessary the asterisk which sometimes has been used with OJ *töwo* '10' (thus, Ōno 1955: 2.276, and following him, Miller 1967: 337). But even without this *Kojiki* phonogram text, the Old Japanese vocalization of the word for '10' would be quite secure, because of the fact that this same Chinese graph *shih* (5807) is also used as a rebus writing for the first two syllables of OJ *töwoyöru*, a word of somewhat uncertain meaning in the texts, but generally thought to imply 'languid, delicate (of body)', while at the same time there are still other phonogram writings for this same OJ *töwoyöru* that make its own vocalization unambiguous. Thus, *M* 217 has OJ *töwoyöru*, with *töwo-* in phonograms (and *-yöru* written with a logogram), but *M* 420 has the same OJ *töwoyöru*, with the *töwo-* element written in rebus-fashion with Chinese *shih* '10'. Because of the limitations on the occurrence of vowels in successive syllables in Old Japanese, the apparent sequence of *ö* followed by *o* in this word presupposes an earlier, though unattested, OJ **töwö* '10', but this is the only form that requires an asterisk, not OJ *töwo*.

Japanese scholars generally associate OJ *töwo* '10' with various secondary derivatives of the same Old Japanese morpheme *töwo-* with which it happens to be brought into connection by the fanciful rebus orthography of the texts, following, as it were, the etymological suggestions of these ancient writings. The usual candidate in these etymologies is OJ *töwomu* 'bend, be curved' (thus, Ōno 1955: 2.276). The lexical sources unfortunately are rather less sure about the meaning of the stem element *töwo* than they are concerning the meanings of the derivatives in which it appears (*töwomu, töwoyöru*, etc.). Sanseidō (1967: 511ᶜ) can only conclude that OJ *töwo-* is a 'sound-imitative', descriptive of pliant bending.

The implication of all these etymologies is that OJ *töwo* '10' was somehow derived from the concept of bending over, or closing up, the fingers (of both hands?). In the modern language related forms with the *-o-* vocalism do not seem to have survived, but with the ablaut-related *-a-* vocalism we do have J *tawamu* 'bend, be bent', and probably also related here is J *tayamu* 'relax, slacken, flag'. All these forms remind us of the shape and also to a lesser degree of the meaning of OJ *taFaru* 'violate, have improper relations with', as well as the *hapax* OJ *tawomu*, of unclear meaning but usually also taken to mean 'bent'.

As is always the nature of such things, there is no compelling reason not to associate OJ *töwo* '10' with OJ *töwo*, a form that may very well have meant 'bend', and also with J *tawamu*, a form that surely does mean 'bend', but at the same time there is also no compelling reason to do so; and, most importantly, there is no real basis in any of this for concluding that in Old Japanese '10' had anything to do with 'bending' the fingers or anything else.

Somewhat more to the point, perhaps, is a fact that appears to have been overlooked in the Japanese literature relating to this problem, namely that if OJ *töwo '10' does go with *töwo* and *tawamu*, and/or some of the other forms cited in this connection, then it begins to look rather likely that *ta-*, the combining form of J *te* 'hand', was involved somewhere along the line—and this should also be kept in mind in discussing Mo. *tabun* '5'. Also not to be forgotten in this connection is J *taba* 'a handful, a bunch (of something)'. Ozawa (1968: 126, #47) suggests that OJ *töwo* '10' goes directly with Mo. *tabun* '5' (but of course he does not attempt to explain how or why '5' equals '10'—apparently the mere fact that both are numerals is supposed to be sufficient); he further speculates than an 'original word for "5" *tab-'* supposedly demonstrated by this correspondence was driven out of Japanese by the 'innovating' form *itu*, to survive only in the forms J *tawa* and *sawa*, both of which, according to Ozawa, now mean simply 'many'. OJ *saFa ni* 'in great number' is common in the texts (e.g., *M* 36, *M* 485, *M* 894), but its relation to all these forms in *t-* is completely obscure. I cannot trace Ozawa's *tawa* 'many' at all; the form appears to be a ghost generated solely for serving the purposes of his etymology.

In general, this kind of semantic speculation, and all related attempts to establish etymologies for numerals through invoking forms from other areas of the lexicon, are notoriously easy to generate and virtually impossible to refute; but unfortunately they are, by their very nature, also virtually impossible to substantiate. With a little ingenuity, almost any quantities of such etymologies are possible. Of these, many will sound quite 'probable', and more than a few might very well even be historically true, i.e., they actually happened. The difficulty is that hardly any of these etymologies are ever susceptible of rigorous demonstration, be they ever so 'probable.' Nor do we have any guarantee that what actually happened in history was always the 'probable' rather than the 'improbable'—and in this respect, linguistic history turns out to be distressingly like all other human history: often the most unlikely events turn out to be the ones that have happened.

As a general rule, therefore, numerals must be explained by numerals; etymologies for numerals must involve numerals; and such etymologies are by definition weakened to the breaking point as soon as they depart from the numerals and attempt to find their explanations in other areas of the lexicon. It should also go without saying that, in comparative studies of numerals, we must always keep in mind the fact that the numerals are unique among all other semantic categories in the lexicon. With numerals there is neither the need nor the possibility of providing allowance for 'semantic drift' in making comparisons. In all languages, numerals constitute a closed set of forms unlike any other forms, and unique in their ordering (so that '2' follows '1', '6' follows '5', etc., in a way that no other forms follow other forms), as well as in their semantic identity (itself a special function of this same feature of ordering). In other words, because of the very nature of numerals, we cannot (with Ozawa, above) equate '5' in one language with '10' in another, nor (with Lee 1963: 100) equate '3' with '5' or '10' with '9'; '5' can only go with '5', '3' with '3', and so on. To do otherwise is to treat the numerals as if they were some other, non-numeral, set of lexical items.

But Japanese scholarship has traditionally been extremely fond of 'explanations' for both the Japanese and Korean numerals in which nonnumeral lexical items are invoked to provide etymologies for the numerals. Shiratori is responsible for a well-known early contribution (1937) that proposed extremely ingenious and often fanciful semantic 'explanations' for '5', '7', and '9'; but none of his etymologies need detain us long. For '5' Shiratori suggested an association with *ito* 'very', *itaru* 'to reach to, reach as far as', and *itatte*, the gerund of *itaru*. The etymology breaks down the moment we recall that *ito* 'very' is a rather late allegro allomorph, with anomalously shortened vowel, from earlier *itō*, which form itself is a late contraction resulting from the loss of inflectional -*k*- in *itaku* 'extremely', going with the adjective *ita-s-* 'painful'. In '7' Shiratori saw a morpheme *na* 'arrange, count' followed by another homophonous but different morpheme *na* 'not', so that he claimed that the entire form originally meant 'not obtained by counting'. His etymology for '9' was equally imaginative; for Shiratori '9' included *koko* 'bend' and, once more, *na* 'not', to mean originally 'not obtained by bending'. It is not necessary to dignify these fables with formal refutations.

Somewhat more important are the data that Shiratori collected in the same essay showing how the Japanese attitudes toward numerals as lucky, sacred, auspicious, and the like may be demonstrated to have shifted under the pressure of continental influence, particularly from

Chinese culture during the Old Japanese period. In the original Japanese myth, auspicious god lists seem typically to have comprised groups of eight deities, but this soon shifted under Chinese influence so that eventually the favorite total for god lists became seven. This and other sociolinguistic data on the Old Japanese numerals are the only important part of Shiratori's early study of the problem; none of his etymologies will stand up to modern scrutiny.

Inter alia, Shiratori cites one important early text dealing with counting that is worth repeating here, *Kojiki* poem 26 (translation in Philippi 1968: 242):

kaga nabëte	The number of days is, altogether,
yo ni Fa kökönö yo	Of nights—nine,
Fi ni Fa töwo ka wo	Of days—ten.

It was the gerund OJ *nabëte* 'counting' in this text that set Shiratori off on his theories for the etymology of '7' and '9' summarized above; but in this text the form is nothing more than a charming literary figure for counting, used here with reduplicated *kaga* 'days', hence *kaga nabëte* 'lining up, arranging, counting the total of days'. The text is one of the few instances in the Old Japanese corpus in which the word for '10' appears written in unambiguous phonograms, and this is probably its only real importance for the linguistic history of the Japanese numerals.

But by all odds the most prolific speculator in this field was Ramstedt. His imaginative speculations on etymologies for numerals in many of the Altaic languages, based in the main upon ideas of recovering various 'primitive' methods of counting on the fingers, are always interesting and stimulating, but they constitute a variety of imaginative theory that unfortunately is subject neither to refutation nor demonstration (typical examples in Ramstedt 1949: 77 and passim, generally repeated in Ramstedt/Aalto 1952: 62 ff.).

Any possible association between OJ *töwo* '10' and other non-numeral morphemes is, for all these reasons, less to the point than the fact that Tungus has back vocalism in these words, pT *$\check{g}uwan$, Ma. $\check{g}uwan$, and that this goes regularly with the initial of the Japanese forms for '10'. We must note that proto-Tungus front *$\ddot{u}$ goes with OJ *ö* in '4', and also in '9' if the hypothesis about OJ *kökönö-* proposed below is to be maintained, while the proto-Tungus back *u of *$\check{g}uwan$ '10' appears to go with OJ *ö* in *töwo* '10'. Does this point to an earlier pre-OJ *$towo$ > *töwo*, the latter form developing because of the extraordinary statistical frequency of OJ *ö* as against OJ *o* in the language as a whole? We have already noted (§5.2) the implications of the reconstruction of pT **du-wan* as the earlier form underlying pT **ǯuwan* '10'.

The ancient pre-Japanese ('Koguryŏ') fragments from the Korean peninsula have a word for '10' written with the Chinese phonogram *té* (1662) 'virtue'. Murayama (1962[b]: 6, 9) reconstructs **tę* or *tęk;* Lee (1963: 98) reconstructs **tęk*, and suggests an association with OT *toquz* '10'; this seems rather more to the point than his further suggestion (also found in Murayama) that this ancient peninsular form has anything to do with OJ *töwo*.

OJ *kökönö-* '9' is generally explained by Japanese scholars as somehow related to a form which they give either as OJ *kököra* 'very many' or as *kököda* 'id.' Ōno (1955: 2.276) gives *kököra*, but *kököda*, ibid., 296, each time suggesting that the form helps explain *kökönö-* '9', but never making clear which of the two forms he prefers. The hypothesis is not impressive. OJ *kököda*, to accept that form for the moment, appears once in *M* 924, but there it is only a traditional reading of the schools, and the text is actually in Chinese logograms, *chǐ hsǚ* (409, 2825) 'how many?, so many'; hence there is no reliable philological basis here for reconstructing OJ **kököda*. The same is true of *M* 666, where the text again has simply Chinese *chǐ hsǚ;* this the schools traditionally read *kokodaku*, but once again, there is absolutely no basis for attributing the form **kököda-* to Old Japanese. The form *kokora* appears only in Heian texts, and to include the Old Japanese *ö* vowels in a reconstruction **kököra* is to do considerable violence both to philology and to linguistic history.

Fortunately it is by no means necessary to go this far afield to explain Old Japanese '9', nor is it necessary to leave the numeral paradigm to do so. The most widespread Altaic root for '3' is that seen in Mo. *γurban*, Dagur *guarebe*, to be reconstructed as original **γu-*. On more than one occasion in the history of the Altaic languages this particular form was used to manufacture other numerals (we shall see below its encapsulation in Korean *ilkop* '7'); a well-known example is pM **ǯirγuγan*, consisting of **ǯir* (< **-r₂*!) '2' + **γu* '3' (Poppe 1955: 245). Here this same form is transparently involved in OJ *kökönö-*, and this is as a result to be analyzed as '3 times 3', i.e., **γu* × **γu*, followed by the same nasal final suffix that is to be seen in Tungus, which however now appears as the final *-nö-* of the Old Japanese form. Even if this explanation were not superior to the attempt to relate this numeral to a supposed OJ *kököra* (or *kököda*) on semantic and philological grounds, which it is, it would still be a superior hypothesis because it explains the origin of the *-nö-* in *kökönö-*, and this the attempts to relate the word to a *kököra* or *ködöda* can do nothing about. This same kind of construction for '9' is to be observed in pT *xüjägün*, which goes exactly syllable-for-syllable with the Old Japanese form, and effectively substantiates this thesis.

Proto-Mongol *jersün* > *jesün* '9', giving Mo. *yisün*, Dagur *ise*, etc. (Poppe 1955: 246), has been related to pT *xüjägün* '9' in terms of the same anomalous pA *j-* > pT *x-* development that is of great importance for the history of the interrogatives (Poppe 1960: 31; cf. above, p. 192), but with the Japanese evidence in hand, and in view also of the above hypothesis, it is clear that other factors too may have been operative, notably a lenition of velar stop to spirant in Tungus. For the time being, it seems more in keeping with the evidence to regard Mongol *yisün* '9', etc., as innovations postdating the Altaic community (and so also for Turkish *toquz* and its descendants), while Manchu *ujun*, Evenki *jegin*, and the other proto-Northern and Peninsular words for '9' going with proto-Tungus *xüjägün* all show the same formation as OJ *kökönö-*, namely '3 times 3'. Beside *yisün* '9' Mongol also has *yiren* ~ *yeren* '90'; Poppe (1955: 246) apparently takes this combining form of '9' in the decades as the basis for reconstructing pM *yersün* '9'; but probably to be preferred is the formulation of Pritsak (1954) according to which Mo. *yisün* '9' shows the original root for '9' in a singular, beside Mo. *yiren* '90' which shows the same root in an old dual-plural form (*yis-/*yir-*), once again with the suffix *-r₂*. All this makes it possible at long last to remove Japanese *kokonotsu* '9' from the shadowy realm of semantic speculation and shift it instead into the relatively clear light of demonstrable historical developments in well-attested related languages.

This leaves only four Japanese numerals remaining for consideration, the pair '3' and '6', and the individual numerals '5' and '7'. Each presents certain problems, and although none of this set is particularly rewarding on the level of Altaic comparison, even here comparison with related languages can still cast a certain amount of light on the Japanese forms and their developments.

OJ *mi-* '3' beside *mu-* '6' reminds one at once of the vocal alternation in *Fitö-* '1' beside *Futa-* '2'. We have seen that the alternation in the pair '1' :: '2' is simply a reflection of the original Altaic vocalization of older forms for these numerals in each case, and so the apparent parallel between the *i/u* alternation in '3' : : '6' with the *i/u* alternation in '1' : : '2' is not likely to be of major significance on the comparative level. Still, it is not completely to be ignored, and there is always the distinct possibility that, since '3' and '6' are very likely purely Japanese innovations, their vocalization utilized, in a kind of secondary binary progression pattern of derivation, the *i/u* alternation earlier established in Old Japanese '1' : : '2', after that pair had been brought together by the analogic remodeling of the initial of OJ *Futa-* '2' from the earlier **y-* going with Altaic **d-*. Once Old Japanese '1' : : '2' had been established as a pair, intraparadigmatic sequence could then serve as a model for the innovation of a secondary binary progression set within Japanese, in the forms for '3' : : '6'.

There is, however, also a bare possibility that OJ *mi-* '3' may have larger Altaic connections, outside Japanese. Japanese scholars usually attempt to explain this word by means of the verb *mit-u* 'be filled, be full', though they are silent on the question of how '3' is any fuller (or more completely filled?) than any of the other numerals. In Turkish, Chu. *višě* '3' goes regularly enough with OT *üč* 'id.' and forms cognate with the latter, except for the important fact, generally ignored or glossed over in the handbooks, that the initial *v-* of Chu. *višě* cannot fully be accounted for in terms of Turkish materials alone, or for that matter, within Altaic at all, apart from Japanese. Initial *y-* and *v-* in Chuvash are generally dismissed on the comparative level as if they were nothing more than automatic 'Vorschlag' developments in that language, with *y-* appearing before earlier *a* and *ä*, and *v-* before earlier rounded initial vowels (thus, e.g., Krueger 1961: 61); but a glance at the materials makes it evident that this is far from the whole story by any means. To accept this explanation is to run directly in the face of such important etymologies as Chu. *văkăr*, MMo. *hüker*, Mongr. *fuGuor*, Tkm. *ökiz*, all 'ox, bull' (Poppe 1960: 109), where there can be little doubt that the Chuvash initial *v-* is the historical continuation of an original labial initial. Benzing (1959: 707) is somewhat more cautious in his approach to the problem, and surely we must agree with his conclusion that the question of the historical origin of Chuvash forms in initial *v-* is far from settled, requiring a great deal more study in the future. In the meantime it is surely premature to write off all cases of Chuvash *v-* as automatic 'Vorschlag'. In the case of the words for '3' the problem is particularly critical. The initial of Chu. *višě* cannot be explained within Turkish; and we have, on the other hand, OJ *mi-* '3'. At the same time, there is the equally important evidence of Chu. *vătăr* '30', where again the initial is inexplicable in terms of Turkish alone, cf. OT *otuz* '30', and where in addition Qazak *χotïz* '30' shows clearly that the *v-* initial of the Chuvash form is not a Chuvash innovation (Benzing, loc. cit.). Further, there is the evidence of the proto-Chuvash form for '30' in the Old Bulgarian inscriptions, where the word appears written in Arabic script in the form *wṭr* (with the 'emphatic' *ṭ*); this Benzing (loc. cit. and passim) customarily vocalizes as **votur*, following the vocalization of OT *otuz*. The survival of the labial initial in this early form directly ancestral to Chuvash is surely significant, since it shows that the '*v*-Vorschlag' in this particular word, whatever its ultimate explanation, goes back at least to the thirteenth century. Finally, there is the form **mit* '3' in the pre-Old Japanese ('Koguryŏ') fragments from the ancient Korean peninsula. Murayama (1962[b]: 9, 13) wavers between the reconstructions **mi* and **mil* for this form. Lee (1963: 100) reconstructs **mil*, which he then attempts to relate to OT *biš* '5', though why '3' should go with '5', or vice versa, is characteristically never explained. The texts from which this fragmentary evidence has been extracted write the form in question with the Chinese phonogram *mi* (4464) 'secret'. A reconstruction **mil* is indeed possible for T'ang times, but it is rather unlikely for the far earlier date of these materials, for which the reconstruction **mit* is more satisfactory. Finally, we must note that the *-č-* of the Old Turkish and the *-š-* of the Chuvash forms, both of which go back to **-t-*, point in the direction of the modern geminate *-tt-* in J *mittsu* '3'. The importance of the obvious congruity of the ancient peninsular form **mit* '3' both with the Japanese evidence on the one hand, and with Chu. *višĕ* '3', *vătăr* '30' on the other, is immediately evident, even though much of the detail involved remains to be worked out. OJ *mi-tu*, J *mittsu* '3' are not isolated within Altaic; the evidence for the relation of these words to forms in the other Altaic languages is fragmentary, but it is by no means to be overlooked. Once again, comparison with forms of identical meaning in related languages tells us far more about the origin of the Japanese numerals than does any amount of semantic speculation with nonnumeral morphemes. Otherwise, Mongol has the widespread Altaic **γu-* for '3'. Both Tungus and Korean have unique innovations, but Manchu preserves **γu* in *gûsin* '30'.

Whatever the origin of OJ *mi-* '3'—whether it is a Japanese innovation, or whether it is in some way yet to be explained a continuation of an earlier but presently unrecoverable Altaic form also reflected in

Chu. *višĕ*—it is clear that OJ *mu-* '6' is to be explained solely as a secondary development within Japanese, generated on the basis of '3' by application of the binary progression technique through vocalic alternation, this time employing an *i/u* alternation imitated from the '1' :: '2' set. It is hardly surprising to find a Japanese innovation for '6', since it is not possible to reconstruct any common Altaic word for this numeral. Turkish and Korean both have unique forms not known to the other related languages; Mongol fashioned the old compound '2 times 3' already noted; and this form, proto-Mongol *ǰirγuγan '6', was then widely borrowed into other languages, notably into Tungus, where it accounts for pT *ñöŋün and other forms such as Manchu *niŋgun* (cf. Poppe 1955: 245 and 1960: 28).

The Altaic words for '5' present a certain amount of superficial uniformity, and it is possible to make tentative statements about their relationships with one another, but on the whole their apparent uniformity is of a special variety extremely difficult to reduce to a rigorous system, and OT *biš*, which goes with Chu. *pilĕk* etc. (Ramstedt/ Aalto, 1952: 64), is isolated even from this superficial uniformity of the other languages. The exact relationship of Mongol *tabun* and its close cognates (Poppe 1955: 244–45) to the Tungus forms is obscure, but they must obviously be associated in some way, if only as interlingual loans. Within Tungus there is a major unsolved problem. The attested forms, such as Go. *tojŋga*, Ev. *tunŋa*, Lam. *tunŋan*, etc., all '5', should, as indicated in the reconstruction of pT *tuñga, give an initial *t-* in Manchu for a regular correspondence, but instead the Manchu form is *sunǰa* (Benzing 1955: 979; cf. ibid. 1049 for the numeral citations). Poppe (1960: 51) treats Manchu forms with *s* for Tungus *t* internally before *-i-* as loanwords borrowed into Manchu after the time at which the regular change of original *-ti-* > Manchu *-či-* was taking place, but he is silent upon the problem presented by Manchu *sunǰa* '5'. Benzing is undecided; he suggests considering both possibilities, namely that the Manchu reflex here is a secondary conditioned development within Manchu, but also the possibility that here Manchu has preserved a feature of proto-Tungus phonology that all the other Tungus languages have lost (1955: 975–76). He states that the number of examples of this development which can be cited are too few for a definite conclusion (ibid., 979), but he also quotes with seeming approval Cincius' decision to take notice of the Manchu reflexes in such words on the proto-Tungus level and reconstruct for them an original affricate *ts (or, Benzing suggests, perhaps a voiceless or even a voiced spirant? Ibid., 990). Under the circumstances, and given this great uncertainty about all the issues concerned on the part of the Tungus specialists, as well as the great amount of interlingual borrowing attested among the Altaic numerals in general, it is probably best for the time being simply to regard the Manchu word for '5' as an old loanword into Manchu from some nearby Tungus form.

Finally, there are the problems of the Japanese and Korean forms. We have already noted the difficulties with Ozawa's theories about this number (1968: 126). In the Japanese it is impossible not to see some reflection of the Mongol and Tungus forms, which have in the Old Japanese form for '5' for some reason or other acquired the somewhat mysterious Old Japanese prefixed *i-* (on which see Miller 1967: 201–2, 207, as well as p. 100 above). With this prefix removed, and the Old Japanese vocalism in the remaining *-tu-* seen as a secondary assimilation to the earlier generalized *-tu* suffix, it is tempting (even though such speculation cannot be substantiated) to see in OJ '5' some allomorph of OJ *të* 'hand', cf. its combining form *ta-*. This makes an association with the Korean form even more likely (the Korean suffix *-s(ës)* is a pairing suffix here, cf. Korean '6'), since pKJ **t-* corresponds regularly with Korean *t-*, Japanese *t-* (Martin 1966: 205). If the Korean and Japanese forms for '5' are to be associated as inherited cognates from an earlier Peninsular and Pelagic unity, then the Old Japanese vocalism must be regarded as a secondary assimilatory development within Japanese, and the OJ *i-* understood as a separable prefix which was not yet attached to the word in the earlier unity. If, however, OJ *të* 'hand', combining form *ta-*, is to be brought into the picture, then problems arise on the Peninsular and Pelagic level, since Korean 'hand' is *son*. But it is probably best here also to avoid etymologies, no matter how 'natural' or 'logical', that would take the discussion outside the lexical limits of the numeral paradigm. The ancient Peninsular ('Koguryŏ') fragments have a word for '5' written in Chinese phonograms as *yŭ-tz'ŭ* (7592, 6980). Murayama (1962[b]: 3–4, 9) reconstructs **ut^su* < **utu;* Lee (1963: 98) reconstructs **uč*. Both make the obvious association of the form in question with OJ *it-u*, but beyond that it is difficult to go.

In '7', Turkish has an isolated innovation, and Korean a different but transparent circumlocution, for which see below. Proto-Mongol **dal-uɣan* '7' has regular developments in the Mongol languages (Poppe 1955: 246), and the changes in vocalization between the reconstructed form and the forms in the attested languages can be accounted for; the *-a-* vocalization here is original, the *-o-* of the attested languages, secondary. It is not difficult to see how this form must have been borrowed from something approaching its proto-Mongol shape into proto-Tungus, with metathesis of the consonants in the first syllable, as **lad-u-ɣan* > **lad-a-ɣan* > **lad-a-n*, and then, after metathesis, automatic substitution of initial *n-* for borrowed **l-* in Tungus, where initial *l-* did not occur.

This etymology must be treated together with one of the unfortunately moot points of proto-Northern and Peninsular Altaic comparative phonology, namely the history of certain Tungus forms with initial *l-*. Poppe (1960: 74) argues that 'das anlautende *l* im Mandschu-Tungusichen ist sekundärer Herkunft und geht gewöhnlich auf ein anlautendes **n* (meistens vor einem folgenden **m*) zurück . . .' Benzing (1955: 993 and passim) argues for an original initial *l-* in several forms. For two of these, **lümgä-* 'schlucken, verschlingen', and **lāmu* 'Meer', Murayama (1962: 109–10) has pointed out that there are likely-looking Old Japanese cognates, *nömu* 'drink', and *nami* 'wave', in **namita* > **nāda* > *nada* 'sea', with initial *n-*. This is only to be expected, because of course Old Japanese has no *l*, only *r* and *n*, and of these latter two, only *n* occurs in word-initial. Murayama opts for Poppe's formulation, and makes the apparently original initial *l-* in Tungus simply an automatic variant of original *n-* in certain environments. This version of the history would also fit in best with the etymology for '7' proposed here. But since that etymology is one of borrowing and imitation, not of genetic inheritance, it is not susceptible either to proof or refutation by further refinement of the sound laws, and hence, while the problem of initial pT **l-* or **n-* is still relevant in this connection, it is not actually a critical consideration. The ancient Peninsular ('Koguryŏ') fragments have a word for '7' written in Chinese phonograms as *nán-yĭn* (4625, 7448). Murayama (1962ᵇ: 6, 9, 11) reconstructs **nanun*, and Lee (1963: 98) reconstructs **nanịn;* both make the obvious association with the Japanese form for this same word.

In this way, OJ *nana-* '7' is probably at the same time both a borrowing and a further analogic remodeling with Japanese, but not a genetically related or inherited Altaic form.

The methods of formation for the decades and other higher numerals in the Altaic languages are extremely diverse, and do not admit of the reconstruction of any general pattern for the original linguistic unity. Some of the Old Japanese higher numerals have already been treated inter alia above; for examples, see Miller 1967: 337, Table 9 (where the gloss for OJ *ika* should read instead '50' [days]'; also, as already noted, OJ *töwo* '10' does not require an asterisk).

The *Bussokuseki* poem 2 preserves a rare phonogram writing *misotiamariFutatu* '32', with *miso* '30', *amari*, deverbal from *amaru* 'be in excess, be superfluous', and *Futatu* '2'. This citation is of great importance, since otherwise there are almost no phonogram renderings for the higher numerals in the Old Japanese texts, where they are almost always written in Chinese logograms. Modern editors often make up higher numeral compounds for logograph writings, as for example in their readings of dates, on the analogy of this and a few other early examples. Thus, for example, Suzuki in the NKBT edition of the *Tosa nikki* (1957: 27, n. 11; 60, n. 4).

OJ *amari* in this special employment in the numeral system is to be compared with Ev. *hálǝkǝ*, var. *hulǝkǝ*, Lam. *hulǝk* 'darüber hinaus, überschüssig' (cf. Ma. *fulu* 'viel, zu viel', Go. *pulǝ* 'zu viel'), in such numerals as Ev. *ilanǯālǝki* '13', *nadanǯālǝki* '17', etc. (Benzing 1955: 1050), to which it is related both etymologically and in this characteristic semantic employment in the numeral system. An allegro allomorph *mari* often appears in later archaic preservations of these old compound higher numerals. Special vowel-harmony allomorphs surviving in J *futsuka* '20th day [of the month]' beside J *hatachi* '20 years [age]' have already been noted. For Middle Japanese the *Genji monogatari* preserves a valuable example of counting by tens: *towo Fata miso yoso nazo kazoFuru* 'counting 10, 20, 30, 40, etc.' (Nakada 1963: 918[a]).

With this, all the lower Japanese numerals have been accounted for, and it is now appropriate to say a few words in passing about the ingenious innovations represented by Korean '7', '8', and '9'. The most transparent member of this set is '8', which both Ogura and Ramstedt, either following one another or independently, saw correctly as a compound involving Korean *tul* '2'. Ogura Shinpei (1882–1944), the great Japanese scholar of Korean, is credited with the solution by Ōno Susumu (Ōno 1952: 55), but since Ōno gives not a hint of a reference to tell which of Ogura's voluminous works contains the information, it is impossible to trace the matter further. Ramstedt has the same explanation (Ramstedt 1949: 76; Ramstedt/Aalto 1952: 64). Ogura's hypothesis was apparently one step more advanced than Ramstedt's, since the Japanese scholar identified the final element as one meaning 'be nonexistent', while Ramstedt simply notes 'Kor.

[*yëtëlp*] könnte in [*yël*] "zehn" und **tulp* (<*tu* + ?) "zwei fehlend" zerlegt werden . . .' (1952: 64, replacing Ramstedt's transcriptions of Korean with those used elsewhere here). The final suffixal element at issue here, and the form that finally makes it possible to analyze Korean '7', '8', and '9' as compounds subtracting, in turn, '3', '2', and '1' from '10', is Korean *ëp(s)* 'be nonexistent', the negative of *iss-* 'to be, exist, have'. In '7', '8', and '9' this has served as a final element, in strikingly contracted compounds involving *yël* '10' as their first element, '3', '2', or '1' as their second, and *ëp(s)* as their last element. The second-syllable vocalization of the resulting contraction has, in '7', originated in the vowel of the element used for '3', the same pA **γu* for the use of which we have already seen much other evidence above. In '8' the vocalization of the initial *yël* '10' has been imitated in the second syllable after contraction, and the *ëp(s)* element reduced to a zero-grade version in which only the final stop survives. In '9', where the process of contraction has been particularly striking, the final vowel survives to provide evidence of the original but now almost obliterated '1', and once more here, as in '7', the final subtractive element has been analogically shifted to the *-o-* vocalism. In '9', there is also the problem of precisely which prior element for '1' should be identified in the precontraction form; *hana* is perfectly satisfactory, but both *hoth-* 'single' and *hon*, var. *hol* 'alone' are also possible contenders. But the vocalism of the modern Korean form *ahop* '9' argues, to a certain extent, in favor of MK *hɔnah* '1'.

The proposed developments for these numerals in Korean may be summarized as follows:

'7': *yël* '10' + **γu* '3' + *ëp(s)* > *ilkop*
'8': *yël* '10' + *tul* '2' + *ëp(s)* > *yëtëlp*
'9': *yël* '10' + *hɔnah* '1' + *ëp(s)* > *ahop*

This discussion has been based largely on the numerals in modern Korean; if we attempt to refer it instead to the Middle Korean forms established by reference to written records, certain difficulties arise, which do not however by any means vitiate the validity of the above hypothesis. The chief problem is that presented by the initial of MK *nilkup* '7'. It is difficult to know how to interpret such cases of initial *n-* before *-i-* in the written records of Middle Korean. Some of them are undoubtedly of importance for the history of the language, while others appear to be little more than orthographic conventions of the Middle Korean period without significance on the comparative level. The parallelism with '8' suggests that the initial *n-* in this Middle Korean form is simply orthographic, but on the other hand there is also the evidence of the nasal and dental initials in the general Altaic words for '7' already discussed above. We have seen how pM **dal-*, pT **nadan*, Ma. *nadan*, and OJ *nana-*, all '7', must go together in a complex if still partially obscure pattern of borrowing and metathesis. If the initial *n-* in MK *nilkup* '7' is genuine and historic, and not simply orthographic, it must have resulted from early contacts between Korean and other languages in which this word appears (or appeared then) with initial *n-*. At the same time that the word was being borrowed back and forth among other early Northern and Peninsular languages, its early Korean initial was analogically remodeled, thus increasing its overt resemblance to the forms in closely related and contiguous languages; but this analogic remodeling of the initial must have taken place after the contraction of the '10' + '3' + 'be nonexistent' complex, since the first-syllable vocalism *-i-* was the end product of that contraction. In the absence of more information about the linguistic value of the Middle Korean written records, it is difficult to go beyond this admittedly sketchy speculation on the basis of these older forms for the Korean numerals.

From this it can be seen that the fears and doubts entertained by the earlier Altaic comparativists concerning the numeral systems in these languages were completely understandable, even justifiable, but as it now turns out, not completely necessary. Despite the considerable diversity displayed by the numerals in all the Altaic languages, including Japanese, they do prove to provide evidence that is of value in the recovery of the earlier linguistic unity of which all these languages are later, changed forms. The numerals differ from the other areas of the Altaic lexicon chiefly in that here the changes transpiring between proto-Altaic and the attested languages have been particularly sweeping.

5.4 Negation

The Altaic languages are relatively rich in negative and privative expressions, and the normal expectation that Japanese would preserve at least a portion of its diverse Altaic inheritance in this area of the lexicon proves to be completely justified. The Japanese reflexes of the original Altaic expressions of negation may be shown to have undergone extensive change in the course of the isolation of Japanese from the Altaic linguistic unity, as well as during the subsequent history of the language itself, but because of this very fact they facilitate certain insights into the nature of the Japanese relationship to the other Altaic languages that would not be possible without an understanding of the history of these negatives and privatives.

The entire range of forms expressing negation in the Altaic languages was surveyed as the subject of one of the most important of the early comprehensive works in the field (Ramstedt 1924). But it was unfortunate in the extreme that Ramstedt took that occasion to indulge in the elaboration of a 'semasiological' theory concerning the origin and development of the Altaic negatives. The result has been that his findings, even though based on his vast experience with all the languages concerned, are not any longer able to stand on their own as a rigorous accounting for the facts and forms in this important area of Altaic lexicon and syntax. Despite this fatal shortcoming, however, it is still important at least briefly to summarize Ramstedt's theories on the negatives, partly in the interest of bibliographic thoroughness, partly as a tribute to the energy and erudition of the great pioneer in comparative Altaic studies, and partly also because at the conclusion of his 1924 article Ramstedt introduced Japanese data in a short passage of considerable historical significance for the study of the relationship of Japanese to the other Altaic languages.

The heart of Ramstedt's 'semasiological' theory for the Altaic negatives is to be found in a number of fortuitous resemblances between certain of the negatives and other words for 'to be'. Out of this he evolved a theory of 'der wandel "bleiben, sein" = still stehen" > "nichts tun", "nichten" ' (Ramstedt 1924: 199), and then attempted to show how traces of this development could be detected in the linguistic materials. He concluded: 'Hiermit bin ich mit meinem altaischen "sein = nicht sein" fertig. Hamlets frage "sein oder nicht sein" bleibt doch für immer bestehen. Soviel ich finden kann, ist der bedeutungswandel "sein > nicht sein" auch in anderen sprachen bekannt . . .' (ibid., 214). From this, it was an easy progression to his final paragraph, significant enough for the history of Japanese and Altaic studies if not for its actual content to merit citation at length:

Das obige wurden schon am 15. märz 1919 in einen vortrage in der sitzung der Finnisch-ugrischen Gesellschaft bekanntgemacht. Wenn ich es jetz, nach vier jahren und nur mit kleinen redaktionellen korrekturen, veröffentliche, habe ich keine veranlassung, meine damaligen ansichten zu ändern. Nachden ich mittlerweile ein wenig mit der japanischen sprache bekannt geworden bin, kann ich nur hinzufügen, dass der "negative stamm" des japanischen verbums vielleicht am besten in derselben weise seine erklärung findet . . . (ibid., 215).

Ramstedt then went on to present a short summary of the Japanese verbal negation forms, in the following terms:

tor- positiver stamm, in *tori* 'nahme' (n. actionis), *tori* 'nehmend' (conv. imper.), *toru* 'nimmt' (verbales nomen), *toruru* 'nehmend' (adjektivisch), *torite* (>*totte*) 'genommen habend' (conv. perf.), *toramu* (>*toran* u. *torō*) 'wird nehmen' (potential), usw., und der negative stamm ist *tora-*, *toran-* in *toranu* 'nimmt nicht', *torazu* 'ohne zu nehmen', usw.

Ramstedt's early familiarity with the Japanese forms is impressive, as are his assignments of grammatical terminology and meanings. But as late as 1952, this same theory of the 'sein = nicht sein' development is still being presented without alteration: '*-ma-*, des Kennzeichen oder Infix der negativen Konjugation, ist aus der Zusammenziehung des *-m* mit dem alten Verbun *e-* "sein" (=*er-*, *i-*) in der Bedeutung "wegbleiben" enstanden' (Ramstedt/Aalto 1952: 106).

Fortunately it will not be necessary to become involved in the labyrinths of this 'sein = nicht sein' theory in order to survey once more the Altaic expressions for negation. In the process it will, as a matter of fact, turn out to be possible to vindicate Ramstedt's final position after all, namely that the Japanese forms are indeed of considerable importance for a full understanding of the Altaic verbal negatives; at the same time, the Altaic materials will also throw light on the Japanese forms themselves as well as upon their historical development.

1. Old Turkish (von Gabain 1950: 108–9, § 211; Tekin 1968: 115, § 3.114.5; 210, § 4.25). The most important verbal negation element here is the well-known *-ma-/-mä-* morpheme that serves as a verbal enlargement to form negative deverbal verbs: *bol-* 'to become', *bolma-* 'not to become', *bul-* 'to find', *bulma-* 'not to find', *yi-mä-yin* 'ich will nicht essen!', *yorï-ma* 'geh nicht!', *qïl-ma-dïmïz* 'wir haben nicht getan'. With the aorist an additional form is found, with *-z* in place of the *-r* of the positive, and used attributively as well as predicatively: *bilmäz* 'unwise', *säw-mä-z män* 'ich liebe nicht', *tïdïl-maz-lar* 'sie werden nicht verhindert'.

Also to be noted in Old Turkish are the nominal *yoq* that negates *bar* 'exists, to be', and an interrelated series of privatives: *-sïz/-siz*, *-suz/-süz; -saz/-säz;* thus *aš* 'food', *aššïz* 'hungry', *bilig* 'wisdom, intellect', *biligsiz* 'unwise, unintelligent', *ig* 'Krankheit', *igsäz* 'gesund', *ög* 'Mutter', *ögsüz* 'Waise'.

Finally, and also of importance for comparative purposes, there is the denominal verbal suffix *-sïra/sirä* 'ohne etwas sein': *il* 'Reich', *ilsirä-* 'landlos sein'; *inč* 'Ruhe', *inčsirät-* 'beunruhigen' (von Gabain 1950: 68–69, Tekin 1968: 110). This formant clearly goes together historically with the previously mentioned privative, both ultimately to be related to pA *sir_2-*.

Chuvash preserves nothing of exceptional interest as far as the negatives are concerned; it has a verbal negation morpheme *-mă-/mĕ-/ -ma-*, with the allomorphs *-mas-/-mes-* for the durative present, the allomorph *-m-* for the future, and the allomorphs *-ma-* and *-me-* for the preterite (Krueger 1961: 142 ff.). The original Altaic privative *sir_2-* appears as *-săr/-sĕr* (ibid., 110), thus *văisăr šïn* 'a man without strength' (*văy* 'strength', *šïn* 'man'), *šïnsăr* 'without a man'; and there is a set of so-called negative pronouns formed by adding a prefix *ni-* to the interrogatives, and *-ta/-te* after the stem, thus *kam* 'who', *nikan ta* 'no one' (ibid., 138).

It is also important to note that Menges has recently suggested (1954: 1111; 1968: 96–97) that the Turkish privatives do not in fact go back to an original Altaic *sir_2-*, but that instead such forms as OT *-sïz* are to be analyzed as consisting of *-sï*, a formant for denominal privative verbs, plus the suffix *-z* for nouns of verbal stems. The problem is one in the descriptive presentation of the facts of Old Turkish. It provides an excellent example of how our recovery of historical events in the development of any language may often be greatly influenced by the form of the descriptive statements that we take as the point of departure for our reconstruction. The final solution for this particular problem in description must be left to specialists in Turkish; for our purposes here, we can only point out that a portion of the Japanese evidence, which will be cited below, does appear to support Menges's thesis about the historical priority of a *-sï* formant for privative verbs, and also that the Japanese evidence for a formant cognate with this form would favor adoption of Menges's thesis. But this is not the same thing as saying that 'because' Japanese appears to have preserved a cognate privative verb formant appearing in Japanese in much the same shape as Menges's descriptive analysis of the Old Turkish evidence would indicate, it must necessarily follow that his descriptive analysis (together with its historical implications) is by that same token 'correct'.

2. Mongol (Poppe 1955: 286–91). Mongol shows great variety in its forms and morphological processes for negation. The most important forms are the following:

(1) *bu*, a preposed prohibitive particle; thus, *buu uŋsi* 'do not read!', *buu oroja* 'let us not enter!'. This same form entered into composition to form proto-Mongol **bütügey*, another prohibitive particle, attested in Urdus, Khalkha and Kalmuck. Poppe (1955: 286) is no more than alluding to Ramstedt's 'sein = nicht sein' theories when he claims that this form has 'resulted from the imperative of the verb **bü-*'; in the absence of corroborative evidence, which does not appear to be forthcoming, the resemblance in shapes between the two forms is best treated as fortuitous and without historical significance (cf. also Street 1957[b]: 86).

(2) In Written Mongol the indicative forms occur with the negatives *ese* and *ülü*. The negative *ese* is the stem of a negative verb **ese-* 'not to be', a verb that may also be traced in Tungus (Poppe 1960: 65). The negative *ülü* has developed from earlier **üli*. In Middle Mongol both *ese* and *ülü* are found with indicatives; in the language of the *Secret History* the form *ese* occurs with past tenses. The two negatives *ese* and *ülü* are represented by a wide variety of developments in the different Mongol languages: 'in one of the Monguor dialects **üli* has resulted in *li*, but in another dialect there is *ī* < **li* < **üli* .... The negative *li* has merged with many verbs, e.g., *lōtśi-* 'not to drink', *lōli-* < **li ōli-* 'not to become', *lōro-* 'not to enter', etc., resembling Latin *nolo* < **ne volo*' (Poppe 1955: 288).

(3) Finally, nominal forms of the verb in Written Mongol appear with the negative *ügei*, as well as with *ese* and *ülü*.

In spite of the wide variety of these forms, Mongol agrees on a characteristic and atypical location for the syntactic occurrence of these negatives, preposing them to the verbs to which they refer, rather than suffixation or incorporation into the final portions of verbal structures. In this, as well as in its total ignorance both of the *-ma-* verbal negation enlargements of Turkish, and also of the *-siz* and other privatives of Turkish, Mongol stands somewhat apart from the Altaic linguistic community. By and large, each of these three general types of negatives appears to be an innovation within proto-Mongol, and hence seems to have little or nothing to contribute either to our knowledge of the earlier proto-Altaic situation or to our understanding of the developments for parallel forms in Japanese.

For the purposes of comparison with Japanese on the Altaic level, however, the most important Mongol verbal negation forms are not those attested in Written Mongol or even apparently those preserved in any of the living languages, but rather a few precious relics preserved only in the Middle Mongolian text of the so-called *Secret History*. Since the forms in question are both extremely rare and extremely important for ultimate comparison with Japanese, it will be necessary to give the philological data on their occurrences, shape, and meanings in some detail.

Ramstedt first drew attention to these relic forms in his original article on the negatives (Ramstedt 1924: 208–9), where he wrote as follows:

Im Juančaomiši kommen wenigstens zwei sichere belege von *-sar* (*-ser*) vor: *kei-su-mu-ser* 'fällt nicht' und *o-lu-su-mu-ser* 'hungert nicht' (**keis-*['']fallen', **ölüs-* 'sterben' . . .; kalm. *kis-*, *öls-*).

These forms, as a matter of fact, both occur in the same section of the *Secret History*, § 56; Haenisch (1937: 7) read them *keyisumuser* and *olosumuser;* Shiratori (1942: 1/37a) read them *keisümüser* and *ölösümüser.* Street (1957: 39) most recently has read them *keẏ.is-ümser* and *ölös-ümser.* (Despite Ramstedt's gloss, *keis-* is not 'fallen' but 'to blow in the wind.') The Chinese transcription in which the Middle Mongol text of the *Secret History* has been preserved has, for the final elements of both words, *sù-mù-hsīeh-érh* (5505, 4563, 2653, 1759) (Shiratori, loc. cit.), with a small 'diacritic' Chinese character to indicate that *érh* is meant for *-r* rather than for *-l.*

One additional example of this same verbal negative formation may be cited from the *Secret History;* this is a form in § 240, which Haenisch (1937: 79) read *uḥamsar;* Shiratori (1942: 10/18a) read it *uqamsar,* and Street (loc. cit.) now reads *uqa-msar.* The Chinese transcription of the original has *wú-hán-sā-érh* (7173, 2017, 5406, 1759), with a small 'diacritic' Chinese character indicating the back velar articulation for the initial of the *hán* (Shiratori, loc. cit.). Haenisch (1937: 119, Anm. 4 to § 240) has a note concerning this form, which he translates 'ohne sich dessen zu versehen', and adds that it is to be compared with a form that he writes *keyisumser* (*sic*), in 'Abschn. 70', apparently a lapsus for 'Abschn. 56'.

This last form, *uḥamsar,* may also be cited from one of the documents in the *Hua-i I-yü* of 1389, at II,a, IV, fol. 19ᵛ in the Chinese original, where it has a Chinese transcription identical with that found for the same form in the *Secret History*, § 240. Lewicki (1949: 139) read the word in question *uχamsar,* and in his glossary to these texts (1959: 82) included the following entries: *uχa-* 'comprendre, concevoir, discerner'; *uχamsar* 'inaperçu, de façon inaperçue, impénétrable'. Haenisch (1952: translation, 12, text, 23) read the passage

Horim gurun udu'uye. uḥamsar ada eduju. ḥahan anọ ḥaracu tuśimel un ḥar tur ḥorohdabasu, translating it 'Bevor sie aber nach Ho-rim (Hara Horum) gelangten, trat unerwartet die Katastrophe ein, dass ihr Kaiser von der Hand eines untergebenen Ministers ermordet wurde'. In his notes to this translation and edition of the text, Haenisch seemed uncertain of what to do with the suffix on the form in question; once (Haenisch 1952: 38) he lists it in the form *-msar,* which he identifies as 'Cv [i.e., Converbum—RAM] abtemporale', but no such 'Converbum' appears in his list of Converba (ibid., 36–37), and under Chinese *pù* (5379) he lists *-msar* as 'post. negat.' and amplifies this entry with a citation of *uḥamsar* (1952: 39). Further, in the same article, under 'Verneinung (nachgestellt)' there is no entry for *-msar* (ibid., 37).

In the most recent treatment of these Middle Mongol forms they are referred to the converbial particle *-(U)msAr* 'not yet' (Street 1957: 39). Street states that this morpheme 'occurs only four times in the S[ecret] H[istory]', but cites only the three forms from that text that we have already set forth in detail above. It would be possible to conclude that Street wrote 'four' because the third of the *Secret History* forms, that in § 240, is also found in an identical transcription (though in a different passage and context) in the *Hua-i I-yü* documents, but in a personal communication (23 March 1970) Street has clarified for me that 'four' here is a lapsus due to a confusion in his word-files; 'three' is hence correct.

To sum up, what we actually have attested in the Middle Mongol remains are three verb forms involving negation, each with the morpheme *-(U)msAr* suffixed; these forms are, in Haenisch's transcription, *keyisumuser, olosumuser,* and *uḥamsar.* In addition, *uḥamsar* may also be cited from an additional passage in the *Hua-i I-yü* documents, so that the total is actually three or four, depending on how one wishes to count. Descriptively, the morpheme in question is best considered a formant for privative deverbal nouns, rather than a converb (Poppe, personal communication, 11 January 1971).

So much for the actual occurrences of these forms in the texts; what can we say of their shapes? (It goes almost without saying that since the Middle Mongolian text of the *Secret History* has been transmitted only in Chinese transcription, problems in the interpretation of the phonetic shapes of forms found there abound.)

It will have been noticed that Haenisch and Shiratori both follow the Chinese transcribers literally, and in detail, in rendering the

morpheme in question as -*umuser* (∼-*ümüser*) in the first two citations from the *Secret History*, but as -*msar* in the third citation from
that text, and so also for the fourth, last, and identical citation from
the *Hua-i I-yü* documents. But Street normalizes the original transcriptions, writing -*ümser* for the first two citations and -*msar* for the
last. The point to which attention should be directed here is not, of
course, the automatic variation in the vocalization of the final syllable,
where the -*a*- or -*e*- is determined by the vocalism of the entire word
(and where, incidentally, the -*a*- and -*e*- distinction between the first
two forms on the one hand and the third [and fourth] on the other is
clearly indicated in the Chinese transcription), but rather the absence
or presence of the -*u*- (∼-*ü*-) between the -*m*- and -*s*- in the first part
of the morpheme. In other words, should we write, and consider for
comparative purposes, MMo. -*umuser* (∼*ümüser*) or -*mser* (∼*msar*)?
The first would be evidenced by the Chinese transcriptions using *mù*
(4593), the second by the Chinese transcriptions using the original
final of Chinese *hán* < -*m* (2017). Street (loc. cit.) writes the morpheme in question in a morphophonemic notation as -(*U*)*msAr*,
where the *U* and *A* are his symbols for morphophonemes, but we note
that nothing in his notation provides any leeway for the insertion of a
vowel between the -*m*- and -*s*-.

Fortunately, this problem, even though at first glance it appears
to be a troublesome one, need not detain us long. It is in effect nothing
more than still another facet of the so-called Problem of the Mongol
shwa, for which we already have descriptions and analyses by Street
(1962) and Martin (1961); moreover, its relation to the Chinese
transcriptions of Middle Mongol has already been investigated by the
author (Miller 1966). The Middle Mongol phoneme in question here
was the equivalent of what for Dagur Martin calls the 'unstressed
/e/', and of which he writes,

Unstressed /e/ behaves much like French *shwa;* I normalize by postulating
its occurrence as a kind of "neutral syllabic" between any two consonants . . .
even when—as in rapid speech—the release between the two consonants is
not realized. In slow speech, the release is nearly always heard; . . . From
the linguist's point of view, it would seem to be best to say that /e/ is present
whenever there is any release of a consonant (not otherwise accounted for)
and to note that /e/ is in morphophonemic alternation with zero. From the
practical point of view it seems best to write /e/ wherever anyone might con-
ceivably pronounce it, and remember that the actual sound is frequently
reduced to the vanishing point (Martin 1961: 16).

In the Chinese transcriptions of Middle Mongol, still other 'practical considerations' intervened to render the work of the transcribers
still more difficult and further to complicate our interpretation of the
texts. These factors included the syllabic structure and syllabic inventory of the Chinese dialects of the transcribers themselves, and the
occurrences and nonoccurrences of certain Chinese consonants vis-à-
vis certain Chinese vowels in those dialects. We have also noted immediately above how Haenisch, apparently unconsciously, normalizes
one of the *Secret History* forms, and then writes *keyisumser* in his
notes for the form that in his text he earlier writes *keyisumuser*. This
is an excellent example of the difficulties that this feature inevitably
causes. In the particular *Secret History* verbal negation forms of interest here, the *shwa* has been rendered with Chinese *-u-* because of the
influence of the *-m-*; but it is clear that we need not concern ourselves
either with its phonetic realization or with its absence or presence in
these negatives; so that Street's normalized morphophonemic writing
for the form, *-(U)msAr*, is not only a convenient but also a completely
valid shape for further consideration on the comparative level.

The semantics of these *Secret History* forms are unfortunately not
such as can be dealt with in such short order. Street (1957: 39) writes,
'from these few examples, it seems that this particle has a future
meaning'; but this analysis probably pays too little attention to the
Chinese interlinear glosses to these passages, which use Chinese
pù-ts'éng (5379, 6771). In the language of the Chinese *Secret History*,
'[*pù*] is the regular negative, while [*pù-ts'éng*] is the negative term in
opposition to [*ts'éng*] . . . with past time reference' (Halliday 1959:
121). So it would seem that there is little if any basis in our sole and
essential source for the understanding of these passages, i.e., in the
Chinese version, for interpreting the forms in question as containing
a negative particle 'with a future meaning'.

Under the circumstances, it would appear more than likely that
the specialized meaning at which Street arrives is to be understood, if
correct at all, as having been conditioned in the first two *Secret History*
passages by their special literary quality. The two passages are part
of a short section in verse, which apparently either incorporates
traditional sayings or is in some other way related to an extremely
ancient oral tradition. This as a matter of fact probably is part of
the explanation for the preservation here of these otherwise all but
unattested negative formations in the first place. But in view of the
lack of other passages to cite in support of any theory on the precise

meaning of this formation, the wisest course is simply to note its negative sense, and not to attempt any more exact delimitation of its function.

Above all, the important thing to note is that, by a lucky chance, this *Secret History* text, for all its philological and linguistic difficulties, has preserved the remnants of a Middle Mongol negative verb formation that otherwise appears to have disappeared completely from the Mongol portion of the Altaic domain; and that this negative formation is, as chance would also have it, of capital importance for relating Japanese to the Altaic system of verbal negation.

3. Tungus (Benzing 1955: 1093–94; cf. Benzing 1953: 117, 124; Benzing 1941: 57). The verbal negation forms in Tungus were made by means of a negative verbal auxiliary, pT *ä-*. In the original Tungus linguistic unity this form was always used with aorist (i.e., -*ra*, -*sa*, -*da*) forms of the verb (except when used with the imperative). The original Tungus forms may be reconstructed as follows: pT *ä-si-n-bi* ∼ *ä-sī-bi* 'ich (Präs) nicht', *ä-čä̃-bi* ∼ *ä-ci(n)-bi* 'ich (Präter.) nicht'; *ä̃-tä-n-bi* 'ich (Fut.) nicht'; *ä-ǯī* '(Imperativ) nicht'. Along with this characteristic use of the aorist -*a* forms for these negative formations in Tungus, another important feature to note is that the different Tungus languages made different use of the same elements of negation; thus, in the present and preterite in Goldi the above-mentioned proto-Tungus negative elements were suffixed, but elsewhere in Goldi and generally in the other languages they were prefixed, rather than suffixed, to the verb concerned. Thus with pT *gada* 'nehme', Go. *gadasembi* 'ich nehme nicht', but Ev. *ǝsim gara*, 'id.', and Lam. *ǝsǝm gad* 'id.'

Manchu did not inherit this original Tungus negative verbal auxiliary. Instead, it innovated to form negatives with a distinctive negation verb of its own, Ma. *akû*, thus *genembi akû* 'er (man, usw.) geht nicht', *genehe-kû* 'er (man, usw.) ist nicht gegangen'. While this Manchu usage is apparently an innovation, the form itself is not, since it has cognates elsewhere in Tungus, cf. Udh. *anci*, Ev. *acin*, Lam. *ac* 'ohne, nicht' (though the sound correspondences for these etymologies present certain problems [Benzing 1955: 977]), and also probably as we shall see below, in Japanese and Turkish. Note also the use of Lamut forms with prefixed *ac* for privatives, thus, Lam. *ac amn.ā* 'vaterlos' (*aman* 'Vater'); *ac hut.lā̃* 'ohne Kinder' (Benzing 1955: 1031).

4. Japanese

a. Old Japanese

The evidence from the standard Old Japanese corpus may be conveniently inspected and arranged according to the categories of the traditional grammarians, e.g., as in Yamada 1954: 260–75.

The most usual forms are the well-known conclusive verbal negatives formed with the suffix -*zu* added to a thematic vowel -*a*-; these forms are too common to require citation here (for examples of the forms and details of their use in the texts, cf. Yamada 1954: 260–65). We give attention below (pp. 272 ff.) to a number of important and apparently aberrant cases where this negative morpheme -*zu* appears written in the texts with phonograms that can only be interpreted as writings for earlier unvoiced -*su*.

For attributive verbal negatives the standard Old Japanese texts generally have forms in -*nu*, again with the suffix added to a thematic vowel -*a*- (Yamada 1954: 265–67); thus, *M* 888 *siranu miti* 'unknown road' (with *miti* written with a semantogram, and *siranu* in phonograms); but -*nu* forms also appear as conclusives, so that Yamada (loc. cit.) cites conclusive *kŏnu* 'not come', from the *Nihon shoki;* and *M* 892 has conclusive *tamaFanu* 'will not deign to do'.

For nonconclusive, nonattributive verbal negatives, and as a basis for negative verbals entering into morphological structures involving further extensions and enlargements, the standard Old Japanese texts use forms with -*ne* added to the same thematic vowel -*a*-: *M* 3688 *iFaFi matane ka* '[was it because] they did not keep the taboo?'. Forms in which a further layer of verbal suffixes (notably OJ -*ba; -dö; -dömo*) is added to these -*ne* negatives are well known and examples need not be cited here.

Of greater interest and importance on the comparative level are a significant number of forms to be found in the standard Old Japanese texts (where however they already appear to be virtually fossils), in which nonconclusive, nonattributive verbal negatives are formed with -*ni* added to the well-known thematic vowel -*a*-. These formations are more or less limited to OJ *sir-u* 'know', the only verb for which multiple examples of this formation may be cited, plus a rare form here and there from one or two other verbs, notably from *ak-u* 'be satisfied'. For *sirani* 'not knowing, unknowing', cf. *M* 904, *M* 3777, and *M* 3239, among many other texts. *M* 5 preserves two parallel passages of particular interest in this connection; in the first, an unambiguous OJ *sirazu* is written in phonograms, while in the second and parallel passage, the text is in rebus-semantograms, and according to the reading tradition is to be read *shirani*. Texts such as *M* 167 and *M* 207, in which a supposed **sira-* is written in Chinese as *pù-chīh* (5379, 932), with only a following OJ *ni* or *mo* written in phonograms, tell us in principle nothing about the shape of the verb forms involved, and cannot be cited for linguistic purposes, though most Japanese scholars do not hesitate to do so. With *ak-u*, *M* 3991 has *sökö mo aka ni* 'because it is not possible of satiation'. *M* 3902 has *akani semu* 'will probably not be satisfied' (thus in the NKBT edition of Ōno et al.; Yamada 1954: 271 has *akani kĕmu*, a variant that the NKBT edition of the *Man'yōshū* does not register). The *Kokiki* poem 8 has *wasurezi* 'not forgetting', but in the parallel version of the same poem that appears in the *Nihon shoki*, where it is poem 5, the final syllable of the form is written with the phonogram *ĕrh* (1748) a graph that unfortunately is disputed as far as its reading is concerned. Yamada 1954: 271 reads the form *wasurani*, but the editors of the NKBT edition of the *Nihon shoki* and *Kojiki* poems prefer *wasurazi*. This problem in the correct interpretation of the orthography of course makes it difficult to rely upon the form for linguistic purposes. Still, and quite apart from this problem, it is important to note that the *Kojiki* version has the thematic vowel *-e-* and an unambiguous phonetic writing for *-zi*, while in the *Nihon shoki* version the thematic vowel is unambiguously *-a-*, and only the reading of the ending is in dispute, i.e., whether it is *-zi* or *-ni*. On the phonogram in question, cf. Ōno T. 1962: 75; in general the graph *ĕrh* (1748) was used for *ni* in the earlier strata of the Old Japanese texts, and for *zi* in the later layers. In the *Nihon shoki* it appears, in addition to poem 5, also in poem 119, where it is probably intended for *-zi*, and three times in poem 124, once in a negative where it might be interpreted either as *-zi* or *-ni*, and twice in another word where once more it is unfortunately ambiguous. On all these forms in *-ni*, cf. also Yokoyama 1950: 28, n. 31.

Finally, there are the Old Japanese dubitive negatives with *-zi* added to a verb enlarged with the same thematic vowel *-a-*: *M* 4263 *Fakazi* 'probably not sweeping up'; *M* 4107 *arazi ka* 'is it not probably?'. In this last example the phonogram read as *-zi* is, if the reading is correct, a very exceptional writing; generally the phonogram in question, *ssū* (5585), is to be read *-si*; cf. Ōno in *M* 4.289, and Ōno T. 1962: 639. If (as would seem reasonable) this passage too is more correctly to be read *arasi*, then the example in *M* 4107 must be con-

sidered together with the cases of *-su* writings for expected *-zu* negatives (below), as well as together with the evidence of the Old Japanese
privatives, to which we now turn.

The most important of the Old Japanese privatives was the suffix
OJ *-zi-*; this appears in the texts specialized in collocations with OJ
töki 'time', particularly commonly in the expression *tökizi-* 'untimely,
unseasonable (esp. of rain or snow)'. Only one text example has this
OJ *tökizi-* without a following morphological layer involving inflectional *-k-* (*M* 6: *tökizimi*); otherwise it always appears with this additional morphological enlargement, as for example in *M* 26, *M* 317,
M 471, etc. (Other citations in Sanseidō 1967: 489a-b). *M* 25 offers
instructive parallel passages when read together with *M* 26; in *M* 25
the text has Chinese *shíh wú* (5780, 7180) 'time, not', followed by a
phonogram *sö*. (Note that this word-order is Japanese, not Chinese,
even though the text uses Chinese semantograms. Normal Chinese
word-order would have *wú shíh*, an expression that in Chinese ordi-
narily means 'unfortunately, unlucky'.) This sequence the reading
tradition of the schools interprets as OJ *töki naku sö* (or sometimes
reading the final phonogram *zö*, even though this is clearly unjustified
by the text, which has *sö* unambiguously). But in *M* 26 a parallel
passage has Chinese *shíh* (5780) 'time' followed by the unambiguous
phonograms *ziku sö*, so that here the reading tradition cannot but admit the reading *tökiziku sö*. *M* 25 twice has Chinese *chïen wú* (835,
7180) 'space, not' followed by a phonogram *sö;* both these passages
the reading tradition interprets as *manaku sö* 'without interruption'.
Again the word-order of the text itself is Japanese, not Chinese; but
in *M* 26 we find the correct Chinese word-order, *wú chïen*, again twice,
with the school reading *manaku sö* for the first of these two passages,
in which *wú chïen* is followed by a phonogram *sö*. It is almost as if the
reading tradition in these cases has preserved a kind of 'vowel
harmony' situation, with *-naku-* after *ma*, but *-ziku-* after *töki*—or
rather, it would have done, if it had not chosen to read the semantograms *shíh wú* with *-naku-* rather than with *-ziku-*. At any rate, these
and other occurrences of the privative formant OJ *-zi-* in specialized
collocations with OJ *töki* 'time' are important for the history of the
language, and important also for its relationship with the Altaic
linguistic community.

The second of the Old Japanese privatives always appears with an
additional morphological layer in the form of the durative suffix OJ
-F-u (on which see p. 265 below) already in place. This second priva-

tive is OJ *-si-*, and it appears in the texts as OJ *-siF-u* 'to lose sensa-
tion, feeling, or operation in a sense organ'. Common occurrences in
the Old Japanese corpus include the deverbal nominals *mimisiFi*
'deaf' (*mimi* 'ears'), *mësiFi* 'blind' (*më* 'eyes'), *akisiFi* 'blind' (*aki*
'light, brightness'). A lexical source of the period 898-910 also lists
this form with a voiced variant, so that the privative *-si-* appears as
-zi-, thus *akiziFi* 'id.', in addition to listing *FanasiFë* 'an obstructed
sense of smell' (*Fana* 'nose'), and *mimisiFë* 'deaf', apparently nonstandard dialect forms with *-Fë* for standard *-Fi* (citations in Sanseidō
1967: 364[d]–365[a]). This evidence for later *-zi-* beside earlier and more
general *-si-* in the case of this particular privative encourages us in
reconstructing an earlier *-si-* also in the case of the privative discussed immediately above; the importance of both for connecting
these formations in Old Japanese with the Old Turkish privatives
outlined above is obvious. It is also interesting to note that this second
Old Japanese privative is one of the Altaic reflexes in Japanese originally suggested in Boller's pioneer work in this field (1857: 467), in
an etymology that is fully as valid today as when it was first formulated, over a century ago.

b. Azuma Old Japanese

The negatives in the nonstandard Azuma varieties of Old Japanese
are of great importance both for the later history of Japanese itself
(particularly since the modern standard language is in many respects
essentially an Eastern, i.e., 'Azuma' dialect, rather than a Western
dialect directly descending from standard Old Japanese), and for reconstructing the relationship of Japanese to the original Altaic linguistic unity. Fortunately the necessary data concerning these forms
are conveniently available in the literature (Fukuda 1965: 365–70;
Yamada 1954: 623–28; Yokoyama 1950: 84–86; Ōno in *M* 3.31–38 is
also useful, particularly his summary of the verbal negation forms in
ibid., 38–39). Hence it will only be necessary to summarize it in brief
here.

In the Azuma varieties of Old Japanese generally, the verbal negatives were fashioned by the suffixation of a morphological element that
in almost all cases assumed the characteristic shape of *-naF-*; this was
then in turn followed by the usual form-final morphemes of the Old
Japanese verb. Rarely but significantly this Azuma negation morpheme appears with an aberrant vowel grade as *-nöF-*, demonstrating
the assimilation of the original *-a-* vocalization of this morpheme to
the position of articulation of the *-F-* immediately following.

The following representative sampling of nonstandard negative forms, all for the verb OJ *aF-u* 'meet, encounter', will give an idea of the forms appearing in the texts; it happens (apparently fortuitously) that this is the verb for which the widest selection of evidence for these Azuma negatives is available: *M* 3375 *aFanaFu* 'be not meeting [continually]'; *M* 3426 *aFanaFaba* 'when [we] do not meet'; *M* 3524 *aFanaFeba* 'since [we] cannot meet' (cf. *M* 3482, where this same form occurs again, and where in addition a variant for the text of the poem has *aFanedömo* 'even though not meeting'); (with the *-ö*-grade) *M* 3478 *aFanöFe sida* 'the time (*sida*) when [we] do not meet'. Ōno, in M 3.39, identifies these Azuma negatives with the modern Eastern Japanese (i.e., modern standard Japanese) verbal negatives of the type *ikanai* 'does not go' and *toranai* 'does not take', in contrast to the modern Western Japanese verbal negatives of the type *yukan* 'does not go' and *toran* 'does not take', which latter forms he identifies as the direct historical inheritance of the standard Old Japanese negatives in *-z-* ~ *-n-*. (Cf. also Miller 1967: 169, and passim).

c. Ryūkyū

The thematic vowel *-a-* by now already familiar from the Old Japanese forms is in general the only overt morphological marker for the verbal negatives in the several closely related Ryūkyū languages for which we have reliable evidence. In standard Naha Ryūkyū we find *kaka'N* 'does not write', beside two parallel positives: *kacu'N* 'writes' and *kaca'N* 'wrote' (Hattori 1955: 333). The final *-N* in all these forms is probably of diverse origins, but without becoming involved in tracing its sources or attempting a detailed analysis of the forms (cf. Hattori 1955: 334, n. 1), it is clear even from this short paradigm that the *-N* is not the negative verbal morpheme. The thematic vowel *-a-* of *kaka'N* 'does not write' is the only overt marker of negation, and is to be kept separate from the homophonous *-a-* of *kaca'N* 'wrote' on the basis of the palatalization of the root-final consonant **-k-* in *kaca'N*, an indication that the *-a-* in the second syllable of *kaca'N* was not originally an *-a-* vocalization but instead some front vowel that by the time of the recorded form had already been leveled out to become *-a-*, either under the influence of the first-syllable vocalism or due to the pressure of analogy operating in the verbal paradigms.

Negatives of the type *kaka'N* 'does not write' are general throughout the Ryūkyū languages; the variations that appear in this area now may conveniently be surveyed through the data made available in Hirayama (1966: 204, 233, 254, and passim). Among the dialect variations for the negative that he records, the following are of particular importance: *kakam; kaka'i, kakazi; kaka'a; kaka*. Each of these forms is of interest. Hirayama notes (1966: 254) that one of the dialects that has -*m* forms of the type *kakam* also has -*m* throughout for general Ryūkyū -*N*, and that these negatives in -*m* are best interpreted as another example of this over-all correspondence. Ryūkyū forms of the type *kakazi* have obvious parallels from the Old Japanese materials. Forms of the type *kaka'i* probably are also to be associated with the same prototypes as the *kakazi* forms. Of particular interest are forms of the type *kaka'a*, which Hirayama and his collaborators derive from the generalized *kaka'N* forms, through an intermediate with a nasalized final vowel, thus **kakaā*. They note one dialect area where older speakers still tend to have *kaka'N*, while the younger speakers in this same area now generally have *kaka'a*, a situation that seems to bear out their postulation of an intermediate form with final nasalized vowel, i.e., **kakaā*, very well (Hirayama 1966: 254). Ryūkyū forms of the type *kaka* represent simply the final stage in a process of linguistic change, where even the lengthening of the vowel (the only surviving overt trace of the formally marked negative in *kaka'a*) has now disappeared.

With such forms as these from the Ryūkyū area, we may also compare modern standard J *sira* and J *yara* in the clichés . . . *ka sira* 'I wonder if . . .', lit., 'I don't know whether or not . . .', and *dō yara* 'somehow or other' (both examples I owe to a personal communication from Samuel E. Martin). In these expressions, J *sira* and J *yara* are anachronistic survivals of the same truncated verbal negatives that otherwise may be cited only from the Ryūkyū languages and from certain of the Old Japanese texts (OJ *sira ni*, etc., above). One cannot but be impressed with this evidence for the persistence of distinctive forms and syntactic structures throughout the Japanese area, as well as with their survival in time as well as in space. One is also tempted to see a parallel form in J *itazura ni* 'mischievously, to no good purpose', even though unfortunately the etymology of *itazura* is totally obscure, and hence the form is difficult to analyze.

With the Japanese and Ryūkyū evidence thus in hand, one naturally turns to Korean, but here the data are disappointing in the extreme. (Kim 1969 is useful for its references to the literature on the Korean negatives in particular, and to negatives in general.) Even that most catholic and adventurous of all etymological dictionaries, *Studies in Korean Etymology* (Ramstedt 1949), has ventured almost nothing in this connection, and it would be difficult to do better than to emulate Ramstedt in this (for him) rare caution. The Korean negative for simple denials of fact, K *ani*, appears impossible to connect with any other Altaic forms. Even Ramstedt (1949: 10) included cautious question marks along with his tentative attempts to identify Tungus cognates, and the Altaic forms he does cite must surely be discarded. K *ani* is most often identified with OJ *ani*, a rhetorical interrogative implying that a negative or dissenting answer is to follow, as for example by Ōno in M 1.177, in a gloss to *M* 345, a poem that provides a typical citation for this form: *ani masamë ya mo* 'how, why [then can one claim that] it excels?' (the implied answer being, 'it does not'). OJ *ani* is almost always written in the texts using Chinese *ch'i* (544), a Chinese rhetorical interrogative that also implies a dissenting answer, and in later stages of the literary language, J *ani* is all but restricted to use in rendering Chinese syntactic structures involving this same *ch'i* into Japanese.

The difficulties attendant upon any attempt to bring K *ani* and J *ani* into a cognate relationship are only too obvious. J *ani* is an underarticulated allegro version of the common interrogative *nani* (on which see pp. 187–89 above). This allegro interrogative allomorph has been specialized in Japanese for use in these rhetorical interrogative structures, but these syntactic structures themselves are almost surely calques imitated from Chinese. All this makes the possibility of a common proto-Korean-Japanese origin for these forms less and less likely. Most importantly of all, the difference in meaning between the Korean negative *ani* and the Japanese interrogative *ani* is an insurmountable obstacle to connecting the two forms.

Otherwise, Korean has *mos* > *mōt* 'cannot possibly'; perhaps this is a loan from Middle Chinese *mįuat* 'don't!', Chinese *wù* (7208), but at any rate, the form has nothing to do with Japanese or Altaic. Nor does K *ëps* 'be nonexistent'—and with this, we have exhausted the meager Korean data for the negatives.

Now we are in a position to begin to trace these Japanese negatives and privatives back to their Altaic originals, and to identify them as far as possible with the related morphological processes and forms for negation that Japanese inherited from the Common Altaic linguistic unity.

The standard Old Japanese verbal negation forms may for purposes of comparison with other languages best be reduced to the following pattern: verb stem + thematic vowel -*a*- + **-n* + addi-

tional suffixes, these last being forms from *s-u* 'do, make', notably
-su and *-si*. Thus, OJ *arazu* 'is not' is to be analyzed as *ar-* (verb
stem) + *-a-* (thematic vowel) + **-n* + *-su*. The assimilatory process
by which this **-n* voiced the following *-s-* and then in its own turn
disappeared after the secondary voicing had been accomplished is a
well-established part of the generally accepted doctrine for these
forms in Japanese scholarship, both traditional (Yamada 1954: 275)
and more recent (Ōno in M 3.343, gloss to *M* 3239; cf. also Ōno in
M 4.179, gloss to *M* 3902). Thus, for the Japanese scholars the development was *siranisu* > *siransu* > *sira^nzu* > *sirazu*. This begins
to solve, in historical terms, the question of the variation between
allomorphs in *-z-* and allomorphs in *-n-* for the negative morpheme
(Yokoyama 1950: 86, n. 6), but it does not begin to answer two other
equally important questions: a) where did this morpheme, with its
striking allomorphic variation, come from in the first place? b) what is
the role in all this, as well as the origin, of the Japanese thematic
vowel *-a-*, which as we have seen above is in fact the most strikingly
consistent and obvious marker of the verbal negatives throughout all
the Japanese materials, widely distributed though they are both in
time and space? For the answers to these two questions it is necessary
to turn to the other Altaic languages, which will provide the only
'explanations' possible. The answers may best be approached by beginning with the more important question, b), namely the origin of
the thematic vowel *-a-* in the Japanese verbal negatives.

This thematic vowel is to be identified as being cognate with the
common Altaic negative morpheme **-ma-* attested in Old Turkish and
in Chuvash as well as in Turkish generally. In Japanese, as also in
Tungus (and it seems both difficult and unnecessary to separate parallel developments here in these two), in an original and basic morphological process for verbal negation, the proto-Altaic negative morpheme **-ma-* was suffixed directly to the verbal root. In consonant-
final verbs, the **-m-* of this **-ma-* then assimilated to the final
consonant of the root, with simplification of the resulting cluster
following shortly, so that, for example, with OJ **kak-* 'write,' the
development was **kak-ma* > **kakka-* > *kaka-*; and with OJ *sir-*
'know' the development was **sir-ma* > **sirra-* > *sira-*. This at once
explains the historical origin of the thematic vowel *-a-* in the entire
range of the Japanese negatives, from the more usual verbal negatives
down to and including OJ *sira* in *sira ni*, as well as J *sira* in . . . *ka*
sira, and allied forms.

Close developmental parallels exist between these reconstructed changes in Japanese verbs with suffixed *-ma-* and changes that can be documented from various Turkish languages. Immediately relevant is the way in which, in Chuvash, stem-final *-r* drops before this same negative morpheme, so that with Chu. *yar-* 'send, leave, let, release' (cf. J *yar-* 'id.'), the forms are Chu. *yamarě* 'he did not release (him)', *yamasčě* 'he was not letting him go', and *yaman* 'he did not release him', against *yarsan* 'when (you) release (him)' (Krueger 1962: 137). In Altai Turkish, original *ärmäz* 'is not' appears in such contracted forms as Qumandin *äbäs*, and Lebed *äväs* (Pritsak 1959: 579). The historical changes underlying all these forms are quite analogous to those responsible for the Japanese forms, with the difference that in Turkish the stem-final consonant first assimilated to the *-m-* of the negative morpheme, and then itself disappeared, while in Japanese the changes worked out the other way around, so that, with the same (i.e., cognate) verb, Japanese has **yar-ma* > **yarra-* > *yara-*, while Chuvash has **yar-ma* > **yamma-* > *yama-*.

What has been said thus far has considered only those Japanese verbs belonging to the original stop consonant (Class A) and original consonant **-w* or **-y* (Class A') groups revealed by internal reconstruction of the Japanese verb (see Miller 1967: 322 ff.; Ōno 1953). In the last of these three classes, those verbs for which internal reconstruction reveals a vowel in stem-final positions (Class B), the development of the verbal negatives was further complicated by being conditioned by the quality of that vowel. Three main types of developments must be accounted for here. In those verbs of this class with final *-a*, the combination resulting from the addition of **-ma-* to that *-a* was simplified so that *-a* + **-ma-* > **aa* > *a;* we may compare the simplification through parallel changes in proto-Mongol, at an early date, of **nadur* < **namadur*, dat.-loc. of the first-person pronoun (Poppe 1955: 209). In both cases it is probably necessary to take into consideration an intermediate stage with a labial semivowel, thus **-ama-* > **-awa-* > **-aa-*, etc. Also relevant in this connection is the characteristic Japanese underarticulation leading to eventual loss of the labial semi-vowel before *-a*, a phenomenon of great importance for the history of the personal pronoun (see above, p. 161). With the other vowels (*-ö*, *-u*) more complicated morphophonemic simplifications, assimilations, and replacements must be reckoned with:

1) *-ö* + **-ma-* > *-ö* + **-i* > *ï*, and
2) *-u* + **-ma-* > *-u* + **-i* > *ï*;

and it was these processes that resulted in the stem-forms for the verbal negatives appearing in the texts.

At the same time that this original negative morpheme *-ma-* was being suffixed to the verb root, and its initial nasal assimilated to the final consonant of the verbs, the vowel of this same *-ma-* was nasalized in pre-Old Japanese, so that the resulting forms were, at one stage in their development, **kakā* and **sirā* (the parallel between these developments and the Ryūkyū forms cited above will be immediately apparent). When these forms with the nasalized -ā- vowels were then immediately followed by further suffixational materials, such as forms of *s-u* 'do, make', this nasalization was often, and in a pattern that became increasingly generalized, realized in the form either of (a) the generation and subsequent insertion of a syllabic nasal -*n* between the end of the verb form proper and the following suffixational form in *s-* (see Miller 1967: 215–18), or (b) the voicing of the following form *s-* > *z-*, or (c) both the above, but in ways the chronology of which it is now often extremely difficult to unravel from the evidence of the texts. This is an historical approach to the doctrine -*nisu* > -*nzu* > -^{n}*zu* > -*zu* as generally presented in the Japanese literature; it amplifies and expands this doctrine by explaining in comparative terms from where and how the nasal element arises, i.e., that it arises from the **-m-* in the original proto-Altaic negative morpheme **-ma-*.

In forms of the OJ *sira ni* type, the *n-* became initial in its own subsequent syllable rather than syllabic and final in the previous syllable; in other words, in these forms it arose following the original **-ā* as a hiatus marker separating that **-ā* from an immediately following and original suffixed **-i*. But it is impossible either to affirm or to refute a connection between this **-i* and the sentence subject marker K *i* discussed above (p. 29).

Explanations similar to those advanced above are also in order for the well-known Japanese negative gerunds of the type *ara de* 'is not, and . . .', *iFa de* 'not saying, and . . .', and *nara de wa* 'unless it is . . .', to give only a few examples. These forms are to be analysed as original **ara-ma te* > **arrā te* > **arā te* > **ara^{n}de* > *ara de;* all the historical developments here have many parallels elsewhere in the language (see Miller 1967: 215–18). The voicing of the *de* in these collocations is definitive evidence for the earlier presence of the nasalized vowel resulting from the assimilated **-ma-* morpheme.

In this way, the answer to the second question, and the comparative explanation of the thematic vowel -*a-*, proves also to be at the same time the answer to the first question asked above, i.e., that on the origin of the allomorphic variation in the Japanese verbal negation morpheme, with its forms in both -z- and -n-. The -z- forms are due to voicing of the initial s- of suffixed forms of s-u 'do, make', following the originally nasalized thematic vowel, which in turn resulted from original *-ma-; the -n- forms are due to a consonant insertion following the original *-ā- when an additional morphological element was suffixed.

Evidence for the same addition of original *-ma- may be traced to a certain extent in Tungus, where it is the aorist form of the verb (-ra, -sa, -da) with which the negative is used (Benzing 1955: 1093). This provides evidence for the same thematic vowel as in Japanese, and there is no reason not to assign the *-a- of these Tungus aorist forms used with negatives to the same origin as the thematic vowel -a- in the Japanese negatives. This is not to imply that the Tungus aorist forms in -ra, -sa, and -da are themselves of the same origin; they must be traced instead to other more complex developments between an original suffixed aorist morpheme and final consonants in the verb stems (cf. the membership of the verbs in *-n in the -da aorist class [Benzing 1955: 1075], for a clue to how this aorist allomorphic variation probably arose in Tungus). What is suggested is somewhat different. In much the same way that the addition of an original aorist morpheme to different verb stems resulted in the development of the Tungus -ra, -sa, -da allomorphs for the aorist, so also did the addition of the original *-ma- negative morpheme to those same verb stems result in overtly identical allomorphs for the forms to which the additional negative formations were added—forms which thus became indistinguishable from the aorists and are conveniently (and inevitably) described as if they actually, i.e., historically, were aorists. In other words, the problem is one both of description and of historical analysis; and if each of the three classes of Tungus aorists were redescribed to end in -r-, -s-, and -d- (thus, class 1, *anar-, etc.; class 2, *bis-, etc.; class 3, *od-, etc.), then the changes involved in the formation and historical development of the negatives would be even more closely parallel to those in Japanese (*anar- + -ma- > anara-, etc.).

To understand how the nonstandard Azuma Old Japanese negatives arose, it is first necessary to center attention upon the final phoneme in their characteristic negative morpheme -naF-. This -F- is to be identified with the well-known Old Japanese durative morpheme for repeated and continuous action, which in early Old Japanese could be suffixed as an enlargement to a considerable number of verbs, if not freely. The morpheme in question is the *fukugobi* 'secondary affix' *ha, hi, hu, he* of the school grammars (Yamada 1952: 128–30). By the time of late Old Japanese this *-F-* had become more or less fossilized in its attachment to a relatively small number of verb forms; examples that may be cited include *FakaraFu* 'plan', *mukaFu* 'confront', *yobaFu* 'call', *kataraFu* 'speak, say, tell', *sumaFu* 'live, dwell', and *naraFu* 'become accustomed to'. All these are complex forms that show this enlargement with *-F-* when considered alongside their corresponding simplex forms, namely *Fakaru, muku, yobu, kataru, sumu,* and *naru* (Nakada 1963: 980).

Often the addition of this enlargement to the verb was the occasion for an assimilatory change in the vowel immediately preceding the *-F-*, which became *-ö-* as a result; thus, in *M* 892, *susuröFite* 'do [something] continually', for an expected **susuraFite*. Cf. also *uturu* 'move, shift', but *uturöFu* in *M* 4109 (other examples in Wenck 1959: 4.8–9, § 908.8; note there especially *yasumoFu* 'rest' going with *yasumu*, for expected **yasumaFu*). Nor is this assimilatory change unknown even to the characteristic Azuma negative morpheme itself; the allomorph *-nöF-* for this morpheme, in which the *-ö-* is to be accounted for in this same fashion, has already been noted above.

Quite apart from the verbal negation morpheme, and apart too from nonstandard Azuma Old Japanese, what proved in effect to be fortuitous suffixation of this *-F-* morpheme to verbs in final *-n-* had in many other completely independent cases produced homophonous enlarged verbs in final *-naFu*; among the examples that may be cited are the following: *ubenaFu* 'comply, submit' (note that the Senmyō texts have a variant in *-m-*, thus, *ubenami!*); *akinaFu* 'carry on trade, commerce', *izanaFu* 'invite, rule', *uranaFu* 'divine, tell the auspices', and *udunaFu* 'treat with esteem, care' (Ōno in *M* 4.278, in his gloss to *M* 4094). In all these verbs, the original sense of the *-F-* enlargement was fully in keeping with the basic meaning of the morpheme, and partly as a result of this the enlargement was soon fossilized into a form that won out completely in its competition with the simplex. And this, too, must have been what happened in the case of the privative OJ *-siFu*, already noted above (p. 258), for which the only form we know from the texts is the enlargement with the *-F-* already in place.

The same verbal enlargement *-F-* may also be cited from still another Old Japanese verb, and one moreover that happens to be, as far as the historical problems of the negatives are concerned, of more than routine interest. This is the verb OJ *usu* 'lose, do away with', alongside OJ *usinaFu* 'id.' This is a particularly important pair of examples because with the enlarged form we are back in nonstandard Old Japanese territory all over again, but this time we have a standard *-naFu* enlargement looking suspiciously like a verbal negative. But when we consider the semantics of the form, it is not difficult to see how *-naFu* was added to original *us-u* as a kind of redundant negative suffix to the stem, as well as in the durative sense proper of the *-F-* enlargement alone. With the *usu* and *usinaFu*, nonstandard and standard Old Japanese forms converge, and at the same time the Azuma negatives fall together with the standard *-F-* durative enlargement.

We have spoken several times above of the nonstandard Old Japanese verbal negative *-naFu;* immediately above we have provided some of the background for its final *-F-u* elements; what then if anything can be said concerning the initial consonant in the *-na-* segment of this morpheme? This *n-* can only be regarded as the result of a dissimilation before the labial *-F-*, to which it early became attached in the Azuma dialects, of the initial *-m-* of the same original proto-Altaic negative morpheme *-ma-*, so that in adding *-naF-* the Azuma dialects were in effect adding nothing more than the changed remnant of an original *-maF-*, i.e., *-ma + -F-*. Perhaps even this Old Japanese durative morpheme *-F-* may be etymologically connected with pA *-m* for present and future tense, the Mongol 'praesens imperfecti I' (Poppe 1955: 261–62; 267).

It is not difficult to cite parallel cases of the dissimilation postulated here, in which original *-m-* before *-F-* (either as such or in its voiced equivalent *-b-*) may be documented as having shifted to *n-*. Perhaps the most striking parallel is that afforded by the place-name Mibu, for which in the Heian period the dissimilated form *nibu* occurs (Wenck 1959: 4.174, § 980). Another close parallel, with the dissimilation operating at a position still one additional syllable removed, is the place-name *MiraFu*, for which the dissimilated form *niraFu > nirō* occurs (Wenck 1959: 4. 179–80, Anm. 16). Also closely parallel is the dissimilated form *niFodori* 'the little grebe' for the *miFodöri* of *Kojiki* poem 42 (Wenck, ibid., 180, Anm. 16). The well-known Old Japanese form *unaFara* 'the sea' (as for example in *M* 2, *M* 894, and frequently throughout the Old Japanese corpus), shows the same dissimilatory changes in its development from *umiFara* 'field, plain, expanse of the sea', and is in addition of more than routine interest because in the secondary, assimilated form the -*a*- that appears following the secondary -*n*- gives additional retrospective evidence for the labial quality of the original but now no longer surviving -*m*- out of which the secondary -*n*- developed. Finally, *M* 4328 most fortunately preserves an Azuma *hapax*, nonstandard OJ *unöFara*, which shows in addition the same assimilatory shift of -*a*- > -*ö*- before -*F*- that the Azuma negative morpheme -*naF*- ∼ -*nöF*- also displays, and hence rounds out the demonstration of the significance of all these forms. Originating in *unaFara*, the dissimilated allomorph *una*- was subsequently generalized to appear in a few other poetic compounds, and in wider phonetic environments.

An important example that may be cited from the modern Ryūkyū area is involved in the following paradigm of related forms for 'read' (glosses and grammatical functions of the forms are not relevant to the example, and hence are omitted):

> '*juma'N*   '*jumi*   '*junu'N*

Since these forms go etymologically with J *yom-u* 'read', there can be little question that the forms with -*m*- are original, while that with -*n*- is a secondary development. Such a secondary development can hardly have taken place here through assimilation to the final -'*N* (which appears also in the first member of the paradigm), and hence must be accounted for as the result of dissimilation with the -*u*- vocalization that appears before and after the phoneme in question. So also the form *kanu'N* is reported, equivalent to and going etymologically with J *kam-u* 'eat, bite, chew'; and in both cases we are also told that 'there are also speakers who instead use' [the etymological, unassimilated forms] '*jumu'N* and *kamu'N* (Hattori 1955: 333 and n. 3).

This, then, was the historical origin of the morpheme -*naF*- for verbal negation that characterized the nonstandard Old Japanese dialects: it was the result of a dissimilation within Japanese of the original Altaic negative morpheme *-*ma*- > *-*na*-, due to the enlargement of this morpheme, also within Japanese, by the suffixation of the durative morpheme -*F*-, so that *-*ma* + -*F*- > -*naF*-.

The statements above for those cases in which Old Japanese verbs ending in an original stop consonant had the negative *-*ma*- suffixed directly to that consonant must be somewhat modified for those cases in which that final consonant was *-*w*, notably in the two important verbs *s-u* 'do' and *ku-ru* 'come', where the original roots as shown by internal reconstruction within Japanese alone were **sw-* and **kw-* (Miller 1967: 322).

For *s-u* 'do' we would expect a negative base **sö-*, but that form does not appear to be attested except in the Old Japanese prohibitives (cf. below); instead the negative forms for this verb are generally built upon a base *se-*, thus *sezu*, *sezaru*, etc. The exact assimilatory processes involved in the development of this special negative base in *-e-* for *s-u* 'do' are exceptional and difficult to parallel from elsewhere in the language, but as always, any form with *-e-*, including the Old Japanese negative base *se-* for this verb, must necessarily be a secondary development within Japanese, and without significance on the comparative level.

In the case of **kw-*, i.e., *ku-ru* 'come', the developments are somewhat more transparent. In Old Japanese morphophonemics, the combination *w + a* is normally replaced by OJ *ö* (Miller 1968: 323), so it is not difficult to see in the special negative base *kö-* for this verb the results of an original **kw- + ma* sequence, with the *-m-* of the negative morpheme assimilating regularly to the final consonant (in this case, **-w-*) of the very stem in exactly the same way as with the other consonant verbs.

This same verb appears in the *Man'yōshū* in an important series of exceptionally interesting negative formations that may be cited with profit in this connection. There are nine poems in the *Man'yōshū* where the original text has the following writing, in Chinese characters: *pù-lái-ì*, lit., 'not + come + increase'. There seems to be no good reason to question the traditional interpretation of these passages, namely that *pù-lái* (5379, 3768) is to be taken as a sequence of two semantograms, in the sense of 'does not come', and that the final character *ì* (3052) 'increase', is instead a phonogram. This character, however, is not a normal phonogram based upon any of its phonetic values in Chinese but rather a rebus-graph whose phonetic value depends upon its semantic association with the Japanese verb *mas-u* 'increase, add to'; hence, the Chinese graph *ì* in these passages is a phonogram for at least the sequence *mas-*, plus some undetermined final vowel (*mas-u*, *mas-a*, *mas-i?*). In all but one of the nine *Man'yōshū* text examples this expression is phrase-final; in one case (*M* 2039) there is the final addition of the Chinese graph *yǔ* (7533) 'have', so that in this poem the phrase-final expression reads *pù-lái-ì-yǔ*. This graph *yǔ* is fairly common in *Man'yōshū* orthography as a semantogram for the Japanese verb *ar-u* 'have, be', and is customarily so interpreted in reading *M* 2039.

The great difficulty with these nine text examples is that the reading tradition is in anything but uniform agreement about what the correct received readings for these particular lines are. The nine texts are as follows, giving in each case the reading adopted in the NKBT edition of the *Man'yōshū*:

> 680: kimasanu
> 1097: kimasazu
> 1499: kimasazu
> 1501: kimasanu
> 1620: kimasane
> 2039: kimasazaru
> 2929: kimasazu
> 3280: kimasazu
> 3318: kimasanu

In each of these cases the original *Man'yōshū* text has simply *pù-lái-ì*, except for *M* 2039, where it reads *pù-lái-ì-yŭ*.

But even this rich profusion of interpretations, for each of which convincing arguments from semantic, grammatical, and metrical considerations may be cited, gives a misleading impression of uniformity and unanimity. For one single example from the above list, *M* 1097, the following variants have been suggested by various exegetical traditions: *kimasazu*, *kimasanu*, and *imasazu!* Most of the commentators and the reading tradition in general have used the *ki*-base for the verb in these forms, but there is no basis in the texts for this choice; and indeed, in *M* 1097, where the entire point of the poem appears to be a play on several words containing OJ *kö-*, it would seem more meaningful and more in keeping with the over-all sense and style of the poem to adopt a reading in OJ *kö-* for this form too, probably here OJ **kömasazu*.

Thanks to these difficulties and ambiguities of the *Man'yōshū* script, about all that can be done about these forms from a linguistic point of view is to call attention to their existence, and in addition to point out what linguistic features are overtly and unequivocally noted in the texts, namely a) that they are negatives (this we can tell from the *pù* of the semantograms *pù-lái*), and b) that they contained the sequence OJ *-mas-* (this much can be ascertained from the use of the Chinese graph *ì* as a rebus-phonogram based upon its Japanese translation equivalent *mas-u*). It is disappointing not to be able to go beyond this point, and not to be able to join the traditional *Man'yōshū* scholars in their flights of exegetical fancy in writing full and suitably inflected negative forms (*kimasanu, kimasazu, kimasane, kimasazaru*, etc.). In *M* 2039 the use of the graph *yǔ* certainly seems to indicate some form of OJ *ar-u*, so that for this single example we might go so far as to write OJ *k-V-mas-ar-*, but it is impossible to go beyond that. In all these forms, it is impossible to determine the vocalization of the verb base, or to decide whether it was *ki-* or *kö-* or something still different from either of these two. But in spite of all these difficulties, the forms involved in these nine text examples are nevertheless extremely valuable ones—forms in which we can see clearly a stage in which the original negative morpheme **-ma-* had not yet assimilated its initial **-m-* to the preceding final consonant of the verb to which it was suffixed. OJ *-mas-* is unambiguously attested as a negative formant in these examples, and given the nature of the writing system and its many drawbacks, we are fortunate indeed to have had preserved for our inspection these extremely valuable intermediate forms from the history of the developmental process of the Japanese verbal negatives.

By the time of the greater portion of the early Japanese written records, the original **-ma-* negative had produced voicing in the following **-s-* from affixed forms of the verb *s-u* 'do', but it is important to note that there are a number of sporadic instances where the early texts actually do record negatives with unvoiced **-s-* forms, thus preserving overt written evidence for still another intermediate stage in the history reconstructed here for the development of the *-z-* ∼ *-n-* negative morphemes. Even without this evidence, the major intermediate stages in the process could be postulated, and postulated correctly, solely by linguistic methods, but the evidence of early written sources is always particularly welcome when, as in this particular case, it may be adduced both to control as well as to substantiate independent theoretical formulations for recovering the processes of linguistic change.

Before presenting the evidence, it will be necessary to make a brief mention of the way in which these important examples are generally presented (and in effect kept concealed from view) in the Japanese literature. Japanese scholarship on the subject (and Wenck 1954–59 generally follows it in this aspect of its methodology) approaches these texts from the following point of view. It assumes that the form the verb would have in classical (or modern literary) Japanese is the same form that it had in Old Japanese. This a priori assumption is of course totally without scientific or linguistic basis. It then interprets the orthography of the early texts in terms of this baseless assumption, and whenever necessary adjusts the usual, normal interpretation of that orthography to conform to this original a priori assumption. This method, it almost goes without saying, is a reversal of logical order, and one that produces unreliable, and at times even ludicrous, findings as a result.

It will help to understand what is happening here if we take a concrete instance dealing with a single but important Chinese graph, *hsü* (2847). In the *Bussokuseki no uta* inscription, this graph is used 18 times as a simple phonogram for OJ *su* (data for this and other statistical statements on the voicing/voiceless distinction both in this particular inscription and in the Old Japanese corpus in general from Ōno T. 1962: 749–50, which also see for a good example of the traditional approach to the problem). The syllable OJ *zu* is written once in the same inscription with another character, the Chinese graph *shòu* (5840), a normal and expected phonogram writing for this voiced equivalent. But there is one additional case, in poem 3 of the inscription, which is the crux of the matter: we are told (Ōno, loc. cit.; Wenck 1959: 215–16, § 1002, and passim) that since the verb form being written here is OJ *emizute* '[they] were not able to see [it]', that this is a rare case, and moreover the single exception within this entire inscription, where the graph *hsü* has been used to write OJ *zu*. Of course the only logical approach is simply the reverse of all this: we have a great body of other evidence available with which to interpret this particular writing, and that body of evidence affords absolutely no basis for interpreting the verb form in *Bussokuseki* poem 3 as any other shape than OJ *emisute*. The method of traditional Japanese scholarship here has been to begin from what should instead be the end-result, to assume the details of the forms in the text as somehow known a priori, and then to evaluate the orthography of the texts in accordance with these baseless assumptions.

We must, it goes almost without saying, adopt a quite different technique, beginning with the values of the graphs in cases where there can be no doubt of their proper interpretation, and then carefully and cautiously extending that empirical evidence into the areas of difficult or moot readings. What we know of Old Japanese is no more or less than what we find written in the texts; but even this is true only so long as those texts are read as we have received them; and it ceases to be true the moment we start to alter the details of those texts to suit our fancies or in order to conform to preconceived assumptions about how the texts 'ought to read', as distinct from the way they actually do read.

For a fair sample of the method and its pitfalls, a single completely representative example may be cited from Ōno T. (1962: 755). Commenting on the writings for the equivalent of J *nezumi* 'mouse' in an early text, he notes that this same graph *hsū* is used for the middle syllable; then, of this word, he adds, 'perhaps indeed [the word] was *nesumi*, but let us assume for the time being that it was *nezumi* (*ichiō 'nezumi' de atta to mite oku*)'. But then this a priori assumption is immediately used as the basis for citing this same passage as a case where the graph *hsū* is used as a phonogram writing for the OJ *zu!* Nothing could possibly be more exquisitely circular.

Once we free ourselves from this philological labyrinth, we are able to collect the following list of passages where the form that in the later developments of the verbal negatives has become *-zu* is recorded in the earlier, intermediate, and unvoiced stage in which it was still *-su*. (For the traditional interpretation of many of these as 'exceptional writings with *hsū* for *zu*', see Ōno T. 1962: 640.)

1. *M* 809: *aFasu* 'not meeting'. (Cf. the note in the NKBT edition by Ōno, M 2.67, noting that the orthography is 'exceptional', but still maintaining the spurious reading **aFazu* in his text.)

2. *M* 845, *tirasu* '[plum blossoms] not falling'.

3. *M* 4337, *monöFasu* 'saying nothing'.

4. *M* 4364, *iFasu* 'not saying'.

5. *M* 4371, *koFisu* 'not loving'.

6. *M* 4372, *kaFërimisu* 'not looking back'.

7. *M* 4943, *kinakasu* 'come and not [be] crying'. This is a particularly valuable example, because it is possible to cite both the voiceless earlier form and the later voiced form as well. The Kan'ei-bon text tradition of the *Man'yōshū* preserves this poem with the unvoiced form *kinakasu;* other text traditions have the later voiced form *kinakazu*, with the Chinese graph *shòu* (5840) for the voiced *zu*, quite regularly and unmistakably (thus the Genryaku-bon and other texts). Note also that the NKBT editors have chosen these later readings over the one in their own basic text in order thus to remove from their text what otherwise appeared to them to be only one more difficult reading. But in the process they have sacrificed a valuable piece of linguistic history.

For other examples of similar writings, with negatives in -*su* from texts other than the *Man'yōshū*, cf. Ōno T. 1962: 610, 7587 and Yamada 1954: 265. The form *emisute* in *Bussokuseki* poem 3, another parallel example, has already been noted above; we shall return again to that form below in the discussion of its prefixed *e*-.

One further form with earlier unvoiced -*s*- for later assimilated -*z*- is worth citing because the phonogram orthography of the original gives such strikingly obvious evidence for the shape of the form; this is the verb *omoFosasaru* 'not thinking (attributive)' in the *Takahashi ujibumi* of 792. Mills (1954: 129, 133) has followed the traditional circular Japanese scholarship on this point and hence has *omoFosazaru* in his transcription. In the original this form is written with two semantograms, Chinese *pù-ssū* (5379, 5580) 'not thinking', followed by a verb ending written in phonograms, -*păo-tsò-tsò-lĭu* (4946, 6775, 6775, 4080), for OJ -*Fosasaru*. This is a striking example, because the same phonogram, Chinese *tsò* (6775), is used here for both the *sa*-syllables; and to assume, as do the Japanese scholars and Mills, that this is intended for writing the sequence -*saza*- is also to assume that the scribes used one and the same phonogram twice in succession, the first time for voiceless -*sa*- and then immediately following again for voiced -*za*-. The form in the text is clear and unambiguous: we must read [*omo*]*Fosasaru*, interpolating [*omo*] on the basis of the Chinese semantograms *pù-ssū*, and adding to it the unmistakable evidence of the ending in phonograms, -*păo-tsò-tsò-lĭu*, i.e., -*Fosasaru*.

It is not difficult to recover the general pattern of change that eventually resulted in the form attested in the *Takahashi ujibumi* text, even though some of the details remain uncertain. Original *omoFo-ma-saru, a form with obvious parallels to the Middle Mongol forms cited earlier from the *Secret History* (MMo. *keẏ.is-ümser*, *ölös-ümser*, etc.), must have been the starting place for these developments. The -*ma*- in this form may first have shifted to -*wa*- (or -*Fa*-) before assimilating to the following -*s*-, or the assimilation may have proceeded directly from the -*m*-; at any rate, with that assimilation accomplished, we have arrived at the form attested in the text. A completely parallel construction going with both the Mongol and the Japanese forms is found in Chu. *vaska-ma-săr* 'without hurrying'; and taking this together with the Turkish forms in -*siz*, etc., we may reconstruct pA *-*ma-sir*$_2$ or pA *-*m-sir*$_2$, or a conflation of both, as underlying all these formations. (My understanding of the correct historical explanation of these forms has been aided by a personal communica-

tion from John C. Street, 23 March 1970.) The comparison is greatly
strengthened when we recall that original *-sir₂* would have given OJ
-sar-, not OJ *-sat-*, since OJ /s/ was an affricated stop, [tˢ], not a continuant [s], before OJ /a/, and hence OJ *-r-* would be the normally
expected reflex of pA r_2 in these circumstances. This casts still further
doubt on the advantage of the traditional analysis that takes all such
Japanese forms as ultimately containing earlier unvoiced, later voiced
forms deriving from the verb *s-u* 'to do'.

It would certainly also be possible to consider instead that one of
the two attested Old Japanese privatives, *-zi + k-* < *-si + k-* or
-si + F- was involved here; but that alternative has been ruled out
on several grounds. Most compelling is the semantic argument; these
formants are privatives, and as such they would be out of place in a
morphological structure that was already, and before their affixation,
clearly and unambiguously negative in meaning. Of equal importance
is the phonological argument, which is difficult to separate from
morphological considerations in this particular case. The two privatives cited are intimately bound up with inflectional *-k-* in the first
case and the durative *-F-* in the second; this indicates a clear de-
marcation between them and the final morphological elements with
which we are concerned here.

Sporadic anachronistic survivals of the original proto-Altaic negative *-ma-* may be detected here and there in Japanese, most notably
in the two following related words:

1. J *mare* 'rare, exotic; seldom'. For the word in Old Japanese, cf.
Bussokuseki poem 2: *mare ni mo aru ka mo* 'rare indeed are . . .'; and
in composition, with a combining form in *-a*, OJ *maraFitö* (ibid.,
poem 15) 'foreigner, esp., a newly arrived foreigner from the Asiatic
continent'. This word represents a survival of an original asyntactic
negative *-ma-* here atypically prefixed (rather than suffixed) to forms
of the verb *ar-u* 'have, be', hence *ma- + ar-* 'not to have, not to be',
eventually fossilized as OJ *mare, mara-*, in the attested meanings.

2. Closely related to this same *mare* 'rare' is the Japanese defective
verbal suffix *-maz-*; for the grammarians this form, used in the texts
for negatives of dubitative, potential, and necessitative sense, is the
negative equivalent of *-bes-* 'ought to' (Lewin 1959: 188). It is the
proximate origin of the modern suffix J *-mai*, as in *arumai* 'there
probably won't be, isn't [any such thing]', *sumumai* 'probably won't
live, dwell', etc.

It is also difficult not to associate these two Japanese forms with

the Old Turkish negative aorists in -*ma* + *z*, where the characteristic -*r* of the Old Turkish aorist shifts to -*z* with the addition of the
negative -*ma*- (von Gabain 1950: 108, § 211; on dialect variants in
-*mas*-, cf. Benzing 1953: 117). This Turkish morpheme may well be
referred to pA *-*mar*₂, with OT -*z* for pA *-*r*₂; in that case, J -*maz*- <
-*mad*- would go together with this original *-*r*₂ in regular phonological
correspondence (cf. p. 148 above), following the continuant -*m*-. It is
also interesting to speculate on the possible reasons within Old Turkish for the shift of -*r* > -*z* in this particular morphological process;
could there have been an allomorph of the negative morpheme in
pre-Turkish of the shape *-*mä*-, with the original aorist -*r* assimilating
to the position of articulation of the vocalization of that form, to
explain its shift to the palatal *-*r*₂ > -*z*? Nor can we forget that the
-*s*- of J -*bes*- could, as we have seen above, be a regular phonological
inheritance for pA *-*l*₂. All this seems to point in the direction of an
ancient complex of interrelated forms, no doubt rendered even more
involved by borrowings, analogic remodelings, and intraparadigm
shifts on more than one occasion.

   3. One apparent survival of the original pA *-*ma*- negative morpheme in Old Japanese deserves special notice. This is OJ *yumë*, a
form appearing sporadically in a few early texts, where it is explained
by the commentators as a strong prohibitive. It most often is found
with OJ *na* immediately preceding it (thus, *M* 1657, *tirikösu na yumë*
'may they never, may they not fall, scatter'), but texts also occur
with OJ *yumë* in the same sense but without an accompanying *na*
(e.g., *M* 3305).

   In the Japanese school tradition this OJ *yumë* is generally explained
as an imperative from the verb OJ *yum-u* 'avoid, shun, keep a taboo',
but this explanation may not be seriously maintained, since as Ōno
points out (*M* 2.352–53, repeated verbatim in *M* 3.378–79) the imperative of that verb would be OJ *yume*, not the *yumë* in question.
Ōno suggests (loc. cit.) that *yumë* is a compound of the base of this
same verb *yum-u*, plus OJ *më* 'eye', and that the expression was
originally something on the order of 'shun, avoiding looking at, avert
the eyes from', to be associated with ideas of the evil eye in early
societies. Such an explanation for the form can neither be affirmed nor
denied; it is purely speculative and beyond demonstration by linguistic methods.

   The morpheme identification of the first syllable in OJ *yumë* must,
for the time being at least, remain obscure; but there can be little

doubt that the final syllable contains a Japanese development of an earlier *-ma- + -i* sequence, appearing quite normally as OJ *-më*, and that the *-ma-* morpheme that can be isolated in this way is related to the old Altaic negative, here sporadically surviving in surprisingly transparent garb in this Japanese form.

4. Additional examples of anachronistic survivals of *-ma-* due to occurrence in asyntactic initial position might possibly include J *masaka* 'by no means, on no account, surely no', and J *mabara* 'sparse, thin, sporadic', both forms that have no convincing etymologies within Japanese. Finally, J *muzukashii* < *mutukasii* 'difficult' should also probably be mentioned in this connection. Ramstedt (1924, = 1951: 19) suggests connecting it with the verb J *tsukam-u* 'grasp, take hold of', through a semantic intermediary '*not manageable', and would hence see in the form an assimilated version (*mu-* < *ma-* before the *-u-* of *tsukam-u*) of the same negative morphological element. The suggestion is a perceptive one, difficult to affirm and impossible to deny; and the least that can be said in its favor is that it surely is head and shoulders above the usual Japanese school explanation of *muzukashii* as somehow related to the verb *muzukaru* 'fret, be peevish, cross, esp. of a child'.

Attention must next be paid to the important set of Japanese negative adjectives that are based upon enlargements of the morpheme *nak-*, with the allomorph *nas-* for conclusive uses (Yokoyama 1950: 24). Initially it may perhaps be tempting to associate these forms with the nonstandard Azuma negatives in *-naF-*, already treated above, perhaps even deriving the Azuma forms from the *nak-* forms by means of a lenition of [k] through an intermediate spirant [χ] (cf. Miller 1967: 169); but the comparative evidence shows that this would probably not be the best solution for the problem of their origin.

This negative adjective morpheme, both in its forms and in its probable historical development, goes together quite closely with the Manchu verb of negation *akû* (Benzing 1955: 1094). On the nasal initial of the Japanese forms, the instructive parallel from Manchu is the following set of forms for the verb Ma. *tači-* 'study, learn', with which go Ma. *tačin* 'doctrine' and *tačinaku* 'unaccustomed' (Poppe 1956: 206). Murayama (1957: 128, 131) has already pointed out certain suggestive parallels between other Altaic languages and Japanese in the use of an *-n-* allomorph for the original genitive postposition in certain locutions (*n-V ∼ *-n-*), and his remarks have immediate relevance for these developments of the Japanese negative adjective morpheme *nak-*. The proto-Altaic genitive suffix *-n* (Poppe 1955: 187–88) may be traced in Japanese in its unvocalized, i.e., zero-vowel form through the voicing of the second member of such compounds as *hanabi* 'fireworks' < *hana* 'flowers' + *hi* 'fire' in a combining-form with voiced initial, i.e., *hana* + *-n*(-) + *hi* > *hanabi* (cf. Murayama 1957: 128–29, citing the original statement of this important historical insight from Ramstedt).

What appears to have taken place in the original linguistic unity underlying all these forms was the development of contractions involving nasal initials and various forms of an original negative verb (or adjective?) *ak-*, going with Ma. *akû*, OJ (*n*)*ak-*, etc. Composition of the type seen in Ma. *tačinaku* 'unaccustomed' was common in the original linguistic unity. A parallel construction in late Old Japanese would be the often-encountered *yangotonaki Fito* 'nobleman, person of good background and position', with *yan-* ∼ *yamu* < Chinese *yàng* (7256) 'sort, variety' through an intermediate *yaũ* (later folk-etymologized as being instead from J *yam-u* 'stop, quit' !) + *koto* 'fact, thing' + *nak-i*.

In this type of composition the original genitive *-n-* tended to become more closely attached in Japanese to the following *-ak-* morpheme than to the preceding morpheme, unlike the situation in Manchu where eventually the form shifted from a genitive into a simple deverbal noun. The result was that this *n* was soon taken as part of the negative morpheme itself, and this morpheme therefore soon developed into the well-known Japanese negative adjective *nak-*. That this phenomenon was not an isolated one, or restricted to that portion of the original Altaic linguistic unity with which Manchu and Japanese are most closely to be associated, is demonstrated by the parallel contractions that Poppe (1955: 288) reports from 'one of the Monguor dialects', in which the original Mongol negative verb *üli*, in a reduced form *li*, contracts with immediately following verbs to give such forms as *lōli* < *li ōli* 'not to become', *lōro* 'not to enter', etc. But proto-Altaic has no forms in initial *l-* (or initial *r-*); and as we have seen above, forms that might appear from the Tungus evidence to go back to initial *l-* are to be referred instead to original initial *n-*. This brings the secondary negative forms in initial *l-* that Poppe cites from 'one of the Monguor dialects' significantly closer to the Manchu and Japanese evidence; once again, while the details remain obscure, the over-all outlines of the developments are clear.

The Japanese developments resulting in these *nak-* negative adjective forms were no doubt accelerated in their formation and encouraged in their survival by the coexistence in the language, at the same time as these developments, of other semantically related forms of the same general shape, notably certain minor forms with (-)*na*(-). We have already discussed the nonstandard Azuma OJ negatives in -*naF*-, whose very existence in the language must have exerted a powerful influence in the direction of the contraction and false-division ultimately responsible for the development of the negative adjective *nak-* forms. Mention might also be made here of the preposed prohibitive OJ *na*, as in OJ *na yuki sö* 'go not!' (on these forms, cf. Murayama 1957: 129; Miller 1967: 157). One might almost suspect the verb stem (here *yuki*) of being infixed, in these prohibitive constructions, into a morpheme **-na-s* + *ö*, strangely reminiscent of the **-ma-s-* negatives already commented upon above. But such speculation is hardly very productive, and it is rather more rewarding to notice instead that it is in these prohibitives that the special negative base *sö* for *s-u* 'do' does turn up after all, as predicted. Another even less well understood but clearly related form that appears in the Old Japanese texts and deserves at least to be mentioned in this connection is the phrase-final negative morpheme *na* of *M* 230, *M* 802, *M* 1826, and *M* 2900; in each of these cases it appears as the final part of the collocation *motö na*, apparently meaning 'pointless, reasonless, careless[ly]'.

We have already noted that, with one important exception in the interrogatives, Old Turkish has no inherited Altaic forms in initial *n-*, because pA **n-* became **j-* in pre-Turkish. This makes it possible immediately to relate OT *yoq* 'be nonexistent, not to be' with J *nak-*, the Turkish form going with the *o*-grade and the Japanese (and Tungus, cf. Ma. *akû*) with the *a*-grade in the well-known *a/o* ablaut series. The final velar of these forms also reminds us of the inflectional -*k*- in the privative OJ -*zik*- treated above, and a remote, though now unrecoverable, relationship among all these forms is by no means out of the question.

Once developed, this *nak-* itself soon became a form of considerable importance. In the language of poetry, this negative enters into an unusual variety of composition when the preceding word is *kumo* 'cloud', which then atypically appears preceding *nak-* forms in a combining form *kuma-*, even at times when separated from the *nak-*

forms by an intervening postposition. Thus, in the *Kindai shūka* of Fujiwara Teika (1162–1241), poem 74, *kuma mo naki* 'cloudless sky'; ibid., poem 80, *kuma naki* 'cloudless', against ibid., poem 8 *kumo no izuko ni* 'where among the clouds . . .', poem 13, *kumo no anata ni te* 'beyond the clouds' (Brower and Miner 1967: passim). The expression was not limited to poetry, but is also found in poetic prose; cf. *Tsurezuregusa* § 137, *kumanaki* 'cloudless'.

It may also be noted in passing that this morphophonemic alternation of *kumo* with *kuma* provides exceptionally important evidence for an earlier **kumö* (cf. Miller 1967: 185–87), and that the rather mysterious *kumoi* < *kumowi* of Japanese poetry (cf. *M* 52), is probably nothing more than a prosodic survival of the original OJ **-ö* in this word. Compare *M* 17 where OJ *umasakë* 'delicious rice-wine' must be read as five syllables (Miller 1967: 300). The etymologization of *kumowi*, i.e., **kumö* to mean 'dwellers [or, dwelling] in the clouds' is little more than a late popular attempt to account for the vocalization and mora-count of the form in earlier texts.

It is clear that in the language underlying the late Old Japanese and early Middle Japanese texts, verbal negatives of the *araz-* type were in vigorous competition with those of the *nak-* type. In the *Tsurezuregusa* it is particularly interesting to see the way in which these two different varieties of negatives are used in syntactic structures quite parallel to one another; thus, in § 28, . . . *bakari aware naru koto wa arazi* 'nothing is more saddening than . . .', but in § 30, . . . *bakari kanasiki wa nasi* 'nothing is sadder than . . .' It is clear that for Kenkō (?1283–?1350), the author of the *Tsurezuregusa*, the two were completely interchangeable synonymous expressions. Other examples of closely parallel use of these two different negatives that may be cited from the same text are to be found in § 25 with *nasi*, against *arazi* in §§ 1, 21, and 28. Most recently, Kobayashi (1968) has surveyed a large amount of textual evidence for the conflict between these two forms, in a study that is extremely informative, even though it has the great drawback of limiting itself exclusively to semantics and pays absolutely no attention to the phonological aspects of the competition. Nevertheless, Kobayashi's study, providing comprehensive data on the appearance of these two forms from Old Japanese down through the Middle Japanese texts of the Portuguese missionary century, is of exceptional value.

OJ *emisute* 'not being able to catch sight of', in *Bussokuseki* poem 3, has already been cited in connection with the evidence it supplies for a still unvoiced intermediate stage of the negatives with final suffixed forms from *s-u* 'do'. In conclusion, it is necessary to comment briefly upon the prefixed *e-* of this and certain other parallel forms.

On these forms, Sansom noted years ago, 'it is curious that these forms are invariably negative. That the use of *e* prefixed to the principal verb is not a borrowed Chinese idiom is pretty clear from its frequency in the medieval colloquial preserved in the Kyōgen and in dialects' (1928: 161, n. 2). His point was well taken, even though, as it now turns out, his data were incomplete. Haguenauer simply denies the truth of Sansom's assertion, but is unable to refute it. For him, these structures are 'un simple calque du chinois [*pù té* (5379, 6161)] + un verbe' (1959: 530); what Haguenauer is unable to explain is the difference in word order, which should have to be reproduced exactly if the Japanese expression were in fact a Chinese calque, together with the difference in meaning, since Chinese *pù té* means 'must not'. It is, indeed, most difficult to find any reason to associate this expression with Chinese. Quite to the contrary, the distinctive ordering of its morphological elements points away from, rather than toward, a borrowing from Chinese. But although Sansom was thus almost surely correct in identifying this as an original Japanese collocation, his statement that these structures occur only in the negative requires slight modification. *M* 4078 has *e mo nadukĕtari* 'is well named'. Sanseidō (1967: 139ᵈ–140ª) lists a few other text examples in which the positive version of this structure also apparently occurs, though none of them is without its problems. In *M* 2091 the reading itself is difficult; at best, if *e-* appears here at all, it is as a semantic equivalent for Chinese *té* (6161), but other texts have a phonogram *ï* instead, and that is the reading that Ōno and the NKBT editors have chosen for their edition. *M* 3152 appears to have *eseme ya* 'will be able to?', but the phrase is only a semantic equivalent for an original in Chinese language as well as in Chinese script, *té wéi yĕh* (6161, 7059, 7312), and as a result it is not reliable linguistic evidence. The same is true also of all the parallel examples for the affirmative employment of this expression that can be cited from the *Kojiki*, all of which are semantic equivalents of Chinese structures with *té*, and hence hardly admissible as linguistic evidence for Japanese. We may conclude that at least one ancient affirmative example is attested (*M* 4078), and others may be conjectured; but the overwhelming pattern in the bulk of the

Old Japanese corpus is that of the negative potential employment of this collocation. At the other end of the time-span, for this structure in Middle Japanese, cf. *eobomasenu* 'can't remember', in the Kyōgen *Iroha* (Lewin 1965: 263, n. 32).

Kindaichi and Kindaichi (1964: 151) distinguish two main semantic functions for this prefixed *e-*, one indicating that an action is impossible because of some subjective reason, the other that an action will not, or should not, or must not transpire. Thus, under the first, *ehaira de* 'unable to enter, not entering' (*Ise monogatari*), from *hair-u* (with the original *-ma- to be traced in the voicing of the original final *te, thus *hair- + ma te > *hairā te > haira de), and under the second, *eFitosikaranu mono* 'something that will not be, ought not to be equal' (*Genji*).

It is also worth noting that forms with this same prefixed *e-* appear to show a certain tendency for collocation with the potential/dubitative negative *-maz-* already discussed above, thus *eideowashimasumaji* 'sie wird nicht hinausgehen können' (*Taketori*); *e zo arumajiki ya* 'wird es wohl nicht geben können' (*Utsuo*) (Lewin 1959: 188).

Morris (1966: 15) calls this *e-* simply a 'neg[ative] potential pref[ix]', a description that, while probably not intended to be any more than a student's guide to the meanings of some of the forms found in the texts, actually comes quite close to describing both the function and the probable history of the form itself. Morris cites *ekoji* (presumably OJ *eközi*) 'cannot come' from the *Kojiki*, and two additional examples in which the *e* is separated from the verb following by one or more additional grammatical elements, *e mo manebazu* (*Eiga* [*monogatari*]) 'cannot (even) learn', and *e kō wa arazarikemu* (*Mak*[*ura no sōshi*]) 'she cannot have been like this' (ibid.). These forms are interesting but rather aberrant; the most usual occurrences for this *e-* finds it directly prefixed to the verb.

The question then remains, are these forms originally potentials that typically appeared in these characteristic syntactic structures and hence have become negative potentials only by association and syntactic collocation, or are they really negative potentials; in other words, are they negatives in their own right, despite the fact that they are generally used with other negatives elsewhere in the immediate syntactic structures to which they belong?

The answer is difficult to frame. In the first place, the Old Japanese verb *u-* ~ *e-* 'be able' is difficult to separate from OT *u-* 'können' (von Gabain 1950: 346). This form must go directly with OJ *u-* 'be able', and the Japanese allomorphs in *e-* for this verb must all be later developments within Japanese, without significance for comparison with other languages. This they have in common with all instances of OJ *e*, each of which involves some internal development or change within Japanese itself. This is only one aspect of the problem; the other is the existence of the proto-Altaic negation verb **e-s-*, cf. Mo., MMo. *ese*, Ev. *esin-* 'nicht sein', Tungus primary stem **e-* (Poppe 1960: 65, and above). Perhaps these two original Altaic verbs, **u-* 'be able', and **e-s-* 'not be', became contaminated with each other in pre-Japanese, a contamination that then in turn hastened the disappearance of the **-s-* from what few traces we may have in Japanese of this **e-s-* verb. The prefixed *e-* of the Japanese negative potentials would then represent a contamination of these two verbs, the potential sense of the resulting form reflecting the association, through the Japanese allomorph *e-* going with original *u-*, of original **u-* 'be able', and the negative sense (as well as the constant syntactic collocation with an additional following negative) reflecting original **e-(s)-* 'not be'. It is not difficult to cite examples in which the potential sense has barely survived, if at all, thus, *enarazu* 'not ordinary, unusual, splendid', in the *Genji monogatari* and other Heian literary texts (cf. Nakada 1963: 169); in such forms the *e* seems to be simply a redundant prefixed negative, totally without semantic function as an indicator of the potential. The syntactic location of this 'negative potential' *e-* reminds one strongly of the preposed negatives of Mongol (Poppe 1955: 288), but it is difficult to associate the Japanese form itself with any of the Mongol lexical items.

In the later stages of the language this *e-* enters into a wide variety of compounds and idiomatic collocations, often with specialized meanings and employment in the special discourse of literature and poetry. Particularly notable in the language of poetry is the expression *iFeba e ni* 'it is difficult, impossible to say', common in texts such as the *Ise monogatari* (Yamada 1954: 272), as well as in the poetic anthologies (Yamada 1952: 155). For *e ni* in other employments, notably as the focus for elaborate wordplay involving the homophones *e* 'inlet, bay' and *eni* 'karma, affinity of action', cf. Vos (1957: 1.229 and 2.122, n. 36) on *e ni si areba* in *Ise monogatari* § 69, and ibid. (1.253 and 2.145, n. 24) on *e ni koso arikere* in *Ise monogatari* § 96. In their treatment of the collocation *e ni* the grammarians have generally attempted to identify the *ni* as an allomorph of the same *-n-u ~ -z-u* negation morpheme discussed above (thus, Yamada 1952: 155, and

Yamada 1954: 272), but there is little basis for this analysis apart from the opportunities it provides for descriptive symmetry. The *ni* of *e ni* is best left simply as what it appears to be in the texts, namely, an adverbial use of the grammatical particle *ni*.

In this way, it is possible to trace all the important Altaic expressions for negation in the Japanese materials, despite the changes and alterations that most of these forms have inevitably undergone during the long period of time that separates our earliest Japanese texts from the Altaic linguistic unity.

To summarize the findings of this chapter: pA *-ma-* is attested throughout the Altaic area (with the notable exception of Korean), and is also well represented in Japanese. In Japanese it has left its most striking and its most ubiquitous traces in the thematic vowel -*a*- for verbal negatives; this -*a*- is etymologically identical with pA *-ma-*. The process of contraction of negative suffix to verb root responsible for this characteristic form has inherited analogs in the Tungus aorists, as well as in Chuvash (Chu. *yama-* < **yar-* + -*ma-* > J *yara-*). In Azuma Old Japanese, the negative -*naF-* is originally **-ma + F-*, with -*F-* durative and -*n*- resulting from dissimilation of *m* before *F*. The *n* in the characteristic Japanese *n/z* negative allomorph configuration is a trace of this same *m* via *mā*, while the *z* in these forms is the result of voicing an earlier *s* still preserved as such in some of the early written records. Sporadic survivals of early forms in the texts help to substantiate this historical analysis, both in the form of negatives of the type OJ *sira* 'does not know', as well as in the case of a few early forms in which unassimilated and unaltered -*ma*- survives in Japanese. Archaic survivals such as the negative OJ *k* + vowel + *mas-ar-* 'does not come' (*M* 1097) have exact and literal parallels in a few equally rare Middle Mongol survivals (*Secret History key.is-ümser*, etc.). For the privatives, the Japanese forms and formations are identical with those in Turkish. The Japanese negative adjectives (J *n-ak-*) similarly go closely with Altaic, representing an *a*-grade development (pA **ja-k-*) of the same root that appears in Turkish with the *o*-grade (OT *yoq*). The inflectional -*k*- of these last forms also appears in the Japanese privatives. Among the Altaic negatives, only the preposed *e*- negative remains isolated from Japanese on the comparative level, but even here we find forms displaying suggestive parallels in both meaning and syntactic employment, though they cannot be brought into direct relationship at present.

All these correspondences in details of form and meaning must be ascribed to something other than either borrowing or coincidence. They argue strongly in favor of an early linguistic unity from which they were inherited by all the languages involved, including Japanese.

5.5 Gerunds

It is not clear when or by whom the term 'gerund' was first used among Western scholars to identify those Japanese forms of which literary J *kakite*, spoken *kaite*, both from *kak-u* 'write', or literary J *nomite*, spoken *nonde*, both from *nom-u* 'drink', are typical; also included as 'gerunds' are adjective forms such as *nakute* from *nai* 'be nonexistent'. The usage is at least as old as Basil Hall Chamberlain's 1888 *Handbook of Colloquial Japanese* (144, § 245: '. . . to the indefinite form add *te*, observing the rules of phonetic change in the Ist. conjugation . . .'); and from its incorporation into Bernard Bloch's description of the modern language (Bloch 1970: 6, and passim) it has become generally accepted usage among most non-Japanese scholars. For the Japanese school-grammarians these forms are compounds of verb bases plus an affix *-te* that they include in their list of *setsuzoku joshi* 'conjunctional auxiliaries' (cf. Lewin 1959: 87, § 109; 91, § 112). Whatever we choose to call them, there are exact parallels, both in form and in meaning, for these verb forms in the other Altaic languages, notably in Turkish, and therefore they must be held to be part of the Japanese inheritance from the original Altaic linguistic unity.

A convenient point of departure for the demonstration necessary to substantiate the above statement is the fact that Old Turkish has a curious set of forms, *yeg ~ yig* 'better', and based on this, an adverbial *yegdi* 'better, in a better way'; but *ädgü* 'good, benefit', as well as another adverbial *ädgüti* 'well', also appear in the texts. It seems to be impossible to connect all these forms within Old Turkish itself; but they can be related to each other when they are viewed from the perspective of the wider Altaic horizon; and in such a treatment the Japanese evidence will prove to be of particular value. In fact, the Japanese forms will turn out to have a high degree of relevance for the explanation of these Old Turkish forms, while at the same time providing a historical account for the development of the Japanese gerund.

It is first necessary, before bringing the Japanese evidence into the discussion, to arrange the Old Turkish materials into somewhat more meaningful order than that in which they are presently found in the handbooks (Tekin 1968, and von Gabain 1950, the principal sources for the forms cited in this chapter).

OT -*tï/-ti, -dï/-di* is a suffix found with 'adverbs of manner'; it is not particularly frequent in the texts (von Gabain 1950: 165, § 382), but it can at least be cited from the following forms: *ädgüti* 'well'; *qatïγdï* 'hard, firmly', *yegdi* 'better', *yaraqlïγdï* 'equipped with weapons' (Tekin 1968: 157, § 3.243). It also appears in a number of common locative expressions, e.g., *öŋdürti* 'im Osten', *kidirti* 'im Westen', and the like (von Gabain 1950: 165, 314), but these forms are best kept separate for the time being, and must eventually be treated in terms of the Japanese locative . . . *ni te*, rather than immediately in terms of the simple Japanese gerund.

Restricting our immediate attention, then, to OT *ädgüti* and *yegdi*, we find that the employment of these forms in the Old Turkish corpus breaks down into four main varieties:

1. with a locative-ablative of comparison, in the sense of 'better than'. Thus, *ötükän yïšda yïg idi yoq ärmis* 'a land better than the *ötükän* mountains does not exist at all!' (Kül Tigin inscription, A.D. 732, SE 3); *ïγar elligdä* [*ï*]*γar qaγanlïγda yeg qïltïm* 'I made them superior to the peoples who have great states and esteemed rulers' (Bilgä kagan inscription, A.D. 734, E 24); cf. also *ïγar oγlanïŋïzda tayγunuŋïzda yegdi* '. . . better than beloved children and descendants' (Kül Tigin inscription, SE 3).

2. with an imperative verb, in the sense of 'well'. Thus, *bu sabïmïn ädgüti äsid, qatïγdï tïŋla* 'hear these words of mine well, and listen hard!' (Kül Tigin, S 2); *yälmä qarγu ädgüti urγïl* 'place the vanguard and patrols properly' (Tonyukuk inscription, ca. A.D. 720, I N 10).

3. in syntactic structures showing no overt correlation with other forms. In such contexts it is generally translated 'better, well', but the sense would seem more likely to have been 'completely, exactly', though the surviving examples are hardly sufficient to settle the point definitely. The clearest example is [*ilig*] *törüg yegdi qazγantïm* 'I arranged and organized [the state] and the institutions completely (? better?) . . .' (Bilgä kagan inscription, E 36). The example from the Tonyukuk inscription, *arïγu batï yeg tedi*, W 2, is translated 'to become tired is, of course, better (they) said' by Tekin (1968: 288), but this makes no sense at all, either in or out of its context in the inscription;

probably the meaning here too is 'completely (exhausted)'. Unfortunately the third example, from the Kül čor inscription (ca. A.D. 719–23) E 6 is too damaged to be useful (. . . *kü]li čor yeti yašïŋa yeg är[. . .]rti*).

4. finally, there are relatively frequent uses as attributes in noun expressions, in the sense simply of 'good'; these require no special attention and need not detain us any longer here.

Von Gabain has already identified this OT *-tï, -ti, -dï, -di* as 'ein im Türkischen selten gebrauchtes, gemeinaltaisches Formans' (1950: 165, § 382). Ramstedt/Aalto collect a large number of possibly related Altaic forms from a variety of languages (1952: 45–46, § 14), and while it is difficult to accommodate all the forms that they cite under this single rubric (in particular, their Tungus forms cause problems and must in general be associated rather with the instrumental and locative constructions, parallel with Japanese . . . *ni te*, on which see also immediately below), the total evidence for an original Altaic gerund formant *-ti* is still substantial.

The phonology of the Japanese reflex of course causes no difficulties; the Japanese *-e* in this form is the result of the same analogic vowel-leveling phenomenon already commented upon in detail (p. 79 above); the initial *t-* is original, going directly with the Altaic form; and the forms in J *d-* (like forms in OT *d-*) are secondary.

The most important thing to note, in comparing these Old Turkish forms with the Japanese gerunds, is the close parallel to be observed in both form and meaning, as well as in syntactic employment, between these two languages for which we have the most abundant materials. We may also comment upon how neatly the cognate Japanese forms would fit into some of the Old Turkish passages already cited, thus effectively demonstrating the striking semantic and syntactic parallels that still obtained between the two languages, despite the great length of time that had elapsed between the Altaic linguistic community (in which they were, in a sense, not two languages but one and the same language), and the time of our earliest written records. Thus, in the passage already cited from the Kül tigin inscription, note how OT *ädgüti* in *bu sabïmïn ädgüti* is exactly equivalent to J *yokute*, both in sense as well as in the forms involved; so also, *qatïγdï* is exactly equivalent to J *katakute*, from *katak-i* 'hard, firm', again both in sense and in the historical continuity of cognate forms.

In the area of semantics, we should also note the meaning of OJ *yöku* 'completely, fully', as for example in *M* 27, a sense that is important for the further congruency of these Japanese forms with the Turkish examples above. *M* 27 is a famous alliterative poem bringing out many of the multifarious meanings that had become attached to secondary formations based on OJ *yö-* 'good,' by the time of the bulk of the Japanese literary materials. There is a fairly literal translation of this poem in Miller (1967: 304), but the following version brings out more fully some of the wide semantic extensions for these Japanese forms:

yöki Fitö nö	Look well at
yösi tö yöku mite	Yoshino, which the wise men [of old]
yösi tö iFisi	Saw completely that it was auspicious
yösinö yöku miyö	And called it 'good'—
yöki Fitö yöku mi (*M* 27)	Oh noble man, look well!

This poem is a virtuoso lexical exercise, not only using derivatives of OJ *yö-* an amazing number of times, but each time using this same *yö-* in another of its important semantic specializations that by the time of this text had come to be part of the Old Japanese lexical store—'good', 'wise', 'noble', 'auspicious' and 'complete' being the most important and immediately discernible of these categories.

With the essentially adverbial import of the Turkish examples, we must compare the usages of the Japanese gerund that the Japanese grammarians also describe as 'adverbial'. A famous passage is the following from the *Makura no sōshi: yamadori Fa, tomo wo koFite, naku ni, kagami wo misureba, nagusamuramu ito aware nari* 'they say when a copper pheasant cries for its mate it can be consoled if one puts a mirror before it—a very moving thought' (translation Morris 1967: I.47, § 43; cf. Kamei 1962: 133, § 43.18; Lewin 1959: 87, § 109). Here the critical portion of this passage is the collocation *tomo wo koFite* 'when he cries out lovingly, longingly for his mate'. Another example of the same usage may be cited from the *Tsurezuregusa*, § 80, *tuFamono tukiya kiFamarite* 'when [a warrior's] sword is broken and his arrows exhausted' (translation Keene 1967: 69; see Nakada 1963: 786[b], where it is an example of his fourth category, *gyakusetsu* 'adversative').

Now we are able to return to the Old Turkish forms with which we began this discussion, and relate them directly to Japanese. Poppe (1960: 58, 61, 137) relates OT *yeg*, *yig* and *yegdi* to a proto-Altaic root **deg-*, in an etymology that is not without its own problems, since it brings together words meaning, in the various languages, 'fly upward,' 'ascend', 'existing', 'feathers', 'the good', and 'best'. Be that as it may, OT *ädgü* and *ädgüti* must be the results of an early metathesis, in which original **deg-* turned up as secondary **edg-*, resulting in the attested forms. OJ *yö-*, MK *tyoh-* 'be liked, be good', pKJ **jox-* (though Martin 1966: 235, #125 has a different etymology) give evidence for the original stem-final continuant that explains the correspondence of OJ *y-* here with original pA **d-*; otherwise, Japanese simply has the *o*-grade for the original *a*-grade preserved in Turkish. (For another possible Altaic etymology for OJ *yö-*, involving problems in the 'original' Altaic long vowels, cf. p. 36 above).

Finally, we are in a position to understand the far-reaching historical connections of the Japanese locative/instrumental particle collocation J *ni te*, a sequence that has regularly yielded the referent particle *de* in the modern language. In the spoken language, J *de* is either 'by means of' or 'in, on, at' (Bloch 1970: 52); in the written language the uses of *ni te* can be classified into instrumental, causal, locative, and temporal categories (Lewin 1959: 80, § 106), but there is little if any important difference between the first two subdivisions of this list, and for all practical purposes the employment of J *ni te* can be adequately subsumed under instrumental, and locative, the latter including both place and time.

With this we are now able to associate directly, as historical continuations and genetic inheritances of the same original Altaic forms reflected in J *ni te*, the Old Turkish instrumental suffix *-n* (von Gabain 1950: 89, § 184; Tekin 1968: 136–37, § 3.2148), together with the Old Turkish locative suffix *-da, -ta, -dä, -tä* (von Gabain 1950: 88, § 182; Tekin 1968: 133, § 3.2145), as well as the proto-Tungus instrumental suffix **-ǯi* (Benzing 1955: 1035, § 99; in ibid. 1027, table s.v. 'Instrum.', correct **ǯɪ* to read **ǯi*).

The Turkish instrumental suffix *-n* shows that the *ni* in J *ni te* is not to be identified with the 'pseudo-copula infinitive' J *ni* (Martin 1966: 226). Murayama suggests that in J *ni*, 'dieses Suffix ist wohl aus **-n-i* entstanden, dabei gehört **-n* zum Stamm und **-i* ist eigentliches Suffix' (1957: 131, § 6). But comparison with Turkish indicates to the contrary that the *-i* in J *ni* is rather an automatic epenthetic vowel, added in 'vowel harmony' with an original front-vocalism of the following morpheme. The language of the Codex Cumanicus has preserved the original vocalism of this final element, which appears there throughout as *-de;* thus the Codex has *syon-de* 'in Zion', *üčünči kün-de* 'am dritten Tage', but also *kun-de* 'am Tage' (von Gabain

1959[b]: 60, 51), regardless of the vocalization of the forms to which it is suffixed. From this we may assume that the original form, in pre-Turkish and probably also in proto-Altaic as well, was *-n + tä;* this shows its original vocalism in the form of the *-i-* of J *ni* in J *ni te;* and J *ni te* itself is a later changed form of an earlier **ni ta,* with analogical *-e* as a result, once more, of vowel leveling in the phonological context of this particular collocation.

Further substantiation for this historical analysis may be found within the morphology of Old Turkish, where the locative affix in question has the allomorphs *-da, -dä,* as well as *-ta, tä.* The forms in *-d* are used following all consonants except *-l, -n,* and *-r* (a by now familiar morphophonemic set within all the Altaic languages, including Japanese; cf. p. 102 above). In other words, by internal reconstruction we may recover earlier **n + t-* for those cases in which our Old Turkish texts have *-d-,* so that for pre-Turkish we may assume that this locative suffix was uniformly **n + tä,* going regularly and directly with J *ni te.*

Additional evidence for this analysis is forthcoming from Tungus. Here too the instrumental suffix **ǯi* has preserved special allomorphs in Manchu and Evenki, depending upon whether its reflex is added to forms with or without *-n* (Benzing 1955: 1035, § 99); and, to round out the picture of related forms, there is the Tungus 'elativ' ('. . . bezeichnet den Ort, von dem aus eine Handlung beginnt ["von . . . her"]'), a collocation of pT **gī* + the instrumental **ǯi,* just as J *ni te > de* brings together *ni* and *te.* The pattern of collocation of particles is the same in Tungus and Japanese; the two branches of Altaic have here diverged only in their choice of the morpheme to which the final element is to be added.

As so often before, we note here once more that the Japanese and the Manchu developments have a great deal in common—too much in common, in fact, to allow of explanation by chance or coincidence.

First of all, in order to clarify the Manchu developments it is necessary to point out that the morpheme that in the usual descriptions of Manchu is simply called the 'genitive *-i*' is in reality not one but three morphemes; and that each of these morphemes has two phonologically determined allomorphs (cf. Yamamoto 1955, from which the following description is adapted and from which the cited examples are taken, particularly his 520-1 on *-i ∼ -ni,* and 522 on *de.*) The Manchu set *-i ∼ ni* consists of three different though homophonous morphemes; the first is a referent particle; the second marks the subject of subordinate clauses; and the third, the one of interest here, indicates means or method by which an action is carried out. Examples of this last: *suhe-i sacime* . . . 'cutting [it] with an ax'; *juwe jugûn-i dosifi* . . . 'entering by both roads'; others in Yamamoto 1955: 521.

Phonologically, by the time of our Manchu texts the allomorph *-i* had been generalized to appear in all instances except following final *-ng*, where the allomorph *-ni* appears (Yamamoto 1955: 520–21, n. 4); but *-ng*, though common in the language, is not an original inherited Manchu phoneme, and has resulted from borrowings from Chinese (Austin 1962: 19; correct Sinor 1969: 258, who writes 'comme finales nous ne trouvons que voyelles et *-n*'). What appears to have happened in the prehistory of Manchu is the following. In the case of each of these three homophonous morphemes, including the third, the indicator for means or method, the original form was **ni* throughout, and in all phonological contexts. But this was reduced (through something allied with the characteristic underarticulation of initials already noted so often in Japanese?) to *-i* in all cases except when found immediately following one of the (relatively) new Chinese loanwords in final *-ng*, in which case the *n-* was not underarticulated, and hence survived. With this survival established as a regular pattern, the set of phonologically determined allomorphs *-i* ~ *-ni* had come into existence. (Another possible explanation would find in the disappearance of the original initial in **ni* some echo of the reduction of both **ñ-* and **n-* to zero-initial in pre-Turkish.)

At any rate, just as the resulting *-i* ~ *-ni* exactly parallels and is cognate with J *ni*, and is the same form used in the same sense, so also has Manchu developed another particle, Ma. *de*, a marker for temporal and/or spatial location in which an action takes place—and this second form is identical with J *ni te*, which itself later contracts to J *de*. Examples of Ma. *de: emu eme-de banjiha damu deo* 'the only younger brother born of the same mother'; *bi giya-i angga-de simbe aliyara* 'I'll wait for you at the entrance to the street'; *ekšeme boo-de dosifi* . . . 'entering the house hurriedly'; other examples in Yamamoto 1955: 522. This Ma. *de* must have evolved from earlier **ni* + pT **ži* (this last form itself < **di* or **ti* ?), in a fashion exactly parallel with the Japanese development of *de* < *ni te*. But in its vocalization the Manchu form at the same time preserves an important and unmistakable trace of the **tä* in the **n tä* reconstructed above on the basis of the Turkish evidence.

It is not surprising that such similar developments of similar forms have resulted in closely similar structures and collocations in both languages. In all these cases, that these forms and constructions are 'similar' is due to the fact that the forms and constructions being considered were originally not parts of different languages but rather were parts of the same linguistic unity; they were 'similar' to begin with because they were in effect the same, and this original identity continued to be reflected in their parallel developments. As a result, we have Ma. *gala-i žafaxa* 'nahm mit der Hand', with the morpheme *-i ∼ -ni;* but Ma. *gala-de žafaxa* 'nahm in die Hand', with Ma. *de* (Ramstedt/Aalto 1952: 44)—a distinction that is exactly paralleled in Japanese with *te ni tor-u* 'take, hold something in one's hand', against *te de tor-u* 'pick up, grasp something by, with one's hand'. In this set of four parallel examples, Ma. *-i ∼ -ni* exactly parallels J *ni* in sense and form, and is etymologically the same morpheme; and the same is true of Ma. *de*, with respect to J *ni te > de.*

These correspondences in details of form and meaning cannot be ascribed either to coincidence or to borrowing; they can only be explained as resulting from a genetic relationship between the languages concerned.

Bibliography

Abbreviations for certain frequently cited journals and other serials:

AM = *Asia Major.*

BSOAS = *Bulletin of the School of Oriental and African Studies.*

CAJ = *Central Asiatic Journal.*

HJAS = *Harvard Journal of Asiatic Studies.*

JAOS = *Journal of the American Oriental Society.*

JNATJ = *Journal-Newsletter of the Association of Teachers of Japanese.*

JSFOu = *Journal (Aikakauskirja) de la société finno-ougrienne.*

KGtKBG = *Kokugo to kokubungaku.*

KKG = *Kokugogaku.*

KSz = *Keleti Szemle, Revue Orientale.*

Lg. = *Language.*

MSFOu = *Mémoires (Toimituksia) de la société finno-ougrienne.*

NKBT = *Nihon koten bungaku taikei.*

RO = Rocznik Orientalistyczny.

TP = T'oung Pao, Archives concernant l'histoire, les langues, la géographie et les arts de l'Asie Orientale.

UAJr = Ural-Altaische Jahrbücher.

UASr = Ural and Altaic Series.

UASt = Ural and Altaic Studies.

ZDMG = Zeitschrift der Deutschen Morgenländischen Gesellschaft.

Short titles used for collectanea frequently cited in the bibliography under the authors of individual articles:

. . . Fundamenta = Philologiae turcicae fundamenta . . . ; see below under Jean Deny et al.

. . . Gaisetsu = Sekai gengo gaisetsu, An introduction to the languages of the world, Ichikawa Sanki and Hattori Shirō, eds., vol. 2, 1955, Tokyo: Kenkyūsha.

Handbuch . . . = Handbuch der Orientalistik; see below under B. Spuler et al. (cited by Abschnitt number).

Studia Altaica = Studia Altaica, Festschrift für Nikolaus Poppe zum 60. Geburtstag am 8. August 1957. (Ural-altaische Bibliothek, 5.) 1957, Wiesbaden: Otto Harrassowitz.

Aalto, Pentti, see Ramstedt, G. J. (1952) and (1957).

Alderson, A. D., and Fahir İz. 1959. The Concise Oxford Turkish Dictionary. Oxford: Clarendon Press.

Arisaka Hideyo. 1934. 'Kodai Nihongo ni okeru onsetsu ketsugō no hōsoku'. Reprinted in Kokugo on'inshi no kenkyū [zōho shinpan], 1959, 103–16; also reprinted in Yamagiwa, Joseph K., ed. Readings in Japanese language and linguistics, part 1. Selections, 77–91. Ann Arbor: University of Michigan Press.

Asami Tetsu, see Omodaka Hisataka et al.

Asano Kiyoshi. 1963. Hōryūji (Genzai kyōyō bunko, 417.) Tokyo: Shakai shisōsha.

Ašmarin, N[ikolaj] I[vanovič]. 1928–29. Thesaurus linguae tschuvaschorum. Vols. 1–4. Reprinted in UASr 70: 1–4, 1968–69. Bloomington: Indiana University.

Austin, William M. 1962. 'The phonemics and morphophonemics of Manchu'. UASt 13.15–22.

Benzing, Johannes. 1941. 'Tschuwaschische Forschungen. III. Das Nomen futuri'. ZDMG 95.46–58.

———. 1953. 'Remarques sur les langues tongouses et leurs relations avec les autres langues dites ,,altaïques" '. UAJr 25.109–18.

———. 1953ᵇ. Einführung in das Studium der altaischen Philologie und der Turkologie. Wiesbaden: Otto Harrassowitz.

———. 1955. 'Die tungusischen Sprachen, Versuch einer vergleichenden Grammatik'. Abhandlungen der geistes- und sozialwissenschaftlichen Klasse, Akademie der Wissenschaften und der Literatur, Mainz 11.[949–]1099.

———. 1959. 'Das Tschuwaschische'. In . . . Fundamenta, 695–751.

———. 1959ᵇ. 'Das Hunnische, Donaubolgarische und Wolgabolgarische'. In . . . Fundamenta, 685–95.

———. 1959ᶜ. 'Das Baschkirische'. In . . . Fundamenta, 421–34.

Bloch, Bernard. 1970. Bernard Bloch on Japanese, edited with an introduction and analytic index by Roy Andrew Miller. (Yale Linguistic Series.) New Haven and London: Yale University Press.

Boller, Anton. 1857. 'Nachweis, dass das Japanische zum ural-altaischen Stamme gehört'. Sitzungsberichte der philos.-histor. Classe der kais. Akademie der Wissenschaften, Wien 33.393–481.

Brower, Robert H., and Earl Miner. 1961. Japanese Court Poetry. Stanford: Stanford University Press.

————. 1967. *Fujiwara Teika's* Superior Poems of Our Time, *A Thirteenth-Century Poetic Treatise and Sequence.* Stanford: Stanford University Press.

Brugmann, Karl. 1886–90. *Grundriss der vergleichenden Grammatik der indogermanischen Sprachen.* Strassburg: K. J. Trübner.

Chamberlain, Basil Hall. 1888. *A Handbook of Colloquial Japanese.* London: Trübner & Co.

Chew, John J., Jr. 1969. Review of Miller 1967. *Lg.* 45.203–9.

Deny, Jean. 1959. 'L'Osmanli moderne et le Türk de Turquie'. In . . . *Fundamenta*, 182–239.

Deny, Jean, Kaare Grønbech, Helmuth Scheel, [and] Zeki Velidi Togan, eds. 1959. *Philologiae turcicae fundamenta* . . . , Tomus primus. Wiesbaden: Franz Steiner Verlag.

Dickens, Frederick Victor. 1906. *Primitive & Mediaeval Japanese Texts.* 2 vols. Oxford: Clarendon Press.

Dmitriev, N. K., ed. 1951. *Russko-čuvašskij slovar'.* Moscow: Gosudarstvennoye Izdatel'stvo inostrannykh i natsional'nykh slovarej.

Doerfer, Gerhard. 1959. 'Das Krimosmanische'. In . . . *Fundamenta*, 272–80.

Doi Takao et al. 1961. *Nihongo no rekishi⁶.* Tokyo: Shibundō.

Emeneau, Murray B. 1957. 'Numerals in comparative linguistics (with special reference to Dravidian)'. *Bulletin of the Institute of History and Philology, Academia Sinica, Taipei* 29.1–10.

Fukuda Yoshisuke. 1965. *Nara jidai Azuma hōgen no kenkyū.* Tokyo: Fūkan shobō.

von Gabain, Annemarie. 1950. *Alttürkische Grammatik².* (Porta linguarum orientalium, Sammlung von lehrbüchern für das Studium der orientalischen Sprachen, xxiii.) Leipzig: Otto Harrassowitz.

————. 1959. 'Das Alttürkische'. In . . . *Fundamenta*, 21–45.

————. 1959ᵇ. 'Die Sprache des Codex Cumanicus'. In . . . *Fundamenta*, 46–73.

Gō Minoru. 1959. 'Fukisoku dōshi ni tsuite'. *Okayama daigaku hōbun gakubu gakujutsu kiyō* 1–22.

Haenisch, Erich. 1937. *Manghol un niuca tobca'an (Yüan-ch'ao pi-shi).* Die geheime Geschichte der Mongolen, aus der chinesischen Transcription (Ausgabe Ye Têh-hui) im mongolischen Wortlaut Wiederhergestellt. Leipzig: Otto Harrassowitz.

————. 1952. *Sino-mongolische Dokumente vom Ende des 14. Jahrhunderts.* Abhandlungen der Deutschen Akademie der Wissenschaften zur Berlin, Klasse für Sprachen, Literatur und Kunst, Jahrgang 1950, N. 4.

Haguenauer, Charles. 1956. *Origines de la civilisation japonaise, Introduction à l'étude de la préhistoire du Japon, première partie.* Paris: Imprimerie Nationale.

Halliday, M. A. K. 1959. *The Language of the Chinese "Secret History of the Mongols".* (Publications of the Philological Society, xvii.) Oxford: Basil Blackwell.

Handbuch der Orientalistik, see Spuler, B., et al., eds.

Hashimoto Shirō, *see* Omodaka Hisataka et al.

Hattori Shirō. 'Ryūkyūgo'. In . . . *Gaisetsu*, 307–56.

Hill, Archibald A. 1958. *Introduction to Linguistic Structures, from sound to sentence in English.* New York: Harcourt, Brace and Company.

Hirayama Teruo et al. 1966. *Ryūkyū hōgen no sōgōteki kenkyū.* Tokyo: Meiji shoin.

Hirohama Fumio. 1967. 'Wo'. *Kokubungaku* 12: 2.28–41.

Ide Itaru, *see* Omodaka Hisataka et al.

Ikegami Jirō. 1955. 'Toungūsugo'. In . . . *Gaisetsu*, 441–88.

Ikegami Teizō, *see* Omodaka Hisataka et al.

Itō Hiroshi, *see* Omodaka Hisataka et al.

Jettmar, Karl. 1952. 'Zum Problem der tungusischen „Urheimat" '. *Wiener Beiträge zur Kulturgeschichte und Linguistik* 9: 484–511.

Kamei Takashi. 1962. *Gaisetsu bungo bunpō, kaiteiban*[5]. Tokyo: Yoshikawa kōbunkan.

Karlgren, Bernhard. 1940. 'Grammata Serica, Script and phonetics in Chinese and Sino-Japanese'. (Bulletin of the Museum of Far Eastern Antiquities, No. 12.) Stockholm: Ostasiatiska Samlingarna.

Kawabata Yoshiaki, *see* Omodaka Hisataka et al.

Keene, Donald. 1967. *Essays in Idleness, The* Tsurezuregusa *of Kenkō*. New York and London: Columbia University Press.

Kidder, J. Edward. 1960. Review of Haguenauer 1956. *Journal of Asian Studies* 19:215–16.

Kim, Soon-ham Park. 1969. 'On the prefixal negatives in Korean, a transformational analysis'. *Language Research (Seoul)* 5.1–17.

Kindaichi Kyōsuke and Kindaichi Haruhiko. 1964. *[meikai] Kogo jiten*[18]. Tokyo: Sanseidō.

Kinoshita Masatoshi, *see* Omodaka Hisataka et al.

Kobayashi Kenji. 1968. 'Futei hyōgen no hensen—"arazu" kara "nashi" e no kōtai genshō ni tsuite'. *KKG* 75.45–62.

Kojima Noriyuki, *see* Omodaka Hisataka et al.

Kokuritsu kokugo kenkyūjo. 1963. *Okinawago jiten*. (Kokuritsu kokugo kenkyūjo shiryōshū, 5.) Tokyo: Ōkurasho insatsukyoku.

Kolpakči, Ye. M. 1956. *Očerki po istorii yaponskogo yazyka, tom 1, Morfologiya glagola*. Moscow: Izdatel'stvo AN SSSR.

Konishi Jin'ichi, *see* Tsuchihashi Yutaka.

Kotwicz, Władysław. 1929/30. 'Contributions aux études altaïques. II. Les noms de nombres'. *RO* 7.152–221.

———. 1936. *Les Pronoms dans les langues altaïques*. (Polska Akademja Umiejętności, Prace Komisji Orjentalistycznej, Nr. 24.) Kraków: Polska Akademja Umiejętności.

Kreuger, John R. 1961. *Chuvash Manual, Introduction, grammar, reader, and vocabulary*. (UASr, vol. 7.) Bloomington: Indiana University.

———. 1961[b]. Review of Poppe 1960. *JAOS* 81.70–74.

———. 1962. 'Morphophonemic change in Chuvash verb stems'. UASt 13.129–40.

Kwon, Hyogmyon. 1962. *Das koreanische Verbum verglichen mit dem altaischen und japanischen Verbum. Zur Typologie des Koreanischen*. Munich: [privately printed].

Lange, Roland A. 1969. 'Documentary evidence for a palatalized /e/ series in Middle Japanese'. *JNATJ* 6:1.47–50.

Lee Ki-moon. 1963. 'A genetic view on Japanese'. *Chōsen gakuhō* 27.94–105.

Lehmann, Winfred. 1962. *Historical Linguistics: An introduction*. New York: Holt, Rinehart, and Winston.

Lewicki, Marian. 1949. *La langue mongole des transcriptions chinoises du XIV*[e] *siècle. Le Houa-yi yi-yu de 1389, édition critique précédée des observations philologiques et accompagnée de la reproduction phototypique du texte*. (Prace Wrocławskiego Towarzystwa Naukowego, Seria A, Nr. 29.) Wrocław: Wrocławskie Towarzystwo Naukowe.

———. 1959. *La langue mongole des transcriptions chinoises du XIV*[e] *siècle. Le Houa-yi yi-yu de 1389, II, Vocabulaire-index*. (Prace Wrocławskiego Towarzystwa Naukowego, Seria A, Nr. 60.) Wrocław: Wrocławskie Towarzystwo Naukowe.

Lewin, Bruno. 1959. *Abriss der japanischen Grammatik, auf der Grundlage der klassischen Schriftsprache*. Wiesbaden: Otto Harrassowtiz.

————. 1962. *Aya und Hata, Bevölkerungsgruppen altjapans kontinentaler Herkunft*. (Studien zur Japanologie, Band 3.) Wiesbaden: Otto Harrassowitz.

————. 1965. *Japanische Chrestomathie, von der Nara-Zeit bis zur Edo-Zeit, I. Kommentar*. Wiesbaden: Otto Harrassowitz.

Maeda Tomiyoshi. 1970. Review of Kokuritsu kokugo kenkyūjo, ed., *Nihon gengo chizu*, dai san-shū. *KKG* 80.78–84.

Mansuroğlu, Mecdut. 1959. 'Das Karakhanidische'. In . . . *Fundamenta*, 87–112.

Man'yōshū, see Ōno Susumu, Takai Ichinosuke, and Gomi Tomohide.

Martin, Samuel E. 1961. *Dagur Mongolian Grammar, Texts, and Lexicon*. (UASr, 4.) Bloomington: Indiana University.

————. 1966. 'Lexical evidence relating Korean to Japanese'. *Lg*. 42.185–251.

————. 1967. 'On the accent of Japanese adjectives'. *Lg*. 43:246–77.

Martin, Samuel E., Lee Yang Ha, and Chang Sung-Un. 1967[b]. *A Korean-English Dictionary*. New Haven and London: Yale University Press.

Maruyama Rinpei. 1967. *Jōdaigo jiten*. Tokyo: Meiji shoin.

Mathews, R. H. 1956. *Mathews' Chinese-English Dictionary*. Revised American edition of the Shanghai, 1931 edition. Cambridge: Harvard University Press.

McCawley, James D. 1968. *The Phonological Component of a Grammar of Japanese*. (Monographs on linguistic analysis, 2.) The Hague and Paris: Mouton.

Menges, Karl H. 1947. *Qaraqalpaq Grammar, Part One: Phonology*. New York: King's Crown Press.

————. 1954. 'Analecta et additamenta'. *Anthropos* 49: 1111.

————. 1968. *The Turkic Languages and Peoples, An introduction to Turkic studies*. (Ural-Altaische Bibliothek, xv.) Wiesbaden: Otto Harrassowitz.

————. 1968[b]. 'Die tungusischen Sprachen'. In *Handbuch* . . . , 3, 21–256.

————. 1968[c]. *Tungusen und Ljao*. (Abhandlungen für die Kunde des Morgenlandes, Bd. xxxviii, 1.) Wiesbaden: Franz Steiner.

Miller, Roy Andrew. 1966. 'Qoninči, compiler of the *Hua-i i-yü* of 1389'. *UAJr* 38.112–21.

————. 1967. *The Japanese Language*. (The History and Structure of Languages.) Chicago and London: The University of Chicago Press.

————. 1967[b]. 'Old Japanese phonology and the Korean-Japanese relationship'. *Lg*. 43.278–302.

————. 1968. 'The Japanese reflexes of Proto-Altaic *$*d$-, *$*ǯ$-, and *$*č$-'. *JAOS* 88.753–65.

————. 1969. 'The Altaic numerals and Japanese'. *JNATJ* 6: 2.14–29.

————. 1970. 'The Old Japanese reflexes of Proto-Altaic *$*l_2$'. *UAJr* 42.127–47.

Mills, D. E. 1954. 'The *Takahasi uzibumi*'. *BSOAS* 16.113–33.

Morris, Ivan. 1966. *Dictionary of Selected Forms in Classical Japanese Literature*. New York and London: Columbia University Press.

————. 1967. *The Pillow Book of Sei Shōnagon*. 2 vols. New York: Columbia University Press.

Murayama Shichirō. 1950. 'Kodai Nihongo ni okeru daimeishi'. *Gengo kenkyū* 15.40–47.

————. 1957. 'Vergleichende Betrachtung der Kasus-Suffixe im Altjapanischen'. In *Studia Altaica*, 126–31.

————. 1962. 'Etymologie des altjapanischen Wortes *irö* 'Farbe, Gesichtsfarbe, Gesicht' '. *UAJr* 34.107–12.

————. 1962[b]. 'Nihongo oyobi Kōkurigo no sūshi—Nihongo keitō mondai ni yosete'. *KKG* 48.1–11.

Murayama Shichirō. 1963. 'Über einige japanische Kulturwörter altaischen Ursprungs'. In *Aspects of Altaic Civilization*, 227–33. (UASr, vol. 23.) Bloomington: Indiana University.

———. 1966. 'Mongolisch und Japanisch—ein Versuch zum lexikalischen Vergleich'. In *Collectanea Mongolica*, Festschrift für Professor Dr. Rintchen, zum 60. Geburtstag, 153–56. (Asiatische Forschungen, Band 17.) Wiesbaden: Otto Harrassowitz.

———. 1969. Review of Ozawa Shigeo 1968. *Gengo kenkyū* 55.78–93.

———. 1969ᵇ. 'Chūki Mongoru-go ni hozon sareta Mongoru-go no hihaseiteki chōboin'. In *Fukuda Yoshisuke-kyōju taikan kinen ronbunshū*, [reprint pp.] 1–21.

Nadelyayev, V. M., D. M. Nasilov, É. R. Tenišev, [and] A. M. Ščerbak, eds. 1969. *Drevnetyurkskij slovar'*. Leningrad: Izdatel'stvo 'Nauka'.

Nakada Norio. 1963. [*shinsen*] *Kogo jiten*. Tokyo: Shōgakkan.

Nishimiya Kazutami, see Omodaka Hisataka et al.

Norman, Jerry. 1967. *A Manchu-English Dictionary*. Taipei: [privately printed].

Okinawago jiten, see Kokuritsu kokugo kenkyūjo.

Omodaka Hisakata, Asami Tetsu, Ikegami Teizō, Ide Itaru, Itō Hiroshi, Kawabata Yoshiaki, Kinoshita Masatoshi, Kojima Noriyuki, Sakakura Atsuyoshi, Satake Akihiro, Nishimiya Kazutami, and Hashimoto Shirō, eds. *Jidaibetsu kokugo daijiten, jōdaihen*. Tokyo: Sanseidō, 1967.

Ōno Susumu. 1952. 'Nihongo to Chōsengo to no goi no hikaku ni tsuite no shōken'. *KGtKBG* 29: 5.46–57.

———. 1953. 'Nihongo no dōshi no katsuyōkei no kigen ni tsuite'. *KGtKBG* 30: 5.47–56.

———. 1955. 'Nihongo: vii, rekishi; viii, keitō'. In . . . *Gaisetsu*, 262–300.

Ōno Susumu, Takai Ichinosuke, and Gomi Tomohide. 1957–62. *Man'yōshū*. (NKBT, vols. 4–7.) Tokyo: Iwanami shoten.

Ōno Tōru. 1962. *Man'yōgana no kenkyū, kodai Nihongo no hyōki no kenkyū*. Tokyo: Meiji shoin.

Ōtsuki Fumihiko. 1932–37. *Daigenkai*. 5 vols. Tokyo: Fuzanbō.

Oyama Atsuko. 1964. 'How did the indicator of the objective case develop in Japan?' In Lund, H., ed., *Proceedings of the Ninth International Congress of Linguists*, 462–66. The Hague: Mouton.

Ozawa Shigeo. 1968. *Kodai Nihongo to chūsei Mongorugo—sono jakkan no tango no hikaku kenkyū*. Tokyo: Kazama shobō.

Paasonen, H. 1908. *Csuvas szójegyzék, Vocabularium linguae čuvašicæ*. Budapest: Magyar Tudományos Akadémia.

Pedersen, Holger. 1938. *Hittitisch und die anderen indoeuropäischen Sprachen*. Copenhagen: Levin & Munksgaard, Ejnar Munksgaard.

Pelliot, Paul. 1944. 'Širolγa - Širalga'. *TP* 37.102–13.

Philippi, Donald L. 1968. *Kojiki*, translated with an introduction and notes. Tokyo: University of Tokyo Press.

Philologiae turcicae fundamenta . . . , see Deny, J., et al.

Poppe, Nicholas. 1924. Review of G. J. Ramstedt 1922. *AM* 1.775–82.

———. 1925. 'Čuvašskij yazyk i ego otnošenie k Mongol'skomu i Turetskim yazykam, III'. *Izvestiya Rossijskoj Akademii Nauk, VI Seriya* 19.23–42.

———. 1926. 'Altaisch und Urtürkisch'. *UAJr* 6.94–121.

———. 1954. Review of Benzing 1953ᵇ. *HJAS* 17.462–71.

———. 1955. *Introduction to Mongolian comparative studies*. (MSFOu, 110.) Helsinki: Suomalais-Ugrilainen Seura.

———. 1956. 'The Mongolian affricates *č* and *ǰ*'. *CAJ* 2.204–15.

————. 1959. 'Das Jakutische'. In . . . *Fundamenta*, 761–84.

————. 1960. *Vergleichende Grammatik der altaischen Sprachen, Teil 1, Vergleich-ende Lautlehre.* (Porta linguarum orientalium, neue Serie, 4.) Wiesbaden: Otto Harrassowitz.

————. 1962. 'The primary long vowels in Mongolian'. *JSFOu* 63: 2.1–19.

————. 1963. 'Die jakutische Sprache'. In *Handbuch* . . . 1, 53–60.

————. 1965. *Introduction to Altaic Linguistics.* (Ural-Altaische Bibliothek, xiv.) Wiesbaden: Otto Harrassowitz.

————. 1967. 'On the long vowels in Common Mongolian'. *JSFOu* 68: 4.1–31.

Pritsak, Omeljan. 1954. 'Mongolisch *yisün* 'neun' und *yiren* 'neunzig' '. *UAJr* 26.243–45.

————. 1957. 'Nikolaus Poppe zum 60. Geburtstag'. In *Studia Altaica*, 7–16.

————. 1957[b]. 'Tschuwaschische Pluralsuffixe'. In *Studia Altaica*, 137–55.

————. 1959. 'Das Neuuigurische'. In . . . *Fundamenta*, 525–63.

————. 1959[b]. 'Das Altaitürkische'. In . . . *Fundamenta*, 568–98.

————. 1963, 'Das Alttürkische'. In *Handbuch* . . . 1, 27–52.

————. 1964. 'Der „Rhotazismus" und „Lambdazismus" '. *UAJr* 35.337–49.

Pröhle, Wilhelm. 1916/17. 'Studien zur Vergleichung des Japanischen mit den uralischen und altaischen Sprachen'. *KSz* 17.147–83.

Ramstedt, G. J. 1915/16. 'Zur mongolisch-türkischen Lautgeschichte. III, Der *j*-laut und damit zusammenhängende fragen'. *KSz* 17.66–84.

————. 1922. 'Zur frage nach der stellung des tschuwassischen'. *JSFOu* 38.1–34.

————. 1924. 'Die verneinung in den altaischen sprachen, Eine semasiologische studie'. *MSFOu* 52.196–215.

————. 1924[b] [= 1951]. 'A comparison of the Altaic languages with Japanese'. *Transactions of the Asiatic Society of Japan* 2d ser. 1.41–54. Reprinted in *JSFOu* 55:2.7–24 (1951).

————. 1949. 'Studies in Korean Etymology'. (*MSFOu*, 95.) Helsinki: Suomalais-Ugrilainen Seura.

————, bearbeitet und herausgegeben von Pentti Aalto. 1952. 'Einführung in die altaische Sprachwissenschaft, II, Formenlehre'. (*MSFOu*, 104: 2.) Helsinki: Suomalais-Ugrilainen Seura.

————, bearbeitet und herausgegeben von Pentti Aalto. 1957. 'Einführung in die altaische Sprachwissenschaft, I, Lautlehre'. (*MSFOu*, 104: 1.) Helsinki: Suomalais-Ugrilainen Seura.

Reischauer, Edwin O. 1956. Review of Haguenauer 1956. *HJAS* 19.202–7.

Sakakura Atsuyoshi, *see* Omodaka Hisataka et al.

Sanseidō 1967, *see* Omodaka Hisataka et al.

Sansom, George. 1928. *An Historical Grammar of Japanese.* Oxford: The Clarendon Press. Reprinted photographically from corrected sheets of the 1st ed. of 1928, Oxford, 1946.

Satake Akihiro. 1945. 'Man'yōshū tanka ji-amari-kō'. *Bungaku* 14: 5.183–95.

————. *See* Omodaka Hisataka et al.

Shiratori Kurakichi. 1937. 'The Japanese numerals'. Memoirs of the Research Department of the Toyo Bunko (The Oriental Library) 9.1–78.

————. 1942. *On'yaku Mōbun Genchō hishi.* (Tōyō Bunko Sōkan, 8.) Tokyo: Tōyō Bunko.

Sinor, Denis. 1968. 'La langue mandjoue'. In *Handbuch* . . . , 3, 257–80.

Sirotkin, M. Ya., ed. 1961. *Čuvašsko-russkij slovar'.* Moscow: Gosudarstvennoye izdatel'stvo inostrannykh i natsional'nykh slovarej.

Spuler, B., et al., eds. 1963–68. *Handbuch der Orientalistik, Erste Abteilung, Der nahe und der mittlere Osten; Fünfter Band, Altaistik; Erster Abschnitt, Turkologie.*

Zweiter Abschnitt, Mongolistik. Dritter Abschnitt, Tungusologie. Leiden/Köln: E. J. Brill.

Stimson, Hugh M. 1966. *The* Jongyuan in yunn: *a guide to Old Mandarin pronunciation.* (Sinological series, no. 12.) New Haven: Far Eastern Publications.

Street, John Charles. 1957. *The language of the* Secret History *of the Mongols.* (American Oriental Series, vol. 42.) New Haven: American Oriental Society.

——. 1957[b]. Review of Poppe 1955. *Lg.* 33.81–87.

——. 1962. Review of Poppe 1960. *Lg.* 38.92–98.

——. 1962[b]. 'Kalmyk shwa'. *American Studies in Altaic Linguistics* 263–91 (UASr, 13). Bloomington: Indiana University.

Suzuki Tomotarō. 1957. 'Tosa no nikki'. (*NKBT*, 20.) Tokyo: Iwanami shoten.

Tekin, Talât. 1968. 'A Grammar of Orkhon Turkic'. (USAr, 69.) Bloomington: Indiana University.

Thomsen, Kaare. 1959. 'Das Kasantatarische und die westsibirischen Dialekte'. In *Fundamenta* . . . , 407–21.

Tōgō Yoshio. 'Heian jidai no "no" "ga" ni tsuite—jinbutsu o ukeru baai'. *KKG* 75.27–44.

Tokieda Motoki. 1967. *Tsurezuregusa sōsakuin.* Tokyo: Shibundō.

Tsuchihashi Yutaka and Konishi Jin'ichi. 1957. 'Kodai kayōshū'. (*NKBT*, 3.) Tokyo: Iwanami shoten.

Tsukishima Hiroshi. 1965. [bibliographical 'headnotes' in] Yamagiwa, Joseph K. *Readings in Japanese Language and Linguistics, part II, Annotations.* Ann Arbor: University of Michigan Press.

Ueda Makoto. 1967. *Literary and Art Theories in Japan.* Cleveland: Press of Western Reserve University.

von Gabain, *see* Gabain.

Vos, Frits. 1957. *A Study of the* Ise-monogatari *with the text according to the Den-Teika-Hippon and an annotated translation.* 2 vols. 's-Gravenhage: Mouton.

Wenck, Günther. 1954–59. *Japanische Phonetik. Band I, Die Lautlehre des modernen Japanischen; Die Geschichte des Lautbewusstseins und der Lautforschung in Japan; Die Quellen der japanischen Lautgeschichte. Band II, Die Phonetik der Manyōgana. Band III, Die Phonetik des Sinojapanischen. Band IV, Erscheinungen und Probleme des japanischen Lautwandels.* Wiesbaden: Otto Harrassowitz.

Wittfogel, Karl A. and Fêng Chia-shêng. 1949. 'History of Chinese Society, Liao (907-1125)'. (*Transactions* of the American Philosophical Society, New Series, v. 36.) Philadelphia: American Philosophical Society.

Wurm, Stefan. 1951. 'The Karakalpak language'. *Anthropos* 46.487–610.

——. 1959. 'Das Özbekische'. In . . . *Fundamenta*, 489–524.

Yamada Yoshio. 1952. *Heian-chō bunpōshi.* Tokyo: Hōbunkan.

——. 1954. *Nara-chō bunpōshi.* Tokyo: Hōbunkan.

Yamagiwa, Joseph K., *see* Arisaka Hideyo *and* Tsukishima Hiroshi.

Yamamoto Kengo. 1955. 'Manshūgo bungo keitairon'. In . . . *Gaisetsu*, 489–536.

Yegorov, V. G. 1964. *Ètimologičeskij slovar' čuvašskogo yazyka.* Čeboksary: Čuvašskoye knižnoye izdatel'stvo.

Yokoyama Masako. 1950. 'The inflections of 8th-century Japanese'. (Language dissertation, no. 45.) Baltimore: Linguistic Society of America.

INDEXES

Index of Correspondences

Each of the following numbered sets of correspondences presents the reflexes of one of the proto-Altaic phonemes in the principal Altaic languages, including Japanese; taken together, these statements sum up the etymologies presented in the present work, as well as a certain number of other Altaic-Japanese etymologies not introduced here. The individual Japanese and other lexical items involved in establishing these correspondences may be located by means of the word indexes for the individual languages, which follow, and to which this Index of Correspondences will serve as a guide.

The numbers in parentheses at the end of each correspondence (except for the first) are page references to Poppe (1960), to facilitate further verification of the non-Japanese data, in particular. 'Strong' and 'weak' following each correspondence-number refer to the special developments of certain proto-Altaic consonants according to their location with respect to the features of the proto-Altaic accent system, and in particular to the interrelationship of that system with the voiced / voiceless (or *lenis / fortis*) contrast in certain original stops (see above, p. 39, and the references cited there).

When more than one reflex is given for a single proto-Altaic phoneme in an individual language or language group, the two following special symbols have been employed: the symbol ' / ' indicates that the multiple reflexes occur in the language indicated in mutually exclusive environments, which allow of rigorous statement (e.g., correspondence #17, below), while the symbol ' , ' indicates that the multiple reflexes appear to occur in free variation (e.g., #21, #22). These latter cases, of course, all constitute a variety of phonological residue, and will require further study in the future, in order to resolve the anomalies that they still present.

In addition, the symbol ' ? ' has been used to indicate that some evidence does exist for the original phoneme in the language cited, but that at present it does not lend itself to summation here; where no evidence has been located, the language name has simply been omitted from the following statements, and the symbol ' ? ' has not been employed in these cases.

1. Consonants

1. (initial zero) :: Mo. Ø, Tk. Ø, Chu. Ø, Tg. Ø, Ma. Ø, Go. Ø, Ev. Ø, Lam. Ø, pKJ *Ø, MK Ø, K Ø, OJ Ø

2. *p- :: MMo. h > Ø, Tk. h / Ø, Tg. *p, Ma. f, Go. p, Ev. h, Lam. h, pKJ *p, MK p, K p, OJ F (10)

3. *-p :: Mo. b, Tk. p, Tg. p, w, Ma. f, p, b, Go. f, p, Ev. p, w, Lam. p, pKJ *p, b, MK p, K p, OJ F / b (43)

4. *-p- ('strong') :: Mo. b, Tk. p, Chu. p, Tg. p, w, Ma. f, Ev. p, w, Lam. w, pKJ * ?, MK ?, K ?, OJ ? (42)

5. *-p- ('weak') :: Mo. γ / w / j, Tk. p, Chu. p, Tg. p, w, Ma. f, Go. p, Ø, Ev. p / g, Lam. b, pKJ * ?, MK ?, K ?, OJ F / m / y / k (46)

6. *t- :: Mo. t, Tk. t / d, Chu. t, Tg. t, Ma. t, Go. t, Ev. t, Lam. t, pKJ *t, MK t, K t, OJ t (13)

7. *-t :: Mo. d, Tk. t, Chu. t, Ma. t, OJ d (49)

8. *-t- :: Mo. č / t, Tk. t, Chu. t, Tg. t, Ma. č / t, Ev. t, Lam. t, pKJ t, c, MK t, c, K t, c, OJ t (50)

9. *k- :: Mo. q / k, Tk. q / k, Chu. x / k, Tg. k / g, Ma. k, Ev. k, Lam. k, pKJ *k, MK k, K k, OJ k (16)

10. *-k :: Mo. g / g, Tk. q / k, Tg. k, Ma. q / k, Ev. g / k, pKJ *k, MK k, K k, OJ k (54)

11. *-k- ('strong') :: Mo. q / k, Tk. q, k, Chu. *k > G, Tg. k, Ma. q, k / x, Ev. k, Lam. k, pKJ * ?, MK ?, K ?, OJ k (54)

12. *-k- ('weak') :: Mo. g / g, Tk. q / k, Ma. k, Ev. g, Lam. g, pKJ *ğ, *g, MK ch, K ch, k, OJ g (56)

13. *b- :: Mo. b, Tk. b, Chu. p, Tg. b, Ma. b, Go. b, Ev. b, Lam. b, pKJ *p, MK p, K p, OJ F, w, m (20)

14. *-b :: Mo. w / b, Tk. b, Chu. v, Tg. b,w, Ma. b, Ev. w, Lam. b, pKJ *p, ?, MK p, ?, K p, ?, OJ F, b (44)

15. *-b- ('strong') :: Mo. b, Tk. b, Chu. v, Tg. w, Ma. b, Ev. w, Lam. w, OJ b, m (45)

16. *-b- ('weak') :: Mo. γ / γ, w / j, Tk. b, Tg. w, Ma. b, w, Go. Ø, Ev. w, OJ b, m, F (46, 48)

17. *d- :: Mo. d / ǯ, Tk. j, Chu. *j > š, Tg. d, Ma. d / ǯ, Go. d / ǯ, Ev. d, Lam. d, OJ t / y (22)

18. *-d(-) :: Mo. d / ǯ, Tk. d, Chu. r / ?, Tg. d, Ma. d / ǯ, Go. d / ǯ, Ev. d, Lam. d, pKJ *r, MK l, K l, OJ r (52)

19. *g- :: Mo. g / g, Tk. q / k, Chu. x / k, Tg. g / ŋ, Ma. g, Ev. g, Lam. g, ŋ, OJ k (24)

20. *-g :: Mo. g / g, Tk. γ / g, Chu. *γ > Ø, Tg. k / g, Ma. q / k, Ev. g, Lam. g, pKJ * ?, MK ?, K ?, OJ k (57)

21. *-g- ('strong') :: Mo. g / g, Tk. γ / g, Tg. g, Ma. χ / x, Ev. g, w, Lam. g, OJ g, k (58)

22. *-g- ('weak') :: Mo. γ / ġ, Tk. γ / g, Chu. *γ > Ø, Tg. g, Ma. χ / x, Ev. g, Lam. g, OJ g, k (59)

23. *č- :: Mo. č, Tk. č, Chu. š, Tg. č, Ma. č, Ev. č, Lam. č, pKJ *c, MK c, K c, OJ t (25)

24. *-č :: Mo. s, Tk. č, OJ t (62)

25. *ǯ- :: Mo. ǯ, Tk. j, Chu. š, Tg. ǯ, Ma. ǯ / n, Ev. ǯ, Lam. ǯ, pKJ *t, MK t, K t, OJ t / y (27)

26. *s- :: Mo. s / š, Tk. s, Chu. s / š, Ma. s, Ev. s, Lam. h, pKJ *s, MK s, K s, OJ s (29)

27. *-s- :: Mo. s / š, Tk. s, Ma. s, Go. s, Ev. s, Lam. s, OJ s (64)

28. *j- :: Mo. j / Ø, Tk. j, Tg. j, OJ y (31)

29. *-j- :: Mo. j / γ, Tk. j, Tg. j, OJ *y > Ø (66)

30. *m- :: Mo. m, Tk. b, Tg. m, Ma.

305

m / *ñ*, Ev. *m*, Lam. *m*, pKJ **m*, MK *m*, K *m*, OJ *m* (34)

31. **-m-* :: Mo. *m*, Tk. *m*, Tg. *m*, Ma. *m*, Ev. *m*, Lam. *m*, pKJ **mp* (?), K *ʷ/ₚ* (?), OJ *m* (67)

32. **n-* :: Mo. *n*, Tk. *j*, Tg. *n*, Ma. *n*, Ev. *n*, Lam. *n*, pKJ **n*, MK *n*, K *n*, OJ *n* (36)

33. **-n-* :: Mo. *n*, Tk. *n*, Tg. *n*, Ma. *n*, Ev. *n*, Lam. *n*, OJ *n*, *r* (69)

34. **ñ-* :: Mo. *n-* + *-i-*, Tk. *j*, Chu. **j* > *š*, Tg. *ñ*, Ma. *ñ*, Ev. *ñ*, Lam. *ñ*, pKJ **n*, MK *n*, *y*, K *n*, *y*, OJ *n*, *y* (36)

35. **-l-* :: Mo. *l*, Tk. *l*, Chu. *l*, Tg. *l*, Ma. *l*, Ev. *l*, Lam. *l*, pKJ **r*, MK *l*, K *l*, OJ *r* (74)

36. **-l* :: Mo. *l*, Tk. *l*, Chu. *l*, Tg. *l*, Ma. *l*, Ev. *l*, Lam. *l*, pKJ **r*, MK Ø, K Ø, OJ *r*, Ø (74)

37. **-l₂-* :: Mo. *l*, Tk. *š*, Chu. *l*, Tg. *l*, Ma. *l*, Ev. *l*, Lam. *l* (?), pKJ **š*, MK ?, K *l*, OJ *s(-i-)* (77)

38. **-l₂* :: Mo. *l*, Tk. *š*, Chu. *l*, Tg. *l*, Ma. *l*, Go. Ø, Ev. *l*, Lam. *l* (?), pKJ **š*, MK *lh*, K *l*, OJ *s(-i-)* (77)

39. **-r-* :: Mo. *r*, Tk. *r*, Chu. *r*, Tg. *r*, Ma. *r*, Ev. *r*, Lam. *r*, pKJ **r*, MK *l*, K *l*, OJ *r* (78)

40. **-r₂-* :: Mo. *r*, Tk. *z*, Chu. *r*, Tg. *r*, Ma. *r*, Ev. *r*, Lam. *r*, pKJ **r* / *l*, MK *l*, K *l*, OJ *r* / *t* (80)

2. Vowels (First Syllable Only)

41. **a* :: Mo. *a*, Tk. *a*, Chu. *ə̂*, Tkm. *a*, Tg. *a*, Ma. *a*, Ev. *a*, Lam. *a*, Jak. *a*, pKJ **a*, **á*, MK *a*, ?, K *a*, ?, OJ *a*, J *a* (94)

42. **ā* :: Mo. *a*, Tk. *a*, Tkm. *ā*, Tg. *ā*, Ma. *a*, Ev. *ā*, Lam. *ā*, Jak. *ā*, pKJ **(y)a*, MK *(y)ë*, OJ *a*, J *a* (94)

43. **o* :: Mo. *o*, Tk. *o*, Tkm. *o*, Tg. *o*, Ma. *o*, Ev. *o*, Lam. *o*, Jak. *o*, pKJ **e*, MK *ë*, K *ë*, OJ *o*, *ö*, J *o* (98)

44. **ō* :: Mo. *o*, Tk. *o*, Tkm. *ō*, Tg. *ō*, Ma. *ō*, Ev. *ō*, Jak. *uo*, pKJ **Ye*, MK *yë*, K *yë*, OJ *o*, *ö*, J *o* (98)

45. **u* :: Mo. *u*, Tk. *u*, Tkm. *u*, Tg.

u, Ma. *u*, Ev. *u*, Lam. *u*, Jak. *u*, pKJ **u*, *ɔ́* / *ɔ*, MK *u*, *ɔ*, K *u*, *a*, OJ ? / *o*, *ö*, J *u* / *o* (100)

46. **ū* :: Mo. *u*, Tk. *u*, Tkm. *ū*, Tg. *ū*, Ev. *ū.*, Lam. *ū*, Jak. *ū*, pKJ ** ?*, MK, K, OJ ?, J *u* (100)

47. **e* :: Mo. *e*, Tk. *ä*, Chu. *a*, Azb. *ä*, Tkm. *ä*, Tg. *ę*, Ma. *e*, Ev. *ę*, Lam. *ę*, Jak. *ä*, pKJ **á*, MK *ɔ*, K *a*, OJ ?, J *a* (103)

48. **ē* :: Mo. *e*, Tk. *ä*, Chu. *a*, Azb. *ä*, Tkm. *ā́*, Tg. *ē*, Ma. *e*, Ev. *ē*, Lam. *ē*, Jak. *iä*, pKJ, MK, K, OJ ?, J *a* (106)

49. **ē̃* :: Mo. *e*, Tk. *ä*, *i*, Chu. *i*, *jə*, Azb. *ė*, Tkm. *e*, Ma. *e*, Ev. *ę*, Lam. *ę*, Jak. *i*, pKJ **a*, MK *a*, K *a*, OJ ?, J *a* (105)

50. **ė* :: Mo. *e*, Tk. *i*, Chu. *i*, Azb. *ė*, Tkm. *ī*, Tg. *ē*, Ma. *e*, Ev. *ē*, Jak. *iä*, pKJ **a*, *á*, MK *a*, *a(ɔ)*, *ɔy*, K *a*, *ä*, OJ ?, J *a* (106)

51. **ö* :: Mo. *ö*, Mongr. *o*, Tk. *ö*, Chu. *va-* / *-ə̂-*, Tkm. *ö*, Ma. *u*, Ev. *u* / *ę*, Lam. *u* / *ę*, Jak. *ö*, pKJ **e* (?), MK *ë* (?), K *ë* (?), OJ *ö*, *o*, J *o* (107)

52. **ō̈* :: Mo. *ö*, Mongr. *ō*, Tk. *ö*, Chu. *va-* / *-ə̂və*, *ə̂va*, Tkm. *ō̈*, Ma. *u*, Ev. *u* / *ū*, Lam. *u* / *ū*, Jak. *üö*, pKJ **e*, MK *o*, K *ë*, *o*, OJ ?, J *o* (107)

53. **ü* :: Mo. *ü*, Tk. *ü*, Tkm. *ü*, Ma. *u*, Ev. *u*, *i*, Lam. *u*, *i*, Jak. *ü*, pKJ **ɔ*, MK *ï*, K *u* / *ï*, OJ ?, J *u* (110)

54. **ṻ* :: Mo. *ü*, Tkm. *üj*, Ma. *u*, Ev. *ī*, Lam. *ī*, Jak. *ṻ*, J *u* (110)

55. **ï* :: Mo. *i*, Tk. *ï*, Chu. *u*, Tkm. *i*, *i*, Ma. *i*, Ev. *i*, Lam. *i*, *ę*, Jak. *ï*, pKJ **i*, MK *i*, K *i*, OJ *i* / *u*, *ö*, J *i* / *u*, *o* (113)

56. **ī̈* :: Mo. *i*, Tk. *ï*, Chu. *jə̂-*, *-u-*, Tkm. *ï* (*ī* ?), Ma. *i*, Ev. *ī̧*, Lam. *ī*, *ē*, Jak. *ī̧*, pKJ **yɔ*, MK *ɔ*, K *a*, OJ *i*, J *i* / *u* (113)

57. **i* :: Mo. *i*, Tk. *i*, Tkm. *i*, Ma. *i*, Ev. *i*, Lam. *i*, Jak. *i*, pKJ ** ?* / *u*, MK ? / *u*, K ? / *u*, OJ *ï*, J *i* / *u* (116)

58. **ī* :: Mo. *i*, Tk. *i*, Tkm. *ī*, Ma. *i*, Ev. *ī*, Lam. *ī*, Jak. *ī*, pKJ, MK, K ?, OJ *i*, J *i* (116)

Index of Forms

Forms in all languages cited are alphabetized according to the order of letters in the roman alphabet; in the case of non-roman letters and special symbols, letters with diacritics follow plain letters, and are followed in turn by inverted or deformed letters or other phonetic signs, which are alphabetized after the normal roman letters (with or without diacritics) that they most resemble, according to the following general order: ā, ä, ă, c, č, d, δ, e, ē, ẹ, ẹ̄, ə, g, γ, i, ï, ị, n, ñ, ŋ, o, ɔ, s, ṣ, š, ʒ, ǯ.

Modern Japanese forms appear in the present work in different systems of transcription, depending on the immediate purpose of each citation (see p. xvii), but in the Index of Forms all Modern

307

Japanese lexical items have been uniformly written (or, rewritten) morphophonemically (thus, *si*, *ti*, *tu*, *hu*, etc., instead of *shi*, *chi*, *tsu*, *fu*, etc.), to permit a single alphabetical order in this portion of the Index, and to facilitate reference by the reader.

JAPANESE

1. OLD JAPANESE

(Standard Old Japanese unmarked; Az = Azuma dialect Old Japanese; MJ = Middle Japanese)

2. JAPANESE

(Standard Modern Japanese unmarked; D = modern nonstandard dialect forms; R = Ryūkyū)

KOREAN

(Modern Korean unmarked; MK = Middle Korean)

TURKISH

(Old Turkish unmarked; Chu = Chuvash; Bas = Bashkir; Jak = Jakut; MTk = Middle Turkish; Oi = Oirot; Osm = Osmanli; Qaz = Qazak; Qql = Qaraqalpaq; Tat = Tatar; Tkm = Turkmen; Uig = Uigur; Uz = Uzbek)

MONGOL

(Written Mongol unmarked; Mgr = Monguor; MMo = Middle Mongol; Shr = Shirongol)

TUNGUS

(Manchu unmarked; Ev = Evenki; Go = Goldi; Lam = Lamut; Olc = Olcha; Sol = Solon; Udh = Udhe)

ǯafaxa 292
ǯakûn 85, 220, 231
ǯalan 86
ǯe- 86, 209
ǯefu 95
ǯeję Ev 86
ǯep- Ev 86
ǯetere 95

ǯolo Ev 120
ǯoromī- Ev 84
ǯugañī Ev 84
ǯuru 84
ǯuwan 84, 220, 235
ǯuwari 84
ǯuwe 220

OTHER
(Modern Chinese unmarked; Lat = Latin; MC = Middle Chinese; OH = Old
Hungarian; Sgd = Sogdian; Skt = Sanskrit)

dharma Skt 103
dhāraṇī Skt 103

gimilc OH 146

mǎ 76

nán 87
nikāya Skt 195
nolo Lat 249
nwm Sgd 195

pù té 281

sè 213, 214
shíh 231, 232
ssŭ 223
ssù 223
śaśaka Skt 116

té 281
té wéi yĕh 281
*t'uŋ MC 133
*˙uo-sįe-γâm MC 116

wù 261

yàng 278

General Index